James Richards
m.
Ruth Hanford

New Canaan, Conn.

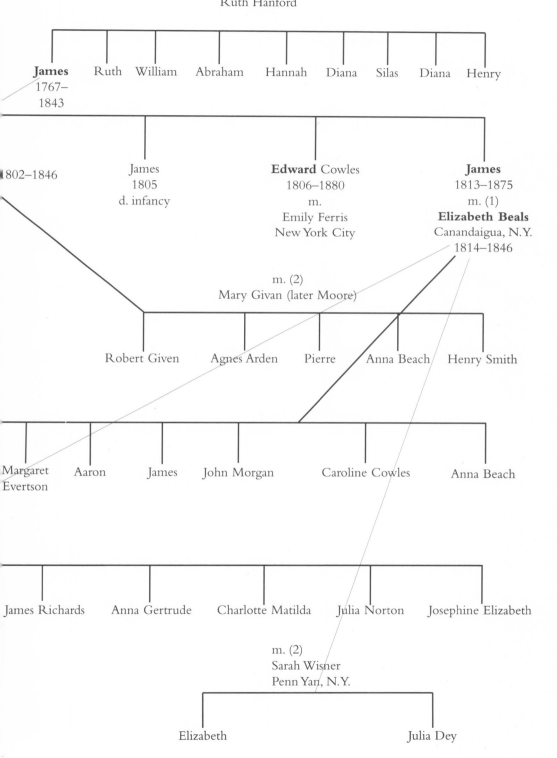

James
1767–
1843

Ruth   William   Abraham   Hannah   Diana   Silas   Diana   Henry

1802–1846

James
1805
d. infancy

Edward Cowles
1806–1880
m.
Emily Ferris
New York City

James
1813–1875
m. (1)
Elizabeth Beals
Canandaigua, N.Y.
1814–1846

m. (2)
Mary Givan (later Moore)

Robert Given   Agnes Arden   Pierre   Anna Beach   Henry Smith

Margaret
Evertson

Aaron   James   John Morgan   Caroline Cowles   Anna Beach

James Richards   Anna Gertrude   Charlotte Matilda   Julia Norton   Josephine Elizabeth

m. (2)
Sarah Wisner
Penn Yan, N.Y.

Elizabeth   Julia Dey

Before
the Throne
of Grace

Before the Throne of Grace

An Evangelical Family in the Early Republic

Laura S. Seitz & Elaine D. Baxter

PROVIDENCE HOUSE PUBLISHERS
Franklin, Tennessee

Printed in the United States of America

03   02   01   00   99   1   2   3   4   5

Library of Congress Catalog Card Number: 99-64726

ISBN: 1-57736-148-2

Cover design by Gary Bozeman

Cover illustration: Main Street, Canandaigua, New York, Circa 1830, *by Agnes Jeffrey, from The Collection of The Ontario County Historical Society*

PROVIDENCE HOUSE PUBLISHERS
238 Seaboard Lane • Franklin, Tennessee 37067
800-321-5692
www.providencehouse.com

For Our Families

CONTENTS

ACKNOWLEDGMENTS

Every book benefits from the help of many others along the way. This one is no exception. As independent researchers, we are grateful indeed to the following persons who kindly assisted our project: Bruce Adams, Timothy Beard, Virginia Calcutti, Robert D. Cross, Michael J. Cuddy Jr., Georgianna Grant, William O. Harris, Thomas Heffernan, Stephen Innes, Seth Kasten, Marilyn Matteson, Natasha Mayers, David McMillan, Eleanor Nashak, Ruth Nightingale, Edward Pessen, Mary Plummer, Norma Stanford, and Barbara Wheeler. Critical readings of drafts of our chapters were crucial to the development of the manuscript, and we are especially indebted to the following persons who generously took time to read and comment: Carol Berkin, Akiko Collcutt, Margaret Davis, Julie Dumper, Paula Fass, Marie Ferguson, Monica Martin, Mirla Morrison, Mark A. Noll, Vera Plummer, Cynthia Read, Daniel Seitz, Roxanne Seitz, Carol Stark, Maureen Steinbruner, Iris Stevens, Jeannie Van Asselt, and Jennifer Watkins. There is one person who was indispensable to the process, who read critically the whole manuscript line by line and gave us the kind of many-leveled criticism that authors hunger for. He also gave us boundless enthusiastic encouragement. To James C. Baxter, we offer our heartfelt appreciation.

Before the Throne of Grace

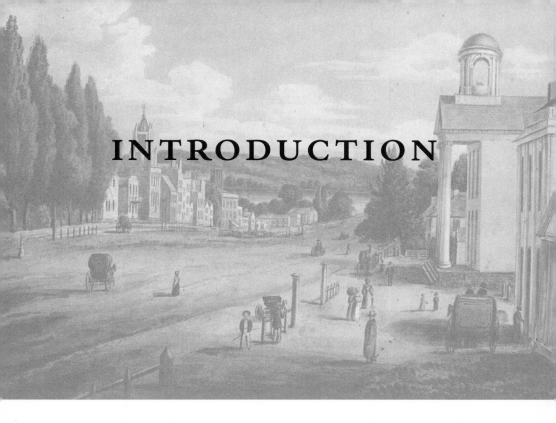

INTRODUCTION

This book tells the story of two generations of the James Richards family, and in doing so, portrays a significant segment of nineteenth-century American society, the northern evangelical middle class. Some books deal with the domestic life of this period and others deal with religious institutions, but this work is unusual in that it deals with both. Based primarily but not exclusively on a collection of family letters, it presents a narrative that weaves together the personal and professional lives of the Richards family. James Richards, D.D. (1767–1843), the family patriarch, was a leader of the Presbyterian Church in a dynamic period of religious transition for this country. Other members of the family were involved in the cotton trade, real estate speculation, banking, law and merchandizing, child rearing and homemaking. Evangelical Presbyterianism of this period was a shaping force in all their lives.

Most of the social units during this era were small. A large town numbered a few thousand, a congregation might be counted in the tens more often than the hundreds, a college graduating class rarely topped fifty, and the faculty of a theological seminary could be three. A family such as the Richardses with many children, often augmented by foster children and servants, constituted in itself a small society which was linked to a network of Presbyterian friends and colleagues across the country. Family and colleagues worked hard to forge personal and institutional ties that would help stabilize a broader American society much on the move.

The story begins with James Richards's boyhood in Connecticut during the Revolutionary War and extends nearly a century to end with the death of his youngest son in the mid-1870s. The elder Richards entered the ministry after experiencing the reorienting power of a religious conversion. He spent thirty years as a pastor in Morristown and Newark, New Jersey, before becoming for the last twenty years of his life a professor of theology at Auburn Seminary in upstate New York. His children settled in roughly the same compass of territory: Anna in Newark, Caroline in New York City, Henry in New York City and Poughkeepsie, Edward in New York City, and James Jr. in villages close to Auburn. The available letters are most plentiful for the years 1809 to 1846. Six chapters (chapters 1–5 and chapter 9) focus on the figure of James Richards, his career amid controversy as a minister and theology professor, and his role as head of an engaging family. The other five chapters (chapters 6–8 and chapters 10 and 11) focus on the adult lives of the five Richards children, who followed different paths and who despite the vagaries of fortune maintained close ties over considerable distance. The last chapter concentrates attention on James Jr. (1811–1875), who had a life and career as a minister both akin to and sharply different from that of his father. His story has arresting features that disclose different aspects of the workings of church and family described in the chapters that precede it.

The Richards family emigrated from England to Connecticut in the seventeenth century. They prospered as farmers and merchants in the area around New Canaan until the Revolution. Unlike many of his renowned colleagues, James Richards did not descend from a family of ministers, which may account in part for his much noted practical sense. His early life and education were affected by the dislocations of the Revolution, so much so that, despite having studied under Timothy Dwight, grandson of Jonathan Edwards and president of Yale, he felt he had been forced to overcome a poor preparation. On reaching adulthood, like many of his generation, he left Connecticut for greater opportunities south and west.

Richards entered the ministry at a critical moment in the life of American churches. Though republicans in the new nation understood religion to be the cornerstone of any moral society, in their enthusiasm for liberty they had opted for the disestablishment of churches. This was a great experiment, and one of its results was that churches were required to muster voluntary support for their activities. Many felt that the fate of the country depended on how well the churches succeeded. Churchmen perceived the world to be remarkably secular and indifferent to religion. To Christians of a Calvinist stripe the world was also threatened by such false doctrines as Unitarianism, deism, and perfectionism.

The solution to this problem, according to James Richards and his colleagues, was to promote the experience of conversion. They regarded "experimental religion," as it was often called, as much more authentic than religion inherited as a social condition. When whole groups or congregations were converted, they spoke of a revival. Properly managed, a revival would lead to lasting spiritual change with profound effects on everyday life. A proliferation of new voluntary societies provided opportunities for the converted to show they were serious. These societies were directed at social betterment for the indigent, the wayward, and the ordinary citizen. Other traditional Puritan adjuncts to religion like community discipline and strong family worship were never abandoned, but the revival impulse was so striking that the period 1800–1830 became known as the Second Awakening.

There were inevitable difficulties associated with this strategy. What after all were properly managed revivals? For James Richards, they required the leadership of ministers with a true understanding of scripture and theology. This in turn necessitated the founding of seminaries. The education of ministers became his passionate lifelong commitment. He helped to found Princeton Seminary and became the acknowledged mainstay of Auburn Seminary. Explosive population growth produced a continuing crisis in the number of ministers available on the frontier, and there were many who advocated a far more lenient standard of training of ministers or even the substitution of zealous enthusiasm for learning. James Richards never wavered in his conviction that seminarians needed a thorough intellectual grounding that could only be acquired in college followed by three years in seminary. For others like Charles Finney, the famous evangelist and later founder of Oberlin College, the spirit was primary, and what he dismissed as all the "hic, haec, hoc" of seminary training was superfluous. Finney and men like him conducted revivals with new techniques that were highly offensive to many, yet, if judged by the number of their converts, were extremely successful. Lyman Beecher, Theodore Weld, Ashbel Green, and a host of others struggled mightily over this issue to the point where the more conservative Presbyterians of Philadelphia finally "exscinded" what they considered their flamboyant and irregular brethren to the north and west. The politics of the situation became so convoluted that the conservative Richards paradoxically ended his life as a leader of the exscinded. Richards's evolving loyalties form a large part of this story.

The issue of proper revivals also revealed a fundamental conflict at the heart of nineteenth-century Presbyterianism which had to do with predestination. On the one hand, there were those who continued to insist on the omnipotence of God and its corollary, the impotence of man unless he was doing God's will. On the other hand, there were those who were convinced that men could choose to be saved and that ministers could persuade the unchurched to commit to the cause of God. The second position was increasingly congenial to an expanding country. It was optimistic, reassuring, and confidence-building. Richards's actions moved him to some extent towards the softer position, but he never lost the nagging fear that the battle against a secular society might be lost. He believed it was in God's hands.

The face of American Protestantism changed in other ways as well during these years. Evangelical denominations, Methodists and Baptists most notably, multiplied and had to be accommodated to the religious landscape. All the churches were trying to create institutions and instruments to meet the needs of both the frontier and the new urban centers. People were on the move, the certainties of class and place were questioned, and old problems such as slavery were seen from new perspectives. The denominations developed strategies of cooperation in some cases, but just as often they were jealous of their purity when brought face to face.

The role of ministers had to be adapted to survive these fluid and rather unsettling developments. In the first quarter of the century, James Richards and his associates mobilized with great success to build an array of new institutions, but by the 1830s the next generation took such institutions for granted. The younger James Richards and his seminary friends dispersed one by one to posts in voluntary associations, missions, private academies, church publications, seminaries, and new congregations where they exemplified a more individualistic approach to ministry. Theirs was a generation that seemed to make little attempt to articulate a common vision. These young ministers were more apt than their predecessors to seek out the right setting for their own individual talents. In a world in flux, they came to look upon themselves as people engaged in careers where their success was measured in moves to increasingly prestigious posts. The ideal of living a whole lifetime in one parish was declining. Ministers were becoming professionals as we understand the term today.

James Richards was in the forefront of all these efforts and disputes. An intimate of church inner circles, a moderator of the General Assembly of the Presbyterian Church, a pastor of two of its larger congregations, a theology professor, and finally at the end of his life the elder statesman of the New School Presbyterians, he engaged himself wholeheartedly in shaping this changing world. Alexis de Tocqueville commented in *Democracy in America* on the phenomenal growth of associations in American civil life and marveled at how successful Americans were at accomplishing a common purpose. James Richards, whom Tocqueville had interviewed when the young Frenchman visited Auburn, honed obvious political skills all his life. He did this among lay and clerical colleagues at the level of parish, presbytery, synod, and General Assembly, on the boards of national associations, and in the committee rooms of Princeton and Auburn. While willing to plot with allies to thwart fanatics and ideologues, he was widely regarded as judicious and fair minded. His opinions were both valued and feared.

Members of the Richards family, living within an active and disciplined church community, often expressed themselves in an inherited religious language. Among family and friends, they were playful and gossipy, but in solemn situations a certain kind of vocabulary came to the fore. As sojourners in a world of deception and a world of strangers, they were taught to meet the world at large with a wary eye, rather than a proffered hand. In their more personal spiritual moments, they sometimes used a language of self-abasement that has all but disappeared today. As the theology began to change, this language lost some of its force. James Richards himself, while frequently urgent in his tone, was rarely apocalyptic. The generation of his children, equally dedicated Christians, lost some of his urgency, the sense of nervous waiting upon God's grace.

Family themes and church themes in this history are often inter-woven. In raising their family, starting around the turn of the nineteenth century, James and Caroline Richards seemed determined on two things above all: that their children should be converted and that they should stay close to one another, as God ordained, through all of life's trials. James Richards saw it as his duty to converse regularly with each of his children about their spiritual development. This inquiry went on throughout their lives. Indeed, the prospects of conversion became a subject of regular, anxious, and sometimes remarkably open dialogue. Though Richards encouraged and importuned, he did not despair when only his oldest and youngest actually converted. He was a powerfully nurturing father, not a stern and distant patriarch. He paid close attention to the personalities and circumstances of each child, and, as in his church ministry, constantly looked for openings to advance his most important paternal responsibility. Youth and personal crises were the friends of such work. Worldliness and idleness were the enemies. He alternated between steadily preparing the ground, that is, making sure his maturing children were placed in favor-able circumstances, and watching for the precise moment in which to make direct, earnest appeals.

Why in a matter of such critical importance was there so little anger and despair at the situations of the three offspring who did not undergo conversion experiences? Part of the answer might be that Richards's even temperament would have allowed him to see that none of his children actually rejected church or God or basic orthodoxy, and in western New York, one saw all of these. Most importantly, his theology supported such an attitude. He continued to believe, contrary to new preachings he judged to be unorthodox, that no one could command divine grace, the ultimate power in a true conversion.

With the three who did not convert, James Richards must have found much consolation in their decency of character, faithful marriages, and useful occupations, which fulfilled another goal for his children, though one more assumed than articulated. Even among such blessings, however, trials came in abundance. Insecurity, bankruptcy, moral lapses, illness, untimely deaths—each of these left its mark on family members. Each also presented an opportunity for spiritual awakening and summoned the family to rally around. Thus it was especially in a crisis that the family was called, individually and collectively, to its most enduring purposes.

Although his primary concern was spiritual, Richards was not indifferent to his children's temporal well-being. He encouraged his children to help one another. He tried to draw each child into a supportive relationship with the others and into alliance with him as occasions presented. The help could be specific and material. They pooled money to start Edward in business and to rescue son-in-law Anthony Dey from business failure. When family members found themselves in a court of law, secular or ecclesiastical, relatives stepped in to testify on their behalf. They also exchanged servants, "help," as they were carefully called. These servants were young people on the move, varying in reliability, quick to turn over, and yet still in some vague way members of the family for whom employers felt residual parental responsibility.

Perhaps the most critical and recurring family assistance was the care of young relatives. The nation, itself in adolescence, seemed to have its hands full with its youth. Illness and the early deaths of parents often caused children to be passed to other relations for long periods of time. The Richards family saw a series of its young boys and teenagers and even a newborn infant require boarding out with relations or near-relations. People seemed to live with a strong sense of contingency and to expect family members to assume special burdens at such times. These burdens could make life difficult for those who tried to help, but, in spite of occasional grumbling, the expected help, at least in this family, regularly came through.

As time went on, especially in the 1830s and 1840s, some of the young males in the family got into trouble and required special "management." The problems of these youths evoked in Richards family members both sympathy and a sense of danger as they set about helping them. James Richards regarded youth as the preeminently formative period, the time to set oneself on the right track in life. It definitely did not represent a time of testing limits or roles. While options varied and each Richards son did something different, the important thing was to settle on a path and comply with its requirements.

Although James Richards regularly supplied his children with both spiritual and practical advice, he expected them to lead independent lives. They chose their own occupations, spouses, and places to live. Only the youngest son, James Jr., remained in the vicinity of Auburn, marrying into the Beals family, also of western New York. Thomas Beals, his father-in-law, was an early town father of the village of Canandaigua and a prosperous banker. The older Beals and the older Richards, both well-established in the region, saw their sons and daughters for the most part go into different lines of work and settle far from home. Family solidarity was compatible with considerable independence.

In a period famous for increasing sectionalism, it is worth noting how connected the Richards family seemed to feel with other parts of the country. The Presbyterian Church, though later split along many lines of controversy, was initially the most geographically widespread of all the Protestant denominations. Through publications and myriad individual correspondences, it maintained a national web of contacts among those engaged in all its far-flung works, and the Richardses knew personally Presbyterians in every region. For members of the family who were engaged in various business enterprises, markets played the key role. These family members included James Richards's younger brothers, in the transatlantic cotton trade out of Savannah; his son Edward, later in the woolens business; and his in-law Henry Beals, in the Erie Canal flour trade. Anthony Dey, Caroline's husband and very much the Jacksonian specu-lator, invested in ventures that included a gold mine in Georgia and a land deal in Texas.

The activities of the Richards family reflected the exciting changes over the decades in business climate and economic opportunity. Before his conversion, James Richards began as a cabinetmaker in the 1780s in an artisanal world that endured for several decades after independence. When he moved a few years later to New Jersey as a minister, new roads had already brought small towns near the coast into new market relations and trade was expanding and transforming material culture. Even so, in the first years of the nineteenth century, he traveled by horseback on missionary tours to areas of New Jersey and New Hampshire that though not many miles away were still regarded as frontier. Meanwhile, his younger brothers moved to New York City, threw themselves into the world of commercial shipping along the coast and with England, and hitched their star to the country's most valuable export, cotton.

From the 1820s on, James Richards and his family took part in the extraordinary development of western New York, an area dotted with towns and villages that had sprung to life in less than twenty years. The family rode stage and sleigh, steamboat and railroad, to cover the miles between them in the coming years. The Hudson River and the Erie Canal connected them to New York City, the country's commercial capital, where Anthony Dey found great wealth investing in new technologies and the Hudson waterfront. The financial panic of 1837 upset his affairs as well as those of the seminary in Auburn and other institutions that counted on the benevolence of the prosperous. By the 1840s, the preindustrial age was passing in towns like Newark, and those of the younger Richards generation who had remained there preferred to leave. Once faraway places seemed closer. More Richardses traveled to Europe or thought of doing so. Their Beals in-laws made extended visits to relatives settled in Michigan and Wisconsin. James Jr. followed the river road to New Orleans.

The oldest Richards son, Henry, also traveled, chiefly for his health. In conformity to prevailing beliefs about the treatment of consumption, he made almost annual trips to the South and later to the Caribbean. Health, or its opposite, was a perennial concern among the Richardses, and, again, typically, its precariousness highlighted both the need for conversion and the reliance on family. The second daughter Caroline survived typhoid as a young mother. Handsome James Jr. in adulthood bore the pockmarks of the smallpox that struck him during his college days. There was much general complaining of dyspepsia and dysentery. Mothers exhausted themselves nursing children through whooping cough.

The most consequential illnesses faced by family members were tuberculosis and alcoholism. The Richards family presents two contrasting studies in the onset and treatment of tuberculosis. Henry Richards exemplifies the chronic case of a male sufferer of professional background, for whom the common prescription was a change of climate. Elizabeth Beals Richards offers a closer study of a young mother who struggled to come to grips with the nature of her ailment while staying close to home on the advice of her doctors. She became ill enough to give up the care of her baby, yet continued to supervise her household and carry out her duties as a minister's wife.

As James Jr. and his seminary classmates illustrate the shifts in the ministry, Elizabeth's activities in the family show an important shift in family life. In the 1840s, she as mother played the role of moral guide to her young children that the senior James Richards as father so forcefully enacted to his older children a generation earlier. Apologetic in her letters for lingering over details of housekeeping, she clearly valued most her duties as minister's wife and Christian mother. The senior James Richards and Elizabeth Beals Richards are the figures of reference for the spiritual nurturing of children in their respective generations.

Any illness could be construed as a chastisement or warning. Alcoholism, in a period when consumption of spirits both reached historic highs and became identified as a singular social evil, was an illness with an especially heavy moral content. Beginning in his middle thirties, James Richards Jr. developed a chronic drinking problem. It deeply affected his ministry and his relations with his family. Surviving documents of two church trials provide eyewitness accounts of its effects on him and his congregations as well as the efforts of his fellow churchmen to balance the discipline of the community and the rehabilitation of the individual. A combination of family and public records helps to sketch a suggestive picture of how the family supported him and his children through his difficulties. The personal and institutional dimensions of this story reveal how alcoholic behavior was viewed and understood in this period and how an individual with his church affiliations managed to cope.

James Richards Jr. is the one family member who has a place in the overall narrative comparable to that of his father. He unites in his person several different themes. Alone of his brothers and sisters, he became a wayward youth, a gambler and tavern idler who was expelled from college. He underwent a life-threatening illness, converted, and became a minister of great promise. His marriage to Elizabeth Beals brought into the family a set of in-laws who further illuminate the workings of kinship. His early ministry, which was marked by obvious accomplishment and won praise, showed how the church had evolved since his father's day. The household he formed with Elizabeth became for a while the emotional center of the whole Richards family as time and deaths reconfigured it. His later life and ministry reveal the ways of church and family in the face of a poignant drama.

This book is made possible by the existence of several sources, most crucially some one hundred and fifty letters preserved by Richards descendents (The Seitz Collection). A similar number of letters written to and by the senior James Richards have been culled from university libraries. The

Richardses also produced two memoirs, a notable diary, and a separate collection of letters with a memorial tribute, all of which touch on significant aspects of the period. Collections of the sermons and lectures of James Richards, with valuable biographical introductions, were published not long after his death. Also available in print are some sermons of his minister son, James Richards Jr. Church, university, seminary, and court records further help to trace the activities of the family.

The Richardses wrote well about their lives, whether the subject was family relations, church politics, spiritual needs, business affairs, or simple gossip. Amused or earnest, their scene-sketching and daily problem solving bring them close to us.

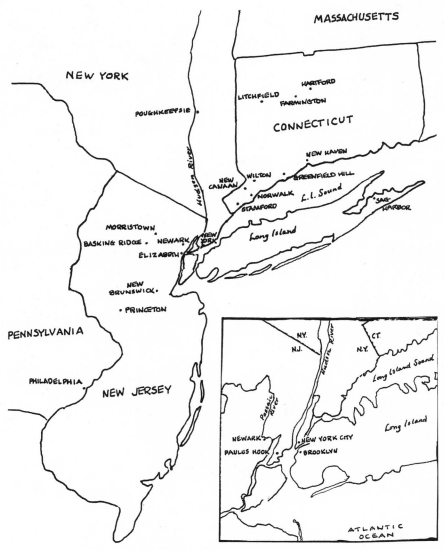

Map of Connecticut, Long Island, New York, and New Jersey.

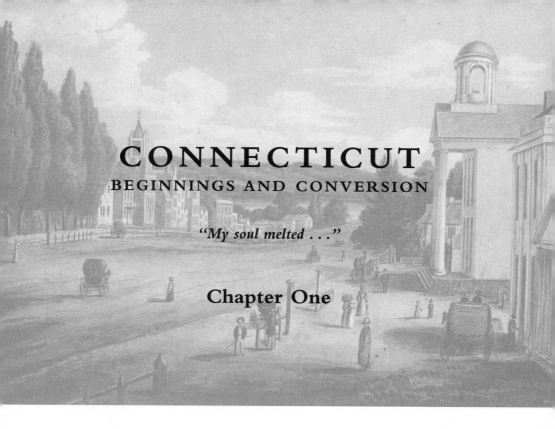

CONNECTICUT
BEGINNINGS AND CONVERSION

"My soul melted . . ."

Chapter One

When the Declaration of Independence was read to the Continental Army in New York City in July 1776, James Richards was eight years old—old enough to feel the excitement of war. His hometown of New Canaan was only a day's ride from where the fighting was soon to take place.

The British fleet had already arrived in New York harbor and landed an army on Staten Island. Although George Washington faced the largest expeditionary force of the eighteenth century, and New York City offered every advantage to a naval power, he had orders to hold it at all costs. The situation appealed powerfully to the imagination. Only six months earlier Boston had faced comparable odds, yet they had driven the powerful British from their shores. The patriots of Connecticut hoped ardently for just such a victory.

However, it was not to be. In short order the British took New York City and Long Island, and Washington retreated across the Hudson to New Jersey. Connecticut, which had sent eight thousand militiamen to New York when the cause looked bright, saw six thousand of them desert Washington at the first taste of British might. They returned home to defend Connecticut, which had now been left to fend for itself.

For young James Richards the war was only beginning. His family was deeply committed to independence. In nearby Norwalk his grandfather James Richards, commonly known as the "Old Squire," was appointed a captain of the Safety Guard by the Committee of Safety. The committee handled all town matters related to the war from seeking out and punishing Loyalists to guarding the shore from possible attack. His maternal uncle, Moses Comstock, also served on the Norwalk Committee of Safety and his great-uncle Samuel Richards became a member of the local patriot guard. Another uncle, Edmund Richards, would later be at Saratoga when Burgoyne surrendered. His own father, James, took up arms as a private in the Connecticut militia.[1]

The "Old Squire," grandfather of James Richards, lived in the original structure of this house in New Canaan from 1762 to 1810. (Courtesy—New Canaan Historical Society)

From the beginning the war went badly for New Canaan and the Richards family. The winter after Washington's retreat, British raiding parties began to cross Long Island Sound regularly in search of firewood, cattle, grain, and anything else of value they could find. There was no one to stop them but the local Safety Guard. On the night of March 13, 1777, Samuel left his substantial house to take his regular turn at guard duty along the shore of Five Mile Harbor, a cove near New Canaan where the Richardses owned a store and shipyard. As the night wore on, he and the other men on watch stepped into the store to get warm. A Tory raiding party chose that moment to sweep into the harbor. Fifteen Americans, one of them Samuel Richards, were taken prisoner and carried off to Long Island. From there they were taken to New York City where the British learned that Samuel was a sea captain with investments in a number of farms, mills, and weaving enterprises besides the store and shipyard. They offered to exchange him for a prominent Tory who had been jailed by the Revolutionaries in Boston. The Old Squire made the arrangements for his brother's exchange and then went to Boston to fetch the Tory prisoner. British prison conditions had been too much for Samuel Richards, however, and he died just one day after his return home.[2]

The English continued to raid the Connecticut shore communities for several years. The final raid, and the worst, left Norwalk burned to the ground in July 1780. Young James's father had been in the local force that vainly tried to defend the town. After the British fires burned out, wartime shortages continued and rebuilding went very slowly. Materials were in scant supply. Fifteen months after the raid, the Old Squire, by then a selectman of Norwalk and a deputy to the General Assembly, petitioned the state legislature to lift the embargo it had imposed so that a ship might sail to a friendly port to bring back boards, shingles, and glass.[3]

Young James Richards himself was directly affected by the local manpower shortage caused by the war. The district school needed a teacher, and called upon him though he was only thirteen. Tall for his age, serious but with a hint of humor, already identified as precocious, he managed to keep order and acquit himself well. The following winter he was asked to teach again.[4] He matured rapidly under the weight of so much responsibility, especially since it was combined with the expectations that naturally fell on an oldest son. In addition he was privy to the conversation of adults who were at the center of the community's efforts to survive.

Whatever ambitions his early experiences may have fostered, they were dashed in the aftermath of the war. His father's finances were ruined. He had lost a vessel at sea and his money had become all but worthless since it was in the form of continental currency. Hoping to recoup his losses, he went west to Ohio with a party of four friends. He spent the winter in the only house in Lazantville, later Cincinnati, but had no luck. In the spring he returned with nothing to show for his pains except severe rheumatism, which incapacitated him for the rest of his life.[5] Under these circumstances he had neither money to educate young James further, nor a position to offer him in the family businesses. The teenaged James Richards now found himself in humble circumstances facing a bleak future.

The situation was particularly galling to a family that had enjoyed considerable property and standing, at least until the latter part of the war. The first Richards, the boy's great-grandfather, had come to the New Canaan area of Norwalk in 1714. He was a weaver escaping from the British army where he had served as a volunteer during Queen Anne's War. He soon prospered and acquired a farm. The next generation of Richardses became sea captains, merchants, and local notables. On his mother's side, young James Richards descended from substantial farmers, the Hanfords, who had moved to the Norwalk and New Canaan area a generation before the Richardses.[6] His mother, Ruth, was the strong one in the boy's family, "a woman of vigorous intellect, of consistent piety, and of uncompromising faithfulness in all matters of social duty." Years later Richards was to say that his mother governed her family with her eye and forefinger, but he also remembered that she often smiled even if she seldom laughed.[7]

In 1782 James Richards at the age of fifteen went to nearby Newton where he was apprenticed to a man engaged in cabinet and chair making as well as house painting. He became seriously ill almost immediately and had to return home for two months. When he recovered, he worked for a time in Danbury and New York City, then found a post as an apprentice in Stamford.

Here occurred the great event of his life, one destined to change his prospects entirely: at the age of nineteen he experienced a religious conversion. Looked at today, it is hard to understand how the events surrounding his conversion produced such dramatic results. When his life changed, he was certainly not a dissolute youth but a regular churchgoer, accustomed to thinking of himself as a serious person on the right road to

James Richards was apprenticed to a cabinetmker at age fifteen. (Drawing in Marshall B. Davidson, Three Centuries of American Antiques, *Bonanza Books, New York, 1979)*

responsible adulthood. In his own unfortunately brief account of the event, he said that one evening in May he joined with some other young men for an evening of fun. Richards, with some of his friends, came in disguise and proceeded to other acts of "unaccustomed levity. But what was meant for mirth became the occasion for the conviction of sin." When recounting this experience, Richards did not elaborate on what sins or thoughts or beliefs suddenly made him feel in jeopardy. Perhaps the mere act of donning a disguise with its theatrical associations, along with drinking, loosened his inhibitions and the results shattered his spiritual complacency. He recalled later that he had remained in great distress for several days, convinced of his guilt until he read the Thirty-eighth Psalm.

Richards never explained why the Psalm afforded him relief from his distress. The psalmist offers no consolation or reassurance to a person estranged from God; rather the psalmist describes his worthlessness and vulnerability and concludes with a cry for help. "O Lord, rebuke me not in thy wrath. . . . There is no soundness in my flesh, because of thine anger. . . . My lovers and my friends stand aloof. . . . Forsake me not, O Lord. . . . Make haste to help me, O Lord my salvation." Perhaps he saw in the psalmist's demand for help the assurance that God was not indifferent. Possibly he heard his own situation perfectly described and heard the psalmist give voice to his own heartfelt prayer.

> I had long cherished the idea that I could be converted when I pleased, that faith preceded conversion and that by exercising it I should lay God under obligation to give me a new heart. The time for the experiment at last came. My sins found me out, and I attempted to believe according to my cherished notions of faith, and thus induce God to give me the grace of regeneration. For several days I struggled, and struggled in vain. I began to see my own impotency, and consequently my dependence on the sovereign interposition of God; and the more I saw, the more I hated. I became alarmed in view of my enmity, and began to feel that I had passed beyond my day of grace, and was rapidly sinking to hell. But at length my soul melted, and the method of salvation I had hated became my joy and my song.[8]

On another occasion, reflecting on his preconversion self, Richards wrote, "I was born an Arminian; but obstinate freewiller as I was, at length, by sovereign power and mercy, I was brought to lick the dust of God's footstool, and accept of salvation by grace."[9] In calling himself an Arminian he accused himself of what strict Calvinists considered a heresy. Jacobus Arminius, a Dutch Calvinist theologian of the seventeenth century, believed predestination was not absolute, but that salvation was open to everyone who sought it. More exacting Calvinists found Arminius's seeming limitation of the awesome power of God heretical. It was Arminius's easy road to salvation from which James turned away. At the moment of his conversion he was overwhelmed by the conviction that his life and fate depended on God alone and this revelation called forth his complete and grateful submission. It felt like an essential reorientation of his basic inclinations and affections.

Richards quickly joined the Congregational Church in Stamford, where he felt compelled to describe what had happened to him to anyone who would listen. At first his enthusiasm was disconcerting to some members of the parish despite the fact that his was a classical experience of personal conversion.

In the early seventeenth century among American Puritans, it was hoped that a child would experience conversion in late adolescence, be baptized, and then enter into full membership in the Congregational Church and the political community. By the middle of the seventeenth century, conversion experiences were occurring less frequently and the church had been able to carry on only by developing a "halfway covenant." Good people, themselves baptized as children, who did not experience conversion, could still be members of the church and have their children baptized. This lukewarm piety became increasingly common as the colonists became distant in time from the founding generation.

Conversions reappeared in quantity in the 1740s under the influence of the Great Awakening. While still an individual experience, conversion now was often experienced in large gatherings under the influence of a charismatic preacher. Known as a revival, the phenomenon often split communities. When the great English revivalist George Whitefield passed through Connecticut, he called for a return to the piety of the early Puritans. He did much to arouse the dormant religious sensibilities of the people against the smug and undemanding church establishment, but he was followed by itinerant preachers who went into many parishes and stirred the people to profound dissatisfaction with their pastors. Congregations split into New Lights who supported the new movement and Old Lights who were shocked. Baptists asked to be exempted from church taxes; Episcopalians made inroads among those who cherished peace and quiet instead of noisy revivalism. Everywhere the power of the laity increased, and the "standing order," the leaders of Connecticut's Congregational Church, was left in disarray. The residents of New Canaan were among those who experienced the excesses of the Great Awakening most vividly. James Davenport, son of the pastor in Stamford, and half brother of one of the founders of New Canaan Parish, was jailed for the local disorders that attended his preaching. He was reputed to have made a bonfire of the books of liberal theologians and then to have fed it with the silks and laces of his female admirers and finally even his own plush breeches.[10]

The ferment died down as the Revolution approached and people were distracted by more secular issues. The confrontation was usually argued in terms of natural and constitutional rights. The educated read Montesquieu, Voltaire, Locke, the Scottish writers, and Thomas Paine as well as the political output of such men as Thomas Jefferson, John Adams, and Benjamin Franklin. There was intense political debate over the nature of man, the legitimacy of revolution, and the meaning of the rights of Englishmen. The confrontation with England was also, however, couched in religious terms; American troops went into battle submitting to fast days and jeremiads that called on God to make them worthy of support against the corrupt English. Thus the Calvinist clergy were in the forefront of the Revolution, and Congregationalism was associated with republicanism.

Once the Revolution was over, clergy and political leaders alike brought a new urgency to discussions about religion. Citizens of a republic needed to vote out of concern for the public good rather than their private interests. Disinterested moral behavior was a necessity if the country was to survive, yet the war had brought an erosion of morality, a loosening of community standards, and a heightened consciousness of individual rights. Churches were eager to take up this difficult aspect of nation building even as others bent their efforts to more secular concerns. By the 1790s the early signs of a renewal of revivals in Kentucky, the West, and New Jersey were noted and enthusiastically communicated. Young James Richards's conversion in 1786 was a solitary experience, but it pointed to the flood of revivals that was coming.

Richards returned to New Canaan a new man and everyone saw it. The boy who had left a "dependent mechanic" came back an aspirant to the ministry. Not everyone was comfortable in recognizing his new character and aspirations, but others "blessed God for the change" and "marvelled." His master saw no point in keeping him to his indenture and kindly excused him from his obligations; his brother William testified that his own life was reoriented at this time by James's example; villagers were moved to attend weekly religious classes that he revived and led. The means were now found for him to attend Pastor Justus Mitchell's school and prepare for Yale. Reverend Mitchell had started this school three years before when young Richards was leaving New Canaan to be an apprentice. Had family circumstances been easier, he might have attended it then. The circumstances had not changed, but his zeal and passion combined with his already recognized ability to make it possible now. His family helped him in critical ways. When he fell ill again for several months to the point that he could not use his eyes, his younger sister Diana read his lessons to him. When he moved to Norwalk to continue his preparation under another minister, Dr. Burnett, his mother's relatives, Sarah and Phebe Comstock, gave him room and board. Finally Richards entered Yale in the fall of 1789, aged twenty-two.[11]

To date his path had not been easy and this did not change. At the end of his freshman year, he ran out of money. He returned to Norwalk, Dr. Burnett, and the Comstocks. Again he became dangerously ill; he was so weak he could not speak for several weeks and was not expected to live. And again a sister, this time Ruth, nursed him back to health, bearing "him in her arms, or placing him in an easy chair . . . , or indulg[ing] him in the grateful exercise of the family swing, as though he were but a child, and as if her own life were bound up in his."[12] Richards was curiously grateful for his terrible illnesses during this time, or rather for his recoveries that he took to be signs of God's blessing on his ambition.

His irregular course of instruction continued for several more years and included independent study in Farmington where he taught school, and formal study under Dr. Timothy Dwight at Greenfield Hill. Dwight was a grandson of Jonathan Edwards, the theologian who had inspired the Great Awakening. He ran a well-known school at Greenfield Hill and had already established a reputation as a poet. He went on to become the president of Yale in 1795, where he was much admired for turning an unbelieving student body back to the church and for enlarging the curriculum by introducing science courses. Known later as "The Pope of Connecticut," he was responsible for preparing many more than James Richards for the ministry before he was finished.

It was while Richards was in Farmington, teaching school and studying independently, that he met a local girl who was "delicate in appearance, pleasing in manner, intelligent, pious, sympathetic and devoted."[13] Time would prove Caroline Cowles and James Richards to be admirably suited to

Timothy Dwight. (Courtesy—Presbyterian Historical Society, Philadelphia)

each other. She came from older Puritan stock than he, being descended on her mother's side from the Reverend Thomas Hooker, founder of the Hartford colony. Her father's family were farmers who had lived for four generations in Farmington. Her mother died when she was ten months old and she was adopted by her mother's childless sister and brother-in-law, Anna (Hooker) Smith and Thomas Smith. She was evidently very fond of them as she later named her first child Anna Smith Richards and her oldest son Henry Smith Richards. By the time she met James Richards, her father had died, leaving her a small inheritance of forty pounds.[14]

Once Richards had completed his education, but while he was still a bachelor, he took the next step in becoming a minister; he presented himself for licensing to the Association in the Western District of Fairfield County. The Congregational Church was organized into independent churches that were joined in regional associations. There were no higher authorities. Once approved by the Association he could preach but he could not be ordained until called to be a pastor. Dr. Burnett of Norwalk claimed him for his first sermon, and he preached in neighboring towns for several sabbaths. He was then invited to go across the sound to Long Island, New York, to the Presbyterian whaling villages of Sag Harbor and Shelter Island. His first efforts at preaching and ministering were well received.

His earnest sincerity as he began his career is evident in a covenant he wrote on December 22, 1793:

> I do now, in the presence of God and his holy angels, solemnly avouch the Lord Jehovah, Father, Son and Holy Ghost, to be my God, and promise, by the help of his Holy Spirit, without which I can do nothing, to devote myself to him in an everlasting covenant, never to be forgotten. As the chief of sinners, I resolve to look up to God for pardon and acceptance, through the blood of his dear son, and to rest my soul on the gracious promises of the Gospel; determining to renounce sin in all its appearances, I resolve to consecrate my time, talents, and all that I have on earth, to the service of God, promising to make his glory the ultimate end of all my actions. It is my resolution to be more watchful and prayerful than I have hitherto been, to see that my thoughts are employed on proper subjects, and in their proper times; to guard against all rash and heedless words, all severe and unjustifiable remarks on the persons and character of other men; taking heed to the door of my lips, that I offend not with my tongue.

I resolve that I will not suffer my passions to take the place of my reason.
. . . Never to be angry without a cause . . . to be faithful in all the
relative duties incumbent on me . . .

Remember, O my Soul, these resolutions and the vows of God which are
upon thee. . . . [15]

He was consciously honing the habits of circumspection that became his
hallmark.

Richards's move to Long Island had more significance than was probably evident at the time. He was leaving Connecticut along with thousands
of others who found too few opportunities there. His father had tried
Ohio briefly at the close of the Revolution, and in the next generation,
James and his brothers Silas and Abraham, all sought careers outside of
New Canaan, Connecticut. There was still hope of success at home as his
cousin Isaac demonstrated by turning the old shipping business into a great
success, but there was not room for all the cousins when families ran to as
many as eleven children.

The move to Long Island opened opportunities for him for another
reason as well. It took him out of the Congregational Church and into the
Presbyterian. Both churches, along with the Dutch Reformed Church,
recognized themselves as spiritual descendents of John Calvin. They all
shared the same fundamental beliefs and a sufficiently similar style of
worship that they could call each other's ministers to be pastors. On the
southern and western boundaries of New England this happened
frequently enough to cause no comment. In all likelihood Richards simply
accepted an opportunity that presented itself, but in doing so he moved
out of a church that was to remain resolutely tied to New England and
into one that was destined to grow much larger as it attempted to understand and answer the spiritual needs of the whole country. In the years
following the Revolution, this could not have been obvious to Richards.
The Congregationalists were the largest denomination in America and the
Presbyterians were a distinct second. Even harder to foresee would have
been the eventual success of the Baptists and Methodists. Hardly a presence
in Connecticut and New York as he began his ministry, by the end of his
life they would be more numerous than either the Congregationalists or
the Presbyterians.

The changing influence of the denominations hinged on organization as much as doctrine. A clear source of the Presbyterians' strength was their hierarchical organization. By 1786 they had grouped their self-sufficient congregations into sixteen presbyteries and these in turn into four synods. Representatives from the presbyteries met once a year in a national gathering called the General Assembly, and this body maintained a permanent presence in Philadelphia. In contrast the decentralized Congregationalists consciously rejected even statewide institutions and were ill-prepared to develop a national strategy of evangelism.

The high degree of centralization in the Presbyterian Church was always associated with doctrinal rigor. The Presbyterians had a long-standing tradition dating back to Scotland and Ireland of demanding adherence to carefully worded statements of faith. Arguably their rigor hindered them at times, while strengthening them at others. During the Great Awakening, they had divided into New Side and Old Side Presbyterians that corresponded to the Congregationalists' New Lights and Old Lights mentioned earlier. To be sure they had come back together again, but they remained a contentious group destined to divide again and again. Despite these differences and some mutual suspicion, the Congregationalists and Presbyterians consulted frequently and looked for ways to cooperate. They both felt beleaguered by the secular spirit abroad in the country. For orthodox New Englanders, there was an additional threat from those they identified as Unitarians. Strongly influenced by eighteenth-century rationalism and humanism, many prominent, well-educated Congregationalists in Boston were moving away from a belief in the Trinity and predestination and towards a more liberal vision. They saw God as loving and merciful; free will opened salvation to all. The Presbyterians to the south were acutely conscious of a different challenge, the pressing religious needs of the rapidly expanding frontier. If the Gospel was not provided in these areas, by default indifference would become the norm in the hinterland as much as in the cities.

As James Richards started to move into the Presbyterian orbit, he was moving into a world that was both familiar and self-consciously different from New England Congregationalism. He would always be identified within the Presbyterian Church as a descendant of the New England tradition with its looser church discipline. At the same time his organizational and administrative gifts would be recognized and put to use in ways that the Congregational Church could not have duplicated.

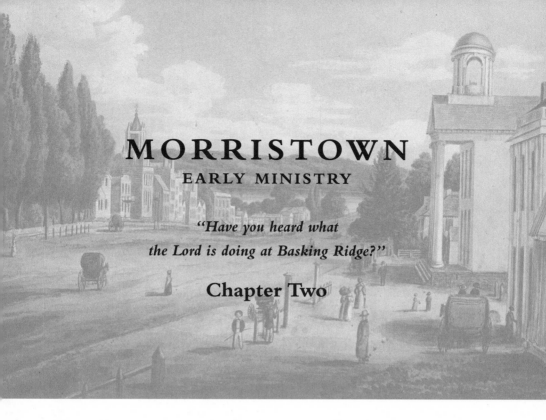

MORRISTOWN

EARLY MINISTRY

*"Have you heard what
the Lord is doing at Basking Ridge?"*

Chapter Two

J ames Richards, aged twenty-seven, rode into Morristown, New Jersey, for
the first time in May 1794. The Morristown Presbyterian Church had
been looking for a pastor for the last nine months and had called him to
preach on a trial basis.

The situation in Morristown was rather touchy. For fifty years Dr.
Timothy Johnes had enjoyed great success as pastor and had won the love
of his parishioners. Two accidents had severely restricted his ability to
perform pastoral duties in his later years, however. In 1788 he fell and frac-
tured his thigh, and then, as he was recovering, he broke his other leg.[1]
With Johnes totally crippled and unable to leave his residence, the Morristown congregation in 1791 called the Reverend Aaron Collins to serve as
"collegial pastor." The new man proved unpopular and within a year some
members of the congregation applied to the presbytery to either silence or
discharge him. Under the circumstances, Collins had resigned and moved
on, leaving behind a considerable legacy of division and ill will.[2] Richards
was not deterred. He had been recommended to the congregation by an
old friend of Johnes from Easthampton, Long Island, for his promising
ministerial character. "The man who on a thorough acquaintance with
James Richards, does not love him, cannot himself be deserving the love of
any man."[3]

James Richards. (Taken from John Morgan Richards, With John Bull and Jonathan, *D. Appleton, New York, 1906)*

Morristown was a handsome compact little town of fifty houses, nineteen miles northwest of Newark and a hundred miles northeast of Philadelphia. Because it was the county seat of Morris County, it had a courthouse as well as a Baptist church and two Presbyterian churches, a small one that the congregation had outgrown and a new one nearing completion. The town was founded in 1710 when a few families moved to the area from Newark and Elizabeth, doubtlessly drawn by the abundance of iron in the vicinity. By the time James Richards arrived, seven iron mines were in operation. Although a few wealthy families like the Schuylers had given the town the reputation of being aristocratic, most of the inhabitants were small merchants and farmers. Nearby Elizabeth was their point of export. Morristown had a proud history of being the winter headquarters of Washington's army during the early years of the Revolution. Because it was relatively self-sufficient, it had survived the Revolution with little damage to its economy.[4]

The Presbyterian church in Morristown drew its original membership from the New England Congregationalists of Newark, as well as from the Huguenots, the members of the Dutch Reformed Church, and the Irish and Scottish Presbyterians who had all joined together to form it. In the Middle Colonies where there had been no established Calvinist church, such an arrangement gave strength and stability to them all. Morristown's congregation now numbered six hundred persons.[5] It found itself in the presbytery of Elizabeth, the Synod of New York and New Jersey, and within two days' journey of the national headquarters in Philadelphia. Since the Presbyterian Church in New Jersey had been formed from all local Calvinists, it was no more unusual for Morristown to consider a

Morristown Presbyterian Church.
(Courtesy—Collections of the
New Jersey Historical Society)

Congregationalist from Long Island as a possible pastor than it had been for his previous church in Sag Harbor.

The business of calling a new pastor was not undertaken lightly; the relationship was intended to be permanent and the Morristown Presbyterian Church had already made one mistake with the Reverend Collins. Aware that Johnes had tended his flock for half a century, James Richards wrote later, "With you I was willing to live, and with you I expected to die."[6] The committee formed to seek a new pastor thought it prudent to begin their search by calling for a "day of humiliation, fasting and prayer to Almighty God." They then invited James Richards to come on a trial basis. In July after Richards had preached for three months to the congregation and privately to Johnes in the parsonage, the congregation was ready to vote. The approbation was overwhelming; 142 were in favor of calling him while two wished to continue the test. They then voted him the rather meager salary of $440 to be paid in quarterly installments, the use of the parsonage except a small part planted with a nursery of mulberry trees, and firewood. They agreed to raise the money by levying a tax on all parishioners in direct imitation of the manner in which state taxes were raised, except that four assistants to the assessor were to be chosen annually whose job it was to see that the tax fell equitably and did not create undue hardship. The salary may have been small but the church trustees were stretching themselves to their limits as they had been building a new church for the last four years and still had to figure out how to pay for the plastering, glazing, and seats.

In James Richards they had found a pastor very much like old Dr. Johnes whom they loved so well. They had both arrived by way of the Congregational Church, Yale, and Long Island, and both were known for their pastoral gifts rather than their literary attainments. For Richards, accepting the offer at Morristown meant that he would be a full-fledged Presbyterian instead of a Congregationalist and that in fact, if not by intent, he would be close to the heart of the Presbyterian Church.

Richards quickly settled into the busy life of a pastor. Initially he helped the congregation resolve the differences that lingered from the dismissal of Pastor Collins. Within a few months of Pastor Johnes's death, Richards took pastoral charge and made plans for his ordination in May of the next year. That same fall he received his B.A. degree from Yale, granted *in absentia* at the instance of Timothy Dwight, his old teacher and now the president of Yale. Then in November he traveled north to Farmington, Connecticut, to marry Caroline Cowles. Everyone said "she had a fine setting out" when she left with a hair trunk filled with clothing, household linens, a feather bed, and six silver teaspoons that had belonged to her mother.[7] It was to be a fruitful and happy marriage that lasted forty-nine years.

There is no question that Richards was comfortable in this church and that he enjoyed the confidence, respect, and affection of his whole flock. He attributed his increasing success as a minister to his sensitivity to God's will, but he also recognized that he benefited from conversation with a cross section of "his people." No intellectual snob, he was invigorated by conversing with the plainest among them.[8] He was finally so much in demand that he was forced to set some priorities in allocating his time.

In this great congregation I had the sick and afflicted to visit, the dead to bury, the wandering to look after, the captious and uneasy to soothe, besides schools to catechise and lectures to preach and prayer-meetings to attend; altogether creating a vast amount of labor, independent of regular family visitations and preparing for the pulpit. Not a little time was consumed in occasional calls upon my people and their calls upon me. . . . It became necessary therefore to . . . attend to those first which were of the most urgent character, leaving others to the dubiousness of an hereafter.[9]

In the seasons of revival, there was no need for anxiety about allocating his time; his job was to set all else aside and enter fully into the joyful work. Thirty years later he could still recall his intense feeling that "The Lord was in the midst of us."[10] During his ministry there were three major revivals, the first within two years of his installation in 1796, a second in 1803 and 1804, and a third in 1808.

The first was remarkable chiefly, from this circumstance, that it came upon the congregation by surprise. None of the church members, that ever I could learn were especially stirred up to desire or expect it. . . . But prepared or unprepared, the windows of heaven were opened, and the spiritual rain descended, and about one hundred souls were hopefully brought into the kingdom. . . . [11]

The second revival was confined to one or two neighborhoods, but the third was more general. He always regarded it as "the most precious" since it seemed so obviously a gift of the Holy Spirit. His congregation had watched as revivals appeared in neighboring towns. They calculated "that the good work would go from congregation to congregation as a matter of course," only to discover that "the cloud of God's presence had come to our very borders, on two sides of us, and was stayed." Then they began to "tremble, and to feel their dependence."[12]

They were describing the same process he had gone through at his conversion. At first complacent, they came to realize that God was sovereign indeed and that the world and their souls were God's to dispose of.

Richards had a role to play in promoting a revival. Although he was always quick to acknowledge God's sovereignty in the matter, he did all he could to prepare his people: "The gospel was preached as plainly and faithfully as I was able and, that publicly, and from house to house." He felt certain that God did not rain down his mercies upon those who were "cold to Him." The failure to have a revival was therefore a rebuke both to him because he had not adequately sensitized his congregation and to the congregation for not caring enough about religion. But he still could do no more than prepare his people, and nurture every sign of "tenderness" among them.

He knew that a revival was trustworthy if it was "solemn" and "deep." Only then could it transform a convert's life. In later years he was pleased to note that "the members gathered during this revival had been peculiarly circumspect, and very few of them [had been] subjected to any church censure."

While only a scattering of revivals took place in New Jersey and elsewhere in the early 1800s, they soon occurred with sufficient regularity that the period was later called the "Second Awakening." Revivals were of enormous interest to the church at large which was struggling with the problems of indifference, competition from Unitarianism, and a shortage of ministers on the frontier. New England clergymen such as Jedidiah Morse of Charlestown, Massachusetts and Timothy Dwight of Yale feared that the battle for a godly nation was being lost. Threats came in the shape of deists, Jacobins, Masonic plots, and unruly, godless students. Revivals that gave people such a vivid experience of God that their lives were transformed forever was one line of defense. Just such a moment of powerful insight had totally reoriented Richards's own life and brought him into the ministry.

Richards and his colleagues spread all encouraging news about revivals that came their way. A letter to his neighbor in Newark, the Reverend Griffin, shows him intensely scrutinizing the working out of revivals in his area:

Morristown, Feby 23rd, 1803

Dear Brother,

My hope that the Lord will do something for us in these parts are not a little raised since I saw you. . . . One man about middle age was exceedingly cut down [moved] - felt as if he could not endure the thought of visiting his habitation again with his old wicked heart. He received his first impressions [inclinations towards conversion] under your sermon at Marsdom. I have since conversed with him; he appears very solemn. The work appears to be spreading in Marsdom. . . . I am ready to say surely the Lord has come. I am the more persuaded of this, because I imagine I see Him sitting on a refiners fire and as the fullers soap.[13] I see old professors [members] are shaken, and looking back on their former barrenness with shame and trembling. It is a good sign with me when the Lord begins his work at the sanctuary.

The letter continues with an account of his visit to Rockaway and Mount Freedom where there were the same hopeful signs. Large numbers of people came out despite the bad weather. He finished by describing the situation in another town:

Have you heard what the Lord is doing at Basking Ridge? . . . That day, through the goodness of God, sounded an alarm to many. On Friday evening . . . about one hundred and fifty persons were assembled of different ages and descriptions, unbeknown to their pastor and sent for him to come among them. He went and found as many as fifty or sixty weeping and lamenting for their sins. Nothing had been said previously to excite their passions. Does not this seem like the footsteps of the Lord?[14]

Revivals were the highlights. The day-to-day business of running a church and nurturing a flock were essential tasks that took up far more of his time. While people expected care and support in times of trouble, they also submitted to the discipline of their neighbors in the church community. Church members were called to do more than avoid scandal; they were to actively cultivate piety at home and in public. Thus careful attention to behavior was another way of advancing the cause of orthodox religion.

Richards regularly sat with the elders of his church in "session" to discipline individuals in need of rebuke. Bethuel Howard appeared before them to explain why, despite the fact that he had formerly entered into covenant with the church and received baptism for his children, he had not attended the ordinance of the Lord's Supper. John B. was advised not to marry Polly A. while he was not legally divorced from his former wife according to the laws of New Jersey. Mrs. C. was told that the excuse of not having decent clothes to appear in public was not sufficient reason for not attending the Lord's Supper since it was due to her want of care and industry and to her extravagant use of opium. Abigail P. was chastised for not attending public worship since her belief that she was persecuted by the congregation was without foundation. Amos P. appeared and acknowledged that he had been guilty of the sin of intemperance but this was not enough; he had to make a public confession before the congregation. A committee was formed to investigate Wm. C.'s neglect of the education of his children. I.C. was chastised for his neglect of family prayers and unkind treatment towards his wife. Nancy B. was required to make a public confession of her sin of "antenuptual fornication" which dishonored her Christian profession. Even if full names were not recorded for posterity, the session did not hesitate to impose its discipline in public.

James Richards and the session members had to come to grips quickly with the problem of who was a member in good standing on whom they could impose the discipline of the church. It was an old problem whose first solutions dated back to the Half Way Covenant. For a long time persons who had at some time in the past professed their religion and who were of good moral character could have their children baptized and were entitled to regular standing in the church. Now in an era when pressure was mounting for a personal experience of conversion and an active response of visible piety, the session concluded it must revoke the privileges of membership for anyone who did not regularly attend the Lord's Supper. At the meeting of September 3, 1795, a few months after Richards's ordination, they decided to review all the church records to arrive at a more accurate list of members. By 1804, members could be required to come before the session to give an account of their experimental acquaintance with religion or to publicly profess their faith under oath. Not all the efforts of the session were directed at greater exclusiveness, however. Older members who had entered the church when regulations were looser benefited from a kind of grandfather clause.

Separate from the elders who met in session with Richards were the trustees. All questions of money, except the provision for poor widows which was reserved for the session, came before the elected trustees of the parish, and Richards did not sit with this group. Six months after his ordination, the trustees were wrestling with the problem of how to raise enough money to finish the new church, now six years in construction. When a committee reported back that it was impossible to raise the money, the trustees decided to abandon the old system of assessments and sell the seats in the new church instead. Number 1 on the east side was reserved for the minister's family, and number 1 on the west side for strangers, and numbers 31 and 32 were for the hard of hearing and the poor. The rest were priced to cover the cost of the remaining work and the minister's salary. When the parish met to consider the new system, it voted to make eight seats free and fixed the assessment on the others at sums ranging from £29 to £120. The front seats brought the higher price. They continued to play with the system, selling some, renting others, reserving some for choristers and some for communicants on sacramental days. The church was finally completed in 1796, so in a sense the new system worked, but it could still not wring money from those unable or unwilling to pay. Notices had to be sent requesting delinquents to make speedy payment on their pews so that the trustees could pay the pastor.

A memorandum from 1797 shows the rental and sale of one hundred fifty-eight pews raised $533. Most of the money went for the minister's salary, and the maintenance of the church, but included in the list of expenses was $24.62 for cider and cake consumed at the yearly "wood-frolick." This event traditionally brought together the greater part of the congregation. The ladies prepared supper at the parsonage, while the men cut some forty cords of wood, the year's supply of fuel for their minister.[15]

Over the years the trustees often had to discuss measures for collecting arrears in Richards's salary. They managed an increase of $125 in December 1803, but in 1808 they were only able to pay part of the balance due him or "compromise by paying him the interest on said balance."

All this discussion of his salary pointed to the very real difficulty Richards was having in living on what he was paid. What had been barely satisfactory in the beginning had become inadequate in the face of his growing family. Anna Smith was born in 1796 and Harriet Caroline, always known as Caroline, in 1799. James Henry, born in 1801, died of whooping cough at one month, but two years later Henry Smith was born. Then another son, named after his father, died soon after birth, this time of smallpox. Edward Cowles arrived in 1806. With four children, the pastor was forced to take in boarders to make ends meet.[16]

The first boarder was Lewis Condict, a cheerful and talkative medical student who eventually became a congressman. His father, the Reverend Aaron Condict, was such a good friend that he baptized two of the Richards children. Later boarders taken into the parsonage were never named in any of the Richardses' correspondence.

As time passed, more of Richards's attention was directed outward to a larger Presbyterian world beyond his parish. Not only did the concern for revivals link clergy but so did a host of other interests, like the production and distribution of religious books, joint missionary activities, the provision of appropriate theological training for new ministers, and cases of discipline that went beyond the individual parish or session to the next administrative level, the presbytery. The presbytery, which met regularly, consisted of representative lay elders and all the ministers within a district. Through these activities Richards developed his talent for organization, and his judgment of human character and situations. These abilities grew finely tuned with exercise and were noted by a widening circle of clergymen.

In 1803, the General Assembly, the national organization of the Presbyterian Church, asked Richards to go as a missionary for a month to the back country of New Jersey.[17] This missionary activity was conceived as a way to provide minimal spiritual nourishment to areas that were newly or sparsely settled. A minister would be asked to ride circuit through these isolated communities, stopping for a day or two at each one. Even if the funds had been available to pay for a more permanent arrangement, there were not enough trained ministers in existence to supply these areas. Richards completed two such tours for the General Assembly. When he returned from the first, he reported to the Reverend Dr. Ashbel Green, chairman of the Standing Committee on Missions in Philadelphia.

April 26, 1803

Rev. and dear sir,

I entered on my mission the 2nd Tuesday of Oct. and was out one month, the time specified in my appointment. My first sermon was preached at Mount Pleasant 12 miles north of Morristown at the house of Mr. Moses Tuthill to a very small audience, not more than sixty or seventy persons owing in part to the sickliness of the season by which many were confined.

The letter continued with a day-by-day account of the many small villages he visited. The report leaves a vivid impression of a thinly populated region, grateful to the General Assembly for the occasional missionary whom they sent. He preached largely to Presbyterians but sometimes to Baptists and the Dutch.

> I spent one sabbath at Nominac, with a particular view to the English people who are settled at New Milford on the opposite side of the river. This is mentioned partly as an apology for passing so much of my time among the Dutch congregations who it may be supposed might be supplied by their own Church or synod. I might say also, if it were necessary, that I was totally ignorant of the religious order or state of this part of the country until I had gotten into it and that finding them extremely destitute of the preached gospel I felt myself warranted to pass a little time among them. . . .

The letter concluded:

> This completed my missionary service in the accomplishment of which I delivered 19 sermons, rode 240 miles, and collected on different occasions to the amount of ten dollars which sum is now due from me to the General Assembly and which I shall transmit to you by one of the commissioners of our Presbytery in May next.
>
> I have been particular in stating the places of my preaching and in some instances their distances and bearing from each other, that if the committee should make out another mission into this country which I hope they will do, they may avail themselves of these circumstances in diverting the labour of the person or persons whom they shall employ.
>
> I am with sentiments of high esteem
> your affectionate brother in the Lord
> James Richards
> P.S. Circumstances will not permit of my being employed as a missionary this ensuing year.[18]

The thinness of the population in western New Jersey as late as 1803 makes clear what a monumental task the General Assembly faced in providing missionaries for the West, and that was only a small part of the region that needed missionaries. There was also the Genessee Valley of western New York, the Western Reserve in Ohio, and the whole trans-Appalachian South; the Louisiana Territory and Florida were about to be added. The next year the General Assembly records showed 204 vacant parishes as against 190 settled ones.[19] As can be seen from Richards's comments about the Dutch, there was no established pattern of cooperation between different denominations in New Jersey that might have made the task easier.

The Morristown trustees debated whether to pay him for the month he was away on this missionary tour. Did they resent the loss of his services? Or did they simply hope to strike a shrewd bargain? Whatever the reason, it hardly seemed generous and may have accounted for his declining to do a missionary tour the next year.

Another source of contact between the clergy centered around the printing and distribution of books, sermons, and tracts. Richards promoted Scott's four volumes of *Bible Commentary* over a seven-year period. Written between 1788 and 1792 by Thomas Scott, an English clergyman converted to extreme Calvinism, they were reissued many times since they were considered one of the theological achievements of the age in England. Richards worked with the Philadelphia printer, bookseller, and stationer William Woodward to distribute the commentaries in his area. Letter after letter spelled out the arrangements for delivery, additions to the subscription list, variations in the bindings demanded by different subscribers, and replacement pages that were needed due to printing errors. There was no established distribution system or any regular means of collecting money and safely passing it along, so Richards found himself weighing the advantages of the stage versus shipment by sea to New York where a drop-off point could be arranged, specifying how the packaging should be done, and himself collecting the moneys owed by many of the subscribers. Thanks to all the effort he was willing to make, this latest theological work was circulating in New Jersey a few years after publication in England. He made sure that his brothers in Savannah, Silas and Abraham, each got a set as well as other serious laymen and his fellow clergy.[20] The whole business of publishing runs like a leitmotif through his letters. Next he promoted Bellamy's sermons,[21] then articles for various evangelical magazines, tracts, and sermons for missionary societies. He and his fellow pastors were astute promoters of the written as well as the spoken word.

The pastors in the New York Presbytery gathered once a month to conduct the business of the presbytery and once a year to elect their delegate to the General Assembly. Richards was elected several times. The regular business of the presbytery included the licensing of ministers, the trial of cases that were referred from the local churches, the arrangement of pulpit exchanges, and any other questions that were of common interest.

Letters between Richards and Edward Griffin of Newark suggest the increasing authority with which Richards spoke at these meetings. Griffin, for instance, wrote of a Mrs. Arden who was censured by the session of her church in New York City for leaving her husband without cause. Her husband had made various unsubstantiated accusations against her. Understandably she felt that she had been denied due process and wished to appeal to the presbytery. She was unwilling to proceed, nor would anyone suggest to her that she should, until she had consulted with Richards.[22]

So by a variety of means, James Richards made his mark. The College of New Jersey, often referred to as Princeton College although the name was not officially changed until 1896, granted him an honorary Master of Arts degree in 1801. Conveying still more prestige, the General Assembly of the Presbyterian Church elected him their presiding officer or moderator in 1805 at the age of thirty-seven. At the end of his service as moderator, his sermon was published and heard by the whole Presbyterian Church, even though he himself was not there to deliver it because he was suffering acutely from the "bilious cholic."[23] He left it to the redoubtable Ashbel Green to make the appropriate excuses; Ashbel Green who had been chairman of the Standing Committee on Missions, temporary president of Princeton College in 1802, and chaplain to the Congress of the United States.

Ashbel Green. (Courtesy—Presbyterian Historical Society, Philadelphia)

Richards had now established himself as a member of the inner circle of the Presbyterian Church.

Few things were more important in the eyes of this inner circle than the spread of God's word. This required not only the proper deployment of the present generation of clergy, but the choosing and nurture of the next generation as well. It was expected that a candidate for the ministry would attend a college and then study with a competent clergyman until ready to present himself to his presbytery for examination. If all went well, he would receive a license to preach. It is not surprising that Richards's letters increasingly mentioned worthy students and candidates for pastorates. In April 1807, he was named to the board of trustees of Princeton College, which put him on the firing line as far as Presbyterian education was concerned.

He took on this new role when the college was in crisis: a great rebellion had taken place a month earlier. The whole affair started when three students visited a tavern, used strong liquor, and then insulted the inhabitants of the town and their teachers. They were suspended. Their fellow students got up a petition in defense of the accused, but the faculty saw this as open rebellion. When students occupied Nassau Hall, college was canceled for five weeks, and 125 of the 165 students were suspended. Who was to blame? What was to be done?[24]

The students were probably bored and rebellious. They were put through a dull, tedious, exhausting course of study by an overworked staff.

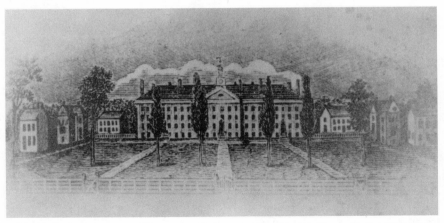

Nassau Hall, Princeton. (Courtesy—Reference Citation, Archives of the University, Department of Rare Books and Special Collections, Princeton University Library)

There was little physical activity to channel the energy of students who were as young as fourteen and fifteen. Moreover, since the Revolution there was a new spirit abroad in the land that talked of liberty, the rights of the individual, and personal dignity, and this spirit was not lost on the students.

The trustees, however, felt that the fault lay with the "pernicious principles and loose morals of some vicious youths" and "the almost unlimited allowance of money or credit given to many others."[25] They wrote to other colleges asking them to refuse to admit the suspended students and were strongly supported. Students everywhere were rebellious and the other colleges were grateful to Princeton for holding the line. The trustees were sure they were witnessing a decline in morality, democracy run amok, and the fruits of deism and Jacobinism. The liberty of the Revolution had deteriorated into license; civic virtue had turned into irreligion. The anger of the trustees was increased by the knowledge that this was the last and the worst in a series of disorders. They blamed President Samuel Stanhope Smith for not being stern enough and wanted him to make it clear to the students who was in charge.

The year after Richards joined the board, enrollment dropped to 112 with no end in sight. The falling enrollment caused loss of revenue which in turn caused a reduction of faculty. Southern boys began to pass Princeton by in favor of Yale and Harvard. But more alarming, the Presbyterian Church was rapidly losing confidence in the college as an appropriate place to educate divinity students. After the riot the Reverend Samuel Miller of New York wrote to the Reverend Griffin of Newark, "Have you heard the terrible news from Princeton? What is the great Head of the Church about to do with that seminary [college]? Is it about to be purged and elevated, or totally destroyed?"[26] To all these worrying questions, the answer of the trustees was discipline and more discipline, and there is no evidence that Richards demurred.

Richards's stay in Morristown came to an end in 1809. His salary was inadequate for the support of his family even with the additional revenue that boarders brought in. At several meetings the situation was laid before the congregation, but the members were slow to respond and nothing was done. The problem was not unique to Morristown. Clergy generally complained of inadequate support in this period. Despite the lifetime commitment he had intended on his arrival, Richards was ready for a change should the opportunity arise, though it would have to be cast as a sign from God to be acceptable.

> When in the summer and fall of 1808, (the year before I went to Newark,) my people refused to unite in an augmentation of my salary, though many were earnestly for it, I found it grieved me, and many things connected with it mortified me and agitated me. I presently discovered that I was getting into a state of mind by no means favorable to my comfort or my usefulness. . . . Though my resolution was to discharge my duty, and leave the event with God, yet I did not infer that I was not at liberty to watch the movings of Providence, and avail myself of any opportunity which should present to change my relations, provided such change appeared to be accompanied with the indications of duty.[27]

Just such a "door of usefulness" presented itself when Dr. Edward Dorr Griffin, his friend and the pastor at Newark, was invited to take up a professorship at Andover Seminary. By the time the call came, the congregation in Morristown was alert to the danger of losing him and did indeed raise his salary. It was too late. The request for dismissal was presented by a member of the Morristown church to the presbytery in Elizabethtown in language calculated to leave no hard feelings:

> [Mr. Richards's] removal I regard rather as the misfortune than the fault of Morristown; and his removal to Newark as an event brought about rather by the providence of God, than by the destination of man.[28]

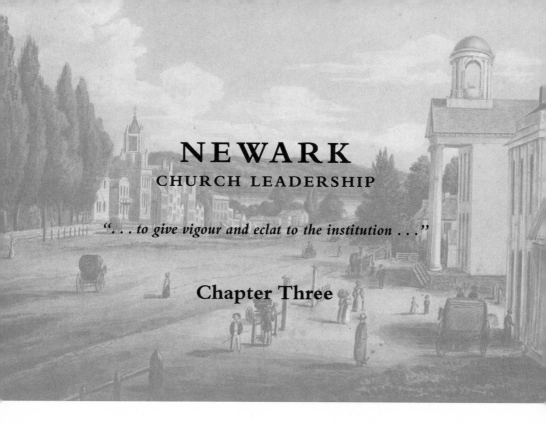

NEWARK
CHURCH LEADERSHIP

". . . to give vigour and eclat to the institution . . ."

Chapter Three

I n the next fourteen years at Newark, Richards immersed himself in pastoral and scholarly activities while enjoying a much enlarged role as a national leader of his church. Strangely, it was in the pastoral role, where his gifts were first apparent and most widely recognized, that his achievement of these years proved the most evanescent. In the early years he experienced great success, in the middle years success with the admixture of painful rivalry, and in the very last years doldrums and frustration.

Although frustrations plagued him in national Presbyterian affairs as well, he unquestionably drew great satisfaction from contributing to the debates and institutions that formed the Calvinist world during a challenging period. At Princeton he played a key role in the shaping of the church's leading educational institutions, an experience that lifted his attention from parish and locality to seminary and nation. Most of his main colleagues—Ashbel Green, Samuel Miller, Edward Griffin—were a few years his junior and superficially better prepared early in life for leadership. They were strong personalities as well. Among them he found an important role as a discreet conciliator with a fine instinct for the middle ground. His colleagues relied on him and his stature grew.

The trend of his career is emblematic of something that was happening in the Presbyterian Church that ultimately hampered the progress of orthodox Calvinism among the American populace over the next half century. Determined to maintain integrity of doctrine and high intellectual standards, Presbyterian ministers became more and more involved with institutions like seminaries and liberal arts colleges that did not directly serve ordinary Americans moving to the frontier or to the larger towns. James Richards was a talented pastor who appreciated the humble among his flock. Fewer and fewer among his colleagues could rub elbows as comfortably and effectively as he. Almost paradoxically, considering his own gifts, in the Newark years he committed his talents increasingly to the formation of institutions that satisfied church organizational standards, but less so the spiritual needs of many Americans.

Newark was nineteen miles from Morristown and presented a familiar face to James Richards. Both towns had been founded by Puritans from his native coastal Connecticut. The restless founding generation had originated in England and then moved to Massachusetts, Long Island, and Connecticut before coming, several dozen families strong, to east Jersey in the 1660s. Before long, some of this group were founding other towns nearby: Montclair, Bloomfield, Whippany, and Morristown itself.[1]

Though Newark was not a prosperous seaport like Charleston or Newport, it carried more distinction than New Canaan or Morristown. When "Parson Richards" looked up Broad Street, he would see above all else the steeple of the First Presbyterian Church, built of stone in 1791, seating seven hundred, "the largest and most elegant of its kind in the state."[2] It was a church rich in exalted Presbyterian associations: the Reverend Aaron Burr Sr., charged with the zeal of the Great Awakening,[3] took up the Newark pastorate in 1744 at the tender age of twenty-one. Burr married Jonathan Edwards's daughter, Esther, and brought her to the Broad Street parsonage where their son Aaron and daughter Sally were born.[4]

In 1754, the senior Burr and others founded the College of New Jersey, intending to make it a stronghold of the New Light followers of Edwards, since Yale then remained firmly in the hands of the Old Lights. After a season in Elizabethtown, the college moved to Newark where

First Presbyterian Church, Newark—"Old First." (Courtesy—First Presbyterian Church, Newark, New Jersey)

classes met in rooms above the town jail. Presbyterians in Philadelphia and the South were numerous and wished to have the new institution located closer to them, hence the final move to Princeton in 1756 and the building there of Nassau Hall. The college at Princeton became the chief training ground of the Presbyterian clergy, and Newark took pride in having fostered it.[5]

After Burr, First Church of Newark was dominated for decades by a Scotch-Irish pastor, the Reverend Alexander MacWhorter, who incarnated the Presbyterian "fighting parson" of Revolutionary days. Richards had known MacWhorter well; the elder man had preached the sermon at his ordination in Morristown twelve years before. It was MacWhorter who had built this impressive stone church, and the old man, dead but two years, was still green in local memory.

MacWhorter's successor, Edward Dorr Griffin, was like Richards a New Englander, who when called to a New Jersey pulpit, had been brought into the Presbyterian fold. Both men were the sons of Connecticut farmers and had studied at Yale. But Griffin's father was a wealthy man of superior education, and the uncle for whom he had been named was a minister at Hartford. Both Griffin and Richards had poor health as children, but Griffin's weakness had spared him from farm work and kept him at school year-round. Though two years younger than Richards, Griffin entered Yale three years earlier and completed the course without interruption, winning honors. During the same period, Richards was out in the world learning to be a cabinetmaker. By the time Richards could finance his single year at Yale, Griffin had graduated.[6]

Both young ministers were quite tall—Griffin was 6'3"—and had developed a presence that combined the dignity and paternal affection considered ideal in their profession in a republican age.[7] Both men won recognition for leading successful revivals. Richards, however, showed a diffidence toward publication that Griffin never shared.[8]

The two first met in New Jersey during the winter of 1800. The Griffins had come "south" for the sake of Mrs. Griffin's health. Through their mutual friend, the Reverend Asa Hillyer, Griffin met "Brother Richards" and occasionally preached for him in Morristown. Staying on to fill the pulpit at nearby Orange, the Reverend Griffin immediately oversaw a revival. The local people marveled at his eloquence, and he was soon acclaimed a new "prince of the American pulpit."[9] This overnight success and his just-published accounts of earlier success at New Hartford, Connecticut, made him a prime candidate for a call to Newark to assist and then succeed the venerable MacWhorter.

Thereafter, the paths of the two transplanted New Englanders, Richards and Griffin, crossed and recrossed. In 1805, James Richards presided as moderator of the General Assembly and Edward Griffin preached the Annual Missionary Sermon. As noted before, they exchanged letters on the subject of revivals in 1803. In 1807 in Newark, Griffin presided over a remarkable revival in which ninety-seven joined the church in one day, 200 in all. A letter from Griffin to the Reverend Ashbel Green in Philadelphia describing the revival was subsequently published in the monthly *Panopolist*, the Boston standard-bearer of the orthodox forces against the Unitarians and a pet publishing project of the energetic Rev. Jedidiah Morse.[10] Morse, the author of several popular geography books, matched his passion for documenting the American landscape with a dogged opposition to the Unitarian heresy and other affronts to orthodox sensibility.

Both Richards and Griffin were achieving prominence in a larger Presbyterian world which cultivated its ties with like-minded Congregationalists in New England such as Morse. After several years of informal consultations, the two denominations had agreed in 1801 in a Plan of Union

Edward Dorr Griffin. (Courtesy—Yale University Library)

put forward by Jonathan Edwards Jr. to cooperate in supplying ministers to the opening West and in combating the rationalist forces at home. In the spirit of that cooperation, Griffin's thriving pastorate at Newark was interrupted in 1809 by a call to Congregationalist New England to assist the orthodox cause in a new endeavor.

Orthodox Calvinism was in a state of alarm. Ever since the Unitarian Henry Ware had been elected in 1805 to the chair of Divinity at Harvard College, Jedidiah Morse, as an aggrieved member of Harvard's Board of Overseers, had worked to marshal the fractious orthodox for concerted action. The issue seemed momentous because faculties in American colleges were so small that a single professor like Ware could dominate theological education. Although orthodox leaders such as Morse were concerned about the state of Harvard as a whole, their immediate focus was the content of the training to be given to future ministers who would fill the pulpits of the rapidly expanding country. Now, with sympathetic friends, Morse set about founding a new theological seminary at Andover, Massachusetts, to educate a pure orthodox ministry ready to counter the influence of liberal thinkers like Ware. Such an idea was not original: Calvinist brethren in the Dutch Reformed Church, without a college to nurture, had established the nation's first theological seminary at New

Brunswick, New Jersey, in 1786. Morse's Presbyterian allies, Samuel Miller and Ashbel Green, increasingly displeased with their own College of New Jersey at Princeton, had for some time bruited in their private correspondence a similar measure for improving the quality and numbers of Presbyterian clergy.

The New Englanders moved more rapidly and reached out to include the Presbyterians of the Middle States in the new enterprise. In gathering the faculty of three for Andover, Morse's first choice as professor of Pulpit Eloquence was the Reverend Dr. Samuel Miller of New York City. Miller, an established voice in national Presbyterian affairs whose focus was on Princeton, refused, but agreed to approach Morse's second choice, Dr. Griffin of Newark. In his letter to Griffin, Miller noted that along with the new seminary, the orthodox community in Boston was determined to build a "large and handsome church" in the "heart of Boston" which would serve the seminary as a "center of orthodox operations."[11] This was the Park Street Church, facing Boston Common just steps from the Massachusetts Statehouse. Griffin accepted the professorship, but he also expressed interest in the pastorate of the new church. Since Andover was twenty or so miles away, the seminary donors demurred, but they agreed that he could preach there half the year and reside there four months of the year. Under this arrangement, Griffin prepared to depart for New England. James Richards, in turn, was now called to fill the vacancy at Newark.

As usual, the first and immediate issue facing everyone was the new pastor's financial support, which even in a more flourishing congregation than that of Morristown tended to be grudging. In a letter written to Richards a month prior to his departure for Massachusetts, Griffin had conveyed the congregation's terms: $1,100 in quarterly payments which was double his salary at Morristown, $100 for wood, and the use of the Broad Street parsonage which Griffin reckoned as worth $400. "The perquisites and presents will amount to from $200 to $400, I expect." He apologized for not getting another $100, "I pressed it out of doors with all my might and with a warmth bordering on anger," but to no avail. At Judge Pennington's urging, the congregation had agreed over some objections to build a second church to accommodate the members added in the previous year. The smaller congregation left at First Church could not afford to pay another $100, so Griffin had let the matter drop. "We have suffered so much from their grumblings about salary, that we are prepared to say, 'Better is a dinner of herbs, etc.' . . . you may be assured it has been strained up to the highest point possible without bucking this harmony, and entailing upon you all the evils [regarding salary matters] which I have endured."[12]

A noteworthy transaction that concerned only Griffin and Richards calls attention to the lingering legal presence of slavery in the state of New Jersey. The previous January, Griffin had sold to his successor "a black boy named Richard aged nine years" for $100 "in hand paid." In May, just two days before Griffin's farewell sermon, the two met again to sign a witnessed agreement that the sale was made "with express condition that the said boy named Richard shall be free on his attaining the age of twenty-five years."[13] Richards also assumed responsibility for a black woman who wished to change masters. Although he did this at her request, legally it made him a slaveholder, a fact which later in life caused him considerable embarrassment.

With these matters concluded, Richards and Griffin embarked on their new assignments, sharing common aims and allegiances. As a Princeton trustee, Richards would follow Griffin's reports on the Andover experiment with particular interest. But differences in temperament and talents would make them at times uneasy partners in the years ahead.

James Richards was now on his own in the town that some of its founders had called "New Work." The pious of Richards's own day liked to spell it "New Ark." Unlike Morristown with its divisions when he first arrived, the Newark church was in excellent circumstances, having just been enlarged and energized by an extraordinary revival. Burr and MacWhorter had accustomed the town to distinguished pastoral leadership, and Griffin had set a high standard for both eloquence and learning. Richards was fully aware of the higher expectations of his new congregation, telling his family that he must make more time for study. He must be scholar as well as pastor and preacher. Here he must make "the full proof of his ministry."[14]

Where Morristown was compact, Newark was built in scattered fashion. The main road was two miles long, and houses had capacious lots for vegetable gardens. For a hundred years, Newark was isolated from the main roads between New York and Philadelphia by three large rivers and vast salt marshes. In the 1760s, however, nine local men raised a fund to build a public road that connected the town to the New York ferry at Paulus Hook (now Jersey City). Newark became a crossroads town, a market town.

Street scene in early-nineteenth-century Newark. (Courtesy—Collections of the New Jersey Historical Society)

The Reverend Richards might have been reminded of his Yale days, for the town of Newark was laid out on the order of New Haven, with a Broad Street eight rods wide (132 feet) and bisecting tree-lined roads of equal width. There were town greens and a common. Small shops selling hats, jewelry, shoes, and hardware lined Broad Street for the block between Bank and Market Streets. Newark was still too small and its harbor too poor to have the kind of wealthy commercial class of the seaports. Most of these shops served the local farm population. Two groups of craftsmen, shoemakers and carriagemakers, produced for a wider market. The town meeting met annually to make provision for the poor. Most of Newark's needs were met, like the parson's salary, by voluntary "subscription." A night watch and three volunteer fire companies were supported this way.

Richards was already acquainted with many of the town's leaders, thanks to the ties of kinship between Newark and Morristown. The artisan class formed the leadership of local society. In preindustrial Newark, the independence and skill of craftsmen and "mechanics" won wide respect and allied them with the small professional class. This network of professionals, merchants, and artisans set the tone. The career of William Pennington illustrates their ease of association: A hatter in his youth, Pennington had taken up the study of law and now served as a judge; in later years he would be elected governor of New Jersey. The lay leadership of Newark's First Presbyterian Church included professional men like

Judge Pennington and Judge Elisha Boudinot, but also Israel Crane who owned a quarry, Luther Goble who made shoes, and Robert Campfield, a Broad Street contractor. "The economic ethic guiding towns like Newark identified 'useful' with 'good.'"[15] So did James Richards, who himself knew how to make a chair as well as a theological argument.

Richards and his wife soon formed a significant friendship with Mrs. Hannah Kinney, who in 1803 had founded the Female Charitable Society of Newark. Women were increasingly active in the work of the church and were encouraged to be so, though a formal role in public worship remained forbidden. Churchwomen like Mrs. Kinney forged loyal, almost collegial bonds with their pastors as they went house-to-house and led small prayer groups, nurturing a female network that proved an important resource in times of revival. The widowed Mrs. Kinney eventually moved to Ohio, from which outpost she peppered Richards with long, discursive letters that regularly called his attention to church developments in the West.

The College of New Jersey had been moved to Princeton, but Newark remained proud of its academy, founded in 1793 and housed in a three-story building on the corner of Broad and Academy Streets.[16] Female pupils had been accepted since 1802, so it is likely that Anna, thirteen, and Caroline, eleven, as well as Henry, six, attended there. Edward at three would remain at home.

Compelled to devote more time to study and to important church tasks that took him away from Newark, Richards must have been pleased to welcome the Reverend Hooper Cumming as pastor of the newly formed Second Church.[17] He and Cumming watched over mushrooming local benevolent societies, placed graduates of Newark Academy in various colleges, and welcomed canvassing agents of worthy causes and institutions.[18]

The Richards family had settled in Newark only briefly when some startling rumors emanated out of Boston accusing Griffin of "improprieties" during his Newark ministry, improprieties unspecified in surviving documents. Newark church leaders sensed a move to discredit Griffin and the new seminary at Andover, and dispatched a letter in his defense. Noting that personal acquaintance with Griffin would serve to silence any slander, the seventeen signers—all of them deacons, elders, and trustees—spoke up, they said, because they saw an "Enmity" to the "truths of the Gospel" behind these slanders.[19] Although the issue died down, the readiness of Griffin's Newark supporters to see the attack as an intentional Unitarian tactic to sully the orthodox cause in Boston shows how charged the atmosphere had become and how alerted lay leaders even in distant New Jersey were to the stakes involved.

The incident could only stiffen the resolve of those in the Presbyterian fold who feared that their own Nassau Hall no longer offered the rigor, piety, or discipline to fortify the next and crucial generation of ministers. Numbers alone were dismaying. In Princeton's early days, nearly half of its graduates became ministers. When the Revolutionary period redirected interest to politics, the proportion declined to one-fifth. Now when the need was greatest, and despite the recent addition of a professorship in theology, only one-tenth of the graduates entered the ministry. Given the increasingly secular atmosphere of the college, it was logical that some Presbyterians began to send ministerial candidates to the new seminary at Andover.

The following winter brought distressing news from Andover about one of them. Lewis Congar, a promising Newark youth who had followed Griffin to the new seminary, had died suddenly after a few days' illness. At the funeral service in Newark, James Richards preached feelingly to the bereaved parents of this only son and especially to the many young people who filled "Old First." Taking as his text, "Be still and know that I am God," Richards pointed to young Congar's own deathbed declaration of God's mercy in calling him home to Himself, and he concluded, "To you, my dear young friends, this is an unusually solemn providence—and to you, above all others, who have recently made profession of religion. . . . Are you prepared to follow him? . . . May God . . . prepare you to meet him and rejoice with him."[20]

The death of a young person, arousing anxiety in otherwise self-absorbed peers, supplied a providential opening to any preacher. Richards could easily cast back to his own complacency when as a young apprentice he thought he had plenty of time. An extract of his sermon went promptly to the *Panoplist*, and the full text of "The Duty of Submission" circulated soon afterwards. This sermon was among the first of many from his Newark pulpit to be published.

Late in his second year at Newark, Richards and John McDowell, the neighboring pastor at Elizabethtown, made a trip to New England with a commission from the General Assembly to examine the condition of the

Presbyterian Church in New Hampshire. Like Richards's preaching tours to the Jersey backcountry, this commission represented a formal attempt by the Presbyterians to monitor developments in outlying or relatively unchurched regions.

The two traveled by horseback through the Connecticut River valley, Richards delighting in the familiarity of the landscape. Pleasant September weather accompanied them as they continued their way along the north shore of Boston to Salem, Ipswich, and Newburyport, where they stopped over with the Reverend Gardiner Spring. This was country new to their eyes, but Richards felt the presence of a two-centuries-old taproot when "after dinner we spent half an hour in the old burying ground examining the ancient monuments of the first settlers of New England. . . ." He was already appraising what he saw.

> [Newburyport] is much larger and far more elegant than we had expected to find it. Indeed all the towns this way carry the marks of wealth and taste far beyond what we had imagined. I should say the town is 5 times as large as Newark and much better built. Salem is perhaps in both these respects before Newburyport—its population I am told is between 12 and 13 thousand.[21]

They spent the next ten days or so visiting Presbyterian congregations in the environs of southern New Hampshire near Exeter, and then attended the examination of the seminarians at Andover on their way back to Boston.

The inspection of Presbyterian churches in New Hampshire where the Congregationalists could expect to be more active and the visit to the Congregationalist seminary at Andover, half of whose graduates would fill Presbyterian pulpits, illustrate the two denominations' efforts to coordinate supply of clergy to areas of rapid growth. It did not all go smoothly. Regional allegiances and suspicions would occasionally intrude. In time the Congregationalists would chafe at the Presbyterian strictures that limited the popular appeal of their alliance, and the Presbyterians would worry even more about the spread of modifications in New England Calvinism which smacked of heresy in Philadelphia.

For now, trips like this one and Mrs. Kinney's detailed letters from Cincinnati helped give James Richards an overview of both the crisis in ministerial supply and the cooperative efforts to overcome it. Concern about the future of the ministry was gathering momentum among his colleagues in the Middle States. How could they fill all of these places? They dismissed any move to rush theological training as exactly the wrong strategy, believing it would dilute the quality of the ministry just when it needed to be strongest in the face of competitive pressures in the world at large and within the fold of religion itself. The Andover model of three years of intensive and specialized training attracted great interest.

Ordinarily the Presbyterian Church looked to Princeton for its best-trained ministers, however small that number had become by 1810. Yet ever since a prominent Virginia pastor, the Reverend Archibald Alexander, had publicly voiced concern for Princeton at the 1808 General Assembly, church leaders increasingly had wrung their hands over a college atmosphere more likely to contaminate than invigorate ministerial candidates. Those supporting the founding of a seminary sent out an inquiry to the presbyteries asking for their preferences among these alternatives: one central theological seminary, a few regional institutions, or numerous synod-based training centers. Responses varied so much as to be inconclusive, with some presbyteries not responding at all. In the face of such uncertainty and irresolution, the Reverend Samuel Miller of New York lobbied strongly for one central institution to serve the whole church, and opinion soon crystallized in favor of a single separate theological seminary on the pattern of Andover.[22] Along with such distinguished college trustees as Miller and the Reverend Ashbel Green of Philadelphia, James Richards, also a college trustee and now a seasoned observer of the Church's needs, was appointed to serve on a seven-man committee to plan the new institution.[23]

Samuel Miller. (Courtesy—Presbyterian Historical Society, Philadelphia)

The committee inevitably had to wrestle with the key issue of seminary appointments. The pool from which professors would be drawn was that of distinguished pastors who, in an unspecialized world, combined many skills in undertaking a variety of tasks. A pastor united in himself both piety and learning and earned recognition through both revivals and publications. To move from a congregation of believers to a community of scholars and future leaders did not seem so great a leap. Yet distinction in the pulpit did not necessarily translate into success as a seminary professor.

To grasp the problem, Richards needed only to contemplate his friend Griffin. The latter, deeply hurt by the rumor-mongering at Andover and Boston, was struggling vainly to master his emotions and his new situation.

> Boston, Nov. 24th, 1810
>
> My Dear Brother,
>
> Your favour of the 20th inst. has just been received. I am ashamed of my neglect: but it is another proof of the distracted state of my mind of late. . . . I am sorry that I have given, or been the occasion of, so much trouble all around; but I am a troublesome creature in the world. I sometimes think it would be better for the world if I were out of it.
>
> After a scene of ceaseless distraction for a year and a half, which has been principally owing, as I now perceive, to my own pride and idolatry, I am quietly housed for the winter, with my family, in the family of one of our congregation, as boarders; having obtained from Andover a dispensation to enable me to devote my *whole* time to the congregation [of Park Street Church] for four months. Having now but one world upon me . . . , I am enabled, without distraction, to devote my whole time and heart to my *favourite* employment, the labours of a parish. . . .

Griffin closed with a request for prayers and again declared he could not henceforward "be connected with *two* worlds."[24] His position at Park Street was only temporary and he was openly anxious about the future.

This letter gave Richards much to ponder. Griffin's case illustrated the difficulty some would have in relinquishing a regular pulpit and adjusting to the requirements of the seminary setting. Presbyterian churchmen traditionally concerned themselves with the institutions of parish, presbytery, synod, and General Assembly. The seminary, designed to provide

professional education, was a new institution that required a new combination of talents. James Richards himself probably was not near the top of
the list of candidates for professional appointment in the new seminary,
for he was not seen as one of the most gifted orators among the Presbyterian clergy. "His trumpet [is] not silver," conceded an admirer,[25] but his
capacities as an institution builder were steadily finding expression and
winning notice. Griffin's letter, which arrived as Richards and others
considered the need to judge rightly the talents of those who would be
appointed to the faculty of the new seminary at Princeton, served as a
reminder that gifts of eloquence and learning, which Griffin certainly
had, were not sufficient.

At the same time, Griffin's letter touched Richards quite personally. As
a friend, he could not but sympathize with Griffin's misery and continuing
uncertainty. Moreover, as Griffin's successor at Newark, he had to reflect
with some discomfort that his friend had given up a successful ministry he
could not now reclaim.

The following March, Griffin enlarged on his troubles, concluding
with a pointed and personal appeal to Richards whose friendship he had
up to then relied upon:

> You can have no idea of the state of parties in this part of the church.
> The party spirit, and struggle for personal influence, among those who
> call themselves orthodox, are beyond any thing you have ever seen or
> thought of. I hope I shall still see my way clear to retire from the *focal
> point* of all this heat, and shut myself up in an affectionate congregation
> in Boston. I am determined to have as little to do as possible in this
> contention *for the balance of Europe.*
>
> One thing which I heard of yesterday will surprise you. Some ques-
> tion, it seems, was put to you and Mr. McDowell, last fall, at
> Newburyport, I supposed by Dr. Spring [pastor at Newburyport],
> respecting the reports at Newark; which, it seems, you did not think
> proper directly to answer. What the question was I have not heard; but
> your silence was construed in a way, which, I know, will give you pain. I
> think it necessary, therefore, to request you to do me the favour to write
> to Dr. Spring, if he was the man, and to give him right impressions.
>
> I conclude that the question was relative to the nature of the reports,
> which you might, very properly, think it not expedient to explain in a

disgusting detail. But whatever was the question, I am confident that your silence was dictated by nothing but *love*. If, however, there *are*, contrary to my former persuasion, any unfavourable impressions on the minds of my *best friends* (such as you and brother McDowell) which would seal their lips when asked *whether my character* has been affected in the church, by those reports, I wish much to know it. If this be the case, my brethren have not been faithful enough to tell me of it. If this be the case,—if my brethren have any difficulties in supporting my character, *without reserve*, they erred in suffering me to come to this region; where it is certain that I cannot live without the *firmest* support from my brethren abroad. Still I wish nothing said but the *truth*. If there be any such state of things, as is barely supposed above, I beseech you to [let me] know of it before I fix in Boston. Is there any idea of *imprudence* in those things, which affects the *love* and *confidence* of my brethren towards me? . . . Dear brother, tell me, *this once, all your heart*, and I will not trouble you, I think, again on this subject. With love to Mrs. Richards, I am, my dear brother,[26]

most affectionately yours . . .

Griffin referred with fresh pain to the charges against him of improprieties that had stunned his former associates in Newark. Made vulnerable by professional unhappiness at Andover and feeling himself a victim of rivalries he did not wholly understand within the orthodox faction at Boston, Griffin tried to interpret Richards's reticence. With little taste for the politics involved, Griffin tended to personalize the issues. Seeking explanations, he focused first on Richards's sense of propriety, then on his sense of expediency, and finally on his characteristic reserve ("tell me, *this once, all your heart*"). The very qualities he intuitively marked in Richards, however, may have inhibited the latter from responding in a wholly satisfactory way.

Before relations took such a turn, however, Richards must have reassured him to some degree, for the tone of a subsequent letter from Griffin reflected the old collegiality. The Andover professor wished to promote to Richards the candidacy of the Reverend Samuel Worcester of Salem, Massachusetts, for an academic position at the college in Princeton.

If you, my dear brother, will exert yourself in this matter, I will consider it a particular favour, and will not forget it. I have introduced Mr. Worcester to four of the trustees besides yourself, viz., to Doctors

Green and Miller, and the two Mr. Boudinots. I have not *spoken out* to either of them; but I have endeavored to prepare their minds for your influence. . . . [Mr. Worcester] knows *all* my affairs, and had done as much as any man to protect me against the assaults both of malice and prejudice. . . .[27]

Although Mr. Worcester did not get a position, Griffin was not amiss in his timing. The college trustees, mindful of the decision to bypass the college to form a separate seminary and anxious to redeem the college from "laxness," were bent on changes of personnel.[28] The vehicle of change would be a new office of vice president. So, in the midst of his committee's preparations to charter the new seminary, James Richards turned his attention to the college in a letter to Green in Philadelphia and ruminated on possible candidates:

Newark, March 24th, 1812

Reverend and dear sir,

My anxiety for Princeton College has induced me to drop a line. . . . I have long supposed such an officer [vice president] would be of impor-tance to the institution, could he be well selected and well supported. . . . But is this the proper time? . . . Would it not be better to postpone . . . until after the meeting of the Genl. Assbly? . . .

But who do you suppose is thought of for [it]? . . . It would be superfluous to say that your own name has been frequently mentioned among your friends. . . . An opinion however has prevailed that you would not, in existing circumstances, accept. . . . Our mutual friend Doctor [Samuel] *Miller* has also been mentioned, and several of the trustees in this quarter [New York Presbytery] are solicitous that he should be appointed. They think him better qualified than any other man *in our reach*, and that if the thing was fairly and honourably tendered to him, he would not decline. I will say nothing of his ch[aracte]r as you know him better than I do. . . .

But there is another person in view, who will be run with great zeal: I mean Doctor Proudfit of Salem, State of New York. I have no acquain-tance with this gentleman—but from information I deem correct I am fully persuaded he ought not to be our man. Besides a diminutive person, and an address far from being prepossessing, I have been assured that his native talent is not above the common standard, and as a public speaker he is *miserable*. From a volume of [his] sermons . . . part of which I have read, I was led to subscribe at once to his piety and industry. But I could see nothing but what was common dressed up with a little more art than is seen in our every day sermon. He seemed to me to deserve the praise of having cultivated his *one talent well*; and though I am far from thinking it small praise, to "have been faithful over a few things," yet more appears requisite in a man who is to direct the studies of youth in the higher walks of literature, and who by his own promi- nence is to give vigour and eclat to the institution over which he presides. . . .

  I am dear sir with great respect your friend and humbl[e] serv[an]t[29]

                    James Richards

Here Richards exhibited the judgment both keen and subtle that his asso- ciates valued. Characteristically, he engaged in the "out of door" preemptive maneuver that he preferred to confrontation. He urged that the college trustees select an outstanding leader as its second officer and not settle for a mere reliable drudge. A wider consultation among those attending the General Assembly, he implied, would help to assure that the new man was well-supported. Richards had taken notice of the many constituencies of a college or seminary.

  In his letter to Green, the Newark pastor set forth the graces of academic leadership so appreciatively that it may have engaged his correspondent's interest in the job. The incumbent college president, Smith, correctly read the move to appoint a vice president as a signal to resign; and, interestingly, it was Ashbel Green who agreed in the end to become president.

  As all this was going forward, another letter arrived from Griffin who was now formally installed as pastor of the Park Street Church. He had heard rumors of a revival beginning in Newark, the first under his friend Richards.

                        Boston, April 22d, 1812

My Dear Brother,

  Your favour [letter] of Feby 3d has lain by me a long time, for reasons that every minister can guess when he looks at his parish. But, my

beloved brother, my heart's often with you. You are among the few
friends on earth whom I love without any *ifs* or *buts*. I am rejoiced to
hear . . . that appearances are more favourable among you. I rejoice for
your sake, as well as for more general reasons. You went to Newark at the
close of a great revival. The thing was *done*, & could not be *continued*. I
had the privilege of being there in *harvest time*; & you came in *the fall of
the year*: a winter followed of course; but a *spring* you will see, & then
harvest. They that sow in tears shall reap in joy . . . may the Lord make
you the Father of many spiritual children in that dear section of the great
family! . . .

Griffin then urged his friend to "take Mrs. R. under your arm & jog along
to Boston" that spring. He and Mrs. Griffin would like to come south, but
"I cannot leave my people so long at present. There are some appearances
I must stay at home to watch. . . ." Some thirty or so were "under serious
impressions" and there were others "whose minds [were] tender."

Griffin next expressed amazement over the renewed divisiveness in
New York City, where the New England–style orthodox and the stricter
Presbyterians vied for influence despite the Plan of Union. The Reverend
Ezra Stiles Ely, a Presbyterian minister of the city, saw a snake in this union
in the form of a deviant brand of Calvinism called Hopkinsianism.
Hopkinsians taught that men were held guilty only for the sins they actually committed and not for Adam's original sin. Hopkinsianism enjoyed
tolerance and even respectability among many New Englanders, who saw
a much greater enemy in the Unitarian heresy spreading among the
Boston elite. However, to vigilant Presbyterians in New York and Philadelphia, the Hopkinsian modification constituted a dangerous watering-down
of the doctrine of total depravity; its effect, they charged, was to deceive
sinners into thinking they could take actions to bring about their own
salvation. The campaign against Hopkinsianism motivated their fervent
support of a specifically Presbyterian seminary, for it meant that fewer Presbyterian ministers would be trained at Andover and become subject to its
influence. On their behalf, the Reverend Ely now took aim at "New-
England religion" with its Hopkinsian taint. To the bemused Rev. Griffin,
who viewed Hopkinsianism with New England tolerance, this was the
proverbial molehill made into a mountain. Of this development, he wrote
to Richards:

> I have had very affecting news lately from my brother in New York. He
> & his friends believe him to have become a subject of grace. I know you
> will rejoice with me. . . . I hope my brother may be of some little
> service to the common cause in this day of agitation in that city. What are
> they doing? What aileth them? Who has stirred up all this strife? . . .
> Have you seen the recommendations of [Ezra Stiles] Ely's book, signed by
> *18* ministers? & the open war which they proclaim against New-England
> religion? & their proclamation that the horrid monster has reared his head
> in the city of New York! . . . Is the land of Jersey shaken with the earth-
> quake? Do the steeples of Newark totter?—Does Dr. Miller stand with
> firmness? Is *your* head upon your shoulders? . . .[30]

A distinct note of amusement crept into the tone of one New Englander
speaking to another, as he beheld the suspicions of conservative Presbyterians toward even the more orthodox of the Calvinist fold in the northern
region. Griffin and Richards were alike in seeing the New England
approach, a focus on revivals and increased numbers of highly trained
clergy, rather than a close monitoring of doctrine, as the hope of a rein-
vigorated Calvinism.

Two weeks later Griffin wrote again to rejoice in the signs of revival
noted in the twenty congregations of New Jersey and the city of New
York. He suggested that Richards revive his preaching tours to the backcountry of New Jersey: "God has blessed them twice before; may He not
bless them a third time?" He then bemoaned the state of his own congregation which had sunk into apathy:

> . . . with habits formed under cold preaching, [they] present a cold
> spectacle, much unlike the congregation at Newark. They must be melted
> down into one mass by an electric shock from heaven. God send the
> shock in His own time!

Griffin's words here capture his feeling of ambiguity about his responsibility
for the state of his flock: If he is successful, he is an instrument of grace and
begets spiritual children; if he is unsuccessful, his preaching must be cold and
the congregation must await the shock of grace from God in good time.

Griffin thanked Richards for showing interest in his brother's case. "I
wish you could see him some time when you are in New York. He needs

help from you." Noting the rumor of Miller's becoming a professor at the new Princeton Seminary, he wondered, ". . . how can he be spared from New York in the present crisis!" Nevertheless, he was soon reaffirming a general optimism that "New England influence is becoming too overwhelming in the city & State of New York to be long resisted; it is *too near morning* for darkness long to reign in any part of our American Israel. Our Andover school will help forward the triumph." Griffin, always a better observer than participant in these struggles, concluded with a report on the latest from Harvard. A bill passed by the Massachusetts legislature to reduce orthodox representation on the Harvard board of overseers had backfired on the sponsors, and as a result "I have lately become one of the overseers . . . the democratick [*sic*] Assembly repealed the law, in their own vindication, & Mr. Thacher & I rode in upon their shoulders. I hope I never may have a worse *horse!*"[31]

Thus aware of the stir in New England and New York, James Richards a few weeks later journeyed to Philadelphia for the annual May meeting of the General Assembly where the new seminary led the agenda. The controversy rocking the New York Presbytery became an instant distraction, however, and Richards temporarily found himself, Miller, and others under suspicion

Princeton Theological Seminary. (Courtesy—Princeton Theological Seminary)

of Hopkinsianism.[32] A dozen leading colleagues met informally at Ashbel Green's house and cleared them of the charge.[33] Of these rancors, Richards mentioned nothing in his letter home to Caroline and the children. He trained his eyes instead on a more satisfying development, the formal establishment of the new seminary alongside the college at Princeton.

> My dear wife
>   I have been so closely occupied with business, that I have not had a moment's time to write. I long to quit this noisy city and return again to my beloved family and flock. The business of the Ass[em]bly has been unusually important and interesting. The theological seminary is located at Princeton after a discussion of the two days & a half, in wh[ic]h much ingenuity and eloquence were displayed. We have a large board of directors to chuse [sic] from different parts of our church and probably one or two professors. . . .[34]

During his Newark ministry, Richards had worked diligently to bring the national Presbyterian Church to this moment and his connections to the college and seminary only grew more pronounced with time as he raised funds, advised on faculty appointments, and otherwise fostered both institutions as a dedicated trustee. His main focus, however, remained on his congregation at First Church, where, sure enough, signs of a revival on his watch had been appearing.

Most of Richards's ministerial activities were conducted in the view of his family, as he worked out of his home, studying, writing sermons and letters, keeping records, and receiving visitors. This routine allowed him to keep a central role in the life of the household, beginning with leading the family in daily religious devotions. The parsonage was a sociable place filled with young faces and led by a lively set of females. His daughters, Anna, the eldest, now sixteen, and young Caroline, fourteen, had been joined by three more girls of similar ages, the orphaned daughters of deceased friends. The premature deaths of adults meant the presence of young wards like these in many middle-class households. Rounding out the household were nine-year-old Henry, six-year-old Edward, probably the black boy named Richard, now twelve, and a servant or two. In the letter Richards wrote from Philadelphia announcing the decision to establish a seminary at Princeton, he also addressed the quintet of adolescent girls:

> I received Anna's letter together with those wh[ic]h it contained from Maria, Sarah, & Julia. . . . Tell Anna that I was pleased with every part of her letter and particularly with the pains wh[ic]h she took with the first part of it. I shall probably get the stockings she has written for. As to a coffee pot I have already made considerable enquiry—& shall make still more. I find as yet only two kinds—*silver* from eighty to a hundred dollars—and block tin . . . at seven dollars.
>
> Tell *Sarah* I was much delighted with the few lines wh[ic]h she enclosed, and shall always be happy to recognise the endearing relation under which she addresses me. Nothing will give me more pleasure than that she and Julia should consider me as their father while I regard [them] as my children. I loved [their] dear parents; how can I help but love them. Early left as orphans, in a world of change and suffering, may the God of Ab[raha]m be their God, and the strength of Israel [their] portion! . . .

Daughter Caroline's letter had asked for books, and he wrote back, "If I can find any books which I think suitable for her I will get them." But he was taken aback by her report that his young wards had recently enjoyed a few hours of music and dancing. He observed that this was

> contrary to the wisdom of their guardian and that I must therefore request that they forbear untill [*sic*] my return. I was not a little surprised that so important a step should have been taken without consulting me. My dear wife, are you aware of the inference which will be drawn from this measure by the pious people in our congregation? It is not exactly now with us as it was at Morristown. But I must leave this subject till I see you. . . . Caroline has my thanks for her letter. . . .[35]

This sharp reproof, folded into so much affection and solicitude, shows that James Richards belonged to a generation of fathers still accustomed to the leading role in guiding the activities of the household. He did not defer to his wife's judgment here.

His family was a great comfort to Richards and he disliked being away from them. Writing letters home solaced him after a day on a dusty or muddy road. On the earlier trip to New Hampshire, he began one of his letters to Caroline, "The clock has just struck ten but I am not willing to retire to bed till I have conversed one moment with you."[36]

There were occasions when the whole family traveled together on trips back home to Connecticut. His wife's home at Farmington was a favorite destination. When Richards had stopped there with McDowell on their way to New Hampshire, he had found himself especially moved to be there on his own.

My Dear Caroline

As I am now in your native town in the very spot where our acquaintance first commenced, I must address you in the language, once so familiar to your ear, and which still accords with every feeling of my heart. I can hardly tell you how much I wish you [were] here to greet your friends and relations with me. They all express a very deep regret that you were not along. As soon as I reached the high ground in Cheshire yesterday—and saw the ridge of mountains at the foot of which you were born—and the seat of your numerous relatives, I could not refrain from expressing my sorrow to Mr. McDowell that I had not contrived to have brought you on with me. I felt as if the prospect was too delightful not to be shared with you; at the same time I was certain that my reception at Farmington would be doubly acceptable if accompanied by you.

We reached this place last evening at a little after sunsetting—found your mother [Anna Smith, the aunt who raised her] and the rest of your friends in perfect health. I halted a moment to see your mother Cowles [her father's second wife] and enquire after your brother's health. He was not at home but the good old [lady] told us he was well and his family—appeared quite gratified to hear from you. I just said how do you do? to your sister Wadsworth as I was passing by and intend to call upon your other sister. . . .

Let us my dear Caroline continue to remember each other at the throne of grace. What a privilege is it that though absent in body we may be present in sp[iri]t, and especially in our prayers. I shall not cease

to commend you & my dear children, and my dear people to the power
and grace of an Almighty most merciful and covenant-keeping God—
and I doubt not that I shall have an interest in your prayers & those of
my flock.

Do not fail when you write to tell me all the news.

Tell my dear children that their father loves them and hopes they will
be dutiful and kind till his return. Have a little care that Henry goes and
returns from school in due season—I am afraid to have him mix much
with the children of the town.

Why did you not bring *little Edward* says little *Mary Cowles* this
morning? who is as great a chatter box as ever you saw. She seems to
recollect Edward perfectly. . . .

Remember me affectionately to the Boudinots, Cummings, Wallaces,
Congars, Kinneys, Hinsdales, Cranes, Allings, Johnsons, Andries etc. and
to all our neighbors.

Kiss the children affectionately for me and believe me as ever invio-
lably yours

James Richards[37]

Delight in his wife and family shines through this letter, and also
caution and care as when he directed Henry to come straight home after
school and avoid mixing with the presumably rougher boys of the town.
As usual, the circle of affection for Richards included all of the local leaders
of the Newark church and their families.

Anna, his eldest child, gave him great joy when she became part of his
first bountiful harvest of souls at the Newark church. Much attached to her
father, she became the only one of the Richards children to be converted
in her teens. It must have made his anxieties for the rest of his children on
this score all the more acute for having had Anna begin so well. Her
personal zeal was impressive, and at the age of eighteen, the fruits of her
conversion were seen in her work of starting up the first Sunday School in
Newark.[38] Such a school for young children was the latest bloom in a
garden of new evangelical ventures in this period that often drew on
female energies. For Anna it was only a beginning. She was to spend the
rest of her life in Newark and in the bosom of Old First, and not surpris-
ingly she always felt proprietary towards its interests.

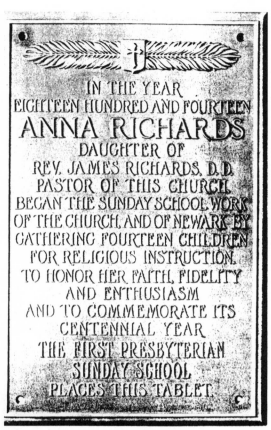

IN THE YEAR
EIGHTEEN HUNDRED AND FOURTEEN
ANNA RICHARDS
DAUGHTER OF
REV. JAMES RICHARDS, D.D.
PASTOR OF THIS CHURCH
BEGAN THE SUNDAY SCHOOL WORK
OF THE CHURCH AND OF NEWARK BY
GATHERING FOURTEEN CHILDREN
FOR RELIGIOUS INSTRUCTION.
TO HONOR HER FAITH, FIDELITY
AND ENTHUSIASM
AND TO COMMEMORATE ITS
CENTENNIAL YEAR
THE FIRST PRESBYTERIAN
SUNDAY SCHOOL
PLACES THIS TABLET.

Plaque placed in the First Presbyterian Church to honor Anna Richards as the founder of the first Sunday School in Newark. (Taken from "The Old First Presbyterian Church, Newark, New Jersey: The Founding Church of Newark 1666–1966," Ecclesiastical Color Publishers, South Hackensack, New Jersey, 1966)

In the great revival that occasioned Anna's conversion, a peculiar accident in September 1812 had a considerable impact. Many who had previously sensed only the tremors of a life change, as it were, saw the ground broken open when they learned that twenty-three-year-old Sarah Cumming had slipped and fallen to her death while on a walk to the falls of the Passaic River. She was a young bride, her marriage to the Reverend Cumming, the pastor at Second Church, just recently celebrated, and she had lived in Newark only a few weeks. Sixteen hundred Newark citizens processed to the gravesite. "Who can trust to the world after this?" James Richards preached:

> Presume not, O sinner, upon tomorrow. Trust not to a sick bed. Tomorrow
> may never come. . . . God in awful majesty is passing by. . . . Our
> prayer is that this wonderful dispensation of providence may issue in the
> conversion of sinners, and in the greater watchfulness and fidelity of the
> Lord's people.[39]

Once again, as in the case of the ministerial student Lewis Congar, the
sudden death of a young person dramatized the spiritual imperative of
conversion. It could not be put off, Richards insisted. Such preaching now
bore fruit. Indeed, the signs of revival in Newark noted by Griffin multiplied in the months ahead and reached a zenith the following year. In late
March 1813, Richards wrote Brother McDowell, "The work of God
increases in this place, notwithstanding all our trials and our fears. I stand
astonished at the goodness of God."[40]

In this fruitful time, after an interval of seven years since Edward was
born, Caroline Richards was again expecting a child. In July a healthy boy
was born. Perhaps this year of grace gave them confidence to try again the
name of James. The father was forty-six, the mother, forty-two. This was
their last child, the only one born in Newark.

In the spring of the following year, Edward Griffin wrote of plans for
a visit to "our dear Newark" on account of his wife's health. She had been
ill for three months. "This is the first day that she has been below stairs.
Today she has rode four miles in a closed carriage . . ." he reported.

> I have no good news [of] our affairs in Boston. It does not please the
> Head of·the Church to refresh us with His influence, and we all remain
> cold and hard as rocks. I am afraid to come among you . . . lest I
> should serve . . . to chill you. But I need to be warmed, though it be
> at your expense. . . .[41]

Richards had been so busy with his flock in Newark that he had fallen
behind in his correspondence. The forlorn Griffin observed, "It is a long
time since I heard from you, though I have *for once* the advantage of
holding you in debt."

In September, Richards was accorded an honor on a par with serving
as moderator of the General Assembly. He was invited to New Haven,
Connecticut, to address the American Board of Commissioners for Foreign

Missions at its annual meeting. The spirit of revivals, growing more fervent and frequent across the land since the turn of the century, was increasingly linked with the spirit of missions, both abroad and among the native peoples on newly settled western lands. Richards was active on the New Jersey foreign mission board where he deepened his acquaintance with Presbyterian "home missions" to the Indians. Earlier in his Newark pastorate, he had written to Green to urge more financial support for the Reverend Gideon Blackburn and his mission to the Cherokee nation.[42]

Until the end of the eighteenth century, Protestant Christianity had not developed a strong missionary tradition, but now missions became an overt part of the general strategy to rally the orthodox. For active believers, missions offered scope to the enlarged sense of duty generated by conversion. The sense of national election, that distinctive Puritan inheritance, would later in the nineteenth century foster among many Protestants the belief in an American vocation to evangelize the world.

In his address at New Haven, Richards urged a view of mission work that went beyond example and prayer. He called for human responsibility and initiative in the spread of the gospel, and in doing so he implicitly imagined a humanity banded together on a common road to a common destiny. To this end he recalled the ancient travels of St. Paul:

> If he had regarded the gospel merely in the light of a good religion, and on the whole perhaps the best religion in the world, you would not have seen him braving all dangers . . . to spread the knowledge of its sacred truths among the nations. He would have left them, as many boasting philanthropists have done, to enjoy their superstitions. . . . But he considered the gospel as an indispensable means of eternal life. . . .

This sense of mission put the individual's response to God at the center of religion. While the revolutionary generation had looked to religion for direct support of republican virtue in the society at large, Richards and his colleagues focussed on personal redemption as the source of energies that would ultimately lift the moral tone of society.[43] The issue of individual salvation transcended any public matter and demanded an urgent tone and, among some, apocalyptic language. Richards told his hearers that it was the task of every Christian to share in the work of calling all people to glory:

What a joy will it be to you, should you then behold some redeemed sinner rescued by your seasonable and pious liberality from the horrors of everlasting death, and made heir of an inconceivable, and eternal weight of glory. Be it some African—be it some Hindoo [*sic*]—be it some tawny savage from the wilderness—the joy will be equal—it is a soul saved from death by your instrumentality.[44]

Conversion still required the divine initiative of grace, but once converted, an individual Christian had the duty and the ability to be instrumental in the conversion of others.

At the end of this unusually busy year, James Richards, in a pensive mood, mused to a friend of his youth, the Reverend Storrs, about the past and the future. He was forty-seven years old.

Newark, Dec[embe]r 19th 1814

My dear Brother

A favourable opportunity presenting, I drop a few lines to assure you that I still have an affectionate remembrance of you and yours. Never shall I forget to my latest breath the kind reception I met with in your hospitable dwelling when sick and full of despondency, I was first introduced into your family. Almost twenty years have rolled away since that event—many changes—many interesting things, have occurred, but the impression is still strong and vivid: and what is this impression? Is it that of mere human kindness? If I am not greatly mistaken, it has a higher character—. There was a mingling of souls; there was an exchange of Christian affection which nothing else on earth can equal, and wh[ic]h is a foretaste of heaven itself. A part of our little company is gone before us to that blessed world—to drink full draughts of Christian love, and to make the place more desirable for us who are left behind.

I begin to think dear brother that it is time for us to be looking away from this world—Our sun has passed his meridian;—all that awaits us now is decline—. Whether that decline shall be gentle or rapid, is for our heavenly father to direct. Long it cannot be, before our sun will be down and our labours ended. May we not be deceived in our hopes which lie beyond this transitory scene.[45]

The glowing memory of this friendship prefigured for Richards a Dantesque reunion of souls. He meditated here on the span of his life, not yet aware that his most significant labors awaited him in the heat of the afternoon sun.

Before that winter was over, a complication arose that would put his present activities in Newark on a quite different footing. He knew his excitable friend Griffin had been consistently restive and uncertain since he had left Newark for Boston six years before. Other Griffin friends in Newark undoubtedly knew this, too. So when an opening occurred at Second Church upon the departure of Cumming, it was perhaps to be expected that the congregation would turn to this beloved former pastor.

The prospect could not have been a welcome one for Richards. It would mean sharing clerical leadership of the town with a man who, besides a patent claim to seniority, enjoyed gifts as a preacher that Richards, solid and appreciated as he was, could not match. Moreover, Griffin would naturally interest himself in the affairs of First Church as his own former parish.

Providence might yet intervene. In a March 1815 letter to that valued and interested observer of the Boston scene, the Reverend Jedidiah Morse, Richards made a discreet attempt to search a way out:

> You have probably learned by this time that the 2d Presbyterian congregation of Newark have made out a call for our friend Doctor Griffin to be their Pastor, in the room of Mr. Cumming lately dismissed. Doctor Griffin has solicited the advice of several of his friends *here*. They are at a loss what to say unless they were better acquainted with things in Boston and the probable effect, which his leaving that place would produce upon the congregation in Park street and upon the general course of orthodoxy in that region. If you could throw any light upon this subject *generally*, or upon the probability of our friend's accepting this call, you would confer an obligation upon one who is placed in circumstances of some delicacy by this singular but providential movement.[46]

Morse wrote back a week later in answer to Richards's "very proper, though delicate, inquiry." Morse observed that, in general, a minister should be considered the "property of the church at large," to be removed only on the advice of local people best able to judge the case if such a move will on the whole "most effectively serve the great cause." He added,

Jedidiah Morse and family with globe. Morse authored several popular geography books. (Family portrait by Morse's son Samuel F. B. Morse, National Museum of American History, Smithsonian Institution)

"In all these changes the evident calls of Providence should always be regarded." Morse expressed surprise over Griffin's call to Newark, saying he had just heard the news. Were he in Griffin's place, "should the proper judges around me approve," he thought he would accept the call. Since Morse was one of the proper judges, he may thus have subtly signalled to Richards his approval of Griffin's call. Morse avoided speculating on the possible effects of Griffin's return to Newark, for his eyes as usual were fixed on Boston.

> It is a time of great trials with us but also of strong and lively hopes. . . . Our hearts are made *inexpressibly* glad by the revival at Princeton. There are hopeful beginnings of a like work at Yale. And we are praying for a like revival at our College in Cambridge . . . may it be brought back from its [Unitarian] apostasy . . . join us in our prayers. . . . There are three of the Theol. Students in our Inst[itutio]n at Andover who are under deep impressions—among them, I bless God, is our youngest son—we have

some hope that our second is in like state of mind, at Litchfield, in Judge Reeve's *Law* School, and under the pastoral instruction of Mr. [Lyman] Beecher. . . . Our kind regards to yourself and Mrs. R.—and to Judge Boudinot.

Yours truly and very affectionately,

J. Morse[47]

Letters between ministers contained little personal information as a rule, but the matter of souls in one's own family was the exception.[48] In a few years, Richards would commence a similar watch over the souls of his unconverted children, one of whom would also attend Judge Reeve's Law School at Litchfield.[49]

In June 1815, when Griffin had discerned his duty and returned to Newark, it fell upon Richards to work out a collegial relationship with this proud and sensitive friend. By now it was clear that James Richards had enjoyed success of his own at First Church as well as in the Church at large. Since a second great revival under him, Old First had grown to a membership of a thousand, making it the second largest congregation in the whole Presbyterian Church.[50] In the next few months, Yale and Union Colleges both awarded Richards the honorary degree of doctor of divinity.

The two ministers would now labor together for souls in a town of about six thousand inhabitants. The arrival of steamboats in 1811 had made Newark the grain, garden, and dairy supplier to New York and would eventually foster Newark's remarkable industrial development. Business was so brisk that Newark, with two banks, was becoming the leading town of New Jersey.[51] On certain projects, Richards and Griffin worked well together. The two men led efforts to form a Newark Bible Society, the new vehicle for local evangelism. This association succeeded his friend Mrs. Kinney's Female Charitable Society. They collaborated with Judge Boudinot and others in forming a chapter of the Presbyterian Education Society for the financial support of ministerial students; Richards served as corresponding secretary at the national level. Griffin held a preaching service for "colored people" on Monday evenings, while Anna's Sunday School at Old First taught interested blacks to read the Bible. Richards acted as the general supervisor of Newark Academy, where one of the instructors he engaged was Matthew LaRue Perrine, formerly a tutor at

Princeton and a close associate in years to come. Though Richards and Griffin made constructive efforts to cooperate, there was one omission and it belonged to Richards: he fended off Griffin's suggestion of regular pulpit exchanges. It may have seemed to him a prudent measure to avoid getting in each other's way.

The challenge of Griffin's return, the conferral on him of public honors, and his deeper involvement in national church affairs marked the next phase in James Richards's Newark ministry. A sharpened sense of time's passing marked it as well. When Richards first came to Newark at the age of forty-two, both his father and his grandfather were still alive. By the time he wrote to his friend Storrs about being past the meridian of life, his grandfather, the "Old Squire," had died. Early in 1816 he received word of his father's death. Although the eldest child of his family and respected for his seriousness and his achievements in the ministry, Richards had not been close to his family in New Canaan in recent years. He did not even now hasten to his mother's side, and some weeks passed before his sister Diana wrote to him the details of his father's deathbed scene that he had requested:

> Our Father went to bed . . . in his usual good health—arose next morning in a severe ague—complained he had lain cold the latter part of the night . . . ate no breakfast—sat sleeping by the fire . . . groaned a good deal . . . I advised sending for a Physician—he said "no, nothing ails me only I am so cold, shall soon get better"—about 11 O'clock we perceived that his limbs failed him, and that he was not sensible [of] what he said. . . .

In the manner of the time, Diana continued an hour-by-hour account of the deathwatch for two more pages. She concluded:

> He then laid his head against Brother William's breast and died without a struggle or a groan—20 minutes past 10 O'clock on Friday morning 7th February—he ended his work—in his 72d year. . . .
>
> There my dear Brother I have endeavored to give you an honest and faithful account. . . . Many things I could say [which] you would gladly hear but they cannot come within the compass of a letter. Our

dear Mother bears this bereavement much better than we could have
expected. . . . She desires me to say she hopes you will come as soon
as the travelling will permit—we want much to see you. . . .

Our Father often complained of your slackness—it is not too late to
make your Mother happy by correcting this fault. Mother unites in the
kindest remembrance to yourself, sister, and all the Children. . . .[52]

James Richards probably hoped to learn about his father's spiritual state at
the time of his death, but Diana was not forthcoming. Was it this matter
that he "would gladly hear" that "cannot come within the compass of a
letter"? Diana had remained at home with their parents, the only one of
his sisters never to marry. Her excellence was in filial duty, and from that
position of virtue she rebuked her older brother. The complaint of his
slackness is interesting in a man otherwise so punctilious. Some aloofness
toward his family may have developed naturally out of residual feelings
and habits stemming from the early independence he was compelled to
assume. His conversion certainly put him on a different road from that of
his brothers, who displayed the family aptitude for commerce. Silently
perhaps a habit of neglect took hold, unnoticed by the busy minister.
Meanwhile, the relatives in New Canaan were proud of him, but also a
little withholding in their pride as he moved forward in the world while
giving them so little of his attention. Thus, Diana now chided rather than
condoled.

James Richards did travel to Connecticut in April when the weather
improved. Before he left, he wrote to Mrs. Kinney in Cincinnati of the
revivals in the surrounding area and of a promising change in his daughter
Caroline, now eighteen years old and always less impressionable when it
came to religion than her older sister. Mrs. Kinney replied:

I did most fervently rejoice to hear about our dear volatile Caroline's
taking an interest in the solemn scenes. Oh that I may speedily hear that
she has come out from the world, and is placed among the believers in
Jesus. . . .[53]

But Caroline's interest did not culminate in profession of religion at this
time.

Both of his daughters had grown into maturity. They soon made marriages very much in keeping with the differences of their two personalities. In 1818, Anna Smith Richards married Aaron Beach, a local man who was the cashier, or the second officer after the president, of the Newark Bank founded in 1804. It was later known as "Old Bank." His father, Nathaniel Beach, a church elder, carried on a prominent carriage-making business. The Beach family typified Newark's prosperous class. Aaron Beach would stay cashier of Old Bank all of his life. His predecessor as cashier had kept his personal rooms on the premises of the bank, but Aaron and Anna maintained a separate residence and soon began a large family.[54]

Two years later, the "volatile" Caroline married into a family more distinguished and moneyed than had her dutiful elder sister. Circumstances found Caroline in a position that was perhaps not unique, if still uncommon, in a time of numerous eligible widowers, but nevertheless notable and potentially delicate: She was courted by two men who were father and son. Anthony Dey was forty-three years old, a widowed lawyer and investor, and his son, Richard Varick Dey, was nineteen years old, a future minister of the Dutch Reformed Church. The elder Dey's suit prevailed, and Caroline's other suitor became the eldest of her four stepchildren, the youngest of whom was ten years old.[55]

In 1817, the spirit of revival again visited Newark. A total of 135 joined the church in a nine-month period. This marked the third of the great revivals under the Reverend Richards. In November, Richards commended one of the converted young to President Ashbel Green for admission to Princeton:

> He is the son of a very excellent Mother, and we hope the heir of her faith. . . . He will bring a certificate from Mr. Perrine, his teacher for the last eighteen months, on whose judgement I think you may rely.[56]

The college at Princeton continued on its uneven path. The season of revival at Princeton in which Jedidiah Morse had rejoiced had been followed by another season of student riots. President Green and the faculty strove to keep the lid on by channeling students' emotional energy into religious awakening and resorting again to stricter discipline. The uproars eventually subsided, and in the following spring of 1817, a wary, relieved, and determinedly stiff-necked Green wrote to Richards:

Nothing can exceed the peace and order of the college from the commencement of the session till the present time. We have not had a case of discipline of any description. But this was the fact also last winter, till within ten days of the riots. I hope the present calm is not the forerunner of another storm. That storm, however, has not hurt but helped us . . . there never was such an accession of students to the college. . . . Such is the issue of gloomy prognostication of some, who probably wished what they foretold. . . . I have always believed and said that the publick would bear us out in a strict [course] of discipline; and that the college would not sink but rise under it. . . . Rebellion was the consequence of a total relaxation of government.[57]

Green went on to ask for Richards's help in finding a new professor of mathematics and philosophy. The board of trustees had recently named the tutor Philip Lindsley to the vice presidency of the college.

The affairs of the Presbyterian Education Society took up more and more of Richards's time and gave him a practical, detailed view of ministerial training and supply in all regions. As corresponding secretary, he kept in touch with presbyteries throughout the country trying to raise money to support needy candidates for the ministry. Memory of his own early struggles made this a cause close to his heart, as he often remarked to his friends.

It was all the more frustrating then that regional competition clouded the effort. The society was strongest in New York and New England. Presbyterians in Philadelphia soon pressured to have the society hold its annual meeting there, a move that was naturally resisted by the northerners who felt this would concede undue leverage to the "brethren to the south." Richards and others proposed instead a compromise whereby the society would alternate its annual meeting between New York and Philadelphia, so that "no predominant influence would attach to either side, but a perfect equality of privilege be secured." This procedure would present "a powerful barrier to all party influence."[58] The compromise prevailed, but the outvoted minority, supported by Samuel Miller and Archibald Alexander, promptly arranged for the establishment of an alternative education society within the structure of the General Assembly. At the 1819 meeting of the General Assembly, Richards and three other officers lodged a written protest. In particular, they objected strenuously to the charge that it was Richards who had acted in a partisan way to block Philadelphian influence. For a while, both societies continued to function until ultimately the older society was absorbed into the upstart one with its official church ties. The experience gave Richards a strong and personal exposure to the sectional rivalry and centralizing tendency within the Presbyterian Church, whose leaders sought every tool at their disposal for the monitoring of orthodoxy. Philadelphia wanted no more eruptions of Hopkinsianism or related phenomena.

The seminary at Princeton had been intended to be a national institution, but its graduates were proving reluctant to settle far afield. Pressing regional needs were now stimulating new ventures in both the West and the South. Four synods of western New York began cooperating in 1818 to organize a seminary of their own at Auburn. James Richards took note of their efforts. He was well acquainted with the Auburn leaders through his work with the Presbyterian Education Society, and they hoped to recruit him as their first professor of theology. The eminent Newark pastor cautiously considered. He was in his fifties, with three sons to educate. Western New York seemed still a distant wilderness to those settled on the seaboard, and his Newark church was still at that point enjoying the afterglow of the last revival. He temporized, then declined. The Auburn organizers, however, did not give up.

Although the prospect of removing to Auburn seemed initially remote, Richards had cause later to reconsider. The close of the decade saw a steep decline at Old First. This was more than lamentable. In an age that prized revivals, it was in no way sufficient for a minister to preside over his flock like a Trollopian vicar—to preach, to christen, to marry, and to bury. Religion must be earnest and vital. If there were no revivals, no "serious impressions," no discernible movements of the spirit among the people, then a parish was adrift, cold, hard, and dead. After the revival of 1817, such was the case at James Richards's church. He could not avoid feeling responsible. Newark was more steeped at present in the new commercial opportunities that internal improvements continued to spur. "New Ark" now paid more attention to its coastal trade in shoes than to renewals of the covenant between God and man.

Richards could not easily turn to his colleague Griffin to commiserate. Their relations had grown tense and formal. Matthew Perrine, now a professor in the new seminary at Auburn, was enough in Richards's confidence on the subject of Griffin that in the spring of 1821 he added this to one of his letters:

> (Private) I am sometimes asked—what do you think of Dr. Griffin? and do you think Dr. Richards would be willing to have him as a colleague [at the new seminary]? I answer as well as I can—but hint I do not think he would do for a professor here. Numbers would urge his appointment as colleague but I hold back and if farther urged will directly oppose—Do I act right?[59]

On Griffin's part, the deteriorated state of religion in Newark aggravated his resentment about the issue between him and Richards long left unresolved: their lack of regular pulpit exchanges. The practice of exchanging pulpits had originated many decades before as a safeguard against the soft preaching that evangelists in the Great Awakening attributed to a "hireling clergy" subservient to its keepers. It was a practice intended to vitalize and challenge Christians in the pews.[60] As a practical matter, it provided to congregations the stimulus of hearing outside preachers without having to pay them fees, and was also a resort when pastors were ill or out of town. Congregations, especially those accustomed to less distinguished preaching, understandably appreciated the variety such a practice afforded them.

For ministers, it could be both convenient and complicated. When James Richards welcomed Griffin back to Newark six years before, he avoided arranging a regular exchange with the "prince of the American pulpit" over at Second Church. Though pained at the omission, Griffin declined to insist or to play the supplicant. And, as long as the efficacy of Richards's own preaching was borne out in the 1817 revival, the matter rested. Now, however, as the cause of religion declined in Newark, Griffin felt compelled to raise the issue anew. The tension between the two was stark in Griffin's decision to address the issue formally in a letter to his neighbor, Richards:

> March 30, 1821
>
> Dear Brother,
>   When I returned to Newark I felt, as I told you, an unconquerable reluctance to offer myself to preach in a pulpit which I had resigned to another, (because I had spiritual children there, and could not think of

drawing their attention; though I did not state this *reason*.) To avoid the pain of having frequently to repeat the offer, (and knowing that the honour of religion required us to exchange) I proposed to have our exchanges *stated*, & named once a month. I did think that, all things considered, I was entitled to have my feelings respected in this matter, especially as they were feelings of mere delicacy to *you*. You thought differently. I then told you that it was impossible for me to *propose* exchanges from time to time, and begged you to understand once for all, that whenever you wished it I always stood ready to exchange, that it would make me happy so to do, and that there was no objection in my congregation.

I can truly say that the only objection I had against returning to Newark, was a fear that I might some how or other disturb the happiness of a brother in a condition where I had been instrumental in placing him. Nothing but a feeling of this sort produced my reluctance to propose exchanges: and that, I must say, would have prevented it to the end of life, had not the loud and increasing complaints of some of your congregation convinced me that the honour of religion requires, and has laid upon me an obligation to break through all my feelings. But to render the task of proposing somewhat less difficult to me, I shall bring it as near as I can to the *stated* form as first proposed. I therefore have made up my mind to renew the offer every other month as my part of the business, and to get as near as I can to the second sabbath in the month, and to the forenoon of the sabbath. But for the month of April, I propose to exchange the next sabbath in the *afternoon* if agreeable to you.

Your friend and brother,
E. D. Griffin[61]

For the nearly six years since Griffin's return this issue had festered. Richards, uneasy in the presence of Griffin's emotional nature and oratorical gifts, had shied away from any arrangement. Whether he made any response to this new initiative on the matter is unknown. The sword that finally severed this knot arrived from outside.

On the fringes of east coast settlement and beyond were many towns that had recently taken up the idea of having a local college. Orthodox religious leaders gravitated to the cause as another way to secure religious influence among local elites, and the Presbyterians and Congregationalists extended their cooperation under the Plan of Union to the establishment of such institutions in a variety of locations. As colleges proliferated and their boards scrambled to find scholarly leadership, there was much raiding of distinguished pulpits. So it happened that, later that spring of 1821, Griffin was called away from Newark a second time to head Williams College in western Massachusetts.[62] The prevailing religious apathy and the economic downturn after the panic of 1819 had led to decreased financial support from his congregation at Second Church, and this, added to the soured relations with his old friend at First Church, moved Griffin now to put aside any qualms about leaving the parish world. He accepted the presidency of Williams, and James Richards had to feel relieved.

During this unsettling period marked by tensions with Griffin and intermittent overtures from Auburn, Richards took more satisfaction than ever from his involvement with the college and the seminary at Princeton. In November 1819, President Green wrote him that the college now had 140 to 150 students, making it "quite as large as it ever ought to be; and we hope we have much fewer rogues . . . than we have usually had."[63] The seminary, under President Archibald Alexander, had about seventy students.

In July 1821, Richards went down to Princeton as a member of the committee to examine the senior class. He studied these young men with more than the usual care, for that fall his eldest son, Henry, hoped to enter the college as a member of the junior class. Upon receiving Henry's application, President Green wrote Richards a rather grumpy letter in which he complained about the preparation of many of the incoming students, acknowledging that he felt compelled to admit them anyway rather than "let other colleges benefit themselves at our expense." As for Henry, Green judged that his "classical reading and attainments" would put him in the middle ranks of the class. Though "not equal to those of our pupils who pass their whole course with us," they certainly did not put "his admission at all on the ground of *favor.*" Green added that Mr. Lindsley was willing to tutor Henry, should he "incline to seek classical accuracy and improvement."[64]

College student bodies, as noted before, were made up of teenagers in this period. Henry, at nineteen, was on the older side. Why he delayed entrance until the junior year is unclear, but this was not at all

Philip Lindsley. (Courtesy—Presbyterian Historical Society, Philadelphia)

uncommon. Finances, the delicate condition of Henry's health, Richards's judgment of the state of the college, and the desire of the family simply to have him at home probably all played a part.

Henry's absence from home entailed the beginning of a regular correspondence between father and son. The latter always addressed his letters solely to his father, while never failing to include affectionate greetings to the rest of the family. As a father, Richards both presided over the Newark household and served as the family's public link to the world outside the home. This form derived from certain established views. Children, it was believed, were born sinful beings into a sinful world, and they required a father's firm moral guardianship. Mothers were thought to be too tenderhearted for this role, as the episode of dancing during Richards's absence would have demonstrated. Henry and his brothers and sisters represented perhaps the last generation of American children reared so visibly on this pattern. Just ahead lay the "child nurture" movement that characterized the emerging industrial age and made mothers instead the special guardians of homebred morals. A letter Henry wrote that November from Nassau Hall captures the spirit of one formula about the father-child relationship of the earlier age, "affection energizing duty, duty controlling affection."[65]

My Dear Father/
Your kind and affectionate letter was duly received by the Saturday's mail—No intelligence could be [more] agreeable to me than to hear that my beloved parents were well, but at the same time I was sorry to hear that Edward's fever has returned and that Sister Anna's children have been so unwell. . . .

You wished to be made acquainted with my studies progress etc—Mathematics is our principle [*sic*] study and will be (as I understand) during the whole of the Junior Year—I think I have quite a relish for this Science—before this I always thought it a dry unprofitable study—not comprehending the beauty and regularity of mathematical demonstrations, of course I could not appreciate their utility—We make a recitation in Euclid every day except Wednesday and have almost completed the first Book—The afternoon I usually devote to the languages, evening [and] morning to Euclid—I have recited but once to Mr. Lindsley—commenced today. . . . He intends to make me a thorough Greco-linguist (as he terms it)—Thinking it to be your wish I have become a member of the Bible Soc. in this place—Another Soc. has been recently formed among the students . . . for . . . the Education of poor young men not merely those who are pious but those of first rate talents for any profession—The society in Coll. is very agreeable, that is, if a person wishes to make it so, as he has it in his power—He can select his own companions and be intimate with whom he chooses—For my own part I have contracted no intimacies—my time is too much occupied in preparing my different lessons to admit of my visiting much, although I have been introduced to nearly half the students—Some of them are very fine young men and others whom at first I thought were able, generous-hearted fellows have proved to be the very worst of characters—Truly this place may be said to be a sink of iniquity—Oh! my dear father much do I need your advice and instruction—much do I need the aid of your judgment and experience. . . .[66]

The anxiety that lies close to surface of this dutiful account is not surprising, given all that he had heard at home about the dangers to be expected from the town boys of his childhood and the "rogues" currently at Princeton. Many of Henry's peers seemed to mystify him. He took refuge in study and approved associations like the Bible Society.

More and more James Richards saw Princeton through the eyes of his son. This meant increased awareness of the young Mr. Lindsley, Henry's tutor in classical languages, who was a significant presence in Henry's life and in the life of Princeton College at this time. Philip Lindsley had been long acquainted with the Richards family. He was related to the Condicts of Morristown and had taught at the academy there when the Reverend

Richards was pastor. At that time Lindsley was not yet eighteen and but a recent graduate of Princeton. He returned to the college in the spring of 1807, the first season of riots, and had been there ever since. Following theological studies with Green's predecessor, Dr. Smith, he was ordained to the ministry. Since Smith's departure, he had pleased the college trustees with his enthusiastic instruction in Latin and Greek, both of which were considered excellent preparation for those students who would enter the ministry. After the riot of 1817, the trustees elected him college vice president. He was known as a learned and exacting scholar and an accessible and popular teacher.

Lindsley boldly spoke his mind and had just published in 1821 a discourse, "A Plea for a Theological Seminary at Princeton," that stirred up the church considerably. "[It] wrought differently upon different minds," understated an observer. One Massachusetts man promptly donated a thousand dollars to the cause of seminary education. Others, however, detected an intemperate attack on older colleagues. In pleading the cause of professional theological training, Lindsley denounced those who had trained in the old private way, who were still the great majority. His ardor sometimes spilled over into contempt: "With a smattering of letters and with abundant self-complacency [the privately trained minister] marches forth . . . and continues through life the same opinionated, bigoted creature that he was at the beginning." It did not help with some that Lindsley himself was privately trained, for his study had been with Smith, the Princeton president so criticized by Green and Miller for "laxness" in administering the college. Moreover, Lindsley was associated with ideals of academic rigor at a time when Green's emphasis had been on restoring discipline and encouraging piety through Bible societies and Bible classes.[67]

The following summer, after ten onerous years in the office, Ashbel Green resigned the presidency of Princeton and returned to Philadelphia to publish the conservative *Christian Advocate.* Enrollment at the college was again on the decline.[68] Despite his controversial discourse, the trustees called on the thirty-five-year-old Lindsley to guide the college in the interim.

Henry began his second and senior year in the wake of this change. Princeton may not have been at a high-water mark, but with energy and a teacher like Lindsley, he could expect to accomplish something. Unfortunately, energy and health eluded him, and he wrote home in January that he was "very much troubled with my old complaint." The problem was dysentery, a common ailment, "which necessarily subjects me to many inconveniences and renders my situation quite unpleasant." He was forced to stay indoors and he believed the resulting lack of exercise was bad for him.

The only exercise which I now use is with dumb-bells, which though very excellent for the heart, does not have . . . influence over the lower extremities. . . . My principle [sic] object in writing is . . . to ask your opinion on the propriety of my returning home until such time when my health should be more established—

This has been the advice of Dr. Van Cleve and others sometime since but I hesitated to propose it to you, until I had thoroughly considered of its expediency—I am aware of its being attended with some disadvantages with regard to my studies, but when I consider that it will expedite my recovery (as I trust it will), and enable me in time to come to review them with more profit and certainly with more comfort, I am inclined to think it advisable—

No person can more deeply regret the necessity of such a measure than myself. This I know is a most important period of my life, and to neglect to improve the opportunities which it affords, will in after life always be attended with regret—I have endeavored to make good use of my time during my indisposition, but I am not able to bear vigorous application without corresponding exercise—I have not made mention of the state of my health in my former letters because I thought it needless to give you any anxiety on my account and even now I hope you will not be alarmed.

In case you should think it proper for me to return I should wish my dear father that you would write immediately. What time I am absent my board and washing and wood will be deducted from the bill. Give my love to my dear mother brothers and sisters and believe me your affectionate son

Henry[69]

Young Henry Richards exercised with dumb-bells. (Taken from Dio Lewis, The New Gymnastics for Men, Women, and Children, *Clark Brothers, New York, 1883)*

Confinement and discomfort had compounded Henry's sense of detachment from his fellow students. He was careful, like the lawyer he became, to anticipate his father's objections: He had been patient, he had consulted a physician, and he had thought through the consequences for his studies and the family purse.

Despite these entreaties, Henry did not leave the college. By the end of March, two months later, he had made it through the winter, and he wrote home in quite a different vein. Perhaps a return to good health put a new light on everything. Earnestness about improving his time and opportunities was now the theme. As his father often reminded, youth was the most important time of life.

My Dear Father

I have no doubt you think me very negligent in delaying to write you for so long a time. I hope however you will receive an old excuse and believe that a pressure of Coll[ege] engagements has hitherto prevented me. The present session has nearly expired—18 days will finish the term. In looking back upon the last 4 months . . . the whole is only as a day, and its scenes appear . . . with the quick succession of a drama. I never was more sensible . . . of the truth of the remark which I recollect once to have heard you make, that the longer we lived the time past appeared shorter. . . . What a fruitful source of gratulation must it be to those who . . . feel a consciousness of having employed their time to the best of their ability. . . . For my own part I see many opportunities . . . for improvement . . . omitted. . . . Mr. Lindsley preached lately a sermon on the improvement of time, which has since been published . . . if I can [obtain] one I will bring it with me. About returning—will you be so good my dear father to let me know as soon as convenient what are your calculations on this head? It is nearly time to make some arrangement respecting it.

As spring arrived much of Princeton speculated on the identity of the next college president. Henry joined in the gossip:

Dr. Rice I understand has intimated in a letter to Dr. Alexander [still the head of the Seminary] that he shall decline the presidency of this coll[ege]. Report says that Mr. Lindsley is going to Nashville [Tennessee]. I don't believe it.[70]

Henry's information about the college presidency was correct. John Holt Rice, the forty-six-year-old Richmond pastor and editor of an evangelical literary magazine, was in close contact with his fellow Virginian, Dr. Alexander. The two men had known each other since their days together in the late 1790s at Virginia's Hampden-Sydney College where Alexander had served as president and Rice had been, like Lindsley, a tutor. Although the conservative Southern Presbyterians were always strongly represented at Princeton, Rice did indeed turn down its presidency and instead chose to head up a Presbyterian theological seminary being established in Richmond. Another new Presbyterian institution found its man, and Princeton now had to reconsider.

Philip Lindsley, young as he was, had reason to believe that the Princeton trustees might turn his way. As acting president, he had been effective. His talents, widely recognized, had led that spring to his "election" to no fewer than three college presidencies, all in the West. As Henry had reported, in disbelief, he had accepted the one at Nashville. But Lindsley's treatment at the hands of Princeton's board of trustees in the end left him shaken and angry.

How active James Richards was in the board's deliberations is difficult to gauge. Lindsley seems to have looked to Richards, a longtime friend of his family, as an ally or at the least an honest broker. At any rate, when all was done, a wounded and reproachful Lindsley poured out his heart to Richards in a letter dated June 11, 1823:

Last fall when the presidential chair became vacant, I clearly saw that duty did not summon me to the post, and I therefore would not suffer myself to be considered as a candidate. Several of the trustees were hostile to me. I thought it all-important to the welfare of the college that the Board should be unanimous in their choice. I therefore cheerfully and promptly sacrificed all private considerations *pro bono publico*. I saw moreover, or thought I saw, that my friends were very doubtful what course to pursue. They seemed to pity my awkward situation—were afraid that I would be mortified and hurt, if I were passed by, etc. I scorned their sympathy and trampled upon all the honour the Board had to bestow. . . . I will not accept the presidency as a *favour* from my friends. If I do not deserve it, then withhold it. I will not seek the office—it will seek me, or I never have it. Such were my feelings. There was more of pride than humility in my conduct, I admit.

This spring I expected similar opposition, and I was prepared to adopt a similar course. The fact is, during the winter I had been left to manage the college almost *solus*. I had four tutors—three of them raw hands. . . . None of us had any *official* rank or dignity to sustain us. . . . And how did we get along? What an accession of students? How much money did we save the institution? When did better order prevail? At the close of the session therefore, when the Board convened, I felt that I stood on high ground in spite of my enemies. . . .

Lindsley was prepared to be treated handsomely or else forego the post. He proved indeed too controversial, however, and though the board did elect him, it was not the unanimous vote he had looked for. Urged on by two of the trustees, he swallowed his pride and "in the morning I suffered myself to say *yes* to the committee." Lindsley's misgivings soon returned as he watched the faction opposed to him maneuver to propose for vice president a man who was unacceptable to the influential Samuel Miller. The board adjourned at this juncture with a plan to reconvene after the college vacation.

I was at a loss what to do. Dr. Miller was the only trustee with whom I conversed much during the vacation. He could not endure the thought that Mr. F. should come and on one occasion, *inter nos*, said, *that I ought not to accept with a chance of bringing him into the Faculty.* You [Richards] were the first and only gentleman who encouraged me to think favourably of the matter. I had but little conversation with you on the subject. I began however to make arrangements to accept. . . .

Richards was also in Princeton during the May vacation, and in a letter to his wife noted, "I lodged last evening at Mr. Johns—but have this morning taken up my quarters at Doctor Miller's by particular invitation. . . ."[71] He said no more of Miller, but his wording indicates that Miller made a point of seeking him out. The topic of mutual interest was almost certainly the college presidency. Miller was pressing Lindsley to bow out. When he became aware that Richards was encouraging the young man to accept the post under the stated conditions, the seminary professor worked to persuade his Newark colleague of the necessity of Lindsley's doing otherwise. Lindsley confided to Richards afterward that he had badly needed at this time the advice of friends but the board was back in session before most of them had arrived back in town.

> You had discouraged me from asking a longer time. When the committee called, I was more in the dark than ever. . . . An answer was expected—*yes* or *no*. I said no, because I did not see my way clear to say yes. . . . Dr. M[iller] knew, or I supposed he knew, the whole difficulty, for he had done more than any one else to create it. Under these circumstances, I felt that my generosity [was] . . . appealed to, to keep the Board out of a dilemma. I therefore sacrificed myself to oblige my friends, to serve the college, and to spare the feelings of Mr. F.
>
> Is it possible that the Board should ever have really wished me to be the president of Nassau Hall—and yet to embarrass me, and hedge me in, so that all the world called on me to refuse. . . .

He felt he had been maneuvered out, that his "no" had been extorted, and that more time should have been afforded him. "Such a procedure," he wrote, "needs no comment. It speaks volumes. And there are some folks of wit to understand it." Was this a dig at Richards?

> When among my pupils, I am at home in the midst of friends, and feel that I could manage fifty colleges. But the Board—the Board—I had rather face the Devil!

Here you have the secret of all my hesitation and vacillation and contradictions, etc. I wished to ascertain how many staunch friends I had on the Board. With half-a-dozen . . . I would not have hesitated. But they must be sterling stuff, not merely true to me at all times but *adamant* to my enemies—not suffering themselves to be deceived, flattered, blinded, cajoled, into compromises and half-way measures by that *cunning littleness* which meets them at every turn. Without such a phalanx I could do nothing. My enemies would be active—they would watch over me with the eyes of an Argoes, and compass sea and land to make me proselyte to their ranks. A president can do nothing if the Board be against him. . . . Now I would care nothing about the Board if they would adjourn . . . and not meddle with my concerns.

But the Board regard me as a boy . . . because they knew me as a youth twenty years ago.

I have served the college during the closing years of one brilliant administration [that of his mentor Dr. Smith] and through the whole of another [Dr. Green's]. . . . I have lost a presidency, but have preserved my honour. . . .

Forgive my scolding and petulance, and believe me respectfully and affectionately your

Ph. Lindsley[72]

Despite his conciliatory closing, it is clear that Lindsley marked Richards among the fainthearted of his friends.

Lindsley linked his own vacillation to uncertainty about his friends who must be "not merely true to me at all times, but *adamant* to my enemies." He came to see Miller as one of his enemies and clearly implied that Richards was among those who were "deceived, flattered, blinded, cajoled into compromises." It may be a fair though heated judgment. Yet Lindsley should have recognized that it was not James Richards's way to draw a line in the dirt in the way he demanded. Richards even at Lindsley's age was never so bold or impassioned in public. More than most of Princeton's conservative guardians, though, James Richards may have felt the appeal of Philip Lindsley. Richards was less connected to the confessional Presbyterianism that tended to be heritage-minded rather than innovative, a group represented by Miller, Green, Alexander, and Rice, and oriented toward Philadelphia and the South. He had personal ties to Lindsley, even perhaps the inclination to be a patron. Most of all, he had a son at Nassau Hall who knew and talked firsthand of Lindsley's gifts. Henry had seen the tutor among his pupils when he felt he could manage fifty colleges.

Yet Miller and Green and Alexander were James Richards's leading colleagues. He was not one easily to jeopardize collegial relationships or to make any institution he cared about the center of avoidable turmoil. Furthermore, he knew from personal experience the suspicions of heresy and partisanship that could dog even a moderate New Englander in the Presbyterian fold. With Lindsley as with Griffin previously, Richards's tact and caution came to be read as a failure of loyalty.

The awkward evolution of these relationships and the continuing stagnation in his Newark parish would weigh on such a conscientious man. As a Princeton trustee, he had seen as well in the Lindsley episode the limits of his effectiveness in that milieu. Whatever the frustrations, Richards had a steadier temperament than either a Griffin or a Lindsley. He strove in his way for the long, less personal view. He continued to find his enthusiasm fired by the fitful progress of his various societies and especially of the new theological seminaries. The need for gospel preachers was great. He could not grieve too much that a man of Lindsley's talents would now be at work in the West, for the burgeoning West had special need for such men.

As events now unfolded, Richards and Lindsley at their different stages of life and in different seats of responsibility had both prepared at Princeton for the major work of their lives. As an officer in the Presbyterian Educational Society and in his various commissions for the General Assembly, Richards knew at firsthand the rapid profusion of congregations that lacked ministerial leadership. But it was as a trustee of Princeton College, a director of Princeton Seminary, a Princeton fundraising agent, and an examiner of Princeton students, that he learned what it takes to launch—and sustain—a new educational institution. When Presbyterians of western New York renewed their invitation to him to be the first professor of theology at Auburn Seminary, James Richards was now ready to accept. Auburn's cause was religion's cause, and as such he would make it his own.

The new task would refresh him. Newark, too, needed a new hand. "Every green thing withers," he had written to McDowell in 1822.[73] In August 1823, he wrote out a thorough statistical report on trends in church membership at Old First in the first quarter of the nineteenth century. His own figures showed that in a fourteen-year ministry, his congregation had roughly doubled in the midteens, only to sink back to its original level by the time of his appointment to Auburn.[74] Since all was in God's hands, this fact in itself might be the hand of Providence showing him the way.

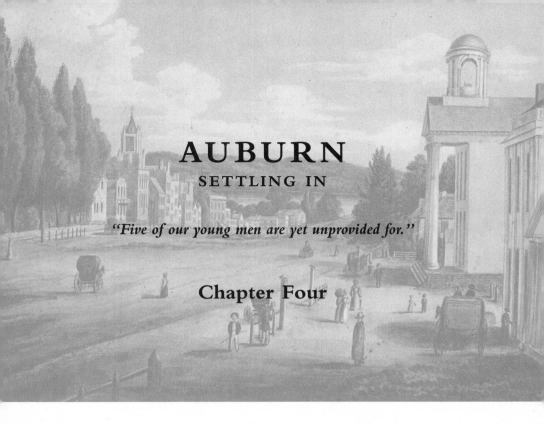

AUBURN
SETTLING IN

"Five of our young men are yet unprovided for."

Chapter Four

James Richards came to Auburn in western New York to be inaugurated as the first professor of Christian theology on October 29, 1823. It was his birthday; he was fifty-six years old. To the man who but a few years earlier had explained that he was "past the meridian of life," it might seem an overly ambitious and risky change, but in a sense he was no longer that man. All that he had done so far suggested that this was the next step in God's plan, and armed with that conviction he descended on Auburn with astounding energy and optimism. The fact that he was choosing to remove himself to a part of the world that he had never seen before, to separate himself from family and friends and longtime close clerical associates to take his chances with a new and financially shaky institution didn't cause him a backward glance; it was his wife Caroline who found the transition hard but then the Lord had not called her.

He appeared the ideal person to establish the fledgling seminary on a firm basis. Although he was a Presbyterian from New Jersey, an insider in the seats of power, he had started life as a Congregationalist from Connecticut, a fact which appealed to the religious mix in western New York. In addition he personified both the evangelical and the scholarly traditions of Presbyterianism. He symbolized all that Auburn was and hoped to be.

93

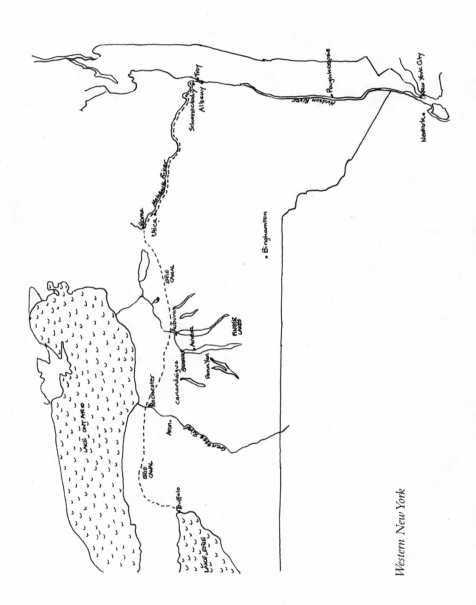

Western New York

This new seminary was western New York's answer to the over-whelming ministerial needs of a region that stretched from Albany to Buffalo and beyond into the former Western Reserve in Ohio. It was an area that had been settled with awesome speed once the Revolutionary War ended and the competing land claims of Massachusetts, Connecticut, New York, and the Indians were resolved. Yankees from western Connecticut left the rocky overcrowded farms of their native state and poured into the Genesee Valley and the plain that paralleled Lake Ontario. In one three-day period in February 1795, the residents of Albany saw 1,200 sleds filled with New Englanders and their household possessions pass through the city; a traveler in 1797 counted 500 wagons a day on the road west from Albany.[1] Settlers also came up through Cherry Valley from Pennsylvania and New Jersey. In the 1790s the Phelps and Gorham Tract, the Holland Tract, and the Military Tract, in fact all the land in western and central New York State from Lake Seneca in the Finger Lakes to Lake Ontario, were opened to settlement; between 1790 and 1820 the census recorded an increase in population from 1,081 persons to over half a million, a 469-fold increase. No other area of the country has ever been settled so rapidly.[2]

And where were the churches while this development was going on? They were struggling to keep contact with the scattered settlements. As late as 1800 there was no settled minister for the 30,000 people living in the Military Tract. The Congregationalist churches of eastern New York and western Massachusetts and Connecticut and the General Assembly all sent out missionaries. Just as James Richards had been sent for a month to western New Jersey in 1803, so others had gone for months at a time to the Genesee Valley. Despite so many settlers having come from "the land of steady habits," as Connecticut was called, "it was a common remark of the day that there was no Sabbath west of the Genesee River, and there was not much of one for a long way east of it."[3] Like all frontier regions, this one was marked by free and easy ways and lawless behavior until communities were established.

Gradually things improved. While there was a revival in 1798 that spread over almost the whole of central and western New York State, the most important institutional development to address the problem was the 1801 Plan of Union between the Congregationalists and the Presbyterians (see chapter 3). Both churches deplored the duplication of effort among scattered people who shared the same Calvinistic faith and simple Puritan style of worship. Under the Plan of Union, a congregation could call either a Congregational or a Presbyterian minister, organize itself according to whichever scheme of government it preferred, and then be admitted to either a Congregational association or a Presbyterian synod or both. It was hoped that the Congregationalists and Presbyterians combined could supply enough ministers for western New York.

The Reverend Dirck Lansing, pastor at Onondaga Valley, first suggested the idea of a local seminary in 1812 to meet the growing need for trained clergy. The proposal went nowhere.

The population continued to grow rapidly. As the need became ever more pressing, efforts were made both locally and through the Presbyterian Education Society to raise money for the new Princeton Seminary and to support "poor and pious youths" for the ministry. By 1818 it was clear that this approach was inadequate, and Lansing, by now the pastor at Auburn, revived his proposal for a local seminary. He thought quite reasonably if an "institution should be established more particularly under the eye and immediate patronage of the good people of this part of the country considerable sums of money and large donations of land might be obtained."[4] A committee was formed to ask for the approval of the General Assembly when it next met in Philadelphia. Despite a professed desire on the part of some Presbyterian leaders to have seminary education centralized, the General Assembly was so preoccupied with establishing the seminary in Princeton that it took no interest in the proposal. The General Assembly sent back word that it had no opinion or advice on the subject and that the Synod of Geneva should do what it thought best.

Now on their own, the committee broadened its base by

Dirck Lansing. (Taken from John Quincy Adams, A History of Auburn Theological Seminary 1818–1918, Auburn, New York, 1918)

calling a meeting of fifty-eight distinguished and varied potential supporters. The new committee included the Reverend Henry Davis, president of Hamilton College, representatives of several Congregational associations and all the presbyteries within the bounds of the Synod of Geneva. Their first decisions were critical. They insisted on only accepting men who had the benefit of a college education or its equivalent against a faction that believed that they could not afford the luxury of insisting on this much prior training. They also decided to establish the new school in Auburn, the largest town west of Utica, on the turnpike running westward from Albany, and the site of a new model prison. The institution was placed under the supervision of a board of commissioners who represented all the presbyteries of the Synod of Geneva.

The first fund-raising efforts were crowned with success. On November 30, 1819, the committee proceeded to break ground in a colorful ceremony. Lansing held the plow when the outline of the first building was marked off. A large number of citizens then pitched in and worked through the morning. At one o'clock, when they had all stopped for a cold lunch, they heard the unexpected sound of the bugle horn at the state prison. A band played as the captain of the prison guard sallied forth with forty workers, their spades held at attention. Everyone worked again through the afternoon until just before sunset when the prisoners returned inside their walls. Then two hundred strong they formed a procession headed by twenty-three teams drawing wagons, carts, and plows and marched through the village to the public house. There they received the thanks of the committee and suitable refreshments before "every man repaired to his house with apparent pleasure and satisfaction."[5]

After the first flurry of interest, donations slowed substantially. It was six months before the cornerstone was laid and four years before they succeeded in attracting James Richards as a professor of theology. They appealed to him repeatedly. They first offered him an annual salary of $1,000, fifty cords of wood, and the use of a "dwelling house." The salary was too small for a man of his responsibilities, but for a number of years all the professors at Auburn would have to come at a financial sacrifice. Another six months passed while he considered the offer before turning it down; he did not think that the fledgling seminary had enough money to succeed. However the committee attracted two of his proteges, the Reverend Henry Mills as Professor of Biblical Criticism and Oriental Languages and the Reverend Matthew

Matthew La Rue Perrine. (Taken from John Quincy Adams, A History of Auburn Theological Seminary 1818–1918, *Auburn, New York, 1918)*

La Rue Perrine, D.D., as Professor of Ecclesiastical History and Church Government. This was the same Henry Mills whom James Richards had prepared for the ministry back in Morristown and the Matthew Perrine he had supervised at the Newark Academy. They were each to get $600 and the use of a house. Rounding out the faculty was the indefatigable Dirck Lansing as Professor of Sacred Rhetoric. He agreed to serve without pay since he continued as the pastor of the Presbyterian church in Auburn.

When the committee made Richards a second offer and he again vacillated, Perrine was delegated to write him a letter urging him to come:

July 15, 1820

My Very Dear Brother,

I am constantly pressed to give my opinion with regard to the probability of your accepting the call—I can only say I fear not; But I know Dr. R. will give it serious consideration, that he will feel willing to pursue that course in which it shall appear to him he can serve his Lord best, and that there is sufficient ground to make the application, etc. . . . Now D[ea]r Brother where can you serve your Lord better than in the Theological Seminary at Auburn, in being the first professor in an institution which is evidently designed to be intensively influential, and in giving a direction to such an institution. The whole of this subject will present itself to you at once—the entire unanimity and the ardency of the united wish of this country that you should be the first professor, or the founder of the theological instruction of this seminary must be viewed as a coin from heaven.

Perrine playfully noted the presence of two new benefactors with the same names as the two distinguished New England theologians Jonathan Edwards and Joseph Bellamy.[6]

Two gentlemen a Mr. Edwards and a Mr. Bellamy have agreed to endow a professorship. The first professor will of course be called the Edwardian Bellamy or the Bellamy Edwardian or the Edwards and Bellamy Professor—a wonderful coincidence of events and circumstances. My hearts desire and prayer is that Doctor James Richards may be the Edwards and Bellamy Professor—and come to teach what Edwards and Bellamy taught and then go and mingle your praises with those good and labourious men. . . . By this means I may secure a plan from which I can very often go and see the E & B Professor.[7]

Their arguments did not touch him sufficiently, and the seminary opened without him. The board of commissioners was both optimistic and ambitious. Princeton Seminary had started with only two professors and after twelve years had three departments. Andover also had started with two professors but had not increased the number in eight years. Auburn was beginning with three professors and four departments, although with very little money and not much assurance of funding in a region that was still partially supported by mission funds.

By now enough money had come in to finish the first building and furnish some student rooms. Some of the support was in-kind, fruits of a man's orchard or the product of another's bees. Fifteen associations of young men had been formed to cultivate a portion of land for the benefit of the seminary. Richards's son-in-law in New York, Anthony Dey, gave the rights to a flax and hemp machine that he established in Cayuga in 1822, a year in which the seminary was unsuccessfully soliciting his father-in-law. Fourteen hundred books had been collected in New York, Philadelphia, and several towns in New Jersey. Expenses had to be kept down since there was no tuition and the cost of board was not to exceed a dollar a week, in contrast to Andover and Princeton where the cost was two dollars a week.

The eleven students in the first class were representative of the classes that followed: seven were Presbyterians and four were Congregationalists; eight of them came from New York and three from New England; three of them were graduates of Union, two of Williams, one each of Hamilton, Middlebury, and Yale; and three were not college graduates.[8]

A year after their last offer, the commission was again urging Richards to come and asked Perrine to write once more. This time Perrine enclosed a little map[9] of Auburn and a list of the prices of staple grocery items.

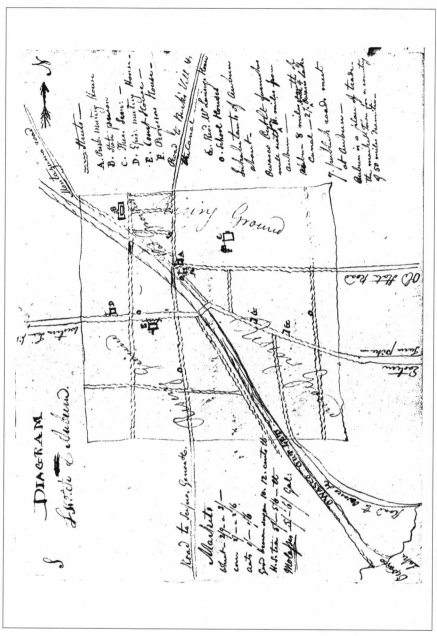

Perrine's drawing of the countryside around Auburn. (Courtesy—Auburn Theological Seminary Library of Union Theological Seminary, Letter of Perrine to James Richards, Otisco, New York, March 14, 1821)

                                                             March 14, 1821
Dear Brother,
    So many communications have been made to you on the subjects
alluded to in your letter that there is nothing left for me—If you are a
good Yankee you will be able to guess something of my statistical report
from my Diagram—to that I refer you—There appears to be very little
doubt among the clergy generally but that your salary will be safe and
punctually paid. . . . Numbers feel . . . that it is time now to have
your decision—that a professor must be obtained so as to be able to
publish it to the churches by May or June. . . . But my very dear
Brother, you do not know the general anxiety which is felt with regard
to your answer—some hope, some fear, some tremble—If you should
negative the call I cannot tell what the consequences will be—Tho a few
talk, we can choose another if Dr. Richards refuses, yet these few would
sigh were they obliged to make another choice—All wish ardently that
you may see the way clear to come to Auburn.[10]

Finally the faith of the founders was rewarded. The notable philan-
thropist Arthur Tappan sent a check for $15,000 to endow a chair of
Christian theology. He and his brother Lewis were prominent silk
merchants in New York City who lent their time and considerable
resources to all manner of benevolent enterprises.[11] Armed with these new
funds the commissioners of the seminary lost no time in once more
seeking out James Richards for the chair of Christian theology, this time at
a salary of $1,200 and house, thirty cords of wood, and $200 for moving
expenses. He accepted at once.[12] The conjunction of stable funding at
Auburn and declining conversions in Newark prevailed and he went west
to be inaugurated.
    In leaving Newark, the Richardses were moving from one of the most
cosmopolitan areas in the young country. They knew western New York
by reputation as a fast growing and needy frontier area, but, in fact, the
frontier phase had passed. In the twenty years since Auburn was settled, it
had become a thriving market town of a little over 2,000 people set in the
midst of fine farmland. Presbyterian, Episcopal, Baptist, Methodist, Roman
Catholic, and Universalist churches had been established, as well as a
Sunday School for "colored people." A state prison was built in 1817 that
was a model of the latest thinking in penology,[13] and there was an

academy, newspaper, county medical society, and agricultural association. Its future seemed bright, so bright in fact that it had hopes of becoming the capital of New York State and went so far as to name the main street Capital Street. Although it was on the main road from Albany to Buffalo, and its population had increased 100 percent in the last five years, the future was destined to be more circumscribed than anyone realized. Unfortunately Auburn was not on the Erie Canal that opened for traffic in the fall of 1824, one year after the Richardses arrived. Auburn may well have merited its high opinion of itself, but Caroline Richards approached the move from Newark with a sense of sacrifice. Within a few weeks she wrote her first impressions back to their daughter Anna:

November 23rd, 1823

My Dear Anna,

We have just received your very affectionate letter; nothing could have been more welcome. I think our better plan will be to write every fortnight. That will prevent a disappointment every time the mail comes in. We live directly opposite the post office where we are awoke every morning about daylight by the western mail. The eastern mail arrives every evening about six o'clock, and leaves here every day at twelve. From my chamber window I can look directly into the post ofice and see the young man sort the letters hoping to hear something from my dear children.

We are also amidst all the bustle of the village, a circumstance you know I do not dislike. I think I never saw so busy a place. It does seem some days as if everybody was upon the move. I think there must be a great deal of business done here. There are several very large stores of dry goods and groceries and confectionaries. I can purchase raisins and lemons and everything of the kind as good and as cheap as you can at Newark.

I don't think there ever was people made more welcome than we were when we first arrived, and when we first went to housekeeping. My pantry looked like a cookshop; every thing that was nice was sent in. I did not expect them to take such an interest in us. The society is much better here than I had any idea it could be so far west; for my part I cannot see any difference either in their dress, manners or style of living from that of Newark. You thought my sofa would cut such a dash here, but I can assure you that it looks very mean compared with some of my neighbours, with their Brussels carpets and every other thing answerable.

So much for the easterner's sense of superiority! The West was not so uncivilized after all. She continued with a description of their neighbors, the warm reception they had received, and the comfort and charm of their house. All the same, nothing compensated for the loss of her family in New York and New Jersey.

But after all my comforts and agreeable disappointments, I find to be separated from children, and grandchildren and others who are near and dear is no small sacrifice. At times I can truly say that I feel like a stranger and a pilgrim on the earth, and my daily prayer is that this and every trial may be sanctified to us all. How are your dear children? No tongue can tell how I long to see you all. I dreamt the other night that I met Susan [a Dey servant] in the street with both of Caroline's children and that little Laidlie could walk. As soon as little C[aroline] saw me she put her dear little arms round my neck and when I awoke I was weeping for joy, but I wept more at the disappointment when I found it a dream. . . .

Do write to us soon and tell us all about. . . . every body and everything and remember me very affectionately to all my friends. . . . Give my love to Caroline and tell her that I really think hard of her. She has not written a word either to your father or myself since we have been here. We recieved [sic] Mr. Dey's letter on Tuesday evening and intend answering it very soon. You must remember us very affectionately to him, and all his family, and also to your dear husband and Mrs. Beach [Anna's mother-in-law] and all the children and kiss them for their grandmama. . . .

In a P.S. she urged her daughters to make up their minds to visit the next summer, "for I do not think I can live till next fall without seeing you both."[14]

The house adjoined the grounds of the seminary, and they could look out upon its lawns dotted here and there by tall locust trees. The parlor resembled other parlors of the era: a sofa and chairs covered with

black haircloth, ingrain carpet on the floor, a center table of mahogany
with the family Bible on it, window shades rolled on a rod from the
bottom and tied at the top, and a mantel over the woodburning fire-
place. In time at the base of the mantel stood two conch shells brought
back from the Pacific by a student turned missionary. There was no heat
in the halls and none in the sleeping rooms but the kitchen was a warm
and pleasant room. The wooden floor was painted pumpkin yellow. Here
Caroline did her baking twice a week, first the meat and pies, then the
bread and biscuits and a weekly loaf of pound cake in case anyone
should drop in. Caroline roasted her coffee at home, cut her sugar for
the week on Friday from a coneshaped loaf wrapped in purple paper,
and made her own soap and candles. She had a smokehouse where she
preserved her ham and bacon and a cellar where she stored her winter
vegetables, apples, and homemade sausage, lard, and mincemeat. Her
granddaughter, Julia, remembered Caroline papering the walls and
ceiling, doing the upholstery, dying her own wool, and always going
about with her knitting fastened at her right side so she could knit as
she talked. She also carried a lucky bone and a piece of sulphur, dried
hard, to keep away rheumatism.

Two smoke bushes and two white lilacs bordered the walk leading up
to the house and a matrimony vine climbed up the veranda, while locust
trees shaded the rooms overhead. In back there was a flower garden with a
path down the center and several crosspaths running at right angles. Here
Caroline grew phlox, sweet William, and cinnamon pinks, while along the
back fence stood a row of sunflowers. There were also crimson peonies,
bleeding hearts, hollyhocks, and across the front a border of box and raspberry bushes.[15] While Caroline concentrated on their private garden, her
husband interested himself in planting and nurturing ten elm trees along
the seminary's sidewalk. Richards saw the trees as the embodiment of the
growth and development of the seminary.[16]

Soon after their arrival Richards wrote to his daughter Anna. The
Newark church of which she was a prominent member was having a difficult time settling on his replacement, and the decision was of much
interest. He also relied on her to raise money there.

> My dear daughter,
> Tell Mr. T[uttle] that I have not the least idea that Mr. W. of Ithaca
> would suit Newark. He is a man of strong sense but not of much taste in

composition nor of much force in delivery. He is not regarded as a popular preacher even in this country so far as I have heard. An excellent man—but better adapted to his present sphere of action than to any important congregation in your part of the country. I regret that Mr. Fisher makes no deeper impression among you. But the Lord knows what is best and you must all wait upon him.

The number of students in the seminary is yet small—only one was added the last year, so low were the hopes of the public in regard to it. Things are now changed. 9 were recieved [*sic*] at the commencement of this term and more are yet expected. Tell me if Newark will give us her good wishes and fifty dollars as the proof of them.

affectionately,
J. Richards[17]

Richards's presence had immediately caused an increase in the enrollment. He assumed personal responsibility for the improvement in the seminary finances that this required. Despite his age, he travelled every vacation for as long as six weeks at a time to solicit funds; and when he was not travelling, he wrote letters appealing for money.

The move to Auburn had been received with interest by his mother and sister Diana. It has already been noted that he had grown apart from them as he pursued his ministry, so the formality of Diana's note and her emphasis on filial duty lent an edge to her good wishes.

December 20th, 1823

My dear brother and Sister,

Mother is often reminding me of my duty and among other duties, that of answering the letters of our very dear friends is not forgotten. She says, "Do write your brother James and thank him for all the interesting matter which his letter from Auburn contained." Indeed, my dear brother, it was very gratifying to hear from you direct. Your pleasant journey from city to city, the delightful situation you now inhabit, the disposing of your interesting sons for business, improvements of your health, and your happy prospect of comfort and usefullness are all topics that call forth our gratitude to our Heavenly Father that his goodness and mercy has continually surrounded you. . . .

We lately had a very interesting letter from Anna. She appears more feelingly to lament your loss than any friend I have heard express their views. And having no spiritual guide appears to lay with great weight upon her mind. Mother writes the most affectionate remembrance of you both and your dear children. . . . You my dear brother will I hope write often. It makes mother so very happy that I feel it your incumbant [*sic*] duty.

> very affectionately
> your sister Diana[18]

If the congratulations seemed a little out of touch with the hard financial realities, it may have been in part because he minimized the uncertainties of his new position. ·

Richards's frequent fund-raising trips certainly increased Caroline's yearning for her daughters and grandchildren. After being in Auburn only three months he visited Troy and Albany. He would return with $1,200 and the good news that he had established a support society in each of the churches he had visited. While on the road he offered news and attention to his lonely wife in several letters.

> Utica, Feby 5, 1824

My dear Mrs. R. –

We reached Rome, the place of meeting, about 12 oclock after a ride of a couple of hours in an open sleigh. The cold was pretty sharp— but I felt no inconvenience from the exposure. . . . During my stay at Rome, I was located in the family of Mr. George Huntington, a man about 60 years of age and of the most agreeable manners. I was charmed with the whole family, with parents and children. Left Rome this morning about ten oclock, dined at Whitesborough—and arrived at this place about 3 oclock where I was cordially recieved at my old quarters. . . . The cold is somewhat increased but as the mail coach is close and well lined I trust I shall not find it very unpleasant. I hope to find a letter for me at Albany tomorrow evening. My health continues good but the prospect of doing much for the seminary is not great.

Remember me affectionately to the children and Mr. Seymour[19] and all enquiring friends. I write in great haste and must bid you good night.

> your ever attached husband
> James Richards[20]

Open sleigh. (By Currier and Ives)

Troy Feby 14th 1824

My dear Caroline,

I had hoped to leave this place before this, but I am obliged to take time to wait upon those whom I wish to solicit. In many instances I have to make several calls before I can find the individuals at home and suitably disengaged. I expect however to finish here today and be in readiness to open my attack on the city of Albany on Monday. The season is rather a bad one for begging, as the Greeks[21] and the sufferers of Alna and Wiscasset have just preceded me. My subscription stands this morning at $404 and I have no doubt of its rising above five hundred before I close my calls. . . . Yesterday I took dinner at my cousins, Mr. Lewis Richards, who has a charming family of nine children about the age of ours. But I did not come hither to eat and drink. The attentions however which I have recieved are very gratifying to a beggar. My health continues good. Shall keep sabbath in this place and preach for Mr. Beman.

In great haste and with much affection, yours

James Richards

My love to the children, best respects to Mr. Seymour and all enquiring friends. No letters had reached Albany post office for me on Thursday morning. I have not heard one word from Auburn since I left it.[22]

Albany Feby 18, 1824

My dear Caroline,

I need not tell you I long to set my face towards Auburn, but the business which brought me to this place is not yet closed. Begging is rather a toilsome and discouraging business at any time. It is peculiarly so at the present as the business men have been able to do but little this season. The want of snow has prevented people from coming to market with their produce and notes running in the bank must be looked after. I returned from Troy to this place yesterday and made preparations for my begging operation. I perceive already that I have many prejudices to combat and the loving money principle the greatest of all obstacles to overcome. . . . I believe that I am in a good cause and that the Lord is on my side. With the blessing of God on my exertions I shall do something—but much cannot reasonably be expected. The present effort I consider in the light of an entering wedge, but the wedge I shall drive as long as I can percieve that it moves at all. You may tell Mr. Lansing and the other professors that I shall remain in Albany till all is done that can be done at this time. My subscription at Troy amounted to $562.50 and I have received a pledge that it shall be made up to $600. . . . I very much doubt however if it [Albany] will come up to Troy. The field of operation is wider, but the people have been heretofore taught to look exclusively towards Princeton. Time alone with good management can induce the Albanians to turn their attention to Auburn. That they will eventually do this I have no doubt.

Three letters reached me from Auburn yesterday: the intelligence that you were all well was peculiarly gratifying. . . . By the return of the mail I wish you just to say if you are all well and what you have heard from Newark. Have the people there yet sent for Mr. Russel of Norfolk? . . .

Give my love to the children and believe me very sincerely and affectionately yours

J. Richards

P.S. My best respects to Mr. Seymour and all enquiring friends.[23]

It was a strenuous trip in midwinter but it by no means exhausted his efforts on behalf of the seminary in these early months. He wrote to

Anna urging her to press the cause of Auburn. "Five of our young men are yet unprovided for, and though we have expected from various quarters, I am anxious for the result. I want you to state the fact to our pious and benevolent female friends in Newark."[24] He also wrote to his fellow clergymen in New Jersey, especially Asa Hillyer, his friend of long standing. Hillyer wrote back with obvious affection—"I could not refrain from dropping a tear at the recollection of scenes which are past and which cannot return. Once an hour's ride could bring us together, but now vast mountains rise between us."—but he could raise no money. As he explained:

> At present we can do nothing for you. We are called upon by the Missionary Society and by the Jews Society and are daily expecting the agent for the professorship at Princeton. You know the agent is appointed by the Synod and we must submit to the higher powers. I do hope the time will come when we shall be able to do something for Auburn.[25]

Letters from Hillyer also kept him abreast of the struggle over his replacement in Newark, a situation about which he was intensely curious. Hillyer had presided over a series of meetings at which prospective candidates were considered and the last of these had turned angry and divisive.

Orange, 11th of March 1824

My Dear Brother,

The state of the old congregation in Newark is truely alarming. It is divided into two strong and apparently unequal parties. Last Monday I was called again to preside at a meeting of the congregation for the purpose of choosing a Pastor. The first question was, is it expedient to proceed now to the election of a minister? . . . After a discussion of several hours in which much fire and not a small degree of improper spirit was discerned, this question was decided in the affirmative by a majority of thirty-eight votes. They then proceeded to the election. No name was proposed but Mr. Russel. The vote was taken by ballot when it appeared that there were for Mr. R. one hundred and fifty one and against him one hundred and seven. After this the parties continued to dispute and to accuse each other of improper motives and dishonourable conduct until after nine oclock in the evening. I was at Newark yesterday [and] had the opportunity to see

some of the most influential of both parties. I was informed that the
majority were determined to go forward and settle Mr. R. and that the
minority were determined to oppose them in every step. Perhaps no
political question has ever called forth more of an electioneering spirit
than was discovered on the above occasion. Such persons as W . . . , Ky
. . . , and L . . . S . . . were seen going around the church with their
hands full of tickets and urging people to the poll and frequently such
young men were heard during the discussions with loud vociferation
calling for the question. . . . At one time I was compelled to rise and
declare that unless the house would come to order and continue so I
would leave my seat and dissolve the meeting. . . . Mr. R. appears to be
a pious man and is an eloquent preacher. . . . I can only say that I do
not think him the man for Newark.[26]

The division that this election caused never was resolved. In the
end the opponents of Russel formed a third Presbyterian church in
Newark under a Mr. Hamilton, leaving Russel and his supporters in
control of the First Presbyterian Church. Six months later young
Henry Richards after a visit to Newark wittily described the ongoing
rivalry:

Last sabbath I had the pleasure of hearing both the Apollos: I endeavored
to hear them dispassionately and without prejudice. Russel's delivery I
like best, but Hamilton is in my humble estimation by far the better
writer, and discovers more ingenuity in the development of his plan and
more mind in the general outline of discourse. Russel's forte lies in his
delivery and in a superabundance of tinselled ornament which like
Horace's poet he tacks on without a great deal of taste upon every unoc-
cupied spot, so that when his sermon is completed it looks very like to a
patchwork bedquilt. Perhaps this is speaking disrespectfully but "what is
written is written."

But he had hopes for a happy resolution:

Notwithstanding all the trials and the animosities and unkind feelings
which have existed and do yet exist among our friends here, I do not
percieve [sic] that their affection has abated towards you or any of your

family. My reception with both parties has been marked with attention and kindness and cordiality and I cannot but hope that when so much good feeling can be exhibited towards an indifferent person, it will expand until it shall reach and be reciprocated by every heart. Indeed I think the heat of the contention has nearly subsided, the rash and head-strong are becoming more temperate, the lukewarm quite moderate, and the indifferent pleased.[27]

However absorbing the conflicts in Newark were, they were not truly Richards's problem. His energy had to be directed towards Auburn. In March he was writing to his colleague, the Reverend Sprague, in West Springfield with enthusiasm over the increase in admissions even as he worried over the shortage of funds.[28]

Auburn March 1, 1824

Dear Sir

Our seminary is yet in its infancy, but its prospects are daily bright-ening, both as it respects the increase of students and of funds. We have now twenty students, 13 of whom have been recieved [sic] since last fall, the greater part very promising. We have about twenty five thousand dollars productive fund and need fifteen or twenty thousand more to place us on a safe and permanent footing. A student here can pass through a three year course for a little more that $150. Board is forty dollars a year, room rent and books gratis. Let us have an interest in your kind wishes and prayers.

Very respectfully and affectionately yours,

James Richards[29]

In late spring Richards was off again. This trip was to last over two months, well beyond the four-week spring vacation, and take him from New Jersey to Boston. The first letter that remains from this trip is from Newark where he was staying with Anna.

Newark June 2nd 1824

My dear wife

I returned from Morristown yesterday afternoon where I preached on the Sabbath and spent a day or two in soliciting funds for finishing and furnishing a room in the seminary. I obtained $77 which with a hundred and twenty three already received from

Auburn Seminary in the mid-nineteenth century. (Courtesy—Auburn Theological Seminary of Union Theological Seminary)

Newark will be sufficient for two rooms. Miss Woodruff and Mrs. Arden have given the seminary 212 acres of land. . . . I told these dear ladies that they had so much trouble with this land they had better give it to our institution and they very cheerfully consented. . . . What it is worth I know not. I should suppose, however four or five dollars an acre. . . . Judging from the eye, I should think it best to take the 212 acres on the southwest corner of the lot . . . which is said to be timbered with oak, ash, elm, walnut, and butternut. . . .

While in New York I saw some of the principal members of the Education Society to which Mr. Nevins belongs and they gave me assurances that they would pay $75 for the support of Mr. Adams in our seminary and his friends in New Jersey think they will help him to the rest. Mr. Adams closes his college course at Princeton next fall and wishes to enter our Institution. Though I have tarried longer in this region than I expected yet I am not sure but my agency has been as productive as if I had been in Massachusetts.

My cough is still very troublesome but I have begun to try Mrs. Lavage's Elixir, which has heretofore been of such service to me. In two or three days I hope to be well enough to bend my course to the east. . . .

Anna complains that she has no letter from you in three weeks. I hope there is one on the way for her. She and her husband with all the little folks unite in love to you and the boys. What would I give if my mission was ended and I was once more in my own family. If I journey again I must not go without you. Have I not power to lead about a wife or a sister as well as Dr. Rice [head of the seminary at Richmond]? He never goes abroad I believe without taking his better half along.

My best to Mr. Seymour and all friends. Remember me affectionately to my brethren the professors. Tell Mr. Mills his friends at Morris are all well.

> Most sincerely and affectionately your devoted husband
> J. Richards[30]

He continued into New England out of duty. As always the letters became increasingly affectionate as the time away from home lengthened.

> West Springfield June 1824
>
> My dearest friend,
>
> It is six weeks to day since I left home; to me it seems more like six months. Were it consistent with duty how gladly should I set my face to the West; but my detention so long in New York and in New Jersey imposes on me the necessity of postponing my return to Auburn for a week or two longer. I left N. York on Friday of last week, spent the night at Greenwich with my sister, visited New Canaan on Saturday where I remained till Monday, made a few calls in favour of the seminary and reached Sagatuck in the morning.

This was the first visit to his family in Connecticut since he had arrived in Auburn the previous fall. Such an opportunity was not to be missed even if it meant a detour.

> On Tuesday I went to Greenfield for the purpose of laying my object before Mr. Branson, the Nabob of that part of Connecticut, but as Providence would have it the bird had flown just before I arrived. On enquiry

I found the prospect of doing any thing with him was not great on account of a sour and gloomy state of mind in which he appeared to be thrown for some days past. I left the business with Mr. Dey [his daughter Caroline's stepson, now pastor of the local Congregational church] and after soliciting a few dollars from two or three friends in the village of Greenfarms I set out for New Haven and reached that place about 4 oclock at night. I put up with our old friends Mr. and Mrs. Atwater, who I need not say received me very kindly. I took stage for Hartford on Thursday morning and went by the way of Middletown. While the stage stopped for dinner, I had an opportunity of calling for half an hour at Mr. Crane's where I found Mrs. David D. Crane, Mrs. Kinney, and Mrs. John Burnet, a cluster of dear old Newark friends all together. I recieved [sic] their kind wishes and departed with a charge to remember them all most affectionately to you. Passed Thursday night at Hartford and preached for Mr. Hawes. Finding that nothing could be done for our seminary, I took up my line of march for this place where I arrived yesterday about 4 oclock. I am to spend the sabbath here and shall go to Boston in the early part of the coming week. From all that I can learn, I shall have my labour for my pains. The large towns in New England seem so perfectly engrossed with their own immediate objects that very little I fear can be done for our Institution. I expect to take Northhampton and Amherst in way to Boston and if nothing important can be effected in any of the central towns of Massachusetts, I shall be on my way home in about ten days. I expect that Anna will meet me in Albany and accompany me to Auburn unless some good opportunity shall occur to enable her to make you a visit sooner.

My cold which oppressed me so long has entirely left me, but the Rheumatic affection in my back continues much the same and occasionally annoys me as I am travelling in the stage.

Not one word have I heard from you since I left home except through Henry's letter and letters which you have written to Anna and Caroline, [and] except occasionally by our Newark friends who have called. I shall be woefully disappointed if I find no letters waiting for me at Boston.

Remember me affectionately to the children, Mr. Seymour and all friends and believe me your affectionate husband.

James Richards[31]

When he finally got to Boston, instead of the loving letter he longed for, he must have found a letter full of recriminations. The trip was now into the second month.

Boston July 3rd 1824

My dear wife

Yours of the 26th ultimo has been received. It is easy to perceive how impatient you are for my return and that much of your wonder at the slowness of my progress is to be imputed to the circumstance connected with the little acquaintance you can possibly have of the many things which occur to retard me. I was prevented nearly three weeks from setting my face towards Boston by a cold which was attended by some threatening symptoms and which for several days confined me to the house. Having determined to take N. Haven in my way I found it would make the difference of only two or three days to go by N. Canaan and spend the Sabbath there which was a circumstance more agreeable than to spend it at N. Haven. I passed two nights at the latter place, one at Hartford, three at W. Springfield as I arrived there on Friday and could not leave according to previous engagements till after the Sabbath. Taking Northhampton in my way I passed one night there, one at Amherst, and reached Boston on the Thursday evening following. As soon as possible I began to sound the gentlemen I was introduced to on the subject of my mission. I found great difficulties in the way and that a sudden push would almost certainly prove abortive.

If I succeeded at all, time I perceived was necessary and things must be taken by the right handle, and strange as it may seem to you, I have not yet asked a man to give me a farthing. I have talked, I have preached, and am to preach again tomorrow. Things however are in a train and I expect to begin a direct application on Monday. No doubt I shall obtain something but my caputations are not large. A thousand other objects are putting in their claims and they who give for the support of evangelical principles are not many. Of course as they are often applied to, their charities must be proportionally smaller.

If you suffer by my absence, I suffer more. If you feel as if you could never consent to another such a separation, so I feel. But I am out and engaged and cannot think of quitting the ground till all is done that can properly be done at this time. I am in hopes of leaving Boston before the close of next week, that is in five or six days, but I make no promise. When I finish my business here, I shall hasten to N.York by way of Providence and thence for Auburn with all the speed practicable.

I am much concerned about Edward. You say nothing of him in your letter. Tell him he must not think of leaving Auburn till I return. I shall write you again before I leave this, that you may calculate with more certainty when to see me. I am quite well, better than you have seen me these many months. May God preserve our lives and health and permit us soon to meet again.

Your affectionate husband,
James Richards[32]

Despite the defensive tone of his last letter, he did not hurry home. He was clearly irritated by her lack of understanding about the time required to raise money and was not about to cut the trip short while it had any chance of success.

Boston July 9, 1824

My dear wife

I hoped to have been on my way to N. York before this, but the difficulties in the way of my agency have been such that I have been obliged to proceed with caution and with all the address in my power. Yesterday was the first time I put my hook down, after spending two weeks in baiting and getting ready. Three pretty clever fellows were taken in the course of the day worth one hundred dollars apiece [sic] and one estimated at 30 dollars. The prospect is less favourable to day but I hope my labour will not be lost. The prosperity of the institution is an object very dear to my heart and I trust I have been enabled to create some interest for it in the hearts of others.

This afternoon I expect to go to Dorchester and to spend the Sabbath with Dr. Codman.[33] He is very rich and has promised to do something. If possible I shall leave Boston on Tuesday next but I may be detained a day or two longer. I know your impatience and that of my dear Anna. I feel myself as if I could not wait another moment. But I must do right and not sacrifice the interests of the institution to my personal feelings. Through the goodness of God I continue quite well and thrive under my fatigues.

Mr. Brown of Auburn is here and expects to leave today. He will probably return to the West about the time that I shall. He looks very spruce; almost smart enough to be upon the look out. I am glad to learn from him that Mrs. Arden's and Miss Woodruff's land is not quite so poor a catch as you seem to suppose and that the poor old man's will at Awaseo [?] Flat is an object of so much hope to the seminary.

By the time you receive this, I shall probably be on my way home. May the Lord preserve us to meet again and fill our hearts with gratitude in the remembrance of all his mercies. My love to the boys and my kindest regards to Mr. Seymour and the brethren.

Most affectionately and truly yours
J. Richards[34]

Clearly Caroline had found this separation unacceptable even though it had been broken by a visit from Anna. After this there were no more trips of two months duration. Despite the suggestion that Caroline accompany him there is no evidence that she ever did. Instead they worked out a way of life in which Richards travelled briefly during the seminary holidays, combining New York, New Jersey, and Philadelphia business with fall and spring family visits. The rest of the fund-raising for the seminary was done either by mail or by sending an agent to solicit funds. His enormous efforts on behalf of the seminary had proved in any case that New England was not worth the effort. Auburn was destined to be the responsibility as well as the focus of the western New York presbyteries.

NEW YORK CITY

THE RICHARDS CHILDREN, 1823–1833

"It is now a most interesting period with you."

Chapter Five

James Richards had made the Presbyterian Church his community and labored at its tasks wherever he went. The world of affairs beyond the church he regarded warily; it was the soul's testing ground, and a good Christian should never put his trust in it. His letters and sermons drove home this theme. At the same time, he also assumed that the virtues practiced by a good Christian would carry one forward in the world.

Some preachers, such as Lyman Beecher, desired, almost demanded, that all their sons become ministers of the gospel. Richards did not. "I know that a man may be useful to the cause of religion, while pursuing any lawful calling," he wrote to Henry at one point.[1] Richards did, however, press without ceasing for the conversion of his children. And, like most revivalists of the Second Awakening, he perceived that conversion came most easily to those who had not yet assumed the many burdens of mature adult life.

The five Richards children struggled in youth and early adulthood to strike the balance between the church world and the world beyond the church. Each struck the balance differently. Anna, the eldest, converted early and became the representative to her generation of her father's world. Caroline flirted with conversion and had a rich husband who gave generously to the church, but she was absorbed by her complicated domestic life and usually more occupied by immediate worries. Henry, although he underwent a spiritual crisis and a medical crisis, did not convert. He became an upright professional man and one of those "hopeful onlookers" toward whom so many preachers directed their sermons. Edward seems to have had no overt flirtations or struggles over religion. He grew into a public-spirited merchant who remembered the church and the seminary among his charities. James Jr. laid a special burden on his father's heart by behaving with reckless extravagance, yet he surprised and gratified everyone by a sudden youthful conversion.

Each of these personal dramas took place largely out of the view of the Richards parents. From 1823 on, the life of the Richards children was centered more and more on New York City, already notable for its frenetic pace and pluralistic, commerce-driven public life. Caroline, Henry, and Edward came to live there. Anna remained in nearby Newark. James Jr., although the only one to make his home in the West, left Auburn regularly on his vacations to visit his relatives in New York City and after the age of sixteen lived away from home at college.

The Richards children on the eastern seaboard saw their family network become extended over great distances when their parents moved west to Auburn. Connections endured well enough that family members cooperated to care for orphaned relatives, lend money for business, and share the services of valued servants. James Richards exhorted his children to keep close to one another. The world was full of strangers. One remained loyal to many others, but for reliable friendship one trusted to immediate family.

ALTERNATIVE WORLD: THE RICHARDS BROTHERS AND ANTHONY DEY

In New York City, the grown Richards children received their father's admonitions through letters, but before their eyes they saw a world that was both continuous with, and quite different from, the traffic of ministers and elders they had known in their father's house. As the public authority of ministers seemed to wane, civic leadership passed to Yankee merchants like their uncles Silas and Abraham Richards, who prospered in the transatlantic cotton trade, and to local speculators like the lawyer Anthony Dey, Caroline's husband, who parlayed connections with the old Dutch and English elite into farsighted investments.

While ministers sought to influence society through revivals, Bible societies, colleges, and seminaries, the merchants of New York laid the foundations of the city's commercial leadership. The entrepreneurs at the Tontine Coffee House who thirty years before had built up the marine insurance industry were now focussed on the prospects for inland shipping offered by the Erie Canal. With the canal about to open in October 1824, New York City verged on a growth of spectacular proportions. The canal had immense personal significance for the Richards family, for it became the vital waterway that linked those in the city with those in the West. It was somehow auspicious that Silas Richards, representing the merchant tradition of the family, served on the seven-man committee to organize the grand celebration of the canal's opening.[2]

The Richards children saw that Manhattan was being transformed by transplanted Yankees like their uncles. As New Englanders from the inland hills had poured into western New York, so Yankees from the New England seaboard—from New Canaan in the case of the Richards brothers—had captured the port of New York City by 1820.[3] Their dominance of the city's trade was clear to all.

Silas and Abraham Richards were in their twenties when the cotton trade began to surge around the turn of the century. They joined the quiet Yankee merchant influx into the southern cotton ports of Charleston, Savannah, Mobile, and New Orleans. As cotton soon became the premier American export, the enterprising northerners saw to it that New York became part of a "cotton triangle" in the flow of goods from the American South to Liverpool, England. The Richards brothers secured a foothold in Savannah, a hundred miles farther south than Charleston but smaller, newer, and less exclusive.[4]

As their involvement in the cotton business grew, the brothers found it necessary to establish the merchant house of A. and S. Richards in Liverpool, where Silas moved in 1808 with his wife and three young children. Abraham stayed on with his family in Savannah until 1817, when they moved back to New York. Afterward, he continued to make frequent coastal trips south to look after business, and the Savannah press continued to report on his business activities in both cities.

The Richards brothers invested in both goods and ships. Abraham's move to New York presaged the firm's acquisition of at least three commercial vessels. Two of them, the *Corinthian* and the *Silas Richards*, came from the busy yards of master shipwright Isaac Webb, and both sailed in the first regular transatlantic packet service. The *Silas Richards* was among the inaugural ships of this service, which began at this time and contributed profoundly to making New York the country's mercantile capital.[5] The brothers invested in at least one other ship: A Savannah newspaper notice of 1823 noted Abraham as the owner of the ship *Vulcan*, just arrived after a seventy days' crossing.[6] Thus, in the early 1820s, with Silas in Liverpool and Abraham in New York, the Richards brothers flourished in the cotton trade.

Equally well-established in New York commercial life was Caroline's husband, Anthony Dey. The first of his forebears in the New World, named Dirck, had arrived in New Amsterdam before 1641 as a young soldier with

The ship Corinthian *of the firm of A. and S. Richards. (Courtesy—The Mariner's Museum, Newport News, Virginia)*

the Dutch West India Company.[7] Dey involvement with New Jersey began in 1654 when Dirck received a patent from Governor Stuyvesant for a parcel of land across the North River (as the Dutch named the Hudson).[8] Eventually the family built and occupied a manor house on a 600-acre plantation in Bergen County.

In 1774, as patriotic protest took hold in Jersey, Dirck's great-grandson, Theunis Dey, was appointed to the county's Committee of Correspondence. Anthony Dey, grandson to Theunis, was born in 1777. His mother was a Pierson from Puritan-settled Long Island. Anthony's father and maternal grandfather fought side by side in the militia, and the Dey mansion was used as headquarters for Washington and his staff on three occasions.

Despite intermarriage with Puritans, the Deys maintained their ties with the Dutch Reformed Church. In 1799, Anthony married Catherine Laidlie, the daughter of a Dutch mother from the Hudson Valley and a Dutch Reformed minister, the Scottish-born and Edinburgh-educated Rev. Archibald Laidlie, known as the first Dutch Reformed minister to officiate in the English language.[9]

As a young man, Anthony Dey went to New York City to study law in the office of his father's cousin, Richard Varick, a lawyer who had been secretary to General Washington during the Revolutionary War and who afterwards served as mayor of New York from 1789 to 1801. The much older Varick became Dey's business partner and was godfather to Dey's first child, a son named for him.

Dey's roots were among the New Jersey Dutch gentry, who were accustomed to mixing with a variety of ethnic and religious types. While the Dutch still led

Anthony Dey. (Taken from Harriet M. Stryker-Rodda, Ancestors and Descendants of Frank Lusk Babbott Jr., M.D., and His Wife Elizabeth Bassett French, Polyanthos, Princeton, 1974)

society in Albany and parts of the Hudson Valley, they were by this time one group among many in New York City and New Jersey. Comfortable in his relations with the city's Episcopalian social elite, the childless Varick may have advised Dey to send Varick's godson and namesake to Columbia College, an Episcopalian institution, rather than to a college with a Calvinist coloration. Interestingly, the younger Dey upon graduation chose the Dutch seminary at New Brunswick for his theological training.

Theunis Dey had raised six sons. By 1800, opportunities in western New York had beckoned all five of Anthony's uncles. Dramatizing the appeal of the West even more was the decision of Anthony's parents in 1811 to sell the plantation by the Passaic River and join them. His father died suddenly in a fall from a horse, but Dey's mother went ahead with the move, taking along the rest of her children. After six generations of the family's continuous prominence in local affairs, only Anthony of all the Deys remained in the New York City-New Jersey area.

Despite many years of residence in New York City, Dey always maintained substantial investments in New Jersey. The most significant of these was the 1804 purchase of Paulus Hook, now the site of Jersey City, through the vehicle of a corporation he formed with Varick and Jacob Radcliff.[10] The purchase, which included ferry privileges, was divided into one thousand shares for public sale. Although Jersey City was incorporated in 1820, the full return on investment was delayed for years pending resolution of a New York-New Jersey boundary dispute. Only then could the investors proceed with the development of the Jersey City waterfront facing lower Manhattan across the Hudson.

The cotton trade, the Erie Canal, the development of the Hudson waterfront—these enterprises were the making and unmaking of fortunes. Such enterprises gave shape to the public world of the grown Richards children.

ANNA AND THE NEWARK "PARSONAGE"

Anna and Aaron Beach had been married for five years and had three children by the fall of 1823. A fourth child had recently died in infancy. Where Anthony Dey dabbled in scores of enterprises, Aaron Beach, a

Newark native and the son of a carriagemaker, spent his entire adult life as the second officer of Newark Bank and Trust. He hailed from that artisanal elite that ran the town. Active in local business, he was in private life a sedentary man, unlike the Richards men who were always urging one another on to exercise and fresh air.

Anna's family was in many ways a continuation of the world her sister and brothers had known in their Newark childhood. Her delight in the company of ministers gave her home the family nickname of "the parsonage." Her teenage conversion continued to bear fruit in her adult church activities and her active solicitude for the souls of all about her.[11] She greatly loved her father and took a keen interest in his activities and welfare. In October, 1824, Richards visited Newark and stayed at her house. In a letter to her mother, Anna described how on a rainy evening her fifty-seven-year-old father had just put on his slippers and seated himself by the fire when there came a rap on the door. He was wanted at a prayer meeting:

> [Papa] hesitated & told the young man at length he would think of it, but not to wait for him. He said sometimes it cured his cold to speak & as it was so near, he'd a mind to try the experiment . . . So he put on his cloak & I accompanied him. The school room was very full & papa expounded in a very interesting manner, part of the 11th of Matth. commencing at the 20th verse. He spoke loud, got much engaged & consequently slept but part of the night. It hurt him I think—

The next day, Saturday, he had expected to go to Princeton but a problem with the stagecoach meant postponement until Monday. He made some calls and then dined and took tea with Anna's family. On Sunday morning,

> Papa attended our ch[urc]h . . . Mr. Hamilton . . . came down out of the pulpit & asked papa but he declined. People were a good deal disappointed that he did not preach. However he has promised to preach for us when he returned.

He knew better than to overextend himself a second time, for he had to leave before dawn the next day. Anna's account shows how close town life still was to country ways:

On Monday morning a little after four papa called us all up (as we had requested) to get his breakfast. We made a nice dish of coffee, had some difficulty to get milk so early. At our place they told the girl they weren't going to get up that time of night to get milk for any body. At length some person gave his permission to milk the cow in the street. He ate his breakfast & about 6 went off in the stage to Elizabeth & got to Princeton in the afternoon . . .

The next day a young minister named Holt called on the Beaches, who were "much pleased" with him. "[He] was fond of papa I could see. . . ." Later, "Mr. Holt sat half an hour with me & I had some interesting conversation about Bellamy—an author he is as partial to as myself."[12]

Anna worried about the spiritual condition of her sister Caroline and her brother Henry in the same way her father did. In fact, she was an

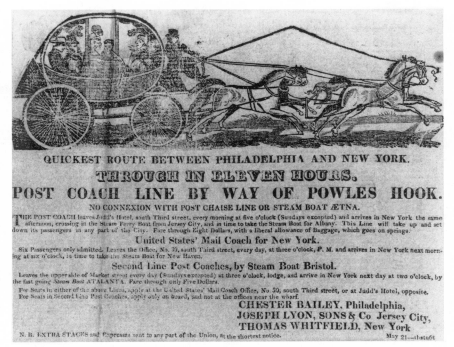

Advertisement for Post Coach Line by way of Powles (or Paulus) Hook, later Jersey City. (Published in the United States Gazette and True American, *Philadelphia, May 28, 1818, Museum of the City of New York)*

informal missionary to all, including servants. When a Dey servant named
Sarah showed promise of conversion, "was very solemn the other day,"
Caroline turned to Anna and asked her to speak to the young woman.
Anna did so and noted wryly afterward that Sarah "may get into the
kingdom & her mistress be shut out." With Caroline herself, "I fear the
work does not progress."

Letters from Anna always contained a great deal more. She often
seemed to leave a letter open on her writing table, ready for additions
whenever she could spare a moment. It was still the case in this period that
those on the receiving end paid the postage, and so, like most correspondents, Anna felt an obligation to fill up the page with news of all kinds.

> Ann Canfield is to be married in about a fortnight to Mr. McClure, from
> a small country town in South Carolina & to set off immediately by land.
> She had refused him but about a fortnight since things are brought to this
> turn. He is about 40 they say, a large man not at all prepossessing in
> appearance & a merchant, likewise an irreligious man—but wealthy 'tis
> said. Poor Robert I can't help thinking he had thoughts of Ann. But we
> all need trials. . . .
>
> Dr. McDowel [her father's old colleague at Elizabeth] is certainly going
> to N[ew] Y[ork]. His people don't mean to oppose it any more—they
> think he has behaved so dishonorably about it after having promised to stay
> & they had raised a fund for Mrs. McDowel . . . Mr. McD. is quite
> pleased, but Lydia says she don't believe she [Mrs. McD.] will like it, for
> "sister always likes to rule" & that she can't do in N[ew] Y[ork]. As to
> Phebe's [servant with Richardses in Auburn] things, I don't know when
> she will get them . . . You need not look for them under two weeks
> from this time I should say. What do you expect to do for help? It is very
> scarce with us. Eliza Taylor is with me yet & Eliza Budd a girl about 16
> does pretty well. We call the former Miss Taylor by way of distinction.
> Mother Beach is quite unwell with rheumatism. Has been blistered but
> does not seem to relieve her. . . .
>
> I believe I have told you all the news. The baby [Henry Nathaniel] is
> better. Tho his face looks bad yet. Is rough. Little Sarah told her father
> the day after papa went away, "Father I should think you had better have
> prayers after breakfast."

Now my dear mother as soon as you receive this . . . be kind enough to sit down & write to me a letter about every thing. I feel interested in all that relates to you & yours, both temporal & spiritual. Want to know how you get along in papa's absence . . . Now don't disappoint me. I must go to my mending . . . My husband unites with me in love. It was a great disappointment to him that mamma did not come as well. . . .[13]

CAROLINE AND THE DEYS

In 1820, Caroline married Anthony Dey, twenty years her senior. They made their home at the corner of Cedar and Nassau Streets in the heart of the old Dutch lower Manhattan. Dey had his law office nearby.[14] He still owned large tracts of land in New Jersey between the Hackensack and Passaic Rivers as well as the entire tract of land that became East Newark. He invested in ditching and draining the salt marshes and in stockraising on his farmlands. The Deys maintained a second house in East Newark and this allowed for casual visiting with the Beaches and other Newark connections.

Dey's son, Richard Varick Dey, was now twenty-two years old. Shortly after his father's marriage to Caroline, he married a young lady from New Brunswick, Lavinia Scott. After a period of study at the Dutch Reformed seminary, the couple settled in Greenfield Hill, Connecticut, at some remove from both their families, where the new young minister took charge of his first pulpit at the Congregational church.[15]

Still living in the Dey household were the teenage daughters of Dey's first marriage, Maria and Kate, and eighty-year-old Mrs. Laidlie, a widow for forty years who had survived all her children and who continued to live with her remarried son-in-law. By 1823, Anthony and Caroline were already the parents of two babies, a girl named Caroline for her mother and maternal grandmother, and a boy named Archibald Laidlie for the long-deceased husband of the widow Laidlie. A third child was on the way.[16] The Deys would name the new baby James Richards.

The complications of such a family could be overwhelming to a young wife. Caroline, fine-tuned in temperament, nursed anxieties about the place and prospects of her own children in so large a brood. Ironically, Richard, who had once courted her, now became her rival as she watched her husband dote upon his firstborn. When a crisis occurred in Richard's marriage, it stirred feelings in her far from sympathy. A concerned Anna shared with their mother what she could deduce about the disordered state of her sister's family and feelings.

> Thursday I spent with Caroline. She walked down to our ch[urc]h on Sunday & she thought it injured her. Says she has not felt quite as well for several days. She had not digested so well. The fact is she has been worrying . . . about their affairs. Richard's wife has gone back to her father's & has told every body she won't live at Greenfield any more. It is currently reported that she has separated from him. She is jealous of him somewhat & don't like it there & thinks it don't agree with her health. On Wednesday he came down to N[ew] Y[ork] & she heard of it & came from New Brunswick to meet him, but from what I can learn still persists in not going back with him. Indeed I believe he has promised never to ask her to come—however this must not be mentioned. They are an unhappy couple. Caroline thinks R. is his father's idol & expects all his property to go upon him & have nothing left for *her* children. I tried to argue with her upon the folly of her anxiety & beg her to seek for herself & her children a portion that nothing can destroy. She says she wonders she don't feel more but the troubles & cares of this life occupy all her thoughts.[17]

The nature of Richard and Lavinia's marital unhappiness is not clear. They were both quite young. Only sixteen when she wed, and still not yet nineteen, Lavinia had already buried an infant son and given birth to a daughter. The separation came just four months after the birth of this second baby, and it proved a temporary one. They stayed another five years at Greenfield, eventually returned to New Jersey, and had a total of eight children. Caroline's seeming distance from their troubles and the anxieties they seemed to prompt in her suggest a sense of insecurity and powerlessness that was probably inherent in the situation of a second wife. She may have regretted not being able to rise above such feelings, yet she held to them candidly, even insistently.

Caroline was unwell that fall, and her worries could only have made things worse. City dwellers like the Deys were subject to irregular epidemics of typhoid fever and cholera, and by the next spring the susceptible Caroline became so ill with typhoid that she lay close to death. Her mother journeyed to her bedside. Remaining at home in Auburn with Edward and James, her father prayed for her. He wrote to his wife, "This is of unspeakable moment. Long has God waited upon her, and much has been done . . . to arrest her attention . . . from this fading world to another and better state of being." A few days later, he wrote again:

> I am distressed. . . . But what can we do—? She is in the Lord's hands . . . He knows what is best, and will do what is best. It is our privilege and duty to supplicate, and no less to submit. . . . O, if her immortal soul were but safe, I should contemplate the trial with different feelings . . .[18]

Caroline recovered, but the spiritual consequences for her were not what her father hoped.

HENRY: SPIRITUAL CRISIS

Henry, the oldest Richards son, recently graduated from Princeton, decided to live and work in New York City when his parents and two younger brothers moved to the West. He lived in the Dey household and found employment as a clerk in a law office, taking the first step to becoming a lawyer. Convenient ferry service made it possible for him to visit often at the Beaches'. He knew his father's keen interest in the old set at Newark, and in a letter home dated August 18, 1824, he painted the following scene:

> By this time you have greeted Mr. Dey [visiting in Auburn] and he has informed you probably what are my prospects here so I say no more on that score. Both Caroline and Anna have endeavored to make it as agreable [sic] to me as they can and thus far I have spent my time very delightfully. Every body is inquiring of me how you are and when you are coming down. Mrs. Kinney and Mrs. Rodgers most crazy to see you & mother. Mrs. Kinney got hold of me in church the other day and I could hardly get away she held on so tenaciously—and Mrs. John Burnet

grasping my hand at the same time, I did not know but I should have
been rent asunder.[19]

He was much pleased with himself for having spotted an instance of
plagiarism by a minister of their acquaintance. The young legal apprentice
had a personal copy of the unpublished original which could be found in
manuscript in the library at Nassau Hall.[20]

Anna observed Henry closely and found him too preoccupied with the
world around him at the cost of what really mattered. He went to church,
but he was not really engaged there. Conversion was considered not merely
a general positive direction, but a decisive personal transformation. The
most propitious time for this event, his school and college years, had passed.
Anna pondered the situation in a letter to her mother:

> At present I think [Henry] gives no evidence of a saving change, yet
> time will shew [*sic*]. I do not know how to give him up. Those Chris-
> tians who are recovered from deep backsliding sometimes appear more
> humble & devoted than others. Look at David, Peter, & others. If he is
> a child of God I think he will be brought back with the end. Perhaps
> the idol of his affections may be [unreadable]. However, we are of
> *yesterday* & know nothing . . . at any rate his situation is awfully
> criminal & dangerous.[21]

Richards encouraged Henry in his clerkship, assuring him, "Every
expense wh[ic]h is necessary I shall be willing to incur while you are
prosecuting your studies. But I must remind you that great frugality will
be indispensable." In a pastoral vein, he noted, "My dear children are in
one way or another all objects of my unceasing solicitude. Their interests
both temporal and eternal lie near my heart, but chiefly the latter. . . ."[22]
In his letter of December 7, 1824, Henry responded:

> I cannot express to you, my dear Father, how I long to see you and
> converse with you. You have considered me, I know, a heedless unre-
> flecting [omitted]. I have been. But I trust my eyes are being opened. I
> confess to you that I am unhappy. I feel that there is something more
> desirable than the cares and enjoyments of this life, that the worldly

prospects are too vain and transitory. Though I have everything around [me]: my situation is agreeable, a sister who has a family who treat me with the utmost [kindness], friends who take & feel an interest for me, a pro[fession?] I admire—still I am unhappy, still . . . a void within . . . , I sometimes weep . . . I read my Bible, I bend my knee in prayer, I supplicate in my imperfect manner . . . I am conscious, however, my prayers will avail nothing, but . . . if you would interest yourself in my behalf . . . God in his infinite mercy would condescend [to] bless me. I fear that this may prove nothing more than a mere animal excitement . . . But if it is indeed [a matter] of God striving with me, I hope I may not be [pushing] him away . . . Oh pray for me . . . My love to my dear mother. I love her much. Write me soon. I need advice & instruction as well as your sympathy and your prayers—Ever your affectionate son Henry S. Richards[23]

Writing again two weeks later, Henry agonized more urgently. He knew that hope rested on the frankest assessment of his feelings and on vigilance against insincerity. He focussed equally on what he felt—the struggle or "storm" within—and on what he failed to feel.

My Dear Father,

. . . How grateful should I feel that God has given me such a father to whom I can apply for advice. . . . It is a privilege among innumerable others I do not sufficiently appreciate and I desire to be deeply humbled on account of it. There is so much of depravity & deceitfulness in my heart that I can scarcely unfold to you the real state of my feelings—the more I examine it the more do I discover of its innate defilement and corruption, its enmity to God and its inordinate attachment to the world. But notwithstanding . . . I do not mourn over it as deeply and sincerely as I ought. Obduracy . . . does not break and dissolve within me at the remembrance of my great & manifold transgressions and at the loving kindness and mercy of God . . . they do not awaken that lively gratitude which they are calculated to inspire and to lead me to that unfeigned sorrow and heartfelt repentance in having despised such mercy and rejected such love—I do not *feel*. I carry in my bosom a *storm* Oh! what reason have I to abhor myself and lie low in the dust before God. The world, my dear Father, holds a strong influence over me and subjects me to great temptations. But I have more powerful enemies to resist and contend with, in my own corrupt immaginations [*sic*] and passions. I have reason to believe I commit more sin in *thought* than in any other way . . . I have not believed on the Lord Jesus Christ & submitted to him . . . Should he not grant me . . . mercy . . . I am undone, for I know that I can do nothing of myself. But I do not plead this as an excuse or in extenuation of my guilt . . . [Pray] that the Lord would grant me his aid and direction . . . without it I shall go back again to the world & become more wicked & polluted than before. Do not forget me. I know you will not. . . . [24]

Not all of the father-son correspondence of this period survives, but a letter from Richards written to Henry the following month reflects the new intensity in their relationship:

My dear son,

. . . I cannot tell you, my dear son, how much I long to see you, and hear from your own mouth the dealings of God with your soul. Much as I always loved you, I must say, I feel a new species of affection towards you—and recognize [a] new relation between us—a relation of unspeakable tenderness . . . better felt than expressed. The Lord grant that neither you nor I shall be deceived in this most interesting of all concerns. I was much gratified to learn that you had connected yourself with Dr. [Gardiner] Spring's Bible class & that you found the exercise a pleasing one to you. You cannot become too familiar with that best of all books—the only sure light to our feet while passing through this world of darkness and sin. Now is your time to study it with care and attention. The understanding is quick and the memory retentive. More can be done in a little time now, than in years of after application, when the [torn] are more sluggish, and the mind engrossed with domestic and other cares. . . .

Your mother & brothers join in love to you and all the family. Believe me your affectionate father, James Richards[25]

Despite such encouragement, Henry continued to express profound frustration and self-reproach three months later in March of 1825:

My Dear Father,

Your affectionate remembrance of me, & especially your anxious solicitude for my spiritual welfare makes a deep impression upon my heart. I would that it were in my power to afford you that strong and convincing evidence of a genuine and radical change wrought by the spirit of grace in my heart . . . Frequently have I asked myself the question "do I hate sin on account of its intrinsic evil or because of the penalty attached to the commission of it?" My heart falters & I know not what to answer. But the difficulty is I do not *hate* sin with that *cordial hatred* & feeling that deep self-abasement on account of it that I ought. I transgress every moment. The cares & temptations of the world beset me on every side in my devotions, in my walks, in my business & intercourse with society. . . .

Henry demonstrated an exact understanding of and sympathy for his father's view of conversion, and he grieved over his own failure to experience the feelings he knew to be requisite for the profession of conversion to be true. He found himself still the hopeful onlooker. Beyond this, at present he could not go, and did not pretend to his family otherwise. On the subject of his health, he could be more positive.

I have confined myself too closely to the office this winter. Now the weather has become pleasant I shall endeavor to ride out every afternoon on horseback. The same course would be serviceable to sister Caroline, I am convinced.[26]

EDWARD AND THE COMMERCIAL WORLD

Edward completed his schooling at a private academy in Auburn. There is no record that he contemplated college. Like his uncles, he was headed for business and the best training for that was on the job. He seems to have clerked sporadically in local Auburn stores, but the family consensus was that a period of work in one of the New York City merchant houses offered the best opportunity for advancement. In a January 1825 letter, Richards queried Henry, "Have you found a place yet for Edward—he is still uneasy and wants to find a place in the city."[27] On March 18, 1825, Henry reported on his efforts and warned Edward off a tempting possibility:

As yet I am unable to find a situation for Edward & I think it will be somewhat difficult to obtain one where he will receive a sufficient salary. I hope he will not be so foolish as to go to Pennsylvania with Husted . . . not a very unexceptionable character . . . He had better not link himself. . . .[28]

Edward remained in Auburn over the spring and summer. His father was pleased to note to Henry that "Edward seems very steady now and attentive to business."

In the September vacation, Richards traveled to the city and came upon a scene to give him pause. As usual, he went first to the Deys' house, but since they had gone to their house in East Newark, he walked a mile uptown to see his brother Abraham on Franklin Street. Here he found a full-blown crisis. To his wife he wrote:

Spent the night at my brothers. They are in great trouble. The cotton speculation has ruined hundreds and he is among the number. The house in Liverpool [is] not executing his orders with promptness—has caused both him and them to stop payment—Perhaps he may have enough to pay his creditors—but it is not very likely. Sister bears it well—her even mind seems not much disturbed by this reverse. She thinks her bread and water will be sure. It presses more heavily on my brother and especially as his failure will injure some of his best friends. . . . —Such my dear wife is the world—"a broken reed at best, but oft a spear—." Let us endeavor to lay up our treasure in heaven. . . .[29]

The cotton speculation of 1824–1825 was the ruin of many. Prices started to tumble in Liverpool early in the spring of 1824, but word was slow in reaching New York where merchants continued to briskly order more shipments from the South. Bulletins with the alarming news began arriving in New York in May. Silas died as these events were unfolding, and Abraham had to carry on alone. To cover their firm's mounting losses, Abraham drew bills of exchange for varying amounts that were endorsed by other merchants, including some for as much as five thousand pounds endorsed by Thaddeus Phelps, one of the city's leading commission merchants and cotton brokers. Abraham sold these particular bills for cash to some merchants named Sheldon who paid in full for them. On September 12 came the news that the firm of A. and S. Richards had failed. James Richards encountered Abraham at this low moment.

Now Abraham's troubles worsened: He had many creditors, several friends among them, as he told his brother. Thaddeus Phelps, for one, immediately applied to Abraham for security against his endorsements. Abraham, "under pressure and confusion . . . and under the influence of very strong representations" by Phelps whose own firm was on the brink of failure, agreed to transfer his title to three ships, the *Vulcan*, the *Corinthian*, and the *Silas Richards*. When he had "time to reflect," Abraham "became convinced" that he could not do this without violating his duty to others equally entitled. But Phelps insisted, took the case to court, and mutually-agreed-upon referees decided for Phelps. Phelps's own firm soon collapsed, and Abraham joined a legal suit by the Sheldons, who wanted the ships applied toward payment of the bills they had purchased from him. On October 25, a judge restrained Phelps from disposing of the property. The surviving paper trail from the case ends there, suggesting an out-of-court settlement.[30] These were hard times, but many shared them. Phelps was a bigger figure in New York commerce than the Richards brothers, and he, too, had been overtaken by events. Though Abraham continued in business in the city for another twenty-five years, he never managed to restore his wealth to its previous level.

It was against such a possible decline in fortune that Richards hoped to steel Edward's character. Business networks were such that it was not just a matter of coping with one's own disaster, but also with its effect on valued associates. The conscientious merchant must bear the burden shrugged off by the callous. Trust, in the end, was the durable coin of business, and Edward had to learn this. To that extent at least, eternal and temporal interests were joined.

Some months later, presumably chastened by tales of the speculative fever that toppled his uncles' firm, twenty-year-old Edward Richards arrived in the city to begin his commercial career. A suitable place for him had at last been found, and in view of his recent steadiness, Richards was ready to give him his blessing. Edward joined Henry in the spring of 1826 as a roomer in the Dey household. This left their younger brother James, twelve years old, the only child at home with Dr. and Mrs. Richards, who were now nearing sixty. On April 17, James wrote to Edward from Auburn:

Dear Brother,

I received your letter a day or two since and was glad to hear that you were all well. We received a letter from Caroline on Tuesday evening she mentioned that you had got in Mr. F[torn] store. I should like to know how you like it. I long to have you come home as I expect to stay alone here in Auburn. I go to school to Mr. Seymours. I am studying Virgil, Mains introduction, Arithmatic [sic], Writing & Geography. I hope you will send me a watch. I do not care what kind of a one it is, by Pa or some of the merchants. Husted['s] goods were sold last week, on the last day of the auction. I hapened [sic] to be passing by and they were selling papa's Morses geography in two volumes [authored by Rev. Jedidiah Morse—see Newark chapter] for one dollar. I saw pa's name in them and I claimed them and they gave them to me. Every thing went high . . . Carson said the whole auction amounted to 4 thousand dollars. I shall leave the rest of this letter to be filled up by Ma & pa. And believe me your affectionate Brother James

My dear son,

James has left a little room for me to fill, which I shall do with the greater pleasure, as I wish you to know that I am gratified that you have found a place of business, which bids fair to be of advantage to you. I hope you will think nothing of the *toil* or the *humiliation* which your employment may occasion you. You must take your turn before the mast—before you can expect to reach the cabin on the quarter deck. The drudgery of the youngest Clerk is a business no less useful to you, than a more honourable or lucrative station. I trust you will know how to appreciate the opportunity which is now afforded you of becoming acquainted with mercantile operations in the city. Do not spare yourself in the duties of your clerkship—but be ready, prompt and faithful in the discharge of every duty. Treat your fellow clerks with courtesy and affection, and your employer with respect. Convince him that you look to *his interest with care*, and that he may safely confide in you.

Beware of forming intimacies with any body. Let your acquaintances be *few*—; the fewer the better for the present. You have acquaintance enough among your relatives—and those to whom they may naturally introduce you. Be *frugal*. This is indispensable in your circumstances, & the mere habit will be of much consequence to you in future life.

Edward was less cautious and more self-willed than Henry. Richards tried to impress on him the risks of such an attitude.

> You know my apprehensions on the score of morals in a gay and dissi-pated city. But remember God is there. His laws cannot be violated with impunity even in the present life—but the most solemn reckoning is in the world to come. Keep out of the reach of temptation; and think not that you can take fire in your bosom, and your clothes will not be burnt, or that you can walk on hot coals and your feet not be burnt. I could wish you were more [sensible] of your danger—as you would [then] conduct [yourself] with caution. It is now a most interesting period with you, both as it respects the commission business, and the formation of moral ch[aracte]r. You cannot feel too deeply, how much is staked upon a few fleeting months or years with you.
>
> Let me not only advise, but injoin [sic] it upon you to reverence the sabbath. Whatever temptation may present to neglect or violate this sacred Institution, do not allow yourself to encroach upon the prescribed duty of this day. Be regular and constant in your attendance upon Ch[urc]h; nor let any trifling exercise detain you from the house of God. Your moral ch[aracte]r is closely allied to this counsel and in all proba-bility your eternal destiny. . . .[31]

HENRY: PROFESSION AND MARRIAGE

Shortly after Edward's arrival in the spring of 1826, Henry made a decision. He had devoted two and a half years to a private clerkship, the then usual path to a legal career. Now he wished to cap his legal education with more systematic study at the renowned private law school in Litch-field, Connecticut. Litchfield was not far from his mother's original home in Farmington; in fact, an older sister of hers, Abigail, lived there, the widow of Luke Wadsworth. This meant Henry could again find lodging with relatives, a circumstance certain to reassure his parents.

The Litchfield Law School, established a half-century earlier in the 1770s, represented the first successful effort to professionalize legal studies in the United States. As such, it was a forerunner of the seminaries that were professionalizing theological studies. The school had been founded by

Judge James Gould. (Courtesy—Collection of the Litchfield Historical Society)

the late Judge Tapping Reeve and was now carried on by his associate, Judge James Gould. Henry had reason to respect what it had to offer, for the school provided a supervised legal education unique in its day. As many as thirty or forty young men from around the country were enrolled at any one time, and the full course of study lasted up to eighteen months. Gould lectured for an hour and a half every weekday morning; students spent the rest of the day transcribing notes and poring over books in Gould's library on the week's lecture topics in preparation for the Saturday afternoon examination. On Monday evenings a moot court was held. Students could enter the course at any time during the year, and Henry enrolled for the summer term that began the first week of June.[32]

Toward the end of July, Henry received a letter from Anna in Newark which led off with the usual family warning about new friends. It was common usage to say "friends" when referring, in fact, to one's closest relatives.[33]

My very dear brother,

Your very kind letter together with one to Caroline have both been received. I was much gratified to hear so particularly of your situation & with the description you gave of Litchfield, etc., & that our good cousins are so very attentive & hospitable. But they are *new* friends, Henry. Suffer not *any* of them, even the most *fascinating* with all their *solid* charms, to supplant in your affections old & *tried friends*. Emily Cowles [a cousin] I think I recollect. She must be on the old maid list, was once engaged to be married to a gentleman in N[ew] York whose name begins with K. I don't recollect exactly, but who failed in business & the affair dissolved. James Wadsworth [another cousin] quite amused us.

I am happy to find your time so well occupied. But do not neglect your health. Take plenty of exercise. All your future prospects of usefulness . . . for this world depend upon the enjoyment of this blessing.

Elizabeth Green came out on Saturday & returned yesterday morning. I found out that you corresponded still [with Margaret Evertson]. . . . They are going to Poughkeepsie together soon. Elizabeth spoke very highly of her, as if she was a treasure. . . .

James and Edward were out on Saturday. Ed says he saw a Mr. Benedict from Auburn lately, who mentioned that some of the most profligate young men Clerks had become subjects of the revival there. . . . C[aroline] had a letter from papa yesterday. He thinks the work has but just commenced. He & my dear mother both appear quite aroused. He said he thinks frequently & solemnly of his dear children, who are with others rapidly moving forward to eternity & four out of five, he fears awfully unprepared.

Anna then quoted to Henry their father's recent admonition to Caroline, words fiercer and more adamant than those used in previous appeals:

"Have I been faithful in warning & entreating & earnestly commending their case to the Lord? Think my dear daughter, think solemnly of your condition. God demands of you speedy repentance and threatens with eternal death if it be delayed; & he doubtless means what he says. Do you really believe God? I know you will say you believe—but that you cannot help it. But do you *really believe*? If you did you would never have a moments peace, till your soul was lodged in the ark of safety. But your unbelief will not, cannot turn the truth of God into a lie. He will *certainly* save the penitent & believing, & as *certainly* destroy those who are not of this character. O that he himself could speak & cause your heart to hear."

I have quoted these solemn truths, my dear brother, knowing that every thing coming from my dear father has double effect. The word of God is true. I should say a [?] moral and honourable deportment, a life free from dissipation, is not a sufficient passport to the house of rest.

Then Anna cited a verse of scripture destined to become a particular favorite of American evangelicals:

"Verily Verily I say unto thee, except a man be born again he *cannot see* the kingdom of God." Your letter to Caroline was peculiarly interesting. I have given it a third perusal. . . . Every heart beats in unison with every sentiment uttered with regard to our beloved parents. Few, very few, can boast of *such parents*. Let us strive, my dear brother, to be all that they desire, to imitate their virtues & in our turn to fill up their places with usefulness & duty.

Write again soon my dear brother. I quite long to see you. Caroline won't write under ten days probably so that our letters may not arrive together for the future. . . . I love my dear brothers & their welfare lies near my heart. Daily do I think of you. My husband sends love too. Excuse this hasty scrawl. I fear your patience will be tried & it is written so badly that I fear it is almost unintelligible . . . In great haste . . . believe me as ever your truly attached sister, Anna[34]

A few days later, Henry wrote to his father at Auburn describing his new routines at Litchfield. As Anna's letter made clear, his spiritual crisis had not resulted in conversion. Perhaps the move to Litchfield was the most tangible outcome of his period of turmoil. Henry was a disciplined young man. Anna's observation that a life free of dissipation is not a sufficient passport to heaven indirectly acknowledged this. Henry's letters to his father now emphasized the cultivation of character, something which lay more surely within his grasp than the grace of conversion.

My dear Father,

I have arisen earlier than usual this morning for the purpose of writing you in answer to your favour rec[eive]d several days since. My time is occupied constantly & systematically in pursuing my professional studies & unless I break in upon my regular hours I am obliged to use some such expedient to keep up a correspondence.

. . . Every thing goes on very regular here as usual. I have changed my boarding or rather my dieting house this week, & now take my meals with A[unt] Wadsworth's family in the same home where I room. I find the [change] for the better, especially in rainy weather, tho' the fare is not quite as good. Still we have what is wholesome and clean.

And what I value more than any other article of food, milk, we have in abundance. I prefer it & use it night & morning instead of tea & coffee, and I think my health is the better for it. Dyspepsia is still an irksome companion tho' I am not without hopes of shaking him off before I leave here. The exercise I take is only walking which I endeavor to do sufficiently to keep up my usual tone of health & spirits. I have been on horseback but once & that happened in the way of an impressment to escort some ladies on an evening ride. I should like to ride much, as I put more faith in that method of exercise as adapted to my complaint than any other. But there is scarcely a horse in the whole village that can be procured, except ex speciali gratia & then paying double what it is worth.

Henry learned that some of the local citizens knew his parents. Colonel Talmadge, a revered veteran of the Revolutionary War, was said to be one. Henry wrote home, "If he is a friend of yours I will call & become acquainted with him." There was also a Mrs. Lord who "claims a sort [of] connection with Mother, says she was quite intimate with her when they were girls & Ma used to visit Litchfield." In general, he took little time for social life, but did visit two prominent sisters, the "Miss Pierces." One was now in the West, he wrote, "making a trip to Niagara. I took the liberty of giving her an invitation to call on Mother at A[uburn]." The Pierce women had founded the Litchfield Female Academy, where several sisters and cousins of the law students received their education. Harriet Beecher Stowe and Catherine Beecher had recently studied there when their father was the pastor in Litchfield. The young ladies Henry escorted were probably enrolled there. Social calls aside, though, the center of Henry's Litchfield world was the judge himself.

Judge Gould says he has heard you preach & if I mistake not that he has been in company with you. We are all much pleased with the Judge. He is affable & very familiar with his students even to a fault. His style of writing is concise & technical & free from all attempt at embellishment. His conceptions are remarkably clear and so accurately defined as never to have the student at a loss as to the extent of his meaning.[35]

Henry found in Judge Gould a man like his father, the same age and noted in Litchfield for a calm and dignified manner. It was a manner that distinguished him from his intense and impetuous predecessor, Judge Reeve, much as the judicious Dr. Richards might be contrasted with the passionate Lyman Beecher. Judge Reeve had died a couple of years before. Judge Gould's relative familiarity with his students must have been a change for Henry from the distance and deference commended by his father and preferred by his professors at Princeton. It seems from his report ("even to a fault") that this manner at times discomfited Henry.

When his term at Litchfield came to an end, Henry once again inclined toward New York City. His father sent him fifty dollars to enable him to close his account at Litchfield and return to the city, "where I hope he will be able to do something for himself."[36]

Before doing so, Henry accompanied Dr. Richards during the September vacation to the Yale commencement in New Haven. They met some of the Richards relatives there and saw Abraham's son graduate. Then James Richards pressed on to Farmington alone to visit his wife's dying sister, Diadema Cowles Deming.[37] He wrote to his wife:

> I am now again in your native place surrounded by those friends who were the companions of your early years. But this circumstance rather gives pain than pleasure. Every thing is so changed from what it was, that it throws a gloom over objects otherwise delightful. Many of our best friends in the grave—others bearing the marks of advanced years, and indicating by their countenance that they are soon to be numbered with the dead.
>
> I reached here yesterday about 11 . . . —found your Sister Deming past speech and evidently sinking into the arms of death. . . . I have never before seen a case where life ebbed so slowly away. . . . Others are indeed affected—but all nature seems to consent that the aged & infirm should die.
>
> It was chiefly on your account that I came to this place. I thought you would desire it in the circumstances . . . and I know our Farmington friends expected it. Now I cannot leave till after the funeral. . . . I shall go to . . . N[ew] J[ersey] . . . and pass a day or two in N[ew] York.

> Your Sister Wadsworth is here—came from Litchfield yesterday. . . .
> I cannot say how much I long to see you—I shall have many things to
> say to you then. . . .[38]

Henry, meanwhile, returned to the city to open an office at 30 Wall
Street and take up law practice. Princeton recognized his recent studies and
granted him a Master of Arts degree. He no longer lived with the Deys,
but found his own lodgings on Lispenard Street, around the corner from
his uncle Abraham.[39] This new domestic arrangement was short-lived. In
February, in a letter addressed uncharacteristically to both his parents,
Henry began with straight face:

> My dear Parents,
>   Nothing of much importance has transpired since I wrote you last
> except what you must have been informed of through the medium of
> Anna's & Caroline's letters—Every thing has gone on, comparatively
> speaking, very smoothly during the progress of the winter, with the
> occurrence thus far of few or no incidents to give variety. . . .

He then confirmed what they had been anticipating for some time, eking
out what suspense he could from the announcement.

> An affair, however, is now in agitation, & I expect it will shortly be
> consummated, of which I think proper to inform you the first of any of
> our family, and I hope the intelligence will be received with a pleasure
> and satisfaction equal to that with which it is conveyed. In a word then
> *I expect soon to be married*—To whom I fancy you will be at no loss to
> conjecture and although I have not formally asked your approbation yet
> I believe I have acted with the knowledge, and tacit consent at least, of
> both father & mother.

After a droll beginning, Henry settled into the sobersided persona more
usual in his letters home:

> The relation I am about to assume is I am well aware pregnant with the
> most decisive & weighty results & will exert a corresponding & powerful
> influence upon my future prospects & circumstances in life. In proportion

to its magnitude & importance I trust has been the seriousness & deliberation with which it has been viewed. It is a step I am convinced that unites every wish & gratification of my heart & which at the same time my sober judgment cordially approved.

Margaret is a girl of principle. Her education has been conducted, her character formed with a strict regard to the preservation & advancement of a high tone of moral & religious feeling. As she is not fond of fashionable gaity [sic] & dissipation & seldom indulges in their pleasures she has not imbibed any of their concomitant immoralities & vices that so frequently mar the beauty & sully the excellences of female character. I never knew a person more conscientious in the performance of duty or in the general regulation of their conduct. She is *consistent* in her behavior, *prudent* & *economical* in her expences [sic], *neat* & *particular* with her person, *kind* & *benevolent* in her feelings & disposition & *has always treated her mother with attentive affection & respect*. She has been a *dutiful daughter* & I doubt not will make "a faithful, affectionate & obedient wife."

I know she has been accused of hauteur & maintaining a dignified distance of manner, but nothing is more unlike her real character & a short acquaintance with her never fails to remove so mistaken an impression.

Henry defended Margaret against a charge that resounded in a society marked more and more by the sentiment of equality. While rejecting the impression created as false, he voiced once again his own preference for dignity over familiarity:

The day is fixed for the 7th of next month & will it be too much to ask you to come down to be present on the occasion. I am aware that Father will be occupied at home so as to render it almost impossible or out of the question, but not so with Mother & I hope she will come with Edward & wait till Father arrives in the vacation.

You may ask why the 7th was appointed instead of sometime in the vacation? Mrs. E[vertson] expects to move on the first of May to the upper part of town & it will be 2 months before they will be settled & this circumstance will put them to a still greater inconvenience. We expect to live with Mrs. E. for sometime to come as long as is agreeable.

Edward I hope will be here & honour us with his attendance. But I have not time at present to finish . . . Remember me to James etc. & I doubt not that if Margaret had been apprised of my writing she would join with me in tendering her dutiful love & respects to her (intended) Father & Mother. Will not Father write *us* & give us all that advice & counsel which the affection & tenderness of a parent would dictate on such an occasion. . . .[40]

The young couple probably met through the Deys. Dey's business partner, Radcliff, was originally from Poughkeepsie where the Evertsons were a prominent Dutch family. Margaret's father, Nicholas Evertson, had died when she was a child, and the family subsequently lived in New York City. Margaret's mother, born Eliza Howe, had been a widow for many years, and Margaret was the eldest of her three children.[41]

Henry and Margaret were married on March 7, 1827, a Thursday evening, as they had planned. Their first child was born on Christmas Eve of that year and named James Nicholas after the two grandfathers.[42]

EDWARD AND THE DESIRE FOR INDEPENDENCE

Anna, Caroline, and Henry, whatever their differences, were now all settled into domestic life. Edward, ambitious and unattached, was more restless. As Anna's letters attest, their acquaintances were departing every month for points west and south. Edward caught the fever and chafed to end his days of dependency and strike out on his own. Family members gently colluded to keep him steady and close to them. With Henry settled into profession, marriage, and fatherhood, Dr. Richards consulted him more freely on the subject of Edward. Already in the previous summer in Litchfield, Henry had offered this comment:

I heard from Edw[ar]d a day or two since. . . . Anna informed me that he had an offer to go to the South & wished me to dissuade him from it. I really think it would be a pity for him to leave his situation & prospects in Town & embark on some new scheme the result of which is totally uncertain.[43]

Edward had backed off of this idea, but when his clerkship came to an end in March 1828, he resisted seeking another. He proposed instead to go into business for himself in Auburn. His impetuosity and presumption in the matter stunned his father. Dr. Richards wrote back promptly to quash the idea, and then, still worked up, dashed off another letter to Henry, reiterating all his points, that Henry might reinforce them:

My dear son,

I have just written a letter to Edward in answer to his . . . which reached me this morning. It seem from his own confession, that he has not made very vigorous efforts to find a place in the city—; that he has declined one offer at $350.00 a year, and that he is still strongly bent on setting up at Auburn this spring or at least next fall. He talks of being able to command about fifteen hundred dollars to begin with, calculating I suppose upon [torn] 00.00 to be advanced by me. I have strongly remonstrated against such a course, on the ground that he wants age and experience. Another year at least ought to be spent in a Clerkship—and perhaps even longer, unless he could be associated with some older and more judicious head.

He thinks the time long—and feels as if all the time spent in a Clerkship was so much time thrown away. It appears to me as if he imagined that life would be quite a different thing, and far more desirable could he but be in business for himself; that then the days would glide smoothly along, and naught but enjoyment would attend his course,— *more money, more independence, more respectability, more every thing*, which goes to make this span of existence of any value. He does not seem to reflect what new cares & perplexities must necessarily involve him— what danger of failing at the threshold—and what deplorable consequences to himself & his friends should such a failure occur. He wonders that his friends should not think as he does upon this subject, and imputes their [reluctance] to assist him to [their] attachment to [their] own private interests.

I have told him that in this he labours under a great mistake. I judge them by myself. I have always intended to give him 500.00 as a pittance to begin with—and this is the *whole* of what I ever intended, or now intend to do. I am as willing to advance that sum this spring as at any future time could I see it to be a prudent measure. But I do not wish to throw it away. I wish to give it in circumstances which promise a favourable result. I do not find these circumstances to exist.

[Be] assured, that Mr. Beach always intended to assist him, though he never said exactly as much. At this moment probably he would not do it. He wants to see more coolness and caution, and less anxiety to press forward in a particular course: he wants to see more stability of ch[aract]r, more maturity of judgment—more modesty of opinion, and more teachableness of sp[iri]t. Age and experience he doubtless thinks will contribute to effect this change. Should he therefore decline to come forward this spring to make any advance or incur any responsibilities on Edward's account, I see not but this would be a sufficient reason for my declining also were I otherwise satisfied of the wisdom of the measure.

Have another conversation with Edward—and with all the tenderness and kindness of a brother endeavor to persuade him to take the advice wh[ic]h I have given. If by post-poning business for himself for a year, or eighteen months, or even two years, he could commence under advantageous circumstances, & at the end of five years he would be far better off, than to plunge headlong into such a concern now,—though he were sure to make no failure.

I cannot say all that I would, but I hope you will befriend him in the best manner you are able . . . I received your letter [and] one addressed to James. It gave us much pleasure to learn that Margaret & the little boy were doing so well. . . .[44]

Richards was clearly exercised. He wrote hurriedly with an agitated hand and made small errors he usually avoided. Perhaps Henry was a good advocate for these views, or perhaps the simple withholding of financial backing carried the day. Edward delayed going out on his own and found satisfactory employment with the Messrs. Frost on Pearl Street by the busy docks on the East River. Here he learned the textile business.

Eighteen months later in a letter dated November 2, 1829, Richards had a new concern about Edward. Where once he worried that his son presumed too much on the generosity of family members to set him up in business, now the senior Richards cautioned Edward against any neglect of his relatives. The immediate family circle, counting in-laws and step-relations and recent offspring, was considerable and now numbered nearly thirty. One's truest friends were found there, his father reminded

East River docks of New York, circa 1834. (Aquatint by William James Bennett, "South Streets from Maiden Lane," I. N. Phelps Stokes Collection; Miriam and Ira D. Wallach Division of Art, Prints, and Photographs; The New York Public Library, Astor, Lenox, and Tilden Foundations)

him. Next might come the extended family and acquaintances in church and business, and after that the world at large, God's children but strangers. Richards did not confine his advice to this point.

> My dear son,
>   . . . I rejoice to hear . . . that your situation is still agreeable to you. I need not say how much it is your interest as well as your duty to do your utmost to give satisfaction to your employers. Let it be seen by them that you are a man of business, and of unshaken integrity, employing your time diligently in their service . . . It is in this way that you are to form habits, all important to you in future life, and to acquire character and estimation among your acquaintance. I hope you will be particular and select in your associates—intimate with few, but just and kind to all. Keep up a frequent and fraternal intercourse with your brother's and sisters' families, and with your other relatives in the city, and in Newark as you

have opportunity. They who would have friends (and who can do without them?) must show themselves friendly. I like to see affection among relatives. God has linked us together in these social bonds for very important purposes;—and while we are not to lean upon them with too much confidence; nor to expect more from them than is rational and becoming, still we should cherish those kindly feelings which the ties of blood and relationship were intended to kindle and to strengthen.

Do you get any time to read? I do not ask whether you acquaint yourself with the news of the day. This almost every young man without any great effort at husbanding his time will be enabled to do. But do you find leisure for . . . that permanent improvement which you ought to seek as an intellectual being, and as a member of an enlightened community? Above all do you read your Bible, the best of all books, and which is able to make you wise unto salvation? As a creature accountable to God, and who has an eternity to provide for, I must entreat you not to forget the word of life. "Wherewith shall a young man choose his way?" says the Psalmist, "*by taking heed thereunto according to thy word.*" For instruction in morals and for wisdom to direct, in the general conduct of life, there is no book like the Bible. And as to religion, it is the only infallible standard of truth and of duty. Other books may be read to advantage on these topics—but none speaks either with the clearness or authority of the Bible. . . .

There is no record that Edward underwent a spiritual crisis like Henry's. His father's tack with him was more indirect: to keep him close to the regular spiritual influences of family, Sabbath observance, and Bible.

A natural way to draw Edward into family concerns was through a mutual interest in the member closest to him in age, young James. That fall of 1829, sixteen-year-old James entered Hamilton College in western New York. There he would study under the paternal eye of his father's friend, the Reverend Henry Davis, president of the college and a member of the Auburn board of trustees. Richards conveyed to Edward the latest about James and expressed a familiar hope:

A letter from James this morning informs us that he is well and much pleased with his situation and prospects. He has an agreeable room mate, a son of Judge Storrs of Whitesboro. This circumstance I regard as of no small moment. The young man I am told is possessed of talent—is studious, and withal hopefully pious. My hope is that his example may exert a beneficial influence upon your brother, as it respects his habits of application and his moral character.[45]

ANNA: "IN THE ARK" IN NEWARK

Meanwhile, Anna continued throughout the late 1820s to post the news from Newark. To Henry she recounted the local commemoration of that remarkable coincidence, the deaths a few hours apart of John Adams and Thomas Jefferson on the fiftieth anniversary of the Declaration of Independence, July 4, 1826. Among neoclassical touches of urns and drapery, a local minister served as chief public eulogist.

> After the 4th, the public attention was much called forth to pay the last tributes of respect to our deceased ex-Presidents. The old revolutionary citizens, together with other respectable inhabitants [assembled] around the Flag staff where they formed a procession. Had two black urns lighted at the top with the names on them, Adams & Jeff[erson], followed by 30 mourners with long crepes on their hats (among whom was my husband) & a number with lighted torches. They marched in this style to the 3rd Church which was [clad] in mourning & a very appropriate address [was] delivered by the Rev. Mr. Hay. I was confined to my bed at the time with an attack of dysentery which prevented my attendance. . . .

In the same letter, she reported on the examination of female students conducted by the schoolmaster, an event "which was crowded with spectators." Anna confessed herself especially interested because her seven-year-old daughter, Caroline Amelia, was present. The examiners, who included her pastor, Mr. Hamilton, were "very close in their interrogation." A ceremony followed a few days later, when "the young ladies all dressed in uniform with blue sashes, walked in procession with the teachers to the Episcopal ch[urc]h from the Institute." They had built a stage "upon which the faculty was seated & upon which at the close of the address Miss Caroline Taylor & Miss Maria Van Doren ascended to receive their gold

medals for excelling in composition & studies." To Henry, then buried in
law studies at Litchfield, Anna dilated on the address delivered by a male
speaker on the subject of female education:

> I wish you could have heard the address, you would have been so
> amused. His aim seemed to be to point out the deficiencies of female
> Education & raise the standard higher. . . . His remarks to this effect:
> That young ladies now a days who could daub a little on paper, play a
> tune on the piano, adjust a ribbon, [sew] a dress & trifle away in nonsense
> the rest of their time—considered it is all that is necessary. He insisted
> upon our being well informed in culinary arts & said he disliked to see
> ladies encroaching upon studies which belonged to the other sex, as
> much as he did to see gentlemen dangling in the kitchen or prinking in
> the parlour, etc. Some of his remarks were very good.

Anna strung her usual beads of gossip. A John Cumming was
"rejoicing in hope" and possibly on the verge of conversion. A girlhood
friend had given birth to a thirteen-pound baby. One neighbor had just
lost his wife and another was "going fast with consumption." A young
friend was marrying a man from Mobile and going out there in the fall;
"he is in good business." A wedding "the other night" joined a couple
"going out shortly for the Chickasaws & Emeline Richmond is going out
with them. The ladies here met this afternoon to prepare her clothing."

Newark was changing before her eyes. "You have no idea what
improvements they are making in this place. Two brick houses next the
market are under cover." Through her husband at the bank, Anna could
mind the real estate market. "Mr. Wright has bought Dr. Lee's place for
less than 8000 [dollars]. The bank would have taken it, if they could have
procured it for that. But would have been obliged first to call a meeting
of the stockholders & then it would have been run so high that they could
not have taken it."

Health always rated a few lines. "I have really racked my invention to
find something more to say. They are all well at Deys. Caroline has
Dyspepsia but rides about every day." Anna's two-year-old, Henry
Nathaniel, was "very much afflicted with boils, [but] poor little fellow is
very patient considering all things. . . ."[46]

FOR SALE,

The DWELLING HOUSE, WORK SHOP, and PREMI-SES, formerly owned by Mr. Joseph Beach, deceased, situa-ted at the lower end of Broad street, in the town of Newark. The Lot contains about two acres, with a Stream of Water running across the same, and is considered a good stand for a Merchant or Mechanic.—For particulars, inquire of ABNER BEACH or ASA WHITEHEAD.

December 16.   43tf

Advertisement in the New Jersey Eagle, June 6, 1826. (Courtesy—Collections of the New Jersey Historical Society)

At the end of the decade, Anna, the only Richards child "in the Ark," continued to pour forth letters rich in gossip and meditation. She had an insider's fascination with the personalities and politics of the church world combined with a believer's understanding of the salvation drama that provided its ultimate frame of reference. Her father was absorbed in the struggle with the Reverend Charles Finney at this time (see chapter 6), and Richards, a discreet man, cautioned the vivacious Anna to watch herself in conversing about family and church affairs. She responded in a letter dated March 22, 1830:

> I received your joint letters my beloved parents together with James' last week. . . . It had been a very stormy & rather gloomy day & your letters were just what I needed. . . . How much cause for gratitude have we all for the increasing health of my dear father. I don't think I have ever prized him more than I have this winter. I hope you don't think I enter into controversy with any body about our affairs. I am friendly with every body & they are so with me. . . .

Anna did not hang back primly, however, when it came to reporting to Auburn on church affairs in Newark, for she next described a competition that had broken out there between the ministers at First Church and Third Church. Her pastor, Hamilton, had been persuaded by some in the congregation to schedule his Bible class on the same night as Dickinson's so as to keep Old First members from straying over to the latter. Anna did not approve of this rivalry, and recorded with implicit approval Dickinson's own exasperation with it. The questions under discussion at these classes suggest the theological basis for concern among pious Christians for their unconverted brethren.

> Mr. H[amilton] is going to give out questions at bible class, I understand. The question to night at Mr. D[ickinson]'s is, Does God view sinners with compassion? The question last week was, Does the sinner in an unregenerate state do any thing acceptable to God? does God view sinners with complacency? . . . Mr. Dickinson told Mr. Thomas he had had his feelings much tried since he had been here with the feelings of the people, with regard to 1st chh. & 3rd chh. Fears we won't have a revival until it is done away. . . .

Anna planned to read a new manuscript on "the benefit of afflictions" with an acquaintance in the throes of bereavement over the loss of her husband. The widow had recently sold her house, which the new owner had promptly turned into a dry goods shop. Over this Anna sighed, "I am often surprised to see how soon people are forgotten after they [are] dead—& are as tho' they had never been." The case of another neighbor came to mind. The man had suffered an apoplectic fit and it looked bad for him.

> Mr. Dickinson [the minister] called to see him—but he was not anxious to converse much. Gave them to understand that he had not lived so many years without making up his mind on these subjects—He had philosophy enough to meet death—had wronged no man—lived at peace with his fellow creatures, etc.—poor man—The God in whose hand his health is . . . he has not glorified. . . .

Despite overseeing a large household, Anna found time to read the serious publications of her father and his colleagues. These works taught her that pride and complacency also blocked the path of the converted like herself.

> Has papa seen Dr. [Edward] Griffin's sermons in the *National Preacher*—on the prayer of faith & Heavenly mindedness? I cannot exactly understand the former—shall send a list of sermons which I wish my dear father to bring with him when he comes. I understand Dr. [Edward] Payson's memoirs are out, I long to get them. I have just purchased *The Family Minister* by Jones, author of Christian Fathers Present—like it very much. His instruction to parents is excellent as well as to Husbands & wives. I think my dear mother would like it very much. . . .
>
> I am often silenced when I attempt to complain of my minister by thinking how many have never had the gospel at all. I don't think I am unreasonable, dear father, & I do feel willing to give him full credit & should be very glad if I had reason to give him credit for more than I do. I thank you for all your cautions to me—they are very wise & kind. . . . I almost despair ever attaining to a spiritual mind—& yet I do not feel willing to give the matter up—I see what advances others have made. . . . Thirty-three years & more I have lived in the world—About half my life I have been a professor of religion—but alas how little fruit I have brought forth unto God. . . .

She fretted some more over the unrighteous.

> [Samuel Mead] is quite intemperate . . . I feel very sorry James Gambol has turned out so. He has left Williams College & gone somewhere to teach school—writes to his mother he has no religion . . . It opens the mouths of the ungodly & wounds the cause of Christ very much. . . .

Then a tolling bell pulled her thoughts home again.

> The upper bell is now ringing for the funeral of a child of Tommy Davis—a sweet little boy 6 years of age, who died of croup—attended the upper infant school. *I know* how to feel for the mother. . . .

Anna had lost a child of her own, an infant named for her. Her surviving children now numbered six.

C. Amelia is now on her balance. She is very well & sends much love, as
also does Sarah. . . . Edward is very fat & healthy—Little Newton is a
very sweet baby—quite lively, has had a bad cold lately & a little fever—
he sits alone . . .[47]

THE RICHARDS BROTHERS
AND THE BATTLE FOR LIFE AND HEALTH

All three married Richards children had new babies in the summer
of 1830. Henry and Margaret became parents of a second son named
Henry Evertson. Henry wrote to his brother James, still at Hamilton, to
say that, ". . . all the good folks at N[ewark] are well . . . Caroline,
who you knew I suppose had another daughter [is] almost entirely
recovered."[48] Caroline now had three daughters and two sons; and her
stepdaughters, Maria and Kate, had grown into womanhood. In the
rounds of family visits that filled a marriageable young lady's time, Maria
had become acquainted with the minister who served at the Second
Presbyterian Church of Auburn, the Reverend Daniel Axtell. The
couple wed in the fall, and Maria now resided in Auburn with her new
husband.

Henry, never robust, started at this time to show signs of tuberculosis.
He took the symptoms seriously enough to settle Margaret and the children
for the summer with his relatives in Newark so that he might pass the season
upstate in Watertown by the shores of Lake Erie. Whatever the benefits, by
December he was again in sufficient distress that he felt forced to cancel a
planned trip to Auburn to avoid its colder weather. He wrote to his father
of the change in his plans:

I shall be impelled to bend my footsteps in another direction. About the
time of receiving your letter I took a violent cold which has seated on
my lungs & now is rendered extremely harassing in consequence of a
severe cough attending it. The external cold affects me differently this
winter than at any other previous season of my life & I cannot now go
out without being severely incommoded with pain in my heart &
increasing my cough. As the only remedy in which I have any faith, I
have been advised by my physician to resort once more to a milder

climate & spend the severe months in an atmosphere more congenial to my constitution where I can exercise in the open air in preference to locking myself up in the house. I have made my arrangements accordingly to go first to Savannah & from there to Florida & trust with the favor of divine Providence to return sometime in the beginning of April.

It is extremely trying & painful to my feelings to be obliged to break off so unexpectantly from my business & tear myself away from my family & friends & sojourn among strangers. And it is peculiarly so at this time inasmuch as Margaret cannot accompany me being afraid to leave our little Henry who is now about teething & requires all his mother's care & nourishments. Mrs. E[vertson] is also undergoing her terrible operation & although every thing in her care is very favourable yet we cannot divert ourselves of anxiety on her account & she perhaps would feel better satisfied to have Margaret near her.

Margaret is delicate & I think a visit to a milder climate would be of essential service to her & I regret her inability to accompany me on her own account as well as on mine. It indeed requires all my fortitude thus to separate myself again from all I hold dear but I trust the separation will not be of so long a duration as it was before.

Henry's illness revived his sense of sin and he asked for prayers.

I am not so callous I trust as not to see in this . . . another rebuke for my sin & ingratitude. I do not feel it, I am aware, in any manner as I ought & I wish I was now humbled and abased at the reproof. I desire your fervent prayers that this chastisement may be sanctified and that He whose way is in the sea . . . may spread over me his protection while in the mighty deep & return me in health & safety to the welcome bosom of my family & friends—With best love to my dear Mother in which Margaret & her mother join I am my dear father your affect[ionate] son, Henry[49]

After passing some weeks in Savannah, Henry arrived in St. Augustine, Florida. He was making the invalid's tour and met others doing the same. In a letter to his father of February 10, 1831, he reported that a strict diet, much exercise, and mild weather seemed to be doing him good. He was making every effort to hold onto life; caring for his health was a moral obligation.

> When I left home I had . . . the most violent cough . . . [which]
> has abated its violence tho' it still continues . . . at intervals of about
> an hour, attended with some expectoration which has also lost much of
> its vicious appearance. . . . It was and still is a most sore trial to me
> & to my dear wife to be thus separated; but I consider it as an escape
> for my life, and that my duty to my family & myself imperatively
> demands the sacrifice. . . . certainly it does not become us to
> murmur & repine at [God's] dispensations. . . . I never expect to be
> a well . . . man. All that I can hope under the nature of my disease is
> to protract life. . . .
>
> The climate is not as good as has been represented if this season can
> furnish any just criterion, but I understand that this is an exception to the
> generality of the winters in this place. My own opinion is that it is too
> near the seaboard for invalids suffering under pulmonary affection. The
> atmosphere is too saline. . . .
>
> I have made arrangements to go to Tallahassee as soon as the weather
> will permit in company with Dr. Bronson of New York who has come
> here also for the benefit of his health. From Tallahassee I intend to
> proceed (Deo volente) to Augusta, Geo[rgia] & from there home by land
> or otherwise as shall seem most advisable. . . . [50]

Some weeks later Edward, too, was traveling in the South, apparently on business. He wrote to his father about a narrow escape from death while aboard ship. His father replied:

April 6, 1831

My dear son

Yours from Peterborough, V[irgini]a, was received. . . . We were much gratified to learn that you had reached . . . your destination in safety, notwithstanding the trouble and alarm you experienced. How kind was that Providence which so mercifully interposed when you were in danger. Let a remembrance of God's goodness on this occasion long and deeply affect your heart. Thousands have been called into eternity as suddenly as you would have been had the disaster you experienced ended in a watery grave. Such a deliverance ought not soon to be forgotten—

nor remembered merely as an incident, of slight and momentary interest.
It is the voice of God to you, never to overlook ye fact, that in the midst
of life we are in death. . . .

Edward also complained of a cough. A concerned Richards counseled
him against exposing himself to the evening air and damp weather and
urged exercise on horseback.

> Henry I suppose is on his return; possibly you may see him, though
> not very likely. He was much better when we last heard. James was
> well . . . and also your sisters and their families. . . . My own
> health and that of your mother was never better . . . I believe I
> mentioned in my last that a revival of religion had commenced in this
> village. It is still progressing, and many have become the hopeful
> subjects of a new birth into righteousness. . . . How ardently do I
> desire that in this day of God's power my dear children might be made
> the willing subjects of Zion's king. . . . I was sorry that [you were]
> called away from N[ew] Y[ork] just at [present]. But God can find you
> any where and you may find him. Seek him I entreat you, and seek
> him with your whole heart. Now is the time.
>
> I hope you will not think of staying longer in Virginia than eight or
> ten weeks. That is not a climate for you—especially during summer and
> autumn. Our vacation commences in four weeks from to day. It is likely
> if God spare my life and health, that I shall make my semiannual visit to
> my [daughters] in the city and at Newark. It is [doubtful] if your mother
> accompanies me. . . .[51]

Earlier that winter, James, too, had been in poor enough health to leave
Hamilton for recuperation at home. This gave his father an opportunity to
see what a year of college had done for him, and the old gentleman was
not impressed.

JAMES: ERRANT YOUTH

James was seven years younger than Edward and in some ways must
have had a different childhood from that of his older brothers and sisters.

A former Auburn student remembered him as "rather a roguish boy." To illustrate the "stern, yet kind" manner of Richards, the student many years later told a story about the head of the seminary and his youngest son. When Richards was away during one of the seminary vacations, James was put in the care of this student to whom he was supposed to report "at the usual time of recitation." Instead, the boy was found playing in the garden, and when called, "took to his heels and ran." The student "pursued, and caught, and chastised him."

> Immediately after the Doctor's return, James entered a complaint against his tutor. [His father] heard him through, and then bade him go and fetch the young gentleman. He did so; and when the latter arrived, the Doctor said, "Sir, *Jeemes* (he always called him thus) has told me that you whipped him because he did not get his lesson, and ran away, and now I have sent to you to know *if you laid it on well.*" The student replied that he thought he did. . . . "Well then," continued the Doctor, "if you are sure you punished him sufficiently, *Jeemes, you may go this time.*"[52]

The story offers a preview of James's behavior at college and his father's response to it. When the seventeen-year-old youth was ready to return to Hamilton at the end of January, Richards wrote to his friend Davis:

> January 31, 1831
>
> Reverend and dear Sir,
>
> This will be handed to you by my son, who returns to College to morrow. His health I think is pretty well restored, and I hope he will be induced to improve his time faithfully in study. He has done something in the way of study since he has been home; but I fear not much. There are so many attractions here to a young mind impressible like his, that it is somewhat difficult to break away from them, and to pursue a system of regular application.
>
> You have my thanks for the care you have exercised over him hith-erto—and I hope and entreat, that you will not withdraw your supervision. I am anxious about his morals, and his spiritual condition. I think I can perceive that he is less reflecting, & certainly less tender than when he entered College. Will you not be kind enough to exercise towards him the part of a father and counsel him on the subject of his

spiritual and immortal concerns. I trust you have done this—and will not cease to do it. And I mention the subject chiefly for the sake of saying, that I think he will take it kindly and that it will be the means of increasing your influence with him. You know the heart of a Father—and will easily excuse my solicitude. . . .[53]

Here was a new note struck in James Richards's concern for his children.

Henry Davis. (Courtesy—Hamilton College, Clinton, New York)

He had worried over Henry's worldliness, yet he appreciated Henry's habitual introspection and caution. He had found Edward's impatience and straining for independence trying, but these qualities showed to him an unseasoned judgment rather than a flawed character. In James's case, however, Richards seemed to sense a susceptibility to "attractions" and a hardness to reproof that might prove more dangerous. On March 11, 1831, a letter from son James confirmed such apprehensions. His father promptly wrote to Davis:

I received a letter from James this morning which both surprised and distressed me. I am at a loss what to do—whether to put an end at once to his College course, or to try him a little longer. I perceive that he is acquiring habits of expenditure which are as incompatible with the state of my finances, as ruinous to him. When he left Auburn last, he took with him seventy dollars which I supposed were sufficient to cover all his debts up to that time. But a man by the name of Johnson it seems had an amount against him of forty-five dollars, for something I know not what—which he entirely concealed from me.[54] He has borrowed the money, he tells me, to pay this sum—and has transmitted Johnsons receipt for the same. This discloses a state of things with respect to my son, which I was not prepared to expect, and has filled me with the deepest alarm. I am anxious he should receive a liberal education—; but I cannot uphold him in extravagance; nor can I willingly see him ruined by forming habits of indulgence which are equally destructive of his temporal and eternal welfare. I look to you my dear sir, to tell me what is to be done. He has confessed to me his fault, and promises a thorough reformation. I would that he were sincere. But I know not what to think of it. You yourself can much better judge. And I most earnestly solicit your advice, as a friend both of the Father and the son.

. . . I have drawn a check on the Bank of Auburn for fortyfive dollars payable to your order. It can be negotiated I suppose through the Bank of Utica, as it is a certified check. I am sorry to trouble you with this business—but I prefer to have the money pass through your hands—at least forty dollars of it . . . The other five dollars you can give to James to pay a student from [whom] he received it as a loan. . . .

Pray attend to my dear son, and be faithful to his immortal soul. Tell him he has greatly distressed his Father—but his chief concern should be to become reconciled to the God that made him. . . .[55]

The matter lay there for the time being. Richards made good his son's debts and accepted the promise of a "thorough reformation."

A little over a month later, a letter from Caroline in New York raised a new concern about James. Richards put the matter before Davis in a letter dated April 22, 1831:

Reverend and dear Sir:

A circumstance somewhat singular has occurred in reference to my son which seems to require some explanation. I received a letter from my daughter in New York saying that on the 4th instant. Mr. Storrs, member of Congress, and father of Henry Storrs belonging to your College, called at her house, and showed a letter purporting to be written by my son & addressed to Henry and requesting him to meet him at the Bank coffee house that day at some hour wh[ic]h was named. The letter was mailed in the city, and dated March 28th—from which Mr. Storrs infered [sic] that James was then in the city, and was desirous of seeing Henry [Storrs] at the time and plan appointed. Considering this as an ominous circumstance he made diligent inquiry for James but could hear nothing of him. This [led] him to acquaint my daughter Mrs. Dey that a letter of the above description had come into his hands. The impression was that James was certainly in the city though he had not made his visit known to any of his friends.

The object of this letter is to inquire if you can explain this matter. James says it is a perfect mystery to him, that he has not been east of Utica since he accompanied me to N[ew] York—nor away from the College 24 hours this term except when he went with Mr. Corbram to Peterborough, wh[ic]h was on the 28th of March, and from which he returned on the 30th. It does not indeed seem to me probable that he could have been absent from the College long enough for such a journey, without your knowledge—, even if he had been disposed for such a jaunt—. And yet strange to tell the letter is signed James Richards Jun[io]r and my daughter thinks the handwriting appears to be his. Whether this is a mere hoax, by some of his companions—or whether some young man who wished to see young Storrs who was expected in the city about that time took this method to obtain an interview—I know not . . . or whether James actually stole away from you for ten days without your being apprised of it, I cannot tell. It would be satisfactory to me and his friends to know where he was from the 25th of March till he left College to return home. If you will have the goodness to answer this immediately, you will very much oblige me.

James is engaged in reviewing the studies of the term, with an expectation of getting ready for the next examination. His health is much improved since his return. . . .[56]

Davis's response does not survive. Over the seminary vacation, however, Richards happened to run into young Storrs on his way from Utica to Albany. He took the opportunity to question this friend of James about this mysterious episode, for some unknown reason referred to as "the Cazenovia affair." Richards wrote to his wife about their conversation:

Yesterday young Storrs & two or three other students from Hamilton accompanied us from Utica, till we reached the point where the road

turns off to Cherry Valley. . . . I inquired of Storrs about the Cazenovia affair. He says he knows nothing of it and has said nothing of it. It
is his opinion as it is mine, that some body unfriendly to James, or from
a mere principle of mischief was the author of the letter addressed to
Henry L. Storrs through the post office N[ew] Y[ork].

I hope James will learn from all the circumstances of this case how
important it is to conduct [himself] in such a way as to render his
ch[aracte]r above suspicion. Dear boy, how deeply I feel interested for
him both for time and eternity! He is continually on my heart. May
it please a gracious God to incline his heart to that which is good. I
do hope by his kindness and attention to you, and by the general
propriety of his conduct, he will comfort you till I return. I have
confidence that he will. Repeat to him my earnest desire that he will
make a vigorous attempt at Huttons mathematics against the time I
hope to see him again. How delighted shall I be to find that his time
has been so judiciously employed. My prayer however is that his
attention may be directed to an infinitely more important Theme.
Give my paternal love to him, and remember me affectionately to Mr.
and Mrs. Axtell [Caroline Dey's stepdaughter, Maria, and her minister
husband].[57]

Richards unburdened himself to his wife but refrained from disclosing
his anxiety to Henry and Edward during their travels in the South. He
closed his letter to Auburn on a domestic note with directions to the hired
man, John, to "lose no time in planting" corn, pole beans, green head
lettuce, and summer and winter squashes. There seemed to be no thought
of pressing James into this task.

When James was ready to return to college almost two months later,
his father wrote again to President Davis on June 12, 1831:

This will be handed you by my son who returns to College with a
purpose I hope of improving his time better than heretofore. He sees,
I trust, the errors of the past and has come to the resolution of taking
a wiser course for the future. But whether his resolution will be carried
into effect time alone can determine. I have given him my most earnest
advice—and my intention is not to indulge him in expensive habits,

nor in idleness. If he gives himself to his studies—much I doubt not will be gained and perhaps most of his former indiscretions will be remedied. I shall be much indebted to the faculty for their watchful supervision over him—and for any counsels which they may judge it meet to impart.

You will have the goodness to excuse him for not returning to College at the opening of the session—as I wished him to remain at home till my return from the [General Assembly at Philadelphia]. . . .[58]

Seven weeks later, Davis was obliged to inform his friend Richards that his son's conduct had disappointed all hopes. In a letter dated August 1, 1831, Richards replied:

Yours of the 29th ult[imo] has been duly received. I thank you for the kindness and frankness with which you have spoken with respect to my son. It grieves me much that he cannot be made to see where his true interest lies—and to avail himself of the advantages for a liberal education, which the Providence of God has supplied.

As it is, I can see no use in continuing him in College any longer—and have therefore written him to come immediately home & to bring his clothing and books. With respect to his bed and other furniture, I have directed him to leave it as it is, till further orders. I suppose it must be disposed of, at public or private sale—but I thought it not best that it should be done now—or done by himself.

In my letter to him to day, I have requested him to ask for a dismission from College, provided it can be honourably done. My motive for this has been twofold—to protect him from unnecessarily injurious reports—and to open the way for his entrance into some other College if after a suitable probation at home, I shall think such a step advisable. I have I confess very little hope of this; but it may be his mind will undergo some favourable change. Be assured, my dear Sir, I shall never cease to be thankful for the kind and ingenuous manner in which you have treated this business. . . .

P.S. With respect to my son's bills for board, tuition etc., I shall make provision for paying them in due season. Let them be lodged with you or with some person whom you shall designate, and they will receive my attention.[59]

Many years later, a Hamilton classmate of James named George Henry Woodruff reminisced about his years at college. In their class of twenty-two, James Richards Jr. stood out vividly to Woodruff as the "bad boy" of the class in the proverbial manner of the preacher's son. "I suppose that but for the regard felt for his father he would have been expelled." Woodruff recalled an incident when "Jim," though refused permission, slipped away from the college to go sleighing "well wrapped in a buffalo robe." The young rake stopped at a tavern where "he passed with the air of a conqueror thro[ough] the hall" into the large waiting room. "With the loud and boasting utterance, 'I am the cock of the walk here,' he strutted up to the large mirror to survey his handsome physique." In the mirror he also saw, enjoying the fire, the reflection of the professor who had refused him permission. With consternation, James turned around, made for the door, called for his horse, and drove back to Hamilton in time for the roll call at evening prayers.[60]

Taverns, centers of gaming as well as drinking, meant adventure to high-spirited youths like James raised in genteel circumstances. In writing to Davis, Richards did not pin down the nature of James's financial obligation to Johnson, but James's concealment of it suggests it was a gambling debt. Any debt Richards found abhorrent, and he warned James as well as his other children that keeping out of debt was "the only way to maintain one's independence."[61] A gambling debt was doubly abhorrent. Richards had specifically requested that James "never play at cards, nor other games of chance; they are a waste of time and most . . . dangerous things." He had also pleaded with him "not to frequent any of the public-houses . . ."[62] A paternal condemnation of theaters probably applied equally to taverns:". . . that species of amusement . . . will always adapt itself to the *corruptions of mankind*, either more covertly or more openly, and ultimately tend to make a depraved world *more depraved*." His daughter Caroline had found one visit to the theater sufficient to satisfy her.[63] He could wish the same for James and the tavern. But James was less persuadable.

Whatever the explanation for the New York City episode (or "the Cazenovia affair"), the established facts and the manner of his father's inquiry suggest that James was believed capable of such an exploit. It is also possible that he was set up in some way, as Storrs and his father came to believe. Woodruff mentioned twice James's pride in his good looks, and this may have laid him open to envy and mischief born of it.

President Davis's last letter left Richards no choice but to withdraw his son from the college. Richards's reference to Davis's ingenuousness acknowledged an extraordinary patience on his friend's part. The seminary professor, now sixty-four, felt at the low point of his hopes for his youngest child. He was certainly loath to pass any more money through James's hands. He doubted at times James's sincerity.

Nevertheless, he usually found a way to give his son another chance. He had spent many years among the inexperienced young, and for all his misgivings, he felt it part of his duty to keep the path clear for James. There is no suggestion that James was a surly, sulky, obstinate youth. His parents seemed to enjoy his company at home, even as they urged him to use his time more profitably. So despite all the talk about probation, family hopes for this talented son were soon rekindled. James proved a welcome companion on his father's late summer travels. Richards wrote to his wife from Oswego at summer's end, "I found it very convenient to have James along as he could drive while I carried the umbrella."[64] James spent no more than a couple of months at home in Auburn before enrolling at Union College in Schenectady.

Richards was probably persuaded to this course by the reputation of Union's president, the Reverend Dr. Eliphalet Nott, who over a period of thirty years had become rather famous for successfully reclaiming wayward students expelled from other schools. Western New Yorkers had taken to calling Union College "Botany Bay," after the Australian penal colony where English convicts received a second chance. Nott's approach was gentle. He believed the boys were basically good and mainly needed self-discipline; punishment should be "moral and parental."[65] This was the manner that Richards himself had endorsed previously in his letters to Davis.

Henry Richards, more skeptical, saw his brother's case quite differently and prescribed sterner medicine.

As regards James, I know not what to say. I deem his situation about as critical as that of any person in the whole range of my acquaintance. I am afraid that in leaving [Hamilton] for Union he has escaped the whirlpool only to be lost among the quicksands. From what I can learn he is beginning to indulge in his old habits of extravagance, smokes sigars [sic] and idles away that time he should devote to study. This I discovered for myself in his recent visit to N[ew] Y[ork]. I conversed with him freely and he seemed to feel that I was right and he was wrong & promised amendment, but all this amounts to nothing unless a radical change does take place. . . . I do think he requires management of a very strong and steady hand.

His habit of spending money can only be restrained but by making him feel how difficult it is to acquire it. If he should be obliged to support himself he would find it would be at the sacrifice [of] many [of] his now useless and worse than useless superfluities & indulgences. I never spent half the money while I was in College that he has for necessaries or luxuries tho my regular bills were almost double the am[oun]t of his. He must break himself of the habit . . . for he cannot support it & a further indulgence will lead to dishonourable or unlawful means of obtaining funds. I told J[ames] that he now was on his last legs and that on his present conduct depended in all probability his future happiness. And I cannot but believe a pretty sharp and serious reproof will have a good effect. . . .[66]

The sharp and serious reproof that Henry prescribed for James was not long in coming. The following month of January 1832, James was suddenly laid low by a devastating attack of smallpox. His father traveled to Schenectady to watch over him. On February 8, Dr. Richards wrote to his friend, the Reverend Dr. William Sprague.

I shall probably remain in this city until Monday next, possibly longer. Should rejoice much to see you, but cannot well leave my sick son long enough to make a visit to Albany. My son is doing [as] well as could be expected in a case of small pox of the most virulent kind. . . .[67]

James survived, and for once a serious illness proved a sanctifying experience for one of the Richards children. His conversion was recorded at Mr. Axtell's Second Presbyterian Church in that year, 1832. His Hamilton classmate, Woodruff, remarked later that the smallpox "made sad havoc of the features of whose beauty he was thought to be proud."

HENRY'S "CUP OF SORROW"

Henry and Edward were back from the South. The next winter in a letter dated December 20, 1831, Henry reported himself less bothered by the cold than he had been in several years. "I go out in all weathers." He hoped it would last. Margaret, too, was "gaining slowly" and the boys were "remarkably stout & healthy." He forwarded the seminary thirty-five dollars according to his annual pledge. Then he conferred with his father about Edward. Twenty-five years old, Edward had spent five years learning business in the city, and the family now found the time right to rally around him with their financial aid so that he might go into business for himself. Henry had put in his share, but warned that some supervision was still in order.

> I have let Edw[ar]d have the $750 as I agreed in his note, to commence business with, and I presume Mr. B[each] will advance the same am[oun]t. This with what you have already given him will enable him to make a trial of his business talents and with care, prudence & industry to assume a fair standing among his business competitors. He ought not to be placed as to means too much above board, but should be made to feel something of a pressure, something that will operate as a stimulus to constant effort. This in my opinion is necessary in order to overcome his natural love of ease & to bring him to more fixed & settled habits of exertion.[68]

Through 1832 and early 1833, Henry and Margaret continued to guard their delicate health with good results. They looked forward to a summer visit in Auburn with their boys, James and Henry, now aged five and three. On the first of July, Dr. and Mrs. Richards warmly welcomed their arrival. Then, inexplicably, Margaret fell suddenly ill and within a few days died.

Henry was crushed with grief. Richards wrote the necessary letters to convey the terrible news to Margaret's relations. On the day of Margaret's burial, Richards needed to reply to a message from a friend at Geneva. In the evening when he sat down to do so, he related the shock of their sudden loss:

Yours of Wednesday . . . has this morning come to hand. I regret that it is out of my power to visit Geneva next sabbath. My family are in great affliction. To day we have committed to the tomb the remains of my daughter in law, the wife of my dear son Henry, who with his family was on a visit to my house. She has been in very delicate health for the last three years; but being somewhat better her physician recommended a journey. They arrived at Auburn on the 1st instant, and she continued as well as usual until last sabbath when she became more indisposed. We were not alarmed until Wednesday evening of this week. She died on Thursday morning at 9 Oclock. But she died as we believe in Jesus and our consolation is that her immortal sp[iri]t is in heaven. Her mother Mrs. Evertson came with them, and has had the satisfaction of witnessing her last moments. Many mercies are mingled in this cup. Nevertheless it is a cup of sorrow. . . .[69]

Ten days later, Henry was among Margaret's relatives at Wappingers Creek near Poughkeepsie. He wrote to his mother and father from there:

July 22, 1833

My very dear Parents,

I know your solicitude respecting us, and altho' I feel almost incapacitated to write or to make any mental effort whatever, I deem it my duty not to leave you unadvised of our present situation and prospects. We reached here on Friday morn extremely jaded and worn out from the fatigue & loss of sleep attendant upon our return, again to renew our sorrows & mingle our tears with those of our dear friends here who had only the day but one before heard the melancholy tidings. We are indeed an afflicted family. Our dear Margaret had been for so long the object of our tenderest care & so often had our hopes & fears been excited in her behalf that she became more endeared to us from her very feebleness and our loss seems more severe than had she been taken from us in the bloom of health.

True it is that we have every consolation that the truths of Christianity afford, not a doubt lingers about the closing scene, not a shadow hovers over the peacefulness of the tomb yet with all these bright and

unclouded hopes before us supported by the precious promises of revelation, it is hard, very hard to part with those we love. Altho we know
they are but lent to us, are not our own. To submit to the stroke with
becoming resignation I conceive to be one of the sublimest triumphs
of faith. I now pray God that in this righteous dispensation of his Providence we may feel and acknowledge his right to dispose of us and ours
as he sees fit and especially that we may not provoke him by fruitless
repinings and unavailing regrets when we have so many mercies left us
of which we are wholly undeserving. And above all I pray that this
event may be sanctified to our souls' eternal welfare.

My nerves are a good deal shattered & I feel the want of exercise as
I had some return of my old dispeptic [sic] symptoms. . . . I hope &
pray you may not be made sick or suffer in any way on our account. My
dear children are well but require a great deal of management. . . .[70]

A postscript in Henry's letter mentioned a coat belonging to James
that was left on the canal boat. Henry said he wrote the canal boat
captain to have it sent to Union College, where James was back at his
studies.

Edward was now twenty-seven and unmarried. He was bending all his
energies to establish himself in the woolens trade on Pearl Street. The death
of Margaret, who was just about Edward's age, as well as the recent turn in
James's life moved his father to write him that August once again in the
pastoral vein:

You have a large place in your mother's affections and mine; and we never
cease to think of you and desire your truest welfare. We rejoice in all the
prosperity which attends your exertions in business and hope by the good
providence of God and your own prudent endeavours, you may be
happily & permanently established in the employment you have undertaken. But there is another interest infinitely more important. . . . You
have another world to provide for, and you have no time to lose. . . .
Thousands of your age, and many much younger, have had the wisdom to
secure the one thing needful. It grieves us to think that you have
neglected this . . . and we fear the delay may be ominous. . . . Do my
dear son reflect seriously on this subject; you have no security for life—

and life is the only state of probation. What will it signify, if you gain the whole world and in the end lost your immortal soul.

With us life is drawing to a close—It is but a little while we shall remain on earth to comfort you or to pray for you. You must not then think it strange that we call things to your mind which we regard as supremely important. We entreat you for once to pause and take a solemn and steady look into that dread eternity. . . . Welcome to your bosom the glad tidings of mercy wh[ic]h the gospel proclaims—and become happy by yielding to the demands wh[ic]h your own conscience and the word of God make upon you. . . .

. . . I hope [James] has truly reformed not in the [outward] man only, but in the hidden man of the heart. I suppose he is busy in writing to you among his other friends, but I wanted to tell you how your mother and I feel in regard to you. . . .[71]

THE RICHARDS CHILDREN IN 1833

"You must not think it strange that we call things to your mind which we regard as supremely important." Richards knew how absorbing the world could be, but he never gave up.

Few of Edward's letters survive. Perhaps he wrote fewer. In any case, his character must be inferred from the words of others and from his deeds. He was the son who most resembled Richards in "size, figure, and general bearing," but he chose a different path, reverting to the family merchant tradition.[72] He stayed in the city and hurried toward success in the famous "go-ahead" spirit.

Henry, now a widower with two small boys, moved his law office from Wall Street to Nassau Street, a few doors down from the office of his brother-in-law Dey.[73] When Mrs. Evertson died two years later, Henry and his sons moved up the Hudson River to be near the rest of Margaret's family at Wappingers Creek by Poughkeepsie. He withdrew from the bustle of the city. Health remained a paramount concern.

Anna's family in Newark grew until there were ten children in all. She continued to anchor the family network and mark the changes all about her. Her excitable sister, Caroline, had yearned for security for her children.

LA GRANGE TERRACE — LA FAYETTE PLACE.
CITY OF NEW YORK.

In 1834, the Deys moved to 43 Lafayette Place on Colonnade Row, new luxury town-houses built by convict labor from Sing Sing and occupied by the Astors and other wealthy New Yorkers. (Etching done in 1831 by Archibald L. Dick, after James A. Dakin, "La Grange Terrace-Lafayette Place," from Views in New York . . . [The Peabody Views], I. N. Philip Stokes Collection; Miriam and Ira D. Wallach Division of Art, Prints, and Photographs; The New York Public Library, Astor, Lenox, and Tilden Foundations)

That seemed now at hand. In 1834, New York and New Jersey settled the boundary dispute that had blocked development of Paulus Hook. Dey and his partners were free to build Jersey City on the site. As a result, Caroline and Anthony Dey entered the period of their greatest prosperity and moved uptown to the elegant new residential enclave at Lafayette Place.[74]

James finished his college course at Union, and then set off, like his brother Henry before him, to study the law—not in New York City, however, nor in Litchfield where the demise of the law school had followed Judge Gould's recent death. James went instead to study under a respected judge of western New York in the village of Canandaigua.

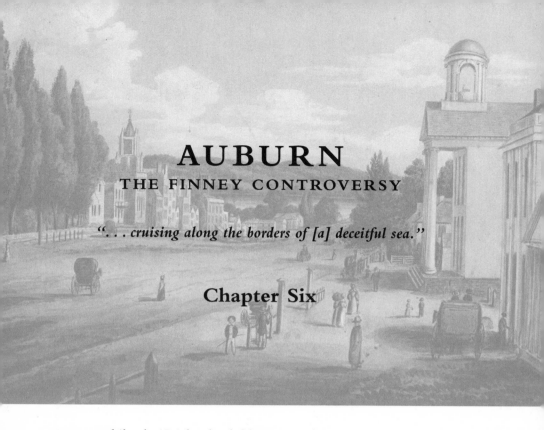

AUBURN
THE FINNEY CONTROVERSY

". . . cruising along the borders of [a] deceitful sea."

Chapter Six

While the Richards children were busy at the tasks of young adulthood, their father faced two new but interconnected problems. The first concerned a local figure, the Reverend Dirck Lansing, and the second concerned a person who was becoming nationally prominent, the Reverend Charles Finney. Lansing, in a sense the real founder of the seminary in Auburn, had raised the critical $15,000 from Tappan that had brought James Richards to Auburn. While living on the salary he drew as pastor of the First Presbyterian Church in Auburn, Lansing had continued successfully to raise much needed money for the seminary and to act as the unsalaried professor of Sacred Rhetoric and Pastoral Theology. All this should have endeared him to James Richards, but unfortunately Richards did not find him congenial. On the contrary he thought him intellectually inadequate for his professorship and quite possibly unorthodox. Things came to a head when the board of trustees wished to change Lansing's part-time voluntary position to a full-time paid professorship.

By 1826 Lansing had fallen under the influence of Charles Finney, the spellbinding evangelist who was taking the Mohawk Valley by storm. Finney was developing a controversial new style of revivalism known as the "New

Charles Grandison Finney in 1835. (Courtesy—Oberlin College Archives, Oberlin, Ohio)

Measures." Part of his message was that there was a substantially easier way to prepare men for the ministry. When Lansing invited Finney to preach his message in Auburn in the summer of 1826, Richards felt a threat to his own vision of the right way to educate clergymen. This galvanized him to undertake the twin tasks of forcing Lansing's resignation and destroying the influence of Finney. Before Richards was done, he would have to beat back three determined assaults by the Finney forces. These problems came at a time when, having made great personal sacrifices to raise money for the seminary, he was ready to spend more time as a professor tending to the needs of his students. This was the primary task that the board of trustees had entrusted to him.

Richards's goals were not easy to accomplish. He was trying to force the resignation of a popular professor who was riding the coattails of the most powerful evangelist yet seen in New York State. Finney had nothing but contempt for the bookishness of James Richards and his insistence on an educated ministry. Finney believed that if a man was armed with the right spirit, he could move from "plow to pulpit" with a minimum of training. He himself was a wonderful example of someone who had effectively evangelized people almost from the moment of his conversion. In fact he had been in such demand as an evangelist that he had found it difficult to complete even a shortened private theological course of instruction. This was a siren song to presbyteries that were chronically short of ministers and to whom the idea of seminary training was a new idea in any case. In contrast, Richards was committed to sending men into the field with four years of college and three of seminary training, men who could sustain themselves and their congregations by their intellectual attainments in Greek, Latin, and Hebrew, and their familiarity with earlier theologians, church history, and classical rhetoric. Not only did he have to raise the money for seminary education, but he had to persuade the churches of the region that it was desirable.

The first recorded intimation of Richards's desire to deny Dirck Lansing a permanent professorship came in a letter to the Reverend Henry Davis of Hamilton College. Davis had gone to Yale in 1793, the year James Richards received his degree *in absentia,* and had also studied under Timothy Dwight. An impressive scholar, Davis was appointed professor of divinity at Yale in 1801, but he had been unable to take up the post because of his bad health. He recovered by the unlikely expedient of a visit to the coast of Labrador. In 1817 he was offered the presidencies of both Yale and Hamilton and chose Hamilton.[1] He arrived in time to participate in the formation of Auburn Seminary and since 1820 had sat on the board of trustees. No doubt as a consequence of his influence, the seminary was a common next step for Hamilton graduates who intended to enter the ministry.

By 1826 Davis and Richards had discovered their mutual appreciation for institutional standards and a common taste for academic politics. His letters to Davis often referred to matters obliquely as if to avoid public clamor should they come to light. They also reflected an instinctive turning away from anything that might seem self-serving or mean-spirited and an effort to caste his objectives as farseeing and balanced. He wished to be seen as a man of conscience. On January 10, 1926, Richards wrote a letter to Davis about Lansing marked STRICTLY CONFIDENTIAL.

> For more than a year I have perceived movements which led me to conclude that there was a desire to get into the active discharge of . . . a certain professorship in this institution. . . . Now matters are coming to a crisis.

Davis, who was part of the faction on the board of trustees that favored getting rid of Lansing, had advised his fellow trustees to take a poll of the three professors at the seminary before making any move. Richards pointed out that this would put him in an awkward position.

> For us [the professors] to be silent was to oppose [Lansing] and could not fail to be construed into an act of decided hostility and to approve *unqualifiedly* might not be honest. I said to the gentlemen who broached

the matter to me that as things were, the professors were the last persons in the world to be consulted on the subject.

Richards told Davis that he preferred someone like Griffin "distinguished for his scholarship, his taste, and intellectual vigour." Lansing suffered, he believed, not only from intellectual inadequacy but a taste for flamboyant clothing and an inability to speak English with sufficient eloquence since his first language was Dutch. His hesitation in coming out and saying so stemmed largely from his fear that such a move would alienate potential donors to the seminary. Lansing was after all a longtime resident of the area and an extremely successful leader of revivals. He had increased his flock from the paltry forty-seven members who had called him in 1816 to a church with over 500 members.[2]

Although Richards tried to avoid being polled, the trustees apparently had such confidence in his judgment that they pressed him for an opinion.

> Thus I was brought to a point. . . . "My opinion on the case is briefly this—that the expediency of the measure in contemplation will depend much on the public sentiment. It has been suggested to me that this sentiment is not exactly uniform, but how far any diversity exists is more than I can say. . . ."[3]

After thus straddling the fence, on March 9 Richards again wrote a confidential letter to Davis. He was well on his way to gaining his goal but could foresee the backlash that was likely to follow.

> The evil hour which I have for some time anticipated has at length arrived. Our brother L[ansing] as you have probably seen by the papers has tendered his resignation to the board of commissioners. . . . I apprehend that pains will be taken to make the community believe that this has resulted from the want of cordial support on the part of some who could not see the wisdom of bringing him here at this time fully into the occupation of his department in the seminary. I hear it thrown out already that a certain president of a college and a professor nearer home have committed their influence to oppose a man who differed from them on some points of theology. . . . And no protestations to the contrary will for the present be of any avail. I exceedingly deplore

this state of things and know not what is to be their end. The mere fact of any discrepancy in sentiment or unpleasantness of feeling can augur nothing but evil.

After considerable efforts at camouflage, he was caught in the midst of unseemly public partisanship, a position that he found acutely uncomfortable and that threatened his future freedom of action. The students, the professors, and the larger community were angry and divided, yet they continually turned to him for advice as he was known to be "wise in the ways of the human heart." With some, like Professor Perrine, even now trying to persuade Lansing to reconsider, Richards needed all his powers of persuasion to smooth things over while letting the resignation go forward.

A few are asking if it will not be in the power of the Board of Commissioners to arrest it [Lansing's resignation] and still retain his services in the institution. . . . Some would be sorry to have his connection with the institution dissolved and others would not think it a misfortune. . . . But it is in the Lord's hands. I exceedingly want to see you and lay the whole thing open to the core. But I know not that any human aid would be of any utility at this present moment. Let me have your prayers and may God enable us all to carry the matter sincerely and humbly to his throne. If anything strikes you as important in this critical hour, let me hear from you soon. . . .

P.S. March 10th, I purposely delayed forwarding the above until today—hoping that some change in our seminary horizon might appear. That change, blessed be God, has appeared. Yesterday I was apprehensive that Dr. Perrine would send in his resignation too, unless we would consent to inflict expulsion on some individuals[4] who had ventured to express a doubt of Brother Lansing's powers. I was willing to counsel and reprove but not to chastize [sic] so severely. Today the dear good man. . . . is willing my policy should prevail. All is well . . . I have had some severe buffetings in my life before, but never any equal to this. . . .[5]

It seems likely that his extreme discomfort came in part from the fear that his true feelings and behind-the-scene manipulations might come to

Henry Dwight. (Courtesy—Geneva Historical Society)

light. He was no longer a supporting player as he had been in Princeton during the Lindsley affair. Now a central figure who could manipulate the faculty but not order it to fall in line, he worried that a false move on his part could put the whole Auburn enterprise in jeopardy.

Hoping, but not sure, that the matter was finally resolved, he went off for the rest of March to raise money in the region west of Auburn. He was the public face of the seminary. As such he still made short trips in his region even if he no longer made the long trips that had been so distressing to his wife.

Geneva, March 18th 1826

My dear wife,

I reached this place yesterday a little after 2 o clock P.M. and found myself in no degree fatigued with the jaunt. I dined at Dr. Axtell's—passed the night at Mr. Dwight's—and expect to take the stage this afternoon for Canandaigua. I hope I shall do a little for the seminary at Geneva though I think not much—the times are so difficult. I shall write you again from Canandaigua and hope to make a more interesting statement. May a kind and gracious Providence have you and all that is dear to you in his holy keeping.

Your affectionate husband
J Richards[6]

Mr. Dwight was a younger brother of his old professor, Timothy Dwight, a friend and a supporter of Auburn. After retiring from the ministry in 1817, he had become president of the Bank of Geneva. He was also one of the founders of the American Home Missionary Society.

The next leg of the journey proved unpleasant. The weather was bad; Richards suffered from his usual anxiety about his health, and he became increasingly homesick as the trip went on.

Geneseo March 25th 1826

My dear wife

It pains me to think that I am two days journey distant from you and a great deal of mud between. I reached this place yesterday at 5 o clock P.M. and found I could do nothing unless I spent the Sabbath here and not a very flattering prospect even then. But as it is a country town and some very influential and wealthy individuals in it I judged it best to become a little better acquainted with them as it might exert a favourable influence in time to come.

If the Lord please I shall go to Moscow on Monday and then return as early as possible. You may expect me probably on Wednesday evening, though there is no calculating with certainty on account of the irregularity of the stages. The travelling in this country is truly *dismal*. I have not visited half as many places as I might have done in the same time if the season and the travelling had been pleasant. It is well that I did not attempt the journey in a sulky as the storms from above and the mud beneath would have rendered travelling next to impossible. . . .

No tongue can tell how much I long to be at home again. It will not be a trifle which will hereafter carry me abroad at this season of the year. The last evening I was at Canandaigua. I took a slight cold which has hung upon me ever since. It is accompanied with no fever but attended with coughing and expectoration. I expect some difficulty in performing public service tomorrow. Never did I wish to hear from home more, but expect to be kept in ignorance of everything there till I return. Make my kind respects to all inquiring friends—give my love to James and believe me to [be] very truly and affectionately yours,

James Richards[7]

His last stop was the lakeside village of Canandaigua. Although the ostensible purpose of the trip was to raise money, he was delighted to find himself in the midst of a revival and pitched in. The activities provided a restorative contrast to the agitations at home.

Canandaigua, March 26th, 1826

My dear Wife,

I reached this place on Saturday afternoon at about 5 o clock and took up my quarters at Mr. Eddys. I find Mr. and Mrs. Eddy much engaged in the things of the kingdom and that the Lord is visiting the congregations in mercy. I preached three times yesterday to very solemn assemblies and expect to preach again this evening. It is refreshing to be once more in a place where the spirit of the Lord is to be seen in the effects of his convincing and sanctifying power. It is not known yet how many we awakened or hopefully converted—but a considerable number of young persons of both sexes and of the first families are subjects of the work. This is the first revival ever witnessed in Canandaigua—the work is silent, but I think genuine. May the Lord make it extensive.

How much I shall accomplish by my journey I know not—I have done a little in Geneva—and shall secure the amount of Judge Howel's pledge in this place—say fifty dollars. To morrow if the Lord pleases I shall visit east and west Bloomfield and hope to get matters in such train as to return at the close of the week; but I shall write to you again in a day or two. Let us not forget each other at the throne of divine grace. My journey has been of service to my health notwithstanding the fatigue.

My love to James and kind regards to all friends. Your affectionate husband.

James Richards[8]

On his return home he found a letter from his nephew, J. K. Richards, telling him that his mother, Ruth Hanford Richards, had died. There was little to be done at such a distance except to record the melancholy tidings.

My dear Uncle,

Aunt Diana is unable to write to you on this mournful occasion because she is so much overcome with fatigue and anxiety. I will briefly mention the particulars of my dear Grandmother's sickness and death. She was taken with the prevailing influenza a fortnight to day. . . . Sometimes Grandmother had doubts with regard to her future state but when Deacon Heacock conversed with her and prayed for her she felt much better. A little while before her death she said that she felt resigned to the divine will and was happy to be in the hands of her saviour. She had her reason to the last hour but was so feeble that she could not converse much. She was particularly careful that family prayer should not be neglected and when she was so far gone that she could not speak, she signified her wish that the family should be called and that Uncle William should pray.[9]

Still governing her family by "eye and forefinger" as she had when Richards was a child, she called the family to prayer even as her life was ending. Now no parent stood between him and eternity.

On turning his attention back from family affairs to the trip he had just completed, he must have found it comforting as well as reassuring to have taken part in the revival in Canandaigua, a revival that was carried out properly. He was only too aware that this familiar style of evangelism was being compared unfavorably to Charles Finney's more sensational efforts in Utica. Richards found himself in the unpleasant position of having his most treasured ideals identified as ultraconservatism. Exercising his capacity for ironic detachment, he wrote to Davis on his return:

> The truth is the clergymen in that direction [Utica] feel a repugnance to certain ultra Calvinistic peculiarities, and they will never cordially cooperate in sustaining an institution [Auburn] where these peculiarities are urged as the grand palladium of truth and virtue. . . . I have heard that our brother L[ansing] is to start for Utica today. Whether anything is in foot to prepare the commissioners to decline receiving his resignation is more than I can say.[10]

Lansing was on his way to see Finney in Utica and invite him to come to his church in Auburn to lead a revival during the coming summer. If Finney's revival were to take hold in Auburn, James Richards would have much to worry about. At the very minimum Lansing's resignation would come undone while at the worst Richards's vision of seminary education might be stopped cold.

Finney was a versatile and charismatic man whose style and popularity inspired unease in the deliberate and methodical James Richards. Without benefit of college, law school, or seminary he had become first a lawyer by studying privately with a judge and then an ordained minister after his conversion in 1821. Since 1823 he had been sent out by the Utica Female Missionary Society as an itinerant evangelist. Although the area around Utica may have been ripe for evangelizing, he was fortunate to arrive in the winter when the Erie Canal was closed for the season and economic activity was slow. The area ignited and Finney felt himself "pulled 40 ways at once."[11] The excitement did not finally abate until the fall of 1829, by which time the whole area was becoming known as the "Burned-over District."

This is not to say that there were not lulls in the excitement; the summer of 1826 was one of them. In the spring just when the revival was slowing down in Utica due to renewed activity on the canal, Finney had been invited to Hamilton College by a twenty-three-year old admirer and imitator, Hiram Huntington Kellogg. Kellogg was a graduate of Hamilton and in his senior year at Auburn. He wished to conduct a revival with Finney at Hamilton, but the local clergy including Henry Davis resented Finney's intrusion. Due to their opposition the revival never occurred. It was not only Finney's intrusion they resented; they were also alienated by his emotional style of preaching and the self-righteousness of young Kellogg.[12] Finney was saved from obvious embarrassment by Lansing's invitation to come to Auburn. He arrived towards the end of June and stayed until late August. His presence constituted a direct challenge to Richards, who was in Auburn most of that summer.

Dirck Lansing, an experienced evangelist in his own right, worked closely with Finney according to a well-developed plan. Lansing preached the Sunday morning service. Finney addressed an informal "meeting of inquiry" in the afternoon and a more formal worship service in the evening. Meetings of inquiry continued during the week, eventually becoming "anxious meetings" in which the emotional level of confrontation intensified. Here sinners groaned and wept as Finney told them they were no different than the legions of hell and called on them to submit to Christ. Meetings sometimes went on all night and "sinners" who were absent were prayed for by name.[13] It was this that constituted the most obvious attack on Richards because he was one of those who was prayed for. His own students were imploring the Lord to soften Richards's heart and bring him to a consciousness of his sinful state.

Awakened sinners were then asked to come forward to sit on an "anxious seat" at the front of the congregation where special prayers and exhortations were directed at them. Finney told them they had no time to waste. Most converts were under thirty years of age and only here and there was an "aged sinner seen coming to Christ."[14] They were pressured to reject their elders (understood by all to be a euphemism for their professors), and make a commitment immediately. Direct confrontations in small groups and in individual religious conversations were kept up throughout the week.

Despite all the pressure, nothing like a general revival took place. There were only fifty-four converts that summer, a number far short of the numbers that had joined the church in earlier revivals conducted by Lansing alone.[15] By the end of the summer it was clear that Finney had suffered another rebuff and the seminary was safe from his incursion.

Almost certainly James Richards's determined opposition was critical in inoculating Auburn against the seductive power of Finney's anti-intellectual approach. It took a characteristic form—refusal to be drawn in while commenting in private. His public silence and noncooperation nevertheless spoke loudly. Later a witness and Richards's supporter who had been at Auburn that summer reported:

> He was an attentive and deeply interested observer of the inroads of that fanatical spirit which began its desolating operations in western New York. He was ready to admit that as in days of old, there might be some co-mingling of good with the evil; but he entertained not a doubt that it was chiefly a ministration of fanaticism and error; and with this conviction, he set his face against it as a flint. He resisted at the expense of being denounced as an enemy of revivals; at the expense even of being most offensively not to say calumniously prayed for by some of his own students for with all the precaution that he could use the storm swept through the seminary; and while some were swept away others prudently bent to the blast, and others still stood up with their venerable professor in the attitude of stern and dignified resistance.[16]

What exactly was Richards opposing? A compilation of objections to Finney's New Measures, was drawn up by Lyman Beecher of Litchfield,

Connecticut, in January 1827 in preparation for a meeting held later in the year at New Lebanon, New York, between the New England revivalists and the Finney forces from western New York. It was based on the criticisms of those who had witnessed Finney's revivals. Richards would presumably have concurred with them all.

1. Hasty recognition of converted
2. Severe and repelling mode of preaching
3. Facile assumptions about the unconverted
4. Use of provoking epithets
5. Produces imitators
6. Female prayer in promiscuous assemblies
7. Bold or imprudent expressions
8. Unbecoming familiarity with God
9. Coarse, blunt or vulgar expressions
10. Harsh and severe mode of addressing sinners
11. Misguided reformers
12. Self-sufficient and daring state of mind
13. Opposed to courtesy in civilized intercourse
14. Accepting success as vindication of what is done[17]

To a great extent these criticisms concerned style which Richards was later able to overlook. However, they also concerned theology in that the Finney group tended to allow more latitude for free choice in conversion than he thought was possible. He later referred to this Arminian tendency as "cruising along the borders of [a] deceitful sea."[18] Richards was not entirely immune to this line of thought himself. He was already urging his own children to actively seek conversion in his anxiety to see them saved. He was clearly prepared to accept some diversity of interpretation on the point. What really angered him was that Finney threatened the very life of

Lyman Beecher. (Courtesy—Yale University Library)

the seminary. Finney's appeal to the students was that if they truly believed, because they believed, they did not need the seminary, but could go forth and preach effectively. Richards made a point of collecting horror stories about freewheeling enthusiasts who preached without adequate training, destroying thriving parishes, and loosing forces they could not control.[19]

A measure of how pressed he felt for the well-being of the seminary can be found in a letter he wrote to Griffin in the summer of 1826 asking him to join the faculty at Auburn. His relations with Griffin had ended on a decidedly sour note in Newark, and it is unlikely that time and distance had softened his memory of those events. But the seminary was at stake and he knew Griffin to be an able theologian and a successful president of Williams College. For the sake of his institution he was willing to forget the old rivalry. The letter was written while Finney was still at Auburn and he was mustering all the help he could find to defeat him.

Auburn July 27th, 1826

My dear Brother,

I have this moment learnt that the bearer Mr. Remington leaves to morrow morning for Williamstown. I am unwilling to lose so good an opportunity of tendering my cordial affection and of saying that I have thought much on the subject I named to you at our last interview. I pretend not to know what is best but it appears to me exceedingly desirable that you should occupy a place in our institution, which has been recently vacated, and which I have now very little doubt will be so declared at the approaching meeting of the Commissioners.

This is not said because I fear at all the result of this resignation. I am as certain as I well can be of any thing future, that it will be productive of good rather than of evil. The prospects of the seminary were never brighter than they are at this moment. But I am anxious that it should be completely organized and that we should bring to it such talents and acquirements as under God may give us increasing public favour and enable us to act with superior efficiency.

I have said next to nothing on the subject except to my brethren the other professors, because I thought it on several accounts to be premature. But I can assure you, should providence open the door for your taking part with us in our labours, you would receive a cordial welcome on the part of all the professors and the brethren and churches in this region. Humanly speaking there is nothing wanting, but such a man as you to make this seminary one of the first in this country and to render it an intensive and permanent blessing to the Church and the world.

You will excuse me for saying that I always thought you peculiarly fitted for the professorship in question and that I verily believe you would enjoy yourself better and do more good in such a station than in any other that can be named. Still should things go well at Williamstown and the contemplated fund be secured, I know not how you could well be spared from your honourable and responsible charge. We must wait to see what the Lord will do, but I thought it would not be amiss to tell you in what channel our thoughts are directed. I expect every moment the bearer will call and I can only say that Mrs. R unites with me in a kind remembrance of yourself, Mrs. G and daughters.

Most affectionately and respectfully yours

James Richards[20]

As it turned out, funds amounting to $25,000 were raised at Williams and Griffin never came to Auburn.

Finney's program was a very real threat as can be seen in the statistics for the classes of these years.[21]

ENROLLMENT AND GRADUATION 1824–1828

Year	No. Enrolled	No. in Class	No. Who Left	% Graduated
1824	11	7	4	64%
1825	9	5	4	55%
1826	15	5	10	33%
1827	36	21	15	58%
1828	24	19	5	79%

But the example of Richards's principled opposition seemed to have worked; the seminary survived and grew. By the end of the summer of

1826, Lansing's resignation from the faculty was accepted by the commissioners and Finney moved on to the Eastern cities.

Although he had won the first round with Finney, Richards had not seen the last of him. A letter he received a month before Finney's arrival at Auburn in the summer of 1826 suggested the next round would be fought more directly over the length and cost of theological education. The letter was from the Reverend Gideon Blackburn, whom Richards had supported earlier when Blackburn was a missionary to the Cherokees. He wrote from Louisville, a town close to the scenes of ecstatic revival that began in Cane Ridge and that had alarmed the General Assembly twenty years earlier. The Cane Ridge revivals continued to reverberate as the prototype of frontier revivalism that conservative presbyteries abhorred.

Louisville, May 17 1826

Dear Brother

This will be handed you by Mr. James Carnahan who is hereby committed to your care by the Presbyterian Church of Louisville in order that he may enjoy the advantages of Theological instruction at Auburn. . . . He has been a beneficiary of this church for some time past and we wish him to prepare for the ministry of the gospel as speedily as may be consistent with propriety—our funds . . . accumulate slowly. We have not much more on hand than will convey him to you, but we hope to be able to meet the bills . . . when the money will be needed . . . if you will be kind enough to let us know the periods when the money will be needed or if you will make yourself responsible for it we will refund it. Perhaps in the vacations he could be so employed as not to be at cost and if you can devise any means to forward or assist him I should feel gratified both for his sake and because temptations have been thrown in his way from other institutions but we wish an opening made to Auburn.

He is a good Latin and Greek scholar and has studied some of the sciences but I wish to tax your friendship with giving him an opportunity of acquiring a knowledge of some other branches aside from the Theological course. The reasons why I make this request are that we had no college convenient where we could put him. Our funds were not equal to sending him long to college. We kept him longer at private schools. The interest of our people who are just in the infancy of such exertions [is] . . . excited . . . when they know [that what is] necessary is going forward in a theological course and I thought it important to take the tide of feeling.

I hope you will find him pious studious and attentive—He has been raised in a part of the country where theology was not much studied but I think he will be able to acquire a sufficient stock for usefullness in a reasonable period in your institution. . . .

And now I remark for myself that I had expected to send you two others but for the present one disappointed—perhaps one or both may reach you by October next. . . .

There followed a rare reference to national politics. Evangelical Presbyterians in general were anti-Jackson and pro-Whig no matter what part of the country they came from. The fact that Jackson had fought duels and his party had not condemned him for it was felt to be symptomatic of their indifference to morality. It also reflected an intemperate spirit that they found repellant. For many, ecstatic revivals, dueling, and the vulgarities of the New Measures were of a piece.

We have nothing very cheering on the subject of religion and clouds and darkness drift on the political horizon. From the flagrant instances of public crime preached at Congress by our rulers I should not be surprised if the effect should be felt throughout the union inciting to deeds of murder. I have long been resolved that I will never give my vote for any place of public confidence to be filled with a man who has fought a duel unless I have good evidence that he is penitent before god. If such bloody murderers rule the people must mourn. May divine providence bless you my Dr. Brother and your colleagues in the work of your institution and enable you to send forth [men] who shall assist to change the moral features of society. I am recd dear sir yours affectionately in the gospel of christ.

Gideon Blackburn[22]

It is clear that sending Carnahan to Auburn was costing Louisville dearly. Was an Auburn degree worth the effort, or was there a shorter route to ordination that would do just as well? Finney believed there was, and his old mentor, the Reverend George Washington Gale, proposed to put the idea into practice in Utica in the spring of 1827.[23] Gale planned to create a new school called Oneida Institute at which young men could combine a course of study with manual labor, thus providing a steady source of income for the school and low tuition. He hoped that the enthusiasm of the new converts could be quickly channeled into an alternative, shorter, and more lively preparation for the ministry that minimized "all this hic, haec, hoc, and no God in it."[24] Finney and his followers endorsed a natural and colloquial style of communication, spontaneous preaching, and "a praying heart" that risked being dried up in the formality of a seminary like Auburn.

This scheme put Richards in direct competition with Finney enthusiasts for students and funds. It seemed entirely possible that western New Yorkers would reconsider their gifts of money to the American Home Missionary Society and the American Education Society, both of which were staunch supporters of Auburn students, if there was a cheaper and equally satisfactory alternative education available. His ally Henry Davis wrote to a friend in Andover in the summer of 1827, "A machine among us for manufacturing cheap ministers, we should deem a public calamity."[25]

Richards and Davis were lucky that Finney had little taste for the humdrum business of soliciting funds. Gale applied to him in vain to mention Oneida in the course of his preaching and to send the funds he had promised for the first buildings. Eventually Gale found a better fundraiser in Theodore Weld, who raised a good deal of money until he redirected his attention to abolitionism.[26]

Richards was having his own trouble with his friends and supporters. By 1827 word of Finney's New Measures had reached the East, and the New England revival establishment, led by the Reverend Asahel Nettleton, was fearful that such unseemly churchmanship would make Presbyterianism the laughingstock of Boston and hamper the struggle against Unitarianism. Nettleton sent a letter to Richards denouncing Finney's New Measures and asked that it be read to the Auburn students. Richards was willing after he had done some judicious editing to remove the most egregious exaggerations that could only weaken their cause. He was soon backing off from such an intemperate ally.[27] Before long Lansing entered the fray supporting the suggestion made by the Reverend Beman of Troy that there should be a meeting between Finney and his eastern critics. The conference was held in New Lebanon, New York, in July 1827. Nettleton, Lyman Beecher of Connecticut, President Humphrey of Amherst, and Jonathan Edwards of Andover came from the East while Finney brought such supporters as Gale, Lansing, and Beman. This meeting and other confrontations either in writing or face-to-face made Richards very nervous and they resolved nothing. The emotional Nettleton had little feeling for the sensibilities of western New Yorkers and continued to over-state the case against Finney by issuing unsubstantiated allegations. Beecher on the other hand was a charismatic evangelist in his own right, capable of imagining that Finney had much to offer the world despite the list of criticisms that he brought to the meeting. Within two years he was inviting Finney to Boston to stimulate a revival.[28] Richards in contrast to other Finney opponents counselled steadfast silence that was universally understood to mean opposition.[29]

By 1828 the proper handling of Finney had become a moot point because Finney again left western New York for Philadelphia, New York City, and Boston. Richards was left to defend his vision of education against Finney's followers. For the next few years he managed to persuade the Western Education Society to back Auburn students rather than Oneida students.[30] A supportive article was published in the *American Education Society Journal* that advocated a thorough course of study since "God has decided that these vacant churches and perishing sinners must wait till the preparation is made by study, for it is not made now by miracles."[31]

His friend and partner in defending educational standards, Henry Davis of Hamilton, was less fortunate in his battles with the New Measures men. Davis was prayed for as an "old gray-headed sinner, leading souls down to hell" and within sight of the college the plea was urged at a prayer meeting that God "would raze the walls of . . . [Hamilton's] buildings."[32] Endless arguments steadily reduced the curriculum to something "more comfortable to modern times."[33] Finally direct confrontations threatened the survival of the school, which at its lowest point consisted of only nine students.

Richards on the other hand managed a successful defense of Auburn and its standards. It seems unlikely that avoiding confrontation could alone explain the survival of Auburn. A more plausible explanation is that the students at Auburn were genuinely fond of him. The words "safe," "judicious," and "sound" were often applied to him, but they do not do justice to the passion he brought to his cause and to the welfare of his students. He clearly called forth a reciprocal confidence, loyalty, and affection. A number of anecdotes that attested to the students' fond memories of their days at Auburn were collected by the Reverend Sprague after Richards's death.[34] Even allowing for the inevitable

James Richards. (Taken from John Quincy Adams, A History of Auburn Theological Seminary 1818–1918, Auburn, New York, 1918)

tendency to collect only flattering material, the stories emphasize over and over his natural instinct for human intercourse and his lack of false dignity that made him easily accessible to students. One wrote after Richards's death:

> Every one that ever knew Dr. Richards must, I think, recall that characteristic smile of his. Again and again have I myself felt its potent influence; and those little collisions of opinion and feeling that sometimes occurred in my Seminary relations, it seems to me that I was oftentimes more controlled by the irresistable effect of his smiling countenance, than by the weight of and pertinence of his arguments and persuasion. Indeed, I sometimes thought that he knew the power of this amiable artillery.[35]

His enthusiasm for the life of the mind and the soul, the seriousness with which he engaged students, and the energy he put into his teaching led another student to write many years later:

> I never shall forget a circumstance that occurred soon after I joined our class. The question to be answered was, Whether conscience always dictated right. I took the position that it did and maintained it with a

force of argument probably unusual for a tyro. This brought me into collision with the Doctor, who took opposite ground. For want of time the debate ended before it was finished. About nine o'clock in the evening following a rap was heard at my door, when who should appear but the Doctor. Not satisfied with the manner in which the debate had ended in the recitation room, he sought this opportunity to resume the subject. The discussion continued till near midnight. I listened with profound admiration to his arguments, and was pleased with the evidence he gave of his anxiety, not so much to triumph as to arrive at the truth and convince me of my error.[36]

Perhaps more surprising are the references to his wit. He was well known for his pithy phrases and his homely illustrations that could relieve the tedium of a long recitation or a dry discussion. An example from outside the classroom came from his Auburn neighbor William Seward, an Episcopalian and an attorney during these years. Before going on to fame as governor of the state, United States senator, leader of the Republican Party, and secretary of state in Lincoln's cabinet, Seward had gotten to know the leading professor of the Auburn seminary. He later recalled:

[Dr. Richards] did not often mingle in the secular concerns of the community in which he lived, but they never failed to call out his opinions and his influence on great and important occasions of general interest. His influence was then irresistable. I remember that in 1825 or 1826, when the struggle of the Greeks for deliverance from their Turkish oppressors engaged the sympathies of the American people, and of the Christian world, our citizens, following the example set before them in other and more important places, moved with earnestness to make contribution for their relief. It was informally agreed that ten persons of considerable wealth and generosity each of whom was pledged to give fifty dollars, should constitute a committee, and that they should be appointed by the chair. A chairman entrusted with the secret was chosen without difficulty. After many eloquent speeches . . . it was moved that the chair appoint a committee. Opposition arose immediately. . . . It was quite apparent that the great object of the movement was in jeopardy and yet no one seemed to be able to satisfy the people that they could safely renounce the power [to name the committee]. In this dilemma, I appealed to Dr. Richards. . . . "Mr. Chairman," said he, "I should agree with the speakers who claim that this committee ought to be appointed by the meeting, that is by every body, if every body knew every body, and everybody was wise. But we all know that every body here does not know every body, and some of us feel that, as to ourselves, we are not as wise as you are, and therefore we who are of that class think it best that you should exercise that power." The effect was complete.[37]

Everyone agreed that he was interesting and often eloquent, but the eloquence derived from his sincerity rather than his literary attainments.[38] And this was undoubtedly another explanation for the hold he had on his students. "I have often seen him, Abraham-like, pleading with God in earnest but reverential tones."[39] A student who travelled with him, shared his room, and thus witnessed his private devotions, reported that "such reverential approaches to God, and such tender expostulations as of a friend conversing with a friend face to face it had never been his privilege to witness."[40]

When the students' course at the seminary was over, Richards was adamant that they leave without debts.[41] He not only spent days on the road during his first years at the seminary raising money, but later was prepared to take a cut in salary for their sake. His wife also took a lively interest in the seminarians. She sent "saucer pies" that she had baked on Saturday to the ones who were cooking for themselves to make their money go further. She stored their clothes in her attic during the summer months, attended to their bedding, and met with other women to mend their clothes.[42] She knew them well. She mothered them and was loved by them. Such devotion went far to persuade the seminarians they were launched on the right track, engaged in worthwhile work with professors who commanded their respect and in whose footsteps they hoped to tread.

Another sign of Richards's sensitivity to the needs of his students during these years was his support for a "house of exercise," a workshop, and a garden.[43] They were provided so that Auburn students could avoid what was presumed to be the short sickly life of the scholar. These additions to the physical plant had a special appeal to a generation but one removed from the vigorous outdoor life of rural America. Young Henry, writing home from Princeton or later from law school in Litchfield, always assumed his father's approval of time spent with dumbbells, on horseback, or in walking. Proper exercise also figured in Richards's discussion of his own health and was part of his regular advice to his other children. It was not lost on him that attention to exercise served as a counterargument to Oneida's farm school.

Against this kind of solidity and piety, Lansing might well appear a lightweight. Certainly his local reputation was not enhanced in these years by his support of the Sabbatarian movement. This crusade was intended to promote a greater respect for the Sabbath by promoting an alternate stage-coach, the Seventh Day Line, that would not run on Sundays. It came up against stiff opposition; businessmen gathered in Auburn to boycott the religious congregations who supported the idea. Despite the division he was causing, Lansing represented his church at the national convention of the Society to Promote the Religious Observance of the Sabbath when it met in New York. This led to such division in the local church, that a Second Presbyterian Church was founded in Auburn that was made up of Lansing opponents.[44] Worn down by opposition to his enthusiasms in both the town of Auburn and the seminary, he removed himself to Utica in 1829 to be closer to the center of Finneyism.[45]

The departure of Lansing marked the end of the second round of James Richards's efforts to maintain Auburn Seminary in the face of competition from the New Measures men. First there had been the frontal attack associated with Finney's revival in Auburn and then there had been the competition with Oneida to be reckoned with. Although he had succeeded again, the struggle was not over yet. The timing of Finney's and Lansing's change of focus, however, was fortunate. Finney went east and Lansing went to Utica just as Richards suffered a bout of ill health and was in no position to devote his usual energy to the fight. In the winter of 1827–28 he had a kind of jaundice, from which it was not clear that he would recover. It was difficult for him to teach, much less travel to raise money. The following spring he was severely injured by his horse which started suddenly while he was harnessing it. He was thrown to the ground and trampled. And then as he was recovering from this accident he developed a cancer in his nose that had to be removed, leaving a considerable scar. Since he was by far the best-known teacher at the seminary, his two years of illness led to a decline in the number of students who matriculated.[46] Hamilton's difficulties and the competition both from Oneida and the newly founded Yale Seminary all played their role. James Richards recovered his health none too soon. It was time to face Finney's final assault on Auburn. This time it took the form of an effort to recast Auburn from within.

In 1830 Finney was back in western New York headed toward Rochester, which was to be the scene of his greatest success. In this third round both Oneida Institute, under Gale, and Auburn, under Richards, were in difficult financial straits. Hamilton, too, was struggling for funds in competition with Oneida. The board of Auburn had raised the salaries of the other two Auburn faculty members to $1,000 each in the fall of 1829, perhaps foolishly since by 1830 they were facing a debt of $10,000 and ideally should have been adding another professor to replace Lansing. Richards agreed to a cut in salary of $190 and the others agreed to forego $200 a year on condition that the board of trustees raise $12,000 within one year.[47] This task fell to Richards who set to work at once.

Meanwhile Gale had developed a debt of $5,000 at Oneida and was appealing to Finney and his former student Weld for help in raising funds. He too wished to add a professor of theology so that Oneida could develop a creditable course of instruction for the ministry. He was trying to persuade Finney's longtime supporter and partner, the Reverend Beman, to leave Troy and join him at Oneida. Beman was a distinguished choice; he was elected moderator of the General Assembly later that year in 1831.[48]

To further complicate the rivalry, Perrine at Auburn had for some time been a convert to Finneyism. Both Richards and Perrine came from the same area in New Jersey, and they had often acted together in the past. Perrine had been Richards's confidant in his troubles with Griffin, and Richards had defended him against charges of heresy when Perrine was pastor of the Spring Street Church in New York City. It was Perrine who had been delegated by the seminary to act as go-between when the trustees were trying to persuade Richards to accept a professorship. Despite the warmth of their friendship, Perrine was a Lansing supporter at the time of Lansing's resignation and then developed into an enthusiast of the New Measures. Ever since Lansing had vacated his pastorate at Auburn's First Presbyterian Church, Perrine had been trying to persuade Beman to leave Troy and fill the vacancy.[49] When this did not materialize, he immediately set to work again and this time succeeded in bringing Josiah Hopkins of Vermont to Auburn's First Presbyterian Church.[50] Together they plotted to force Richards into accepting a shortened course of a year and a half for the students at the seminary, and to place Beman on the Auburn faculty.[51]

It seems remarkable that the seminary could function in the face of such an undisguised fight for its soul.

Once again Davis and Richards cooperated by sharing information and strategies. This came at the time when Richards was beginning to depend on Davis for an understanding of his youngest son. He wrote Davis in January 1831:

> I rejoice to learn that college is filling up and that public confidence is returning. But must not something be done soon in the way of raising funds? If you spend your last shilling or very near it before you appeal to the public will there not be danger of making a crash?
>
> Some are looking forward to the time when your funds will be expended and the college dissolved. And when our Oneida friends will be strong enough to take the premises and carry all in their own way. Without any hostility to them, I can say I should be sorry for such a result. But they are very active and somewhat successful. It was mentioned to me on Saturday, that their agent had recently obtained seven thousand dollars in Rochester and expected to make it ten thousand. If other parts of the country should take up the subject with corresponding zeal, they will soon have the means of accomplishing something.
>
> A short road to learning seems to be the object at which they aim and a road too in which the traveller shall be furnished with the ability of paying his own expenses. The last is a very popular thing, but has more sound than substance. . . . It will make but eighteen dollars difference in a year between Auburn and the Oneida Institute, in the supposition that no labour was performed by our young men. But labour is performed and in some cases to the amount of ten or fifteen dollars a year. . . .[52]

A few months later Richards again wrote Davis, this time because he heard that a revival might be starting in Hamilton.

> I hear that the Lord is proving out his spirit in some measure upon the college. I greatly rejoice at this intelligence and hope that the work may become extensive and powerful . . . I cannot doubt that the officers of the college will feel their amazing responsibility at this time, and by prayer and counsel do all in their power for salvation of the dear youth committed to their charge. Would it not be life from the dead to this

important institution should the Holy spirit descend upon it in his convincing and life-giving power. . . .[53]

Closer to home a revival led by Hopkins was already underway. All the letters Hopkins, Perrine, and others had written to Finney over the the past four months begging him to come to Auburn finally bore fruit.[54] The great man arrived and the revival quickened, thundering to a climax in late April. On May 1 alone, one hundred and fifteen converts were received into Hopkins's flock.[55] Hopkins was jubilant. The Beman appointment and the control of the seminary that came with it seemed within his grasp.

It was not to be. Hopkins was undone by the internal politics of the New Measures men and the foresight of James Richards. Gale and Weld at Oneida Institute, angry at being betrayed once again by Finney's lack of effort on their behalf, insisted that he stop Auburn's attempt to steal Beman from them.[56] Finney for once seems to have taken an interest in an administrative problem and concurred.[57] James Richards had been waiting stolidly in the wings, maintaining a diplomatic silence but preparing to present an alternative candidate in the form of the Reverend

A revival at Union College. (Taken from James H. Smylie, American Presbyterians: A Pictorial History, *Presbyterian Historical Society, Philadelphia, 1985)*

Gardner Spring of the Brick Church, New York City. Although Beman was nominated for the professorship in late April, Richards's stalking horse, Gardner Spring, was elected by a nearly unanimous vote.[58] Finney had already departed.

By December Richards had raised the daunting sum of $12,000 on which all the professors' salaries depended. He could write to his old friend Henry Davis:

> I have never been more pressed in Spirit with any earthly concern than with this 12,000 business. I dreaded above all things a failure—as the consequences in many respects would have been exceedingly disastrous.[59]

The crisis had passed and Auburn Seminary was safe. Although he did not know it in 1831, Oneida's days were numbered, and Hamilton's star was in the ascendant. He wrote a rather optimistic though cautious note to Davis in October 1832.

> The seminary opens this year with better prospects. . . . We have received 25 already and more are expected to join us soon. The newcomers as a body appear to be able young men of considerable promise and well prepared to commence a course of theological study.[60]

James Richards described the manner of the final settling of Beman's relationship with Auburn in a letter to Davis one month later. Apparently there had been another effort to woo Beman to Auburn and it had provoked a bitter fight.

> Your conjecture in relation to Dr. Beman has proved to be well founded; he has declined the call from our seminary. . . . The ground upon which he put it was, *the want of unanimity in the call, and the unwillingness of his people that the pastoral relation between him and them should be dissolved.*
>
> But word came . . . that one principal reason why his people would not consent to part with him was that I had remained silent during the whole business, while Dr. Perrine, Mr. Hopkins and others had forwarded letters expressive of their approbation of the appointment and urging his acceptance.
>
> Mr. Spencer of Auburn who had previously procured a favourable petition from the students to Mr. Beman, called up to their rooms on

Saturday to sympathize with them in their disappointment, and to state the important and distressing fact of my obstinate silence, and to suggest, as I understood, that something should be done by the students in the case. . . . And to give the more effect to his suggestions he very kindly added that I had always opposed the appointment of a man of talents, whenever it had been proposed by the board. Nor is it unlikely that he would put my opposition to Dr. Lansing's coming into the seminary as a permanent and active officer upon the same footing. But perhaps I ought not to be surprised at this, when I recollect the perversity of our poor fallen nature and how apt we are to judge others by ourselves.

He went on to explain how he had dealt with several inquiries from students who had sought explanations for his silence. In contrast to the tone of what he had just written to Davis he presented a bland and mild face to the students. He claimed that he simply did not feel free to speak in the face of a divided board of trustees and commissioners.

I ought perhaps to say before concluding my letter that there is no decided personal opposition to Dr. Beman here, except some, from the fact that he is regarded as a new measure man, would prefer a different candidate. The great reason why the Board was not unanimous in their choice was the time and circumstances in which it was made. It was believed to be unfavourable.[61]

Why was Richards playing down the great controversies of the last six years when they were so well known? He seemed to be reestablishing the outward semblance of an orderly world. The effect of his attitude was to say there is no need for misunderstanding. Some small-minded people are trying to cause divisions among us, but I am above this pettiness and mischief. This half truth may have helped heal the wounds at Auburn and allowed people to work together again more easily, but the underlying rift remained in the Presbyterian Church. Richards had stood with the conservative, hierarchical, intellectual camp, and the New Measures men were more democratic, more trusting of man's abilities, and more pragmatic in their practice. Their differences extended to both style and substance and could not be easily papered over.

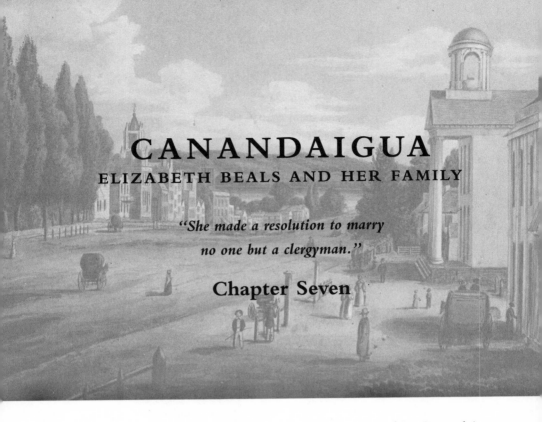

CANANDAIGUA
ELIZABETH BEALS AND HER FAMILY

*"She made a resolution to marry
no one but a clergyman."*

Chapter Seven

I n the fall of 1833 young James Richards appeared in Canandaigua
to study law with Judge Henry W. Taylor. It was to be a short-lived
legal career. In a matter of months he had found a new direction
for his life and returned to Auburn as a student at the seminary.
His family always attributed this abrupt change of direction to the
influence of Elizabeth Beals, an attractive, grave young woman of
whom it was said that "she made a resolution to marry no one but a
clergyman."[1]

There were already a few connections between the Richards and Beals
families. Dr. Richards took part in the first revival in Canandaigua in 1826
when Elizabeth, aged twelve, joined the church. This was the revival he
reported on so favorably to his wife, commenting that "a considerable
number of young persons of both sexes and of the first families are subjects
of the work"[2] (see chapter 6). Richards undoubtedly met Elizabeth's
father, Thomas Beals, on his fund-raising tours as well. They probably soon
discovered that Henry Dwight of Geneva was a mutual friend. However,
in a small village like Canandaigua it did not require any previous connection for Elizabeth and James to meet. Their paths inevitably crossed at
church and in social gatherings.

First Congregational Church,
Canandaigua. (Courtesy—
Canandaigua Historical Society)

Elizabeth Beals was the fourth child of Thomas Beals and Abigail Field, both of whom had arrived in Canandaigua when it was still at the frontier stage. Thomas Beals was born in Boston in 1783. He was descended from Puritans who founded Hingham, Massachusetts, in 1638, and was intensely proud of his Boston heritage. Coming from a bustling urban center set him apart from the other early settlers in western New York, who typically came from the western regions of New England. His father, Samuel Beals, was a prosperous tailor who had dealings with merchants as far away as the West Indies and Charleston, South Carolina.[3] When Samuel died in 1799, he left his wife Rebecca with nine children ranging from the baby Isaac, aged four, up to Samuel, aged twenty. Thomas, the fourth child, was seventeen. Rebecca quickly remarried Richards Jones, coppersmith, and the new family including Thomas left for the West. While the rest of the family moved on to Buffalo, Thomas and his brother John Wilkerson Beals stopped short of the final destination in Canandaigua, arriving in 1803 when he was twenty.[4]

Even though he was not among the first settlers, Thomas Beals came to Canandaigua early enough to be considered a founding father in later years. When Beals was still a youngster in 1788, Nathaniel Phelps of Connecticut and Oliver Gorham of Massachusetts opened up land for settlement between Geneva and Lake Erie.[5] With extraordinary rapidity they gathered investors, extinguished Indian titles, cut a road, and sent agents to open the first land office in the United States that surveyed and sold land. Subsequent financial difficulties and new surveys caused Phelps and Gorham to lose title to some of their holdings, but Canandaigua soon prospered as a boom town with two long rows of log cabins set at wide intervals on Main Street. Local merchants supplied fur traders, land speculators, and settlers pushing farther west. With its idyllic location at the foot of Lake Canandaigua, it quickly became a regional market town, a cultural center, and the county seat. Phelps himself and Gorham's son, Nathaniel Gorham II, settled there. The founders laid out a wide main street with a public square in the center and deeded 6,000 acres for the support of a school. Within the first few years settlers established a courthouse, the Canandaigua Academy, a church, and two newspapers. The log cabins gave way to handsome frame houses set on broad lawns. Census returns showed the population that stood at 103 in 1790 had risen to 1,153 by 1810.

The excitement surrounding the War of 1812 swept Canandaigua when Buffalo was razed and refugees flooded the village. Thomas Beals, already a resident for nine years, was active in organizing the defense that fortunately was never needed. When the Erie Canal went through and Rochester began to gain prominence to the north as the premier American flour milling city, Canandaigua experienced the change as a mixed blessing. It meant Canandaigua would be denied the wealth that comes with large-scale industrial and commercial activity, but at the same time it would be spared the accompanying ugliness, disorder, and poverty. By 1830 Canandaigua was a village of about 5,000. A number of wealthy people besides the Gorhams made their homes there. The most prominent was Francis Granger, who had been postmaster general under Presidents Jefferson and Madison. In both its physical appearance and lay leadership, the town bore a striking resemblance to the Newark Dr. Richards had known twenty years earlier.

Thomas Beals had arrived in the midst of all this hopeful activity to become a teacher in Canandaigua Academy. In a short time he started a dry goods store, where he did well as a commission agent who dealt also in lead, seed, oil, and hardware. Before long he was investing his profits in land bought for speculation and doing very well indeed. In many ways he epitomized the character traits needed for personal and community success in those early years. Cheerful, optimistic, decisive, and willing to take risks, yet sober, hardworking and disciplined, a great reader and collector of books, he was a model New England Yankee businessman thriving on New York soil. Like the serious laymen James Richards encountered in Newark, he put the "voluntary principle" to work and lent his energies to endless civic endeavors. However, unlike Richards, whose true home was the Presbyterian Church, he was the kind of community builder who spent his whole adult life in one place. By the time he died he had established a bank; built substantial parts of the business district including the hotel; subscribed generously to railroads and works of public utility; provided stewardship as a trustee of the Canandaigua Academy, the Ontario Female Seminary, and the Congregational Church; served as treasurer of his church, the village, the county, and the Agricultural Society; superintended the erection of the Congregational Church, the county jail, and the almshouse; and for several years supervised the poor of Ontario County. He had a generous open nature that found it natural to love his family and his fellow man, and rewarding to play his part in the world. At the end of his life his favorite citation from Job, "I shall die in my nest," summed up his satisfaction with the life he had chosen for himself.[6]

Abigail Field arrived in Canandaigua three years before Thomas Beals in 1800 at the age of sixteen. Then known by the nickname Nabbie, she

On left, Abigail Beals. (Taken from Caroline Cowles Richards, Diary 1852–1872, *copyright 1908) On right, Thomas Beals. (Taken from John Morgan Richards,* With John Bull and Jonathan, *D. Appleton, New York, 1906)*

came with her brother Timothy and her sister-in-law to help with their young family when he was called as the first pastor of the newly organized Congregational Church. Small, attractive, and very pious, in later years she was proud to recall that she had come all the way from Connecticut riding postillion behind her brother.[7]

Like Richards, Timothy Field and his brother David Dudley Field both prepared for the ministry under Timothy Dwight. The great Yale educator had roamed the New York and New England hinterland on horseback some years before in an effort to recover his health and as a result took an active interest in promoting missionary activity on the frontier. Dwight encouraged both brothers to look to the New York frontier and recommended Timothy to Canandaigua. The Fields were descended from old Puritan stock. Their mother's family, the Dudleys, had provided Connecticut with two governors. Before entering Yale, Timothy had studied with the Reverend Dr. John Eliot, the famous missionary to the Indians, and had delivered a much admired oration at his graduation in 1797.[8] The fact that Canandaigua could draw such a promising young

Main Street, Canandaigua, circa 1830. (Watercolor by Agnes Jeffrey, 1806–1896. Courtesy—Collections of the Ontario County Historical Society)

minister demonstrates the importance that Dwight and the Congregationalists attached to evangelizing upstate New York.

Abigail Field married Thomas Beals in 1805, and in the same year her
brother left his pastorate in Canandaigua. Fortunately the young Bealses,
far from other family members except for one brother for the rest of their
lives, were launched on a happy marriage that lasted for sixty years. Within
a year the first of their eleven children, Ann, was born. She was followed
by Mary, Lucilla, and Elizabeth, then two boys, Henry and Gorham, two
more girls, Magdalena and Glorianna, and finally Thomas, born in 1828
when his mother was forty-four. Two other children died in infancy.

By the time James Richards came to Canandaigua to study law under
Judge Taylor, Elizabeth Beals was nineteen. All her older sisters were
married. Ann had married her first cousin, Alfred Bishop Field, the oldest
son of Timothy Field. They lived nearby in Avon, a local spa, where he was
a merchant. Mary had married Edson Carr, whose family originally came
from Rhode Island; he practiced medicine in Canandaigua. The year
before, Lucilla had married an attorney, Asher Brown Bates, son of an early
Canandaigua family, and, repeating the pattern of western migration, they
lived with their new baby in Detroit. Elizabeth's younger brother, Henry
Channing, aged sixteen and named after the pastor of the Congregational
Church, was already in New York City clerking for a Mr. Sage who was in
the Rochester flour business. There were still four children at home besides
herself. Gorham, aged fifteen and named for his father's friend and business
associate, was working at least part time. There were also Magdalena, nine,
Glorianna, seven, and the baby Thomas, who was only five.[9]

Elizabeth grew up in a household in which family worship and Bible
reading were central to the daily round. After her conversion, she became
even more devout. Just as her older sister Ann had been sent away to the
Emma Willard School in Troy, so she had been sent to the Female Boarding
School in East Bloomfield. There, aged eleven, she had won a prize of four
leatherbound books called *Irving's Catechisms on Ancient Greeks and Romans*
for leading the school in reading at a public examination similar to the one
that Anna took her daughter to in Newark. Later she had studied at the
Ontario Female Seminary under Miss Hannah Upham, a noted woman
educator, and had graduated the previous year.[10] She filled her days by
helping her mother with the household, visiting her married sisters,
reading, sewing, visiting with friends, and doing church work.

Beehive emblem from Thomas Beals's "Beehive Bank," Canandaigua. (Courtesy— Collections of the Ontario County Historical Society)

A letter to her sister Ann Field, who was setting up housekeeping in Avon, painted a picture of her life in the spring of the year in which she met James Richards. Her letter was full of the local gossip and family news. Their father was in his prime and was building a fine new house on Main Street that the Bealses were about to move into. The year before he had become the treasurer and guiding light of the Ontario Savings Bank, the third bank to be established in Canandaigua.[11] Later he established his own private bank, the Beals Bank, which became known colloquially after its emblem as the Beehive Bank. Although he had been active in many endeavors, from the time of his association with the Ontario Bank he would be identified as a banker.

Canandaigua April 18, 1833

My dear sister,

Your kind letter was yesterday received and altho I am very much engaged about these times, I hasten to reply to it. I had been wondering for more that a week why you did not write, but concluded you were all in confusion and had no time to think of home. We have been quite as busy taking up carpets and packing furniture as you have been in putting down carpets and unpacking. We have all our carpets up and rooms cleared except the front room which will not be disturbed until next Monday when we expect a man to whitewash. I have packed up most of the books and crockery we have in the house. I rather think Papa and Mama will board out until our new house is finished, and scatter the children among the sisters. Our new house comes on finely. The brick is laid almost to the top of the windows of the first story. The chamber windows will be in by Saturday.

Papa has concluded to let me go to Detroit. [to visit their sister Lucilla and brother-in-law Asher Bates] Joe Cole has gone to New England to be married; he will return about the first of May, and I expect to go with them. George Bates is going at the same time.

I shall be very glad to go to Avon, when Mr. Field comes out; that was the arrangement I had made, as I have some sewing to do which I cannot do at home, and what is more, I want to see how you succeed in housekeeping. I went down to Mary's [their sister] this morning where I found Hannah (the black girl which used to live there) washing. I asked her if she would like to live with you. She said yes, and could go immediately if you wanted her. It is quite impossible to get a white girl. . . . We succeeded in finding a girl for ourselves, but she is not such a one as we want. If you would succeed to get Hannah, you had better send me word this week when she shall come and how she shall get there. Mama thinks when you get a good girl, and get rid of your old woman, you will think differently about the curtain.

The recurrent references to problems with servants in this period reflected not only the aversion Americans had to filling this role, but the word's associations with slavery. Mrs. Trollope wrote in her account of her American visit that no matter how much to her advantage being a servant was, a young woman would only consider herself to be a "help" and that but temporarily.

Mary says Mrs. Thompson told her she would like to go to Avon for benefit of her health; if you would allow her to stay with you and pay her board by sewing, she would expect to walk to the springs and not make you any trouble in that way.

I would like to fill this sheet, but I have got to prepare for a wedding which is to take place this evening. You'll wonder who is going to be

married—it is Alfred Bates. George informed me very secretly of the fact
a week since, and at his mother's request, invited me to be bridesmaid,
and stand up with him. Alfred is going to marry the young lady whom
most every one here supposed to be engaged to Jonas Brewster. She is a
daughter of Col. Johnson, lives about four miles from town. I went to see
her on Monday with a whole load of Bates. She is a very pretty girl, quite
young and rather genteel. Alfred will do much better than I ever
supposed he would.

The arrangements for this marriage were reminiscent of the arrangements for Henry Richards's wedding. The ceremony was accomplished
with remarkable dispatch and little preparation or fanfare despite the
seriousness of the commitment.

As to the emptings[12] Mama says the old way is altogether the safest and
most likely to make good bread. She thinks you had better not try any
experiments. Mrs. Hubbell sent me a bundle of tracts for you which I
will bring. She is a little better. Sally Lyman has gone to Buffalo and Miss
Partridge to Rochester.
    Love to Mr. Field, and anyone who inquired for me. The children are
well, who with Mama and Papa would desire an affectionate remembrance.
                                                      Yours truly
                                                      Elizabeth.
    If you expose this letter, you only expose my reputation for letter
writing. . . .[13]

In the fall Elizabeth was again writing Ann and describing her usual
routines.

                                          Canandaigua, Oct. 27, 1833
My dear sister,
    Ever since Mary [their sister] returned from Avon I have been
expecting a line from you; but mail after mail has arrived and brought us
no letter, and now at Mamma's request I intend to tell you something
about affairs at home. In the first place, our family is so small that a feeling
of loneliness comes over us, as we sit around the table, and remember
how great is the contrast between the past and the present. 'Tis true we

often seat a friend at our pleasant fireside, but there is always room
enough for the absent. Mamma says she is afraid Thomas and Magdalena
are staying so long, you will be made twice glad; indeed, your cares must
be very numerous with four such children to take care of. It was Papa's
intention to have gone to Avon for them this week, but he has had so
much business to do, that it was quite impossible; perhaps he will go on
Monday or Tuesday; if so I may go out with him and spend a few days. I
want to see you very much, and I have been waiting this two months for
a convenient season; and lest it should never come, I think I will improve
the next opportunity. . . .

Something of a sentimental homebody, she commented on her sister
Lucilla's wedding anniversary and then reported on the affairs of some of
Ann's hometown acquaintances.

I suppose you thought of Lucilla on Wednesday; it was the anniversary of her wedding day and the weather was exactly the same; it was
gloomy for a week before and that morning the sun came out bright and
beautiful. Lucilla has not written me one word since I left her. I have had
two hasty letters from Mr. Bates. Susan Baxter has gone up to Detroit,
thinking that her profession will flourish better in a new country. I
prophesy that she will come home in a year disappointed. Tom Howell
has got home; he saw Lucilla, and says she never looked better. He was
quite pleased with Chicago, but probably will not go West to reside until
spring.

They are as badly off as we are at Judge Howell's: they have only two
children at home. _____ [omitted][14] has been making entertainments
for her friends the week past; a week ago Mamma and Papa received a
very formal invitation to visit her on Monday evening. It was rather a
singular arrangement, giving her friends such a long time to prepare to
go. I heard Alex. Howell said "it distracted his thought so much, that the
sermons on the Sabbath did him no good."

Monday evening I went to hear the "Tyrolese Minstrels" sing. I
never listened to finer music. I think you would have enjoyed it very
much, but I suppose you have become so much devoted to your
husband and household duties, that your relish for such diversions is
all gone.

Mr. Eddy [the minister in Canandaigua] left us last week to go to New York. Mr. Hubbell is better, though not yet able to discharge deacon's duties. We need a minister very much. Mr. Clarke has read a sermon two Wednesday evenings, to the very few who still go to the Lecture Room. I hope religious feeling will no longer remain at such a low ebb among us.

Mamma and Glorianna desire a kind remembrance to your husband, yourself, and Tom and Mag. Dr. Carr and Mary are quite well. Albert Lester has recently been appointed post-master. Allen Royce has bought out Mr. Hall, and become sole editor and proprietor of the Phoenix. In haste, with much affection,

> I am, as ever your sister,
> Elizabeth[15]

A week after her return from the visit to Avon that was planned in this letter, she was again writing with news of other members of the family. Canandaigua may have been on the frontier thirty years earlier, but by now the residents were attending tea parties, and giving and receiving dinner invitations. Elizabeth's comments on a week's notice for a dinner invitation in the previous letter and her comment about her mother's usual refusal of invitations in this one hark back to an earlier standard of proper behavior.

Canandaigua, Nov. 16, 1833

My dear sister,

It is just a week since I left you. We had a tolerably pleasant ride. L. was not very animated, and I, of course, had most of the talking to do. There were two very severe showers before I got home, but we were entirely protected from the rain, and did not stop. We got home a little after five o'clock. I found that Papa had just put a letter for me into the [post] office, requesting me to come home on Monday. Mother was a little surprised at my staying, but she had not the least objection to make when I told her how much I enjoyed the visit.

Tuesday, we had a long letter from Lucilla; it was purely accidental, her writing. She said she had a dozen pieces of work before her which ought to be done, but her baby was asleep, and she had mislaid her thimble, and, that the time be not misspent, she concluded to write. She seemed in fine spirits. The letters were mostly filled with local matters, which would not interest you. She wished to be remembered to Mr. F.[ield] and yourself.

Monday, Papa had a letter from Henry [her brother]; among other things, he wanted three new shirts. I went down street immediately and bought some cloth, and Mamma and I went to work, and the last stitch in the second is now being taken, and one of them is on the way to New York.

I don't think there is much probability of my being idle this winter. Thursday there was an annual meeting of the Bible Society held in this village. Mr. and Mrs. Dwight, of Geneva [the same Dwights who were good friends of Dr. and Mrs. Richards], came over to attend it, and stopped at our house. They sent word the day before that they were coming. In the a.m. we went to church and heard quite animated addresses. Mamma stayed at home, and prepared, with the assistance of her girl, a very excellent dinner. After having dinner, the gentlemen returned to the church to transact the business of the County Temperance Society. Mrs. Dwight and myself called to see Mrs. Taylor [wife of Judge Henry Taylor] and Mrs. Eddy. Mrs. Greig and Miss Betsy Chapin called and invited all of us up to Mr. Greig's to tea. . . . Mamma, as usual, declined the invitation; I went with Mrs. Dwight, and enjoyed the visit very much. . . .[16]

Elizabeth's next letter suggests broader intellectual interests were making their way in the village with the introduction of French lessons.

Canandaigua, Dec. 5, 1833

My dear sister,

It is with great pleasure I acknowledge the reception of your letter. I have been very much engaged since I left you; we have had a dressmaker for two or three days. It was my intention to have done some sewing for you before this time, but it has been quite impossible. I hear Mr. Taylor expects to go to New York soon on account of his eyes; sore eyes are very prevalent here. . . . Mr. Wood saw Henry in New York; they met in the street. He said Henry spoke first and he did not recognize him for some time. . . .

> Dr. Carr and Mary are taking French lessons. You will think Mary is undertaking too much; but the truth is, Mr. Burgoyne would not take the class unless they could insure him six scholars. They could not make the number without Mary; she seems quite pleased with the study, and Mr. B. pronounces her the best scholar. They meet at Dr. Carr's two or three evenings every week. It would be a fine opportunity for me to learn, but I have no time to attend to literary pursuits.

She next wrote about her younger brother Gorham who was following a business path for the moment. Like Henry Beals and Edward Richards, he began by an apprenticeship in his hometown and then expected to move on to New York City.

> Gorham is out of business again. Mr. Hayes has closed his lower shop, and does not require his services any longer. Papa finds sufficient employment for him for the present; he is in hopes to procure him a situation in New York.

This was Elizabeth Beals when James met her, a young woman recently out of school, busy with a wide circle of family and friends. The handsome, if somewhat scarred, new law student was introduced to her at Judge Taylor's and fell quickly in love. It happened so fast that within three months of entering into his clerkship he gave it up and returned to Auburn Seminary, willing to be away from her because it was the way to her heart.

At the end of her letter to Ann, Elizabeth sidled into the topic that was already making the family rounds.

> You inquire about my Auburn friend. He was quite well last Monday, and making great progress in Hebrew. . . . Mrs. Dwight talked a great deal about Mr. Richards when she was here—she speaks very highly of him; thinks he has inherited his father's talents. I do not think Mrs. Dwight had any idea that I felt peculiarly interested in him; she commenced the conversation accidentally.[17]

The romance progressed rapidly. Only three weeks later she wrote Ann again.

Canandaigua, Dec. 24, 1833

My dear sister

I heard today from Mr. Richards. He does not intend to come to Canandaigua until the 23rd of next month; it was his intention to have been here long before that time, but a meeting of the Presbytery with which he is to unite, and some other things, render it necessary for him to postpone his visit. He often alludes to his visit at Avon; and if it should be good sleighing and other things are propitious, you need not be surprised to see me in about four weeks, with *my minister* as you call him.[18]

This letter written at the holiday season makes clear that the Puritan tradition that celebrated Thanksgiving but ignored Christmas was honored at the Bealses. The new year, however, provided the occasion for a lively social round.

I can say, as you did, we all thought of you Thanksgiving Day, and regretted that you could not be with us. We went to church in the morning and heard one of Mr. Eddy's best sermons. After church there was "a gathering of the tribes"—Dr. Carr and Mary, Thomas and Dr. Morse, with Susan and William Hosmer, together with our family, made out quite a table full. We had a good dinner, and a pleasant visit. . . . Mrs. Duncan gave a very large party on that evening; her guests were invited to assemble at six o'clock; and as ours did not disperse until after that time, I thought best to decline her invitation.

We had a letter from Henry a few days ago; he has postponed his visit until February. His detention is unavoidable, as Mr. Sage [his employer] had made his arrangements to leave for the West the first of January, and they cannot both be absent at the same time. I am very sorry that we have been so often disappointed about seeing him; I am sometimes fearful that it will be a long time before we welcome him home.

We did not celebrate Christmas Day, not feeling in the mood of seeing company, and it was an exceedingly unpleasant day. Mary invited Mrs. and Miss Taylor and Anna Masters to pass the day with her. I saw Mary the next day, and she said she enjoyed the visit very much indeed.

I went up and passed yesterday afternoon with Sophia Johns. There are quite a number of visitors in town passing the holidays; I have not heard of there being any parties, but presume there will be.

As usual her letter included gossip along with family news. There is an edge to some of her comments that seems uncharitable, but a more generous interpretation is that she simply held conservative views of a woman's role, a posture that was admirably suited to her future role as a parson's wife.

As for Mary, she is pursuing her French with great diligence; I think it seems to have a salutary effect upon her, even if she never makes any practical use of it, which I consider very doubtful. It occupies her mind so constantly that she has no time to have the blues. I went down there a few afternoons since, and found her alone in the parlour, with the table covered with books, and she writing her French exercises; she looked quite like a student. I believe Mary used to love study very much; she says, however, she shall be very glad when the studying is at an end for she finds it very confining.

Last evening the Episcopal ladies had a fair at Blossom's [a local hotel]. I presume there was a great display; but as I have not been out today, neither have had any calls, I can give you no information respecting it. I spent an evening last week at Mrs. Taylor's (her husband has gone to New York for the benefit of his eyes), where I met Mr. and Mrs._____ and a few others. Mrs._____goes out a great deal; she is sometimes drawn in her waggon and sometimes rides in the cutter. She has been to Judge Howell's and Mr. Hubbel's repeatedly; she does not walk a step while in the house; she reclines on a sofa or sits in a rocking chair. Dr. Carr and Mr._____took her in their arms as they would a child, and carried her outdoors and laid her in the waggon. . . . How she can consent to such things is more than I can account for. Mamma says that if a wise Providence had so afflicted her that she could not go about as other people did, she would be resigned to her fate and stay at home. I presume this is the language of many hearts, but Mrs._____loves to go and see all that is to be seen.[19]

A letter to Ann the following spring suggests the effort family made to keep in touch despite the difficulty of travel and the distances that increasingly separated them. A visit from Detroit tended to be a long one.

Canandaigua, May 28, 1834

My dear sister,

Being quite at leisure this afternoon I feel constrained to inquire about the welfare of yourself and family. Mamma and I have thought and talked much about your affairs for a few days past. Mr. Bates and Lucilla arrived here [from Detroit] at five o'clock on Saturday. We were very glad to see them. On Monday I sent for some of Lucilla's most intimate friends, and Adele Granger and her cousins, and we had a very pleasant sociable visit. . . . Lucilla and Mr. Bates set out this morning to go and see his relatives. They were invited to dine at Mr. Whites', and they have now gone to Mr. David Bates' to make a sociable visit. Tomorrow all the Bates' family are to meet at Uncle Phineas'. I expect Lucilla will be very tired before her visit is done. I rather think Mr. B. will leave for New York on Friday. Lucilla seems so happy and contented at home, that I hope she will stay another month.

James was by now such a member of the family that he made the considerable effort of traveling eighty miles to see the Bateses.

Mr. Richards came over last Thursday and spent the evening, and left the next morning at four o'clock. It is only forty miles, and a very pleasant ride. . . .

We heard M____ preach on Sunday. He brought home a splendid piano for B. that cost 180 dollars. I expect the people will talk about the parson's extravagance, but probably he does not regard the opinions of men. . . . Dr. Carr has just purchased a new carpet for Mary. It is very pretty and they will soon have it down.

Do write to us very soon and let us know if the baby is well and more particularly about your own health. When Lucilla goes back to Detroit, I think I shall go to Avon and make you a little visit. . . . We all want to see your baby.

Your attached sister
Elizabeth[20]

No more correspondence survives from this period. Elizabeth and James became engaged with an understanding that they would be married when he finished his course of study at the seminary. He visited when he could, sometimes accompanying his father on his fund-raising trips to the Canandaigua area. On at least one occasion

> . . . James with my permission pushed directly on to Canandaigua, which he probably reached by eight o'clock in the evening. He promised to stop one hour on the road and let his horse rest.[21]

During his time at the seminary James established a considerable reputation for eloquence. He developed his natural gift for language and the commanding presence he inherited from his father into an impressive pulpit style and in addition distinguished himself in his courses.[22] Elizabeth was a strong influence on his growing seriousness and purposeful ambition, but he still took pleasure in charming and teasing the ladies, including the servants. He found time occasionally to accompany his parents on their regular visits to their daughters in Newark and New York City where he was a great favorite with his nieces, Caroline Amelia Beach and Caroline Dey. Fiercely competitive with each other, they accepted Elizabeth's place in his heart without question. After a visit in the fall of 1834 [date uncertain] Caroline Beach, now aged fifteen, wrote him with a wonderful flair for romantic self-dramatization, played out with tears, flirtatious asides, and unabashed adulation.

> *Dear, dear uncle,*
>
> As Mrs. Griffin leaves on Monday, I cannot refrain from writing a few lines to inform you how much we missed you and what an aching void you left in every bosom not very soon to be filled. After watching you until out of sight, I returned to the nursery where I gave full vent to my feelings, and found some relief in a flood of tears. As I do not approve of indulging in grief, I endeavoured to divert my mind by reading—but either owing to the dullness of the author, or my own stupidity, it had no effect and I found that even the great Rowland Hill could not gain my attention when my thoughts were constantly following my absent friends. I tried to analyze my feelings, and to ascertain if there was not

some other source to which I could impute my unhappiness, but I at last came to the conclusion that it was *pure affection and sorrow* mingled for the departure of those I *dearly love*.

I *know* that I possess a *warm heart*, although I may not have as happy a faculty of showing it as some others. I enjoyed your visit *very much* dear uncle, but still think that you might have directed your time *more equally*. I do not believe they love you *half as well* in New York [the Deys] *as we do*.

Old Mrs. Patterson called to see grandma in the afternoon and appeared very much disappointed to find she had gone. Mrs. Morris was in a few moments, but except these we were entirely alone the remainder of the evening. Father came upstairs and by way of consoling us, said "*Oh how gloomy*"!

I retired very early and *cried myself to sleep*.—but forgot all my troubles when encircled in the arms of *Morpheus*. I was much surprised when I awoke this morning to find that yesterday was only a *weather breaker* and also in sympathy with our feelings and to add to the dolefullness of the scene it was storming very fast. I have had a sick headache to day, a very unwelcome visitor, I assure you, not half as agreeable as *Uncle James*.

Mother was bled this morning, but has been to preparatory lecture notwithstanding—heard Mr. Seymour from Bloomfield; said he preached by illustration—it was not altogether what she expected. I believe Mrs. McClure had her babe baptized. Tell grandmother that mother comes on finely with her quilt, but will not be able to do anything until Monday in consequence of her arm. I heard today that they talked of building the 3rd Church parsonage on the hill at the head of William St.

I was perfectly astonished when mother told me that you took 6 of Nelson's pills yesterday. I presume you mean to try their virtue effectually this time dear uncle.

I took up my dictionary this morning, thinking to find upon the first page something to remind me of you, but imagine my surprise when on opening it, to discover that the spoiler's hand could not even let this remain unmolested but had divested it of all its greatness and only a small vestige of your handwriting remained. Now I cannot think who did this, unless it was your own "dear self"—no one else would dare to do such a thing and even you ought to be *severely reprimanded*. If you ever do so again my dear uncle, I shall have to complain to Miss Beals and see if she don't put you *in purgatory for a little while*.

Did Aunt Caroline send any thing? I am quite anxious to know.— Ann Evans has just brought me a hat to line for her and I must therefore draw this scrawl to a close—I shall make no apologies for this; as I detest them; therefore you must take this just as it is—good, bad, or indifferent. . . . Give a great deal of love to grandmother & grandfather (dear old people) and believe me to be as ever, your truly attached

and unworthy niece *Caroline Amelia*

P.S. Do write me a long letter as soon as you get home dear uncle and don't be so delighted to see *Aunt Elizabeth* that you will forget all about your other relations. Remember they have a claim upon you still. I hope we shall see more of you the next time you come down. I have not said half to you that I want to. Once more dear uncle Good night. I really envy Aunt C. this evening.

Your poor, foolish, but affectionate niece—C.A.B.

I am most afraid to write to you, there is such a contrast between my letters and those from the magnet at Canandaigua, but never mind—you will take this from where it comes.

Both Ellen and Ann [Beach servants] took a wonderful fancy to you. Ellen says she is going to live with Mr. James Richards when he gets married. She is to be his cook and Ann waiter so you see you are provided for as regards to servants but you must wait until we are done with them.

Did you meet the long expected letter on your arrival to the city, to welcome you? If so what was the nature of its contents? O how I wish that I was going to Auburn with you to spend the winter. I know that I should enjoy myself there.

In looking through the life of Rowland Hill, my eyes happened to light on this advice to a young minister. Thinking that perhaps you may turn it to account I will give you a short extract. It is seasoned with his peculiarities. "Better to feed the appetite of the hungry than to tickle the fancies of the whimsical. This breed of preachers are apt soon to preach themselves out of breath, & come to nothing. May you and I never be the retailers of such whipt syllabub divinity—better keep a cookshop to satisfy the craving appetite, than a confectioner's shop to regale the depraved appetite of the dainty—Good *brown bread* preaching is the best after all."

C.A.B.

I hope you will not fail dear uncle to remove those rags from the interior of the bag, before it goes to Canandaigua, lest perhaps the fair stranger might think they were designed for pocket handkerchiefs. Methinks I hear you say what a beautiful appearance this letter presents. Well you may for it is almost equal to one of yours.[23]

This letter was matched by an equally affectionate and jealous letter that winter from his fourteen-year-old niece Caroline Richards Dey. She began her letter with an apology for not answering his "two letters and 6 messages," a sure sign that he thrived on the girls' attention. She had a precocious interest in gossip about the seminarians. Her twenty-five-year-old half sister Kate and Kate's friend Mary Jackson of Philadelphia were unmarried and "on the lookout." Here is the seminary seen as a pool of eligible bachelors rather than a center of theological controversy.

. . . the information with regard to those in whom I am most interested namely the students was very acceptable especially the news of Frame's engagement as it gave me an opportunity of plaguing Mary. I am very sorry to hear that you have been ill and with regard to your health I think you ought to be particularly careful during the month of March. Mary has just been writing to mother and she says "the most interesting news in your last was the intended marriage of W. Frame to Miss Cadwell" and she "judges that it will be a very good match" having seen the young lady frequently and thinks that she is a very fine girl. However I guess M[ary] felt a little sort of twinge when she heard it. Mary talks a great deal about matrimony this winter and I do not think she would have many objections against entering into that state of (as those who know nothing about it say) supreme felicity. I hope you will suggest this to Friend Foot and send him down to the "city of Brotherly Love" to see whether he cannot excite passion in the breast of Miss Mary.

I wish you would send me a catalogue of the students and tell me how the world goes with Johnathan Cook. The description of your family arrangements amused me very much and I drew a similar picture in my last letter to sister M. [her half sister Maria married the Reverend Daniel C. Axtell of Auburn] I am so very selfish as to wish that instead of going to school all summer I should again visit you and Sister Kate should stay at home. I love Grandma, Grandpa, and you better than any three persons in the world (of course excepting my own family) and I shall always consider my visit to A[uburn] as one of the happiest periods of my life. I hope that you will make us a *long, long* visit this spring though I expect that Aunt A[nna] will keep you all the time. I am very jealous of C[aroline] A[melia] Beach and N[ew] J[ersey] Indeed I think that Aunt Anna's family is preferred by all of you much above ours.

Remember me to Miss B[eals]when you write to her again. You will have to adopt our baby [Josephine Elizabeth Dey] according to your promise when you come down. I expect it was on account of your promise that Father insisted so strongly on its being named E [lizabeth].

I am not in very good spirits this afternoon and do not feel at all like writing. I have not patience to correct any errors so you must excuse three of those which occur in every line. I should like to write a letter to Grandma but I have no time so I hope she will take the will for the deed. . . . I believe every one is well. If they are not I have not time to reccolect [*sic*] who are sick. Give all my love to Grandma, Grandpa, and believe

that I shall ever remain your affectionate niece
Caroline Dey

P.S. Write to me by the very next opportunity and tell all the news.

Tell every person who says any thing about me that I have not forgotten them and that I send my love to them in every letter. I expect Johnathan [Cook] talks as much about me as ever. Now I must go and practice so good bye.

P.P.S. Sister K. says that if all my friends take the will for the act when I send letters my letters come very cheap. Give my love to Sister M. Sister Kate sends her love to all not forgetting Abraham. What a fib. Sister Kate has cracked her jawbone laughing at my mistakes. . . .[24]

Caroline wrote another amusing letter in August of 1835 from "The Mountain of Health," probably a farming village a little way up the Hudson River, where she and the other young Dey children had been sent to get out of the hot city. They were under the supervision of her half sister Kate and her friend Mary Jackson.

My very dear uncle James,

We arrived here last Saturday and find it very pleasant though rather solitairie [*sic*]. The situation of the house is *beautiful*. It is on the side of a hill some distance from the road and surrounded by woods. On one side of the house is a beautifully romantic little brook overshadowed by trees where I should often sit and sentimentalize had I not heard that snakes were very abundant in this part of the country. Directly before the door is a little mound of dirt which is very convenient for the children who are in the daily habit of converting it into pies. A little further on is a puddle of stagnant water which our pets the pigs use as a bath. On the other side is a barn which is useful for a nursery for fleas. The house is very old and looks as if it were just going to fall in pieces. The inside however is very comfortable. The house door is without lock, bolt, or bar and the only way to shut at night is to put up a chair against it.

The family with whom we are boarding consists of three persons, an old servant woman and a father and his daughter named Lewis. Sister Kate and I occupy the parlor while Mary Jackson sleeps in the garret in which is also the nursery. The domestic animals are five cats, hundreds of rats, a number of pigs, chickens, 2 dogs and 5 or 6 fleas which have placed themselves under the protection of Mary Jackson.

We are very industrious and go through a certain round of employments every day, take a dose (dose indeed) of tansy (Mother thinks this is the grand elixir), breakfast at seven, walk from eight until—and sew until twelve which is our dinner hour, until six we read, sew, or walk. I have been out once for blackberries. So you see what a complete country girl I am becoming. In the evenings Mary Jackson and sister Kate usually sing the Hymn Books through. Our fare is excellent and we have once or twice carried the "villanous appetites" of eating and drinking to such an excess that we have been reduced to the vulgar necessity of loosening our belts after dinner.

We expect to remain here three weeks longer, Mary Jackson only one week and I hope that Caroline Beach will take her place. Mother and Father came to see us on Saturday and brought with them a great deal of news. She thinks of going to Saratoga this week. Cousin Henrietta has just returned from there very much delighted. Mother has only

seen uncle Ed once since his return. Aunt Anna has a cook at last!!!!
_____[torn] Frelinghuysen had a party last week and *Fred* is handsomer
than ever. Nothing has been heard from Uncle Henry since he went to
the West—is he dead or alive? Mother has taken a little nigger to bring
up.

Having dealt with family news, Caroline passed on to the romantic
gossip she thrived on; it was also of particular interest to Mary Jackson.
Granted Mary's natural interest in the social life of other young unmarried
people, it is a striking testimony to the interconnectedness of Presbyterian
society that she could inquire about a network of young men and women
that extended from Philadelphia through Newark, New York City,
Auburn, and Geneva, to Canandaigua.

I found by the last "Observer" that your commencement [the seminary commencement but not James's class] is to be next Teusday [*sic*].
I shall expect a full account of all the proceedings together with my
long promised catalogue of the students. Mary Jackson desires me to
tell you that she wished very frequently that we were at Auburn
again. She appears to be still very fond of Rice—one would judge so
from the quantities she devours daily at dinner. This important particular she wishes you to forward to Geneva. Mary Jackson desires me
to tell you that we—no I will not tell you either. Mary desired to
know when Frame is to be married—Has Uncle Ed asked Miss
Hagaman that long waited and wished for question? Mary Jackson
wishes you to answer this letter directly after commencement that she
may have the benefit of it too. . . . How is Miss "Orely" Bissel? Has
she been in Auburn since? Does Mr. Hugh escort her about as much
as he used to or rather does she escort him about. Mary wants to
know which of the Miss Somebody's of Geneva is married. Miss
Gordon she says it [is]. They were in Philadelphia to see her this
spring. How is Johnathan Cook? Compston and A. Mills give my love
to.

Caroline in her enthusiasm for matchmaking happily revelled in James's
love for Elizabeth.

A gentleman said that he had never met with a young lady that pleased him so much with so beautiful a face and whose manners were so innocent. I thought that this complement would please you better than one paid to yourself. I shall never forget my visit—delightful at Canandaigua and the hospitality I experienced there. Mary is very anxious to see Miss Beals, her praise is in every one's mouth, and her curiosity is so much excited that she thinks of going to the West on purpose to see her.

Write me all the news. We are very solitary. Days pass without our seeing a strange face and I think that you would show that your bump of benevolence[25] is very fully developed by answering me immediately. I had meant to write this letter to Grandma but I was afraid that I should never get an answer and that is what I am very anxious for. Do come down this fall. We are all very anxious to see you. Give my best love to Grandma, Grandpa, Miss Beals and her father and mother and everyone else that recollects me. I am tired of scribbling my dear uncle so good Bye.

Your very much attached niece
Caroline Richards Dey[26]

James was obviously fun-loving but he was also making the serious expectations of the Richards and Beals families his own. He completed his course of study at Auburn in 1836. Although not ordained until he had a parish of his own, he was now ready to marry. A few months before the commencement Thomas Beals wrote him a warm chatty letter that suggests a comfortable relationship with his future son-in-law.

Canandaigua 23 Apr. 1836

My dear Sir

Your letter of 21 Mch was recd. this morning at 7 o'clock. You remark that your father is gardening. I want to do so, but I do not get on as fast as usual.

I found my Barn was too near my house—in hot weather; at evening; we could perceive an influence—an odour—I have bought part of the Methodist lot, beyond my garden & paid $75 for the land, with a privilege to use their lane—I now get my horses and carriage off my lot,

and have all "tidy"—In doing this, I have disturbed my garden—pros-
trated my Raspberry Bushes. The fences are now rebuilt.

But my man Richard, who can see as far into a mill stone as the man
who packs it, did last year put a parcel of Raspberrys at the farther end
of my orchard—these he has now taken up and supplied the place of
those which have been crushed by moving the Barn, and I have now the
whole again dressed and plants set and it is done—I do not see as the
barn sustained any damage—Besides—the spot where the Barn stood, is
now in the garden, and we may expect some rare productions thereon. I
have Peas planted, but to day later than last year.

My cellary [sic] has lasted till now and I regret we could not make it
stay until you came—

We have abundance of apples, and I told Mr. P, this morning, he
might sell a few bushells. Gorham left this morning at 5 o'clock for
Geneva—horseback—get there at 8 o'clock, leave at 10 o'clock and get
home at 1 o'clock at dinner.

You see we have method in our small affairs.

I think I shall leave next week for Rochester and West—I am calculating on an appreciable excursion—good company—and shall leave all
business behind—

Gorham will be my only representative here, and I think he will be
able to steer—"somehow."

I was glad to hear from your father and mother and hope at no
distant period I may have the pleasure to salute them in their own house.

I meant to go to New York but think it doubtful, whether I can go
in May—

C. W. Bradbury, the bearer of this letter is going to Skeneatales and
will return on Monday next. If you were ready to come here, perhaps he
will give you a seat. Present my respects to your father and mother, and
future son to be.

Your friend
Thomas Beals
Mr. Bradbury may be found at the coach makers shop.[27]

The long awaited wedding took place at the Beals house on August 26,
a beautiful moonlit night.[28] The wooden partition between the dining

room and the parlor was raised out of sight on pulleys making one big room; here in the bosom of Elizabeth's family they were married by James's father with Harriet Martin and Elizabeth Taylor acting as bridesmaids, and fellow students at the seminary, Samuel Hopkins and J. Brayton, acting as groomsmen. It was later remembered that the elder Richards had said "God bless you, my dears; remember that love is as necessary after as before marriage."

The newlyweds made a wedding tour in a carriage drawn by a pair of white horses as far as Auburn, a distance of forty miles. The trip was broken at Geneva where Henry Dwight invited the entire bridal party to dinner. On their arrival in Auburn the students at the seminary serenaded them and went so far in their enthusiasm as to bring a piano out on the grounds under their window to accompany the singers. From this point James and Elizabeth continued on alone by stagecoach through New York State to Farmington, Connecticut, and then to New York City for a month-long wedding trip.

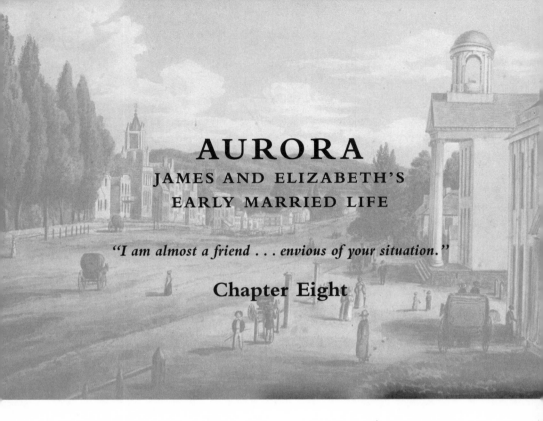

AURORA
JAMES AND ELIZABETH'S
EARLY MARRIED LIFE

"I am almost a friend . . . envious of your situation."

Chapter Eight

Elizabeth Beals and James Richards spent their honeymoon with James's family in New York City. Their transition from single to married state did not seem to require time off by themselves; rather, it was a gala time when everyone rejoiced with them in their obvious happiness.

Back in Canandaigua, however, the Bealses were feeling the loss of their daughter. Anxious to feel part of her new life, Thomas Beals wrote several times and pressed for news.

> Canandaigua 15 Sept. 1836
>
> Dear Children,
>
> I [looked] to you yesterday for mail and looked with confidence for a letter from you this morning. . . .
>
> We encourage the hope that we may have your company next month and you know "Charity begins at home." . . .
>
> I will only add that you are constantly in mind. . . .

He told her that he had received a letter from his sister, Lydia Jackson, soon to become the third wife of Lyman Beecher.[1]

On left, James Richards Jr. On right, Elizabeth Beals. (Both taken from John Morgan Richards, With John Bull and Jonathan, *D. Appleton, New York, 1906)*

She expressed a desire to see you and I have no doubt you would find it a pleasant place to visit. She lives at Cambridge in the mansion House of the late Chief Justice Dana; about a mile east of the college, on the Boston Road. . . .

When a letter finally came, Abigail added a note the next day full of motherly advice and reassurance to her daughter who was coping for the first time with her new role as wife.

My dear Elizabeth,

Long looked for has come at last . . . We are concerned first of all for your health, which it would seem was unfavourably affected by your visit to the seaboard. The kindness of your friends or rather of Mr. Richards' friends is certainly equal to any of your anticipations. I do not see how you could avoid the visit at "the Parsonage" in Newark [Anna Beach's home], and I should have been very sorry if you had not decided as you did just as I shall always expect you to do—with dignity, and propriety—my dear. You have much of wisdom—I pray that you may have it imparted to you—I am glad you have found my letters of as much interest as to repeat the perusal—You know I love you, and therefore I am unwearied in my attention, that I may afford you all the help that my experience suggests—and those helps are all found in the Book of Wisdom!

The former part of this letter is not very satisfactory because it treats of nothing valuable, but I shall send it off this evening, expecting it will reach you Monday morning next—and anything from home will interest you—It seems Miss Beach and Miss Dey love to accompany you to Hartford. I am glad of it and am much obliged to those ladies for their kind attention to you. . . . I conclude that after having returned to New York—you will hardly think it worthwhile to go to Boston. I think it had been mentioned before you left and I had apprised my friends there of your intention. . . . Make all your plans fall with theirs and you will find it comfortable and safe. . . . [2]

Thomas Beals seemed to be having a particularly difficult time letting go of his daughter. Elizabeth treasured these ties no less and so preserved another letter from him.

I feel very much obliged to Mr. Richards for a newspaper, mailed at Farmington, received yesterday morning. I thought I could trace a pencil mark "all well." It was very grateful to me to get such a testimony, but it would have been much more so to have got a long letter from him. . . . I confess that I want to fix some obligation upon you, and from your last letter it would appear, that the limits of a sheet of paper did not satisfy you for our letter. I beg of you my dear to give us as much of your attention as you can. I am sorry I cannot give you some interesting village news; but I cannot. We are very quiet here and nothing has transpired since you left that would interest you. We see but little company. . . .

On Saturday I received a long letter from Henry. . . . from which we hope his journey and visit home was of use to him. His mind has been opened and his views on some subjects enlarged. I hope he will get through with his engagement in New York to the satisfaction of his employers and get a good name for himself and be prepared for usefulness in the world. We have a great desire that our children be found walking in the truth. . . .[3]

When they returned from their honeymoon, James and Elizabeth found another letter from Thomas Beals waiting for them in Auburn. He had written it two days after the wedding.

To James Richards Jun. and Elizabeth his wife,
Very dear Children,

I have thought proper to improve an early opportunity to apprise you by letter under my own hand, that I charge my estate with the sum of Five Thousand Dollars for the Dowery of you, my daughter; and being desirous to provide for your mutual comfort, do make known, that I will, on the first day of every fourth month hereafter, pay the interest on said sum at the rate of 6 percent per annum—that is, on the 1st days of January, May and September in each year, I will pay the sum of one hundred dollars so that you may consider that a permanent provision is made for an income of $300 per annum.

It is proper for me to remark that this property on which this is based consists principally of Houses and Lands that my experience has convinced me, that 6 percent is the extent of income derived from this property exclusive of charges for taxes and other unavoidable expenses tending to the preservation and protection of such property. . . . It is my desire to do all I can to make you happy. I have not the ability to make any other or greater provision for you than that herein declared having just regard to the claims of all my other children; and it appears to me that it is right and proper that you should be made acquainted, thus early with my intentions in this behalf, that you may be just to yourselves, and feel a proper self respect. I remark again—all sums advanced for your outfit will be charged to you on my books. This accords with my business habits and I owe it to myself to keep exact accounts. . . . This arrangement is the first of this kind that I have felt it to be my duty to make, as the other members of my family are happily located in business and makes such provision, as yet, unnecessary—Still—exact justice requires, that they shall, prospectively be as favourably considered. This letter has been read and approved by your mother. She unites with me in aff. regard.

Thomas Beals

Her mother added a spiritual legacy to Thomas Beals's material provision for them.

> My Dear Elizabeth
>   You will not be surprised if I say that I feel your loss, but at the same time I can rejoice that Our Heavenly Father has placed you in a Family that love God, and take delight in his service, and I hope through Christ strengthening you, You will be able to fill your place, so that God may be glorified and you happy both on this day and that which is to come.
>   This is the sincere wish of your affectionate Mother.
>
> Abigail Beals
> My love to your Husband. Remember me to Dr. and Mrs. Richards
> Saturday afternoon[4]

The letter implies that no dowry had been arranged beforehand, so this must have come as a very welcome surprise. A certificate of railroad stock was also enclosed. James was spending a post graduate year at Auburn and had no visible means of support for the moment other than the generosity of his own parents.

As the year progressed the question of what James would do next became pressing. Because of the theological turmoil that had been disturbing the Presbyterian Church since Finney, the choices usually presented themselves as theological dichotomies. James had to decide whether he was pro- or anti-Finney, often couched as pro- or anti-Taylor, and soon to be seen as pro- or anti-New School. Just like Pelagianism and Hopkinsianism of an earlier time, Nathaniel Taylor's theology enlarged the operation of free will at the expense of predestination. At Yale his ideas were seen as an intellectually respectable version of Finney's New Measures and they attracted many who were offended by Finney himself.[5] James discussed his future openly and fully with David Frame, a friend and former classmate who had gone to the new seminary in East Windsor, Connecticut, founded to counter Taylorism. The right decision about his future course rested just as much on a correct assessment of his gifts and his temperament.

January 4, 1837

Dear Broth[er] Richards

I don't know what I have done that my letter addressed to you some months since should never have met a reply. I have been pretty much determined to wait the issue but on second thought I feel that I ought to make very liberal allowances for the peculiarity of your circumstances the few months past and have therefore resumed my pen. As I have never had the opportunity of wishing yourself and Mrs. Richards happiness and all other good things in the relation wh[ich] you have assumed, take it for granted that I do so now. . . .

Since I saw or wrote you no particular change has occured in relation to me. I am still as you will perceive from the caption of my letter in E[ast]. W[indsor]. and shall probably remain here at least until spring and just as likely the next fall. I am very pleasantly and comfortably situated, having every facility for study and so on. Rooming as at Auburn alone and in the fourth story—I preach at most every Sabbath, or more than half the time in adjoining destitute [i.e. isolated] places, and am perhaps as really performing the work of a missionary as if I were in that field. There are several small destitute places within from 5 to 15 miles of this place where labour is perhaps as much needed as almost any where. . . . the places are quite small and of course the remuneration corresponding, but I receive enough to make both ends meet and with this I am satisfied.

Every thing here goes on very agreeably, there are but few of us, but we try to make every thing pleasant and we succeed—Bro Wiles (?) as you know I suppose is at New Haven. I recd a letter from him a few days since in wh[ich] there is something wh[ich] looks as if he intended to go to Illinois. I had not written to him since he went to New Haven and when I replied to his letter, I expressed a little regret that he had not gone elsewhere than where he is. I dont know what he thinks of it, but the truth is that Taylorism whether right or wrong is rather a cumbersome thing for a young preacher to carry, and the suspicion of being a Taylorite he must bear if he go to New Haven. Now I believe it is possible for a man so to preach at the conscience of men that they will never think of inquiring what a man is, but I question whether Br W will do so. He will be apt to interlard and spice his sermons with phraseology wh[ich] will set the curiosity of his hearers all agog and so put their consciences to sleep. This seems to be a peculiarity of at least some of Dr. Taylor's students.

But enough of this—I was at home about 2 months since—the people of West Bloomfield [New Jersey] ripe for building a new church. The matter between the good people there and myself in respect to preaching for them stands as it did a year since—I have no anxiety on the subject any further than to question very seriously whether it would be advisable for me to respond affirmatively to any call which they might make. The reason is that it is my home. It would do better for yourself— There is no difficulty in obtaining a settlement. The only difficulty is in paying the tax wh[ich] will be made upon a man's intellect when placed in such circumstances.

Frame was in as much doubt about his personal life as he was about his professional life. The question of whom to marry was openly discussed among friends. It was expected that these were the people who would introduce you to an appropriate circle and agonize with you over your choice.

I saw Bro William M. Richards at the commencement at Amhurst [*sic*]—he has trimmed up wonderfully. He is as I understand very much respected. I saw also Br Columbus Shumway and lady. He is doing well. Also Br Bisby. He also is doing well. They were all at Auburn while I was there. They are all in the same case with yourself. Conjugated. In this respect I am clear behind the times and I dont see how I am to come up with them.

I should like to have your honest opinion in regard to matrimony. Now no shuffling or smoothing over a bad matter—no polishing up the moon in an eclipse into a sun at noon day—no making the tide seem to move smoothly in one direction while there is a counter current beneath—but tell me. Do right up and down without any starch or ironing what you think of the matter and whether your opinion is that it would sit well upon me. In a few years my life will be on the wane even if I should live the alotted time of man upon the earth. What do you think? Had I best get some one to go down the street of time with me or not? Will it smooth the ruggedness of the way? Will it make me a happier or a better man and enable me to increase the happiness or goodness of others? How do wives behave? Are they as kind and clever after marriage as before? Oh now I know this is all nonsense. You won't tell me.

But leaving aside all matters and adopting a more serious strain as better befits the subject, what do you think and especially what do you think of the matter in respect to myself—I still have your letter of introduction to Miss I. with the seal unbroken in my trunk—it being my present purpose to deliver it in the spring to the proper person or to return it as I received it to yourself. The reason why I have never delivered it has been that I know not how to go. Do you think in regard to that affair as you did a year since? Do you really think she is the one? I think I should find no special difficulty in getting my heart in relation to this affair, into the state of sealing wax ready for an impression, but then I want to move warily and cautiously because the step ever taken cannot be retraced. I wish to make not a solitary movement wh[ich] either party might wish to recall. So far I kept a clear conscience in these matters and I hope to do so still. You have known all my manners of life in regard to this subject and you will not accuse me with guilt or duplicity in regard to it. Spare if you can an hour to answer this.

Yours very truly sincerely
David A Frame[6]

Frame's next letters continued the conversation about possible pastorates for them both.

I received a very pressing solicitation from Rev. A. Granger of Meriden [Connecticut] . . . to come and assist him for a time. As he was an old academical acquaintance, I could not very well refuse. I have now preached here two Sabbaths and twice during the past week. He is anxious to have me stay three Sabbaths longer, have not decided whether I shall. There is a large Baptist Society in Meriden and those who are in the Baptist influence and interest have been for a few weeks past making the most untiring efforts to lengthen the cords and strengthen the stakes of Baptist Exclusiveness. In true New Measure style they have entered into other mens' labors and have seemed determined to carry their point at all hazards, appointing meetings in those places previously occupied by [C]ongregationalists and seizing upon other points to which they have no just claim. I understand that their preaching partakes very much of the nature of that flashy wretched stuff which has so much abounded in western New York.

He went on to describe the distress and division this was causing not only among the Presbyterians, but among the Baptists. Despite his conservatism, he acknowledged, "It has not always been the worst material which has gone off for a while in a tangent." All this was relevant to the choice that James had to make. James, too, was not happy with the implications of Finneyism and was open to settling in other places.

In your last you express an unwillingness to settle in western New York because everything there is so new fangled. The truth is Br. Richards, the churches in many places are wonderfully afloat. You will find even in this land of steady habits a vast deal of *unsteadiness*. In many places there is a restless desire of change, a fondness for feverish excitement and a lamentable disregard of what was once held sacred. Ministers are not so pleasantly situated in C[onnecticut] at the present day as they once were. . . . The ancient landmarks are plucked up. . . . It is all burly. Money-seeking, pleasure-seeking, office-seeking have become the order of the day. It may be severe but I am constrained seriously to believe that even in the once far removed Connecticut they would put the very prince of darkness into office if they might only hold office under him. Oh what a wretched state of things. When I look over the length and breadth of our land and witness the mighty commotion in politics [and] religion, money making and so on, I am sick at heart. . . . My only hope is in him who settled the noise of the seas, the noise of their waves and the tumults of the people. I know that God can bring man back to that original susceptibility of conscience which they seem to have lost. . . . This is solid rock, all else is shadow.

He wanted James to know about the opening in his home town of West Bloomfield, New Jersey.

In regard to West Bloomfield you could not have a better place. If they think about going on or if they are now in a state of forwardness, I will speak to them about you. As to myself, I don't go there; that's settled. A prophet. . . .[7] As I hope to see you very soon, I shall not write more. Only to ask you to convey to all enquiring friends my best wishes and to Mrs. R. and your father and mother especially my kindest regards. . . .[8]

A few months later Frame again addressed the problem of a career. He had evidently been in Auburn for the annual convocation of the seminary, known as the anniversaries, but had missed James. He began his letter with gossip he had picked up about their classmates, and then quickly went on to his obsessive concern with finding a suitable position, riddled with self-doubt as he was. He had been asked to preach at a vacant church in South Street, Philadelphia, with the possibility of a post.

The idea agitated my mind so much that I did not dare and did not go at all. . . . But Brother R., I can't think of such a thing. Why I am hardly fit to settle over a barn, how much [less] upon a church in P[hiladelphia]. Why the very idea sickens me and agues me all over. But after all I presume I need not be frightened. There is very considerable difference between being asked to come and try and being unanimously called to settle. While in Bloomfield received an invitation from the church in Glastonbury in this state . . . and also an invitation from the church in Northfield . . . both in the way of candidating. Both are among the respectable churches, either of them is too good for me. My desire is not to occupy a field when they can support a better man and where one better suited can be obtained.

Last Sabbath I preach[ed] three times at M[eriden]. The congregation is very large and the people are wealthy. . . . They would give a thousand dollars. It is not the place for me. I am not adequate to it. They seemed anxious to have me preach two or three sabbaths. I know their design or guessed at it and rather discouraged them. Told them however that I had no objection to preaching a few Sabbaths but advised them to be on the lookout for an older man, older at least as a preacher. They also want a candidate at Suffield. But I am a little inclined to think that I shall come out near you somewhere in the fall. I am afraid of these big churches. I would like to have people where there is some cultivation . . . but not too much. . . . I do wish that I was fit to preach, really say to preach, so as that I might be acceptable and useful but preaching is a great work. . . .[9]

John Morgan. (Taken from John Morgan Richards, With John Bull and Jonathan, *D. Appleton, New York, 1906)*

In the end, after all the speculation and soul-searching and despite his reservations, James settled in western New York as the pastor of the Presbyterian church in nearby Aurora. It was a charming little village on the picturesque shores of Cayuga Lake, and home of the Morgan family. John Morgan, the son of Christopher Morgan, the oldest of the five Morgan brothers, was a warm friend of James's from undergraduate days at Union, and so he was asked to come.[10] The Morgans were large landowners who dominated the commercial, political, and social life of Aurora and the surrounding area; Christopher sat on the boards of

Village of Aurora on Cayuga Lake; the steeple of the Presbyterian church pierces the horizon. (Courtesy—"Aurora, N.Y., from the North Poplars, 1848," Wells College Archives, Louis Jefferson Long Library, Aurora, New York)

a number of prestigious state institutions and was elected to Congress a few years after James's arrival. In many ways it was an ideal location for James to test his powers and develop his confidence. There was room to grow, but he was unlikely to be overwhelmed. Sixteen miles away in Auburn his father was available to advise and help, but far enough away for James to make the pastorate his own. Elizabeth, too, was close enough to her family to visit frequently; she never evinced any interest in leaving the Finger Lakes area.

The village and church were small so there was no parsonage but they found accommodations in the village. A letter to her parents in the early fall of 1837 captures the flavor of their life.

We feel very much disappointed that Gorham [her brother] has decided not to spend the winter with us, but we hope and believe it will be "all for the best" in the end. Mr. Richards thinks he may make more rapid improvement by being associated with young gentlemen, who like himself are preparing to enter college. I was rather selfish in wishing Gorham to remain here. He was a great deal of company for me and he always seemed perfectly contented and happy.

I have not felt lonely one moment since my sister and brother left me. On Saturday Mr. Richards went to Farmerville and as we had some friends there, I went with him and spent the Sabbath and the minister from that place came here and preached for Mr. R. This was a very pleasant exchange. Farmerville is 8 or 10 miles from here on the opposite side of the Lake. We crossed the lake in a houseboat, and, as the weather was delightful, we enjoyed it very much.

Since our return we have done little else but entertain company. A number of Ladies have been here to make apologies for not calling on Sister Mary [Carr]. On Monday evening John Williams and his wife came here and staid [sic] until almost 11 o'clock. Tuesday evening it rained and I told Mr. R. I believe we should not be troubled with company. To this end we made a good fire up in the study. Mr. R. had seated himself with books and papers intending to accomplish something for the Sabbath. I had taken my sewing in hand and promised not to talk, when we were surprised by a peculiar knock which we knew to be that of Mr. Seneca Wood. He had the "*Hippo*"[11] pretty bad as usual and had come over to have Mr. Richards frighten away the blues. I believe he succeeded for he seemed in good spirits when he left here. Mr. R. saw Mr. Wood soon after reading your last letter and he read to him your receipt for curing *dyspepsia*. Mr. W. said he believed such a course would cure him but he had not sufficient courage to give it a trial.

We agree with you perfectly about the *cider*. Mr. R has given it to me to use for sauce. It is about as good as the best champaigne [sic] and seems to give a relish to a pudding.

On Wednesday Dr. and Mrs. Thompson took tea with us. Mr. R invited them to come and eat *tomatoes*. They have furnished our table with them and I had pickled and preserved some which they seemed to admire very much. Another gentleman and his wife came in during the evening and they staid [sic] until *eleven* o'clock. I was really tired out when they left and felt the next day just as if I had been watching.[12] We have had the wooden clock regulated and it keeps good time and strikes very loud, but it does not seem to frighten away company, and the truth is, the people in this place do not observe good New England rules in the regulation of their domestic affairs. We are resolved to set good examples and not protract our visits beyond nine o'clock. At that hour I always wish to have the family assembled for evening devotions.

I am glad to hear of Henry's [her brother] safe arrival in Detroit. I hope he will be at home in a few days. Mr. Richards thinks he will go with me to Canandaigua on Tuesday next. We intend to go from here in a private conveyance. You must not calculate with a certainty upon seeing us for our plans have been very often defeated. If Mr. R. hears of his Father's return, we shall take Auburn in our way when returning and pass a day or two and be absent from Aurora about a week if the services of any clergyman can be obtained from Auburn. I hope our visit will not prevent Magdalena and Glorianna from spending a part of the vacation with us. I am very anxious to see them here. Mr. R will pay Gorham's tuition bill and talk with you about Gorham's plans when next you meet. He would be very glad to write a few lines but his duties and engagements for the Sabbath occupy him constantly. I was really glad to see it rain this morning for seldom except when it rains is Mr. R. allowed any time alone in his study.

This same letter also responded to the news from Canandaigua that Richard Varick Dey, Anthony Dey's minister son, husband of Lavinia and father of eight,[13] had died on September 20 in New York. Young Henry Beals was a frequent visitor at the Deys and Beaches in New York, so it is not surprising that the news reached them indirectly from the West.

The news of the death of Richard Dey was a great surprise to us. It is two weeks since we have heard from New York and of course we had had no intimation of this sickness. Mr. R. found a number of the N.Y. American, which confirmed your account of his death; probably Saturday's mail will bring us a minute account of his sickness etc. I feel very sorry for Mr. Dey. Mr. Axtell's [his son-in-law and pastor of 2nd Presbyterian, Auburn] death was a great affliction to him, but this will inflict a still deeper wound. Richard with all his faults was very tenderly beloved by his father. I presume he feels as David did when bewailing the loss of his son Absalom.[14]

James Beach, Anna's eighteen-year-old son, visited in the West that fall. He had taken much pleasure in the company of the young women there and on his return to Newark was eager to compare notes with his uncle only six years his senior.

> I will give you a detailed account of my visit as also the attentions shown me by the (once so considered by you) fascinating Misses H's. I recd. a long letter from H. Hills Jun[ior], a few days ago. He gave me a very minute and also graphic description of Animal Magnetism. It was however most too profound for my Comprehension, I should like exceedingly to possess a sufficient quantity to transport me to Aurora. When I get thinking how happy Aunt E. and yourself are I am almost tempted to break the Tenth Commandment (so far as covetousness is Concerned).
>
> Since my return I have become quite a Beau (not in its literal sense however) visiting ladies and attending parties. Last week I attended a bridal party given by Mrs. Jesse Baldwin, Jun[ior] in honor of Rev. Abeel Baldwin and Lady. I had the pleasure of promenading the room a greater part of the evening with the Bride. She told me, as she had refused several gentlemen the honor, that I ought to Consider myself as being very highly favored. On Tuesday of this week I called with Mother & Sister Sarah on the newly made Bride, Katy Graham (a name you know that denotes every thing *unpalatable*). She married her own Cousin, a gentleman bearing the same name. The Bride looked very *youthful ironically speaking* being *only* 30 years of age, the groom but 25. Quite a disparity I think. So we go?

This letter then made one of the rare political references in the family's correspondence before returning to the subject closest to James Beach's heart.

> [Senator] Danl Webster & Caleb Cushing, a distinguished member of the house of Representatives, favored us with a visit the early part of

the week. They received a hearty welcome from the Inhabitants. Speeches were delivered by them on the occasion both of which were listened to with apparently much interest as also attention. Mr. Webster is truly in a literal sense of the word an honorable. I should suppose from the tenor of his speech that he was given much to meditation.

I called on The Misses Condit the other evening (Two of them have recently visited Geneva.) They asked me about my visit to the west. I told them satisfactorily. They recommended to my especial attention Miss Dwight of Geneva. I told them she had already been mentioned to me. Believe me my dear Uncle I shall not engage myself 'till I have seen her. If she is unencumbered tell her the next time you see her that you have a young Gentleman in reserve for her. I think from the description given of her that I would be much pleased with her, at any rate I will endeavor to see her. Don't forget to say a good word for me. If I live till next June or July I shall go on; and get you to accompany me in a visit to Geneva as you promised. If she comes to New York this winter please inform me of the Circumstances.

Henry Beals was up one day last week and staid [*sic*] over night. He is a clever whole souled fellow (not Yankee clever however). We shall be pleased to see him at any time & under any circumstances. If well wishes can avail much in a business point of view he cannot fail to succeed.

I have a favor to ask of you. It is this. Select for me a duplicate of your wife, or to be more explicit a lady like Aunt Eliza[beth], and if I can get her, no matter whether rich or poor, I will go ahead as the saying goes. Miss Dwight is, I should think from all accounts, the proper very identical individual. Excuse me for breaking off so abruptly as time will not permit me to add more. Remember me *kindly, affectionately* and *sincerely* to Aunt Elizabeth as also to her parents, Grandpapa, Grandmama, y[ou]r bro[ther] Gorham & other enquiring friends.

from your attached nephew
James[15]

As Thanksgiving approached that first year on their own, James and Elizabeth expected the Richardses to spend the holiday with them. Dr. Richards wrote to them in November.

We have been much disappointed in not seeing you and Elizabeth at Auburn this week, as we heard in various ways that you intended coming. I hope that no untoward event has detained you. Perhaps you have been afraid to encounter the roads. But how then shall we get over to Aurora next week to keep Thanksgiving with you. It is however our present purpose to come, unless the weather shall prove stormy on Wednesday.

Edward has just left us for Rochester and Buffalo. He came evening before last. It is his intention to return this way when he expects to come and see you. He wishes to do up his business before he spends much time in visiting friends. He left all well at Newark and N[ew]. York. Henry expects to sail to Key West by the last of this week intending to spend his winter on the south side of Cuba.

Edward continued to travel on business and Henry continued to nurse his health at ever more expense and distance. Mrs. Richards added a homey note.

My dear Elizabeth

I have taken up the pen to thank you for your very acceptable letter today by Mr. Williams. . . . We saved a nice roasting peice [*sic*] of beef to send to you by him and kept it till it had almost spoiled and then was obliged to cook it. Mr. and Mrs. Cumpston called here soon after they returned from Aurora—said they were very much pleased with their visit. I am glad your girl behaved so well. What a comfort it must have been to you. We had a letter from Mr. S[amuel] Hopkins [James's close friend and groomsman] this morning. He is going to spend the winter at the South.

Yours Affectionately C. Richards

We were greatly disappointed in not seeing you and James here this week. I hope we shall be able to spend Thanksgiving with you, best love to James and accept a large share for yourself.[16]

The New Year season saw them dividing their time between both sets of parents. It was a long and welcome break from their new duties. On their return, Elizabeth wrote her mother a warm and grateful letter. She

James and Elizabeth's house at Aurora. (Courtesy—Laura S. Seitz)

loved her Canandaigua home and Aurora was a missionary outpost in comparison.

Although I feel somewhat fatigued this evening, yet Mr. R. and myself feel so anxious to know if papa has recovered from his indisposition that I cannot forbear writing by the earliest opportunity. We had a very pleasant ride from Canan[daigua] to Auburn. We never before accomplished the journey in such a short time; it was not five o'clock when we reached Auburn. We found Mr. R's parents very well, and anxiously expecting to see us.

    I never had a more delightful visit at C[anandaigua] than my last. I never left home with more regret, still I should not have been willing to have protracted my stay at C., and been thus the means of disappointing Mr. R.'s parents. James' visits are very precious seasons to them, and I should not like to abridge any of their pleasure. On Sabbath morning we heard Dr. Halsey preach[17] in the chapel, and in the afternoon a Mr. Lewis; in the evening an address was delivered by an agent for the "Seamen's Friend Society," which was said to be very interesting. I did not hear it. We spent yesterday very pleasantly. Dr. and Mrs. Halsey passed the day at Dr. Richards'. Their conversation is always interesting and instructive. I never knew how to appreciate the society of intelligent Christians until I came to this place [Aurora], where there is a dearth of everything of that kind. I would not have you infer from this remark that I am dissatisfied with my home; so far is this from being the fact, that I regard as an additional reason why Mr. R. should make this the place of his continual labours, hoping that thereby a change may be effected in the views and feelings of his parishioners. . . .

We found our house as we left it—in good order, but we had a cold reception. There was no father and mother to welcome us, and no brother and sisters to anticipate our wants, and gratify our every wish; but though we were deprived of such attentions, the family who lie in the cottage in our garden were very kind. One of them took charge of Mr. R.'s horse, and went after Rebecca, and another assisted us in making a fire, so that we had much to be grateful for, though everything by its loneliness reminded us of the home and friends we had left. Mr. Seneca Wood called soon after our blinds were thrown open. He seemed very glad to see us, and said the time of our absence seemed very long to him. Mr. Van Buren preached here on the Sabbath, and gave general satisfaction. I believe Mr. R's friends were very glad to allow him a little recreation. I believe the journey has done us both good.

During our absence Mr. R. had an invitation to go eleven miles south of us, to marry two couples, and has, of course, lost a double marriage fee. He has also lost a visit from a brother minister. He does not at all regret these losses; they were made up to him tenfold.

My New Year's present has been very much admired, and it is very highly prized. I had many things about me before which constantly reminded me of the home I had left, but this Bible has very pleasant recollections associated with it. I cannot express the gratitude which I feel to my parents for their unwearied kindnesses to me. At present I can only acknowledge my increased obligations to them, but possibly when that season arrives, so beautifully described by Solomon, "when the keepers of the house shall tremble, and the strong men shall bow themselves; when they shall be afraid of that which is high, and fear shall be in the way," in this season of infirmity, I say, possibly it may be my privilege to make my parents happy and render them a tithe of what they have delighted to bestow upon me. . . .

Mr. R. most cordially unites with me in love and a Happy New Year to all the dear members of the family circle at home. . . .

I am your very affectionate daughter,
Elizabeth.[18]

In January, 1838, James became seriously ill, but by the end of the month Elizabeth was able to write the Richardses a reassuring letter.

I am very glad to inform you that James continues to improve. From present appearances, he will doubtless be quite well in a few days. He has not been out of the house yet, but hopes to take a short ride tomorrow with Mr. John Morgan. If the travelling should be comfortable, he intends to go to Auburn the latter part of the week, but says father need not make any efforts to get him there, but, if possible, he will devise some means here of getting out. Mr. McCullough arrived here at about two o'clock Saturday p.m. We have had a very pleasant visit from him and he preached very well indeed. James feels very much indebted to him for this "labour of love." Our neighbours continue to be very kind. Mrs. Harriet Morgan sent us a fine turkey this morning. James has turned over a new leaf since his sickness; he gets up at six o'clock in the a.m., and retires at nine o'clock in the evening. I hope he will keep all his good resolutions. I cannot express my gratitude for his recovery; life seems to have new charms now that he is restored to his place at the table and the family altar. . . .[19]

Their seminary friends were inexorably moving away from the seminary base in Auburn. Samuel Hopkins went south as anticipated and in April sent them a vivid description of the sparsely inhabited back country of Georgia and Florida. Letters as much as newspapers were welcomed for their news of such unfamiliar places. Although Florida had been acquired from Spain in 1821, it was still a territory and very much a frontier. Texas had become an independent republic under President Sam Houston two years earlier.

Steam Boat Commerce on the

Chatahoucher [Chatahoochee] 15 April 15, 1838

My Dear Richards

It may be well for our friendship perhaps, that I don't defer writing to you untill I reach Savannah for should I find on arriving there that no letter from you has been waiting for me, I should begin (if I began at all) by calling you various hard names, any one of which should be sufficient to make bitter enemies of even David & Jonathan. But this artillery I keep in reserve. If you have not written, you may suppose a whole broadside discharged at your personage. You will please (with Presdt Houston) "consider yourself reprimanded."

As you see by my date that I am in motion (and you may guess from my Kacography that the motion is none of the smoothest). I will take you briefly over the course I have travelled since I left Savannah about three weeks since. My brother who was engaged with a party of Engineers in Florida wrote me from Tallahassee that he was about to ascend the Ocklockney on an exploring expedition and, expecting to meet with fine scenery and other objects of interest, invited me to come and join him. Wishing to see my brother before returning home, and not unwilling to meet with some little adventure, I packed up a few things and started off in the first coach for Tallahassee.

A journey of three or four hundred miles in N[ew] York with our great facilities for travel and with every thing to make travelling comfortable, is a very small affair, but in Georgia and Florida with long ranges of uninhabited pine woods to traverse, rapid rivers to be crossed in flatboats and liable to rise so much in a single night as to make crossing at all hazardous, if not impossible, accommodations of the rudest and coarsest character etc., it becomes rather a formidable affair. I got on very tolerably however for the first three days of my journey and bore without any disposition to complain [about] those inconveniences to which I had made up my mind before starting. But on the third night, the monotony of the ride was interrupted by a catastrophe rather too striking to be agreeable. I was waked up from a doze by the horses running away with the coach and had hardly time to open my eyes before we came in contact with a stump with tremendous violence, upsetting the stage and leaving it almost to peices [*sic*]. I sprang up from the corner into which I had been so unceremoniously pitched upon the top of two other passengers and feeling satisfied that no limbs were broken, though I feared the blood pouring like rain from my head, I jumped out on the upper side, and as soon as I recovered from the momentary shock, set about helping the others. I heard the horses tearing away through the woods carrying the forepart of the running gear with them. We cut a pretty figure when we had all crawled out. I was almost the only person able to stand. The rest were banged and sprained & dislocated, though not a bone was broken in all the company. Here we stayed in the piney woods from midnight untill [*sic*] near day light with only a single house within miles of us. The [runaway] horses at length were found, one of them having been knocked down by running against a tree, and harnessing them into a common waggon procured with great difficulty, we got onto the next stage. Here even this recourse failed us, and as a last resort, putting one horse into a common cart, and using the others as saddle horses, we managed to get on twelve miles further. And then we stuck fast for the two following days. I got off with a cut in the head ("luckily I pitched upon my head" as some poet says) from which I have been able only within this day or two to remove the bandages.

His final destination was Tallahassee, capital of the Florida Territory, and site of a land boom once the Americans had taken possession of the area. Anthony Dey was among those persuaded that Florida was ripe for development. Since 1832, the Seminoles under Osceola had put up fierce resistance to the American encroachments. Six year later, when Sam Hopkins arrived, Osceola had been captured, but the Indians were still undefeated.

My journey had nothing else worth telling. The entire country from Savannah to Tallahassee (where I arrived at the end of the sixth day) is more dull and monotonous than you can conceive, nothing but the everlasting piney woods, and at this time, too, on fire the whole length of my route, filling ones eyes with smoke, and constantly blocking up the road with fallen trees. In this distance of 350 miles there are only four villages. Two of these, Dublin & Gainbridge, are very favorably represented when I say they are nearly equal to Canossa and the "devil's half Acre." The other two, Hawkinsville & Quincy, have perhaps 4 or 500 inhabitants apiece. Tallahassee has 2000. It is a very rude looking place but pretty well situated. The people are irreligious, quarrelsome & blind to reproval, even here. They have a very clever Presbyterian cler-gyman, however, Mr. Burroughs, to whom I had a letter of introduction. . . .

I went by Rail Road 20 miles to St. Marks, where I found my brother & party. They were encamped on the top of the old Bomb proof fort built by the Spaniards & taken by Genl Jackson, and having finished their survey were about to return to N.Y. without exploring the Ocklockney which was rendered dangerous by the vicinity of the Indians. St. Marks is as mean & contemptible a collection of a few dirty old wooden houses as you can imagine. I had the satisfaction of preaching the Gospel (a thing of which they [torn] know little) on the only Sabbath I was there to quite a numerous congregation in the eating room of the tavern. I left St. Marks a week ago with my brother & his party in two boats to proceed by the Gulf of Mexico to Apolochicola where we arrived on the 12th. My adventures on this cruise and at St. Marks I must tell you at some other time, or rather you can have an opportunity of reading them in any of the papers as I intend to publish them in future [torn] letters in the *N.Y. Observer* and afterwards to collect them [torn] request into six volumes. How many copies will you [torn] subscribe for?

After seeing my brother & his men embark on board the *Washington Irving* last evening for New York, I put myself on this Boat for Columbus; whence I intend, (by the guidance & protection of that Good Providence which has delivered me from six perils & can deliver from the seventh) to cross the state of Georgia to Savannah, and then shortly proceed by sea to N.Y.

Scarce any earthly consideration, my dear friend, could tempt me to stay in this country. Its moral climate is as bad as its natural. Vice and crime seem to think a mark hardly necessary here. The amount of intemperance & the horrible amount of profaneness and blasphemy, the almost total want of the Sabbath [torn] either want of public opinion favourable to religion or virtue, the feebleness of law, all make the country odious and intolerable to me. Apart from all this, you will be surprised, if you have heard Florida spoken of as the "Italy of America" etc. to know that it is the most dismally flat and insipid country one can possibly travel through—swamps, swamps, swamps—sand, sand, sand,— low flat marshy islands—narrow rapid, muddy rivers—and not a hill or any spot that I can ascertain (except you climb a cypress tree) from which you can obtain a view half a mile in extent. The scenery in the Chatahoucher up which I am now travelling is the best I have seen. The banks are covered not only to the waters' edge, but into the water, with a dense growth of forest trees, cypress, palmetto, maple, live oak, bay tree, etc. And every interstice is filled up with the rankest & most luxuriant undergrowth so that your view is absolutely & rigidly limited by the solid walls of trees lining each side of the river. The foliage however is exceedingly rich. There is every possible shade of green and the trees are often of a magnificent height. I hope to reach Columbus in three days if we don't stick fast in this river which is low, and the boat besides is loaded so that her guards rest upon the water.

I am anxious to get to Savannah for letters. I trust that you & Mrs. R continue well. My own health has been uninterruptedly good since I came South. If Providence spare me to get back, one of my first excursions will be to visit you. Please to remember me with particular respect & affection to Mrs. R., to your father & mother & to Dr. Mills when you see them and believe me my dear brother Most truly & faithfully

Your Br—Sam. Hopkins

[Don't] let me forget to mention as one of the blessings of this country, the swarms of most ferocious and insatiate mousquitoes [sic], sand flies, and fleas.[20]

While others were traveling, James and Elizabeth were taking on more family responsibilities. In May of 1838, Henry Beals sent them an order of tea, coffee, sugar, rice, and candles and also a sofa and "a bed and bedding for Anthony" that came from Lavinia Dey.[21] Anthony was the son of Richard Varick Dey who had died eight months before and he was

Family devotions. (Painted by Alexander F. Fraser, "Asking a Blessing" circa 1830–1842, Milwaukee Public Museum)

coming to live with them. His widowed mother could not manage her eight children[22] so it had been arranged that the nine-year-old Anthony would come to live with James and Elizabeth for an indefinite period. Childless themselves at this point, they were playing their part in this extended family by providing a home with a wholesome atmosphere for the youngster.

Within a few months, they also took in ten-year-old James Nicholas Richards, Henry Richards's oldest son. Henry, now living up the Hudson in Poughkeepsie, had married Mary Howe Givan, a niece of his first wife.[23] That spring she had just given birth to a baby boy. Perhaps by summer she found a family of three children more than she could handle; she was only eighteen years old herself and had gone through much of her pregnancy without her husband, who was in Cuba. Despite his ill health Henry, aged thirty-five, had sought another wife and not hesitated to father more children. A Richards child would always be cared for in this extended family. James was ten years old, an age when a boy becomes more interested in his father's world, and one can only wonder what the effect of being excluded from his own family circle had on his behavior. Elizabeth soon shared her impressions of her new charges with her mother-in-law.

> August 7 1838
>
> My dear Mother,
>
> We reached home very comfortably last Thursday p.m., about five o'clock. James did not incommode us at all; he seemed to enjoy the ride very much, and has been apparently contented and happy since he has been with us. He is a much more difficult child to manage than Anthony.

Elizabeth assumed like her elders that the company of the local boys would only compound the situation and was grateful that they had each other.

> His uncle has thus far kept him in good subjection, but their government and instruction make very large demands upon his time. Our house has quite a literary appearance at all times, one room being the schoolroom, and the other the study. I believe the boys are much happier together than they would be alone. They seldom see the boys of the village, and do not care anything about them. . . .
>
> James unites with me in much love to father and yourself. Little James sends love to his grandparents. . . .[24]

A letter to James from David Frame in June reopened the question of where James should settle. Aurora was pretty and pleasant, and the seminary was nearby, but it still had its shortcomings. He discussed with Frame the possibility of leaving Aurora for a parish in Bloomfield, New Jersey. Another letter from Frame in October made clear that the plan advanced almost to the point of being acted upon.

> N.J. Oct 1, 1838
>
> My very dear friend,
>
> Yours of the 28th reached me on Saturday, I had been expecting it for several days and began to think that I should receive its contents viva

voce in propera persona of the writer himself. . . . I thank you very much for the kindly sympathies which you tender me on consideration of the loss of my Trunk etc. The trunk however is no longer a lost Trunk but is in the possession of its rightful owner where it ought to have been and would have been at the date of my last letter if those who are the regularly constituted salaried public servants had been only half as honest and manly as they would try to appear. After their littleness had thrown up its shrivelled visage to receive the full day light of investigation, I found the article in question in the possession of the public functionary at Jersey City, called the ferryman of whom by the way I had made particular inquiries respecting it at two separate and distinct hours just one week before I made the discovery where it was and 2 weeks after it had fallen under his eyes and into his hands. . . . The Trunk is now safely moored in my own harbor. It would have been quite a severe loss in some respects and particularly as it regards the Sermons. They are poor things I am fully aware, and I speak thus disparagingly of them not in the sickly palaver of false modesty but because I feel . . . that they are so, but still they are a convenience until I can prepare better ones.

But enough of this. . . . I know no doubt but that I could have obtained a call for you without any difficulty even as matters now stand and while you are personally an entire stranger to them, but I very much doubt whether this would be the better course. The place, I have no doubt, is yours just as much as if you were already settled. Their minds are fixed upon you and upon no other. Nor have they been brought into this state by exaggerated statements on my part of your capabilities. I have not said to them that you are perfect in any respects. I have been careful not to excite exorbitant expectations. I have said to them that you had been sucessful to some good degree at Aurora, that the Aurora people are an intelligent people and that you are held in very good estimate there, that your intercourse with the people will be kind and conciliatory, that your sermons and addresses are more than usually pleasing, that you have a good voice and a good manner in the pulpit, that you write a good sermon, smooth emotions, . . . and that you often hit off men and things very happily, that your theology is like your father's, that they must not expect of one so young to be a giant theologian, and that your knowledge of men and things is quite as good as that of young ministers generally, that in regard to personal experience as a Christian and so forth they need to bear in mind that it is but about four years since you made a profession. I am aware of the injury which is often done to young men by the wretchedly injudicious encomiums which are passed upon their performances. They are sometimes represented as only second to Gabriel and then the people come together with their eyes and mouths and ears wide open expecting to hear the 8th wonder of the world, and lo what is here? Why a man with a man's voice and a man's tongue. Shocking. What a disappointment! Poor souls they had thought to hear Jupiter. Your modesty will hardly [argue] against any part of the description which I have given above.

He then pointed out the advantages of James's present situation so strongly as to potentially leave James in the same indecisive state he found himself.

But Brother, you now have . . . , so I think, a plain intelligent considerate people. The truth is I know not the congregation I should prefer to it. It is indeed and in truth the most [?] place for a young man that I know of any where. You can exchange as much as you please and as much as you will need to do by driving half an hour, and if you happen to hit the people pretty exactly, why everything will be in your own hands, They are not that restless changeful people you [typically] find in New York nor that self sufficient know everything and more too which a body often meets with out there. They are not disposed to shake off their ministers and undermine them and all that sort of thing. Nothing of this, not a bit. The truth is I know of no better place, prompt and sure pay and every thing to help a man along. I am almost a friend that shall become envious of your situation.

As usual Frame was taking a parish on a temporary basis and was diffident about becoming a candidate for a permanent position.

In regard to where I should settle I cannot say exactly. I have what is equivalent to a call from Montrose but whether I go or not is yet to be

determined. I hear of a new church about to be formed or just formed
in Rahway just below here. I hear that Hanover and Paterson Second
churchs are both vacant. It will all come round about right by and by.
. . . My kind regards to Mrs. Richards and all your household and
believe me to be yours very truly and sincerely

David A. Frame[25]

Despite coming so close to moving, James decided to stay where he
was. He may have enjoyed testing the waters to reassure himself that he
could move if he wished. In any case these explorations with Frame ran
up against a new reality. Elizabeth had become pregnant. With her
intense love of family, she did not appear to share his restlessness for a
wider or at least a different field of activity. Nor did James appear dissatisfied to her. When she wrote to James's parents a few months after
Frame's letter, she painted her husband as a minister fully engaged, with
the leisure and desire to develop his powers. There was no sense of being
up in the air or unsettled. She was six weeks away from the birth of her
first child.

Aurora January 25 1839

My dear Parents,

It was James' wish and intention to spend one day with you this
week, but circumstances beyond his control have prevented the execution of his plans. He made the contemplated exchange with Mr. Mealin
altho the weather was very rough, and he was obliged to go in his Buggy
instead of the Sleigh. Mr. Mealin preached very acceptably and it is the
universal opinion here that he is a young man of uncommon talents. In
other words the good people were very much taken with him and have
spoken in unqualified praise of his exercises, particularly of the extem-
poraneous performance on Sabbath evening. Mrs. Mealin returned with
James on Monday A.M. and brought with her her little daughter who is
just one year old and a very engaging & promising child. They remained
here until Tuesday afternoon and we enjoyed their visit very much
indeed. I was very much pleased with Mrs. M. She is very lovely in her
disposition & she seemed anxious to offer me sympathy and instruction
adapted to my present circumstances and I feel as if her visit had done
me a great deal of good. I shall remember it with gratitude and with

pleasure. James will tell you that Mealin's visit was equally pleasant to him. They parted with reluctance & regret & with mutual promises that so long a time should never pass without their meeting.

Since they left us, James has been constantly in his study except when taken up with company. In the early part of the week, he was very deeply impressed when reading the portion of Scripture contained in Exodus 33 chap[ter] and he concluded to make the inquiry of Moses "Lord, show me thy glory" the foundation of a discourse. The subject has so absorbed & interested him, that he is scarcely willing to sleep or eat. . . .

As often happened, her brother Henry had sent news from New York that she copied out for the Richardses.[26] He had visited the Deys as they were preparing for their daughter Carrie's wedding to Howland Bill.

He says, "I spent last evening at Mr. Dey's and I really wish you could have looked upon the industrious group I found assembled in the parlour. Mrs. D. was making a lace cap, Caroline Amelia [Beach] was sewing lace on the border of a H[andkerchief], Caroline Dey [the bride-to-be] making a lace collar, Miss Catherine [the bride's still unmarried stepsister] putting together a flannel garment with great dispatch, & really it was such an unusual and busy scene that I could not but believe that some remarkable event was about to occur." I presume Henry will not be admitted into the secret until Mr. Bill arrives, but his curiosity to know the facts will be wonderfully excited. He does say that he expects to be present at a wedding before three months shall have expired.

Henry spoke of a visit at Newark. He said they were all well, and that Sarah had gone to Philadelphia with her Uncle Edward to stay 3 or 4 weeks, & that Caroline Amelia was going to spend a month at her Uncle Deys. He said it seemed quite lonely at Mr. Beach's. . . . Brother Henry Richards was in N.Y. last week, and was very well indeed, so he writes.

I made a very pleasant visit yesterday at Mr. Arms. James did not go with me. I was sent for in a cutter & brought home. I have been remarkably well for week past, indeed I was never in better health. I should love to come & see you, but I believe it will not be expedient. I hope you are recovering rapidly from the Rheumatism. We feel very anxious to receive a visit from you very soon & if the weather moderates we hope you will come before the sleighing is gone. Did you ever know such cold weather as we have had? I shivered over the fire all day Wednesday & feel very thankful that there is now a change.

On Wednesday evening I received the parcel you was so very kind as to send to me. I cannot express to my dear Mother the satisfaction her letter afforded me, I am sure she would write more frequently if she knew how much she might thus gratify James & myself. The letters from Anna & Caroline were read with much interest . . . The Boys [Anthony Dey & James Nicholas Richards] are very well & unite with James and myself in much love to you. . . .[27]

A few weeks later, James received another letter from Frame. In rapid succession he had at last committed himself to a wife and a parish. Still unsure of himself and his goals, he had made his peace with necessity by accepting a pastorate that did not make great demands on him.

Your "declination" as Dr. Cox would say has put Samuel Fisher Jun. in West B(loomfied)'s pulpit. . . . I have now been in this place (Succa-suma or Roxbury) for more than three months. This pulpit happened to be vacated just before I went to Phil[adelphia]. I was applied to supply it for a Sabbath or two and have been here since. The congregation is not a very large one, but may become larger. There is nothing particularly interesting about it except perhaps, that there is a very flowering academy in the place and that the location itself is a pleasant one, The country around though not particularly fertile is beautifully level and susceptable I presume of high cultivation. . . .

Mary and myself are both well enough pleased with our situation and are trying to do some good as we go along. A project was started a few days since to paint up the church inside and out, and to create a regularly laid stone wall around the grave yard with other improve-ments and the subscription list already amounts to between 3 and 400 dollars. This for such a church, quite something, and when the contemplated improvements are completed they will add much to appearances. They have agreed to pay me six hundred dollars a year and are quite a willing people.

I might have obtained a more lucrative place and one of more refinement I presume but happiness does not depend on high places. The situation affords me a very fine opportunity for study and this is quite a desideration. How long I shall remain I know not, perhaps a year, perhaps more. There is perhaps as good attendance at church as has ever been in the place, and if matters should continue to wear a favorable appearance and to improve as they have done I may be induced to stay for some time to come.

Recognizing his own saturnine disposition, he was touchingly grateful to have so understanding a wife.

We have not gone to housekeeping as yet, but are boarding with an old school mate of mine. . . . If we should conclude to remain we shall take up that branch of science and discuss it in a few months. I suppose you would like to know now what I think of the married life. Well I take it along quietly. I never supposed that there was a great deal of poetry in it. Imagination and sentiments never entered very largely into my ideas of it, and when I did indulge the dreams of fancy, I was soon brought to my senses by looking around for the originals and not finding them in other cases. I did not dare to hope, nor was I so sanguine as to hope, that I myself should be an exception. I perhaps rather looked on the dark than on the bright side In fact a far more serene sky hangs over me than I supposed would. I am quite as happy as I supposed I ever should be in this state, and more so, I have as good a wife as any one, I care not who he is, and just the one for me, one who understands me and works around all my corners and sharp points exactly. I have every reason to believe that it has been the happiest thing possible that I never got any one else. I might have married in several instances but I should have missed it. I cannot but think that in this thing the very best thing has been done which could have been done. I am perfectly satisfied myself and I am without a doubt but that the satisfaction is mutual.[28]

Three days before the birth of Elizabeth's child came the shocking and wholly unexpected news that her sister Lucilla Bates had died in

Detroit. People were not so jaded by the frequency of early deaths that they did not take care about how they presented such news to a woman close to childbirth. Elizabeth, nevertheless, learned the terrible news and, unable to travel, wrote her mother immediately. She made recourse to all the available formulas of consolation to comfort herself and her mother.

March 3, 1839
Aurora—Sabbath evening

My dear Mother,

Yesterday afternoon we received a letter from Dr. Richards enclosing one from Papa which contained the melancholy intelligence of Sister Lucilla's death. The letter was not designed for my perusal, but it providentially fell into my hands. It was the wish of Dr. R to come & communicate the intelligence in person, but the travelling was so uncomfortable that it seemed impossible for him to do so. He therefore wrote a very consoling letter, and trusted the event to God.

I was entirely unprepared to hear such sad news, and was at first almost overwhelmed with grief. It is true that in two letters received from home it had been barely mentioned that she was seriously ill, but I had not allowed myself to believe that she was to be removed from us by death, and when I received the communication, it greatly agitated me. But every murmur has been silenced, and the troubled spirit is calm. Eternal wisdom ordered the event, and we must cheerfully submit to the will of Him, who never errs in judgment, but who directs all things with relation to his creatures, in loving kindness and tender mercy. If we yielded to our natural feelings we should indulge in immediate grief and with an unsubmissive spirit inquire, why was she cut down in the midst of her days and her usefulness? Why has her name been made desolate, her husband's hopes blasted, and her children left motherless, etc., and a numerous circle of relatives and friends called to mourn over her early grave? But if we have that perfect confidence in God, which ought to calm the Christian when in affliction, we shall have ready answers to such questions. We shall say, and feel too, that we are receiving corrections from our Heavenly Father, who has assured us that he does not willingly rebuke the children of men, but that he does it for their profit. By this dispensation of Providence God has come very near to us, and I feel as if we ought all of us to seek a right improvement of this chastisement from the Lord. It certainly is a loud call to us to prepare to die and this preparation we ought to make when we are in the full possession of all our faculties.

From the nature of Lucilla's disease I have been lead to fear that she was not herself conscious of the approach of death and that she was summoned unexpectedly into the eternal world. If such was the fact, it should be an admonitory lesson to us, and make us feel the necessity of living every day as if it might be the last day of our probation. We should have "our lamps trimmed, our lights burning, and we be like unto men that wait for their Lord, for blessed are those servants who the Lord when he cometh shall find watching." While we deeply mourn Lucilla's death, we have much to console us. . . . I trust the Saviour was her support in the hour of death, that He conducted her Spirit thru the dark & gloomy valley, and that she has reached that blessed abode where "there shall be no more death, neither sorrow nor crying, but where God shall wipe away all tears from their eyes."

Cherishing such hopes and relying upon such a promise as may be claimed for the believer in Jesus, we will not mourn for the dead but for the living. Our sympathies must be keenly excited. I fear Mr. Bates is poorly prepared to endure such an affliction. Had he a cordial trust in God, he would find in Him "a present help in time of trouble." My most earnest prayer is that this mysterious dispensation of Providence may be sanctified to him & that instead of sinking in this season of gloom & adversity, that he may find abundant consolation in pouring his sorrows into the bosom of a compassionate Saviour and in cheerful submission to his will he will say "the Lord gave & the Lord hath taken away." He certainly needs grace & wisdom from above not alone for himself but that he may lead his motherless children into paths of peace and holiness. My heart aches for those dear little boys. They have met with a loss which cannot be made up to them, but the Lord will provide for them. Any distrust or anxiety that I have indulged concerning them is reproved by circumstances which have been developed in my own experience. God in his wise providence has placed under our care two children who were early bereaved each of one parent. Friends have been raised up for them, and they are unconscious of the losses they have sustained. Such will be doubtless the case with Lucilla's children. It is comforting to have such hopes, tho' extremely painful to know that they never can appreciate the worth of their dear departed mother and never can receive those thousand acts of kindness which it would have been her duty, her privilege & highest happiness to have extended to them. I shall feel very solicitous to know what disposition has been made of them for the present.

I hope you will keep nothing from me, which may come to you relative to Lucilla's last sickness or death, or with reference to Mr. Bates and the children. I believe I shall have sufficient Christian fortitude to sustain me under any trial which a chastening God may find it necessary to inflict. I have been reading an anecdote which Dr. Dodridge relates of himself. He says, once when in deep affliction he was riding by a school house & heard a little boy reading a passage from the Scriptures. He stopped & listened and heard these words, "Thy feet shall be iron and brass and as thy day is, thy strength shall be." Such a sweet promise so cheered & consoled him that he went on his way rejoicing. I have appropriated this promise to myself, and I believe that He who has said, "Call upon me in the day of trouble & I will be with thee" will never forsake those who feel this trust in Him.

I hope I may hear that the death of Lucilla has been the means of leading Thomas, Magdalene & Glorianna to make an immediate and effectual preparation for death. We know not who among us may next be called to exchange worlds. The voice which spake to us all "Be ye also ready that the messenger of death may find us so prepared" is the prayer of your affectionate but much afflicted daughter

Elizabeth

Mr. R. unites with me in much love to every member of the family.[29]

In this poignant letter, Elizabeth was especially fearful for Mr. Bates and her brother and sisters who might not be prepared, that is, converted. Nevertheless, belief held the promise of salvation, the world was in the hands of a mysterious but loving God, motherless children would be cared for, no one would be tried beyond their strength, and there was a lesson to be learned about the nature of our dependence on God from such an affliction.

A few days later, in what must have been a confusing leap from tragedy to pure joy, James dashed off a letter to his parents.

Aurora Friday morning
March 8th 1839

My Dear Parents-

I have only time this morning to communicate the joyful intelligence that our Dear Elizabeth is the happy mother of a living son. The little stranger came to town about 1/2 past 6 last evening. All the Ladies regard him as a prodigy. We weighed him a few moments after his birth and to our surprise found that 10 pounds was quite a moderate calculation for his weight. Both Mother & Son are doing remarkably well. Perhaps I ought to add that Elizabeth was as comfortable thro'out the whole labour (which was somewhat protracted, having commenced as early as 7 in the morning.) as could be expected. I hope we are not insensible of the loving kindness of our heavenly Father in ordering this event in all its circumstances so as to conduce to our happiness. May we ever feel the obligations under which we are now placed "to take this child & nurse him for the Lord." Elizabeth and myself are exceedingly anxious to see you. If you could come out on the morrow & pass the Sabbath with us it would be a great comfort to Elizabeth and relief to me. Mrs. Christopher Morgan says the baby is the very image of Grandma Richards, but for one I cannot tell who he looks like. I can only say that he has a very fine open face—high forehead, etc., etc. We propose to keep up the family name.

Most affectionately yours in
great haste James[30]

He then took up the more complicated task of writing to his parents-in-law who needed to hear the good news, but also to be consoled on the death of Lucilla.

Aurora Friday morning
March 8th 1839

My Dear Parents

   Our dear Elizabeth is now the joyful mother of a living Son. The little
stranger came to town about 1/2 6 last evening. (from 7 am) she exhibited uncommon firmness and patience and was comfortable as the
circumstances of the case would allow. Our neighbors are exceedingly
kind and everything is done that can conduce to render her situation
agreeable. There is now every indication of a speedy restoration to health
& strength and accompanied with a solemn determination in reliance
upon [the] Divine and to consecrate the life given & the life preserved
to the service of the best of Masters. My own emotions are indescribable.
No man can look upon the Mother of his pretty babe without feeling
his heart irresistibly drawn toward her.

"Thus for the parents sake the child is dear
"And dearer is the parent for the child."

   I hope I am not insensible to the loving kindness of our Father in
heaven in ordering so mercifully all the circumstances of this pleasing
event, nor am I unmindful of the increased obligations under which I am
placed to consecrate myself & mine to the Service and Glory of God.
   You have been apprised in this both by Elizabeth & my Father of our
having received the intelligence of Sister Lucilla's Death. Our Sympathies
& our tears have flowed forth unbidden at your sorrow, but as we believe
that Jesus died & rose again, So also them that sleep in Jesus will God
bring with him: We Sorrow not therefore as those who sorrow without
hope: Time is the restorer as well as the destroyer of all things and this
simple reflection to the Xian [Christian] should be enough to silence the
murmur of discontent when God lays upon him his chastening hand. We
have it on proof solemn & abundant, that tho' our Xian friends die and
their bodies are committed to the dust, yet shall they be raised at some
future day & when reanimated shall be made shiny and illustrious,
permanent & durable. You my dear parents can never become insensible
to the bereavement which you have recently experienced, yet may your
sorrows be greatly mitigated when you think that God is on the throne,
that he sees the end from the beginning, & that his judgement cannot
err. His ways to us may be past finding out, yet we may be assured that

"all things shall work together for good," etc. My Prayer is that this affliction may be sanctified to us all, but to none more than Bates. Let us all fervently commend his care to God & pray that the engrossing and selfish occupations of life may not close his ears to the loud & monitory voice of this afflicting providence. I intend to write to him soon.

James had an additional practical problem to take up that concerned the care of Elizabeth and the baby James. Their servant woman Charlotte had a son in Canandaigua who had inexplicably left the family for whom he worked. James asked the Bealses to investigate so that she would not abandon them to deal with her own family problems. There was no such thing as a permanent servant in their world, and keeping someone required much attention. He added this postscript:

P.S. I ought to add that our little boy weighed last evening soon after his birth ten pounds. All the neighbors say "he is a proper child" and we are not sceptical on the subject—For

"Where yet was ever found the mother
"Who would give her baby for another.
"No child is half so fair & wise
"She sees wit sparkle in his crying."

Tho others may be far from agreeing with the enraptured parents.[31]

Elizabeth's brother-in-law, Dr. Edson Carr, immediately sent a letter explaining their serious responsibilities as parents. As a doctor and an experienced father, he felt free to advise them. His counsel was entirely compatible with the new norms of child rearing that were emerging. The old belief that sinful Adam existed in a newborn babe required parents to "break a child's will" early on. Replacing it was the

Dr. Edson Carr. (Taken from Caroline Cowles Richards, Diary 1852–1872, copyright 1908)

belief that children best learned their roles by example within an affectionate family circle. This letter focuses on the father's role when many others were concentrating on the mother's.

Canandaigua March 10th 1839

My Dear Brother

Your letter to Mrs. Beals announcing the birth of a Son, was recd this morning and was a welcome message to us all. I cannot suffer this interesting occasion to pass without offering a cordial gratulation as we welcome the little stranger to this theater of joy and sorrow, pleasure and pain.

And has an immortal being entered upon a state of conscious existence who will ere long look to you, the voluntary author of its being and call you Father?

What thrilling emotions should this awaken. What fond and anxious thoughts cluster around this endearing relation. What visions of the future. Yea what dread responsibilities have fallen upon you. Does it not seem almost the waking into new being?

And now my dear brother, allow me to make a few suggestions by way of advice and instead of looking upon this almost unconscious infant; let us for a moment contemplate its future developments, its formation of Character, the part you are here to perform, the influence you are destined to exert in the unfolding of its future capabilities and consequent destinies.

Here I believe parents are in danger of making a fatal mistake, in the management of their children by supposing that the formation of character depends chiefly upon the establishing of proper rules for their conduct, inculcating right principles & Doctrines. Now these things are right in their proper place, but this is not the way in which character & habits are formed, nor is it here that we must look wholly or chiefly for the greatest and most permanent influences. We are creatures of imitation and almost unconsciously adopt the habits and characters of others, and especially is this true of children, before they are scarcely able to distinguish between right and wrong, truth and error. Depend upon it. Children are influenced vastly more by what they observe at home in the ordinary family intercourse, then by all perceptible teaching at home or abroad. Our habits of speaking, acting, feeling and almost thinking become theirs.

How important then that we should be what we desire them to be! How important that we should watch and guard ourselves and give place to no words, actions, feeling, or even thoughts which we should regret to have repeated by them and incorporated into their very being.

Let me then entreat you as you enter upon this new and interesting, as well as awfully responsible relation, to learn to be perfect Master of yourself. Amid all the cares, trials, vexations, and disappointments of life (and these will surely come) let your Offspring Never learn that it is possible for you ever to exhibit anger or be thrown off your guard in any way or under any circumstances. Govern Yourself perfectly and you can govern others. Fail to do this, and you fail every where. The first failure here, you lose a hold upon your children which you can never regain.

There is as much truth in the proverb "Train up a child in the way he should go and when he is old he will not depart from it," as when it was first uttered, but to train him we must first teach the pattern we would have him follow.

A word to the wise is sufficient. Brother Thompson desires me to say that the 'Tobacco Story is foul slander, that he has taken no other tobacco than Chamomile Flowers, since he saw you. He also tenders his most sincere congratulations.

Much Love to Elizabeth. Tell her that Mary will make her a visit as soon as the weather and roads are comfortable.

Yours truly—Edson Carr[32]

While James and Elizabeth took their family roles seriously, James's professional duties continued to expand. He was active in clergy exchanges and was now often sought out as a preacher in local revivals. The activities of his friend Sam Hopkins showed the other face of the religion of the era, the benevolent societies. Back from Florida, he had taken a job with the American Bethel Society. In March he wrote from Geneva in his usual breezy style.

Geneva 12 March, 1839

Dear Richards

I don't know whether the calm repose that usually pervades your quiet village has been violently interrupted by the report that I am at present endeavoring to sustain the functions of Cor[reponding] Sec[retary] to the American Bethel Soc[iety] or not. If not perhaps you had better not make any great ado about it as I rather avoid the applauses of the multitude, and should not perhaps have time to reply to the congratulatory addresses they might send me on the occasion. However such is the fact—and (to be serious) I am at present on a visitation of a few weeks to the churches in this region for the purpose of addressing them on the subject and receiving the annual [collection]. I have probably only two Sabbaths now to spare at present, and on them must visit Lyons & Palmyra. If I can afford a third before returning to Buffalo I shall try and reach Auburn, but a visit to you which I had promised myself I shall be obliged to forego.

Now I wish you to know that I have a very contemptible opinion of all agents and their vocation, and, if I was a Bishop, would not let a mother's son of them into my Pulpit. In consistency there-fore I endeavor to persuade all Pastors I can to keep me out, and themselves do all the preaching I want done. This, besides a great many other good reasons for it, will have the advantage of econo-mizing time, and enable me to do much more in a limited period than I otherwise could. Now as it will be entirely out of my power to visit Aurora at present, at all events, I want you to do me & the Bethel Soc. the favor to address your people on the subject next Sabbath (if convenient) and take up a collection, i.e. if this has not been done during the year.

You need not, of course, devote a whole sermon to the subject, but after preaching (as usual) could make an address of ten minutes or so, setting forth the moral wants of boatmen & sailors, their vices, irreligious influences upon society, early deaths, etc., and the efforts which the Bethel Soc. is making with very inadequate means, to supply them with the means of religious instruction and evangelize this mass of American Heathen. You will of course do it with earnestness & feeling & much better than I could, were I there. Tell John Morgan I'll thank him to make himself Life Director by a donation of $50.00 (with my love). I shall make this my head-quarters for a fortnight longer & anything collected you can send me here, for which I will send you a receipt. With sincerest regards to Mrs. R., I am my dear friend

Very truly yours Sam M Hopkins[33]

There continued to be visits back and forth to Canandaigua and Auburn, although never enough to satisfy the grandparents in Canandaigua. Elizabeth received a letter from her father clearly expressing his dissatisfaction with the amount of time they found for him. The letter includes an ambiguous suggestion of increasing his financial support of them.

17 Oct. 1839

I have been anxiously waiting to get a letter from you (Mr. Richards does not love to write to me) that I might know when to expect a visit from Mr. Richards and yourself, and Master Richards! Do put us at ease upon this subject and let us know when to expect you, and if you do not do so, then I will go and see you and will give you no intimation of my visit, and come upon you without notice.

You do not know how much I want to see you, how many enquiries I have to make about you and from Mr. Richards about his journey and a great many things I cannot now recount. Besides all this I have many things to say to you and am fain to think you would be glad to know something about my journey, and of all the things I saw and heard and more than this, I should not be surprised if you wanted some more substantial proof of my regard for you.

Do let me see a line from you very soon.

Your mother is sitting by and unites with me in affectionate regards to you and Mr. Richards and by you to convey much love to your parents at Auburn whom we should be right glad to entertain.

affectionately yours,
Thomas Beals[34]

Auburn was sixteen as opposed to forty miles away, and so visits with the Richardses were exchanged more easily. Besides, there was the professional tie between James and his father with which Thomas Beals could not compete. It goes without saying that Dr. Richards took a lively interest in his son's spiritual development and his activities as a pastor, but in addition it was an uncertain time, rife with rumors (see next chapter). James, who was in touch with other ministers, could keep him posted on the state of affairs around his region. Even so, James was not always able to meet his father's expectations for visits. In a letter of January 1840, James explained that he could not come to Auburn because he had a parishioner who was dying, had to consult the next day with two colleagues about the state of the congregations in the vicinity, and had to preach in the afternoon. He also had to prepare a day of fasting and prayer and lectures for his own congregation as the Communion season would occur the next Sabbath. In the midst of all this activity he did not forget the seminary.

I am very much pleased with the course which you marked out in your letter to me and shall pursue it, but whether any means will bring about the wished for result is known only to the Son of the Virgin. To him I daily look for a blessing to descend upon the word preached but not with so much earnestness and importunity as I ought. Pray for me, my dear Parents, and pray for this people.

On Sabbath afternoon I design to present the needs of the Seminary. How much can be accomplished I am not able to say, probably 75 dollars. I intend to make a personal application to each member of the ch[urc]h for one dollar. If they are able to do more than this I shall ask it. Then I shall apply to others not in the Ch[urc]h. This course has been advised by the Elders.

I should like to have you send James [Henry's son who was boarding with them and was visiting his grandfather] home as soon as is practicable. His term commences today at the Academy and it is desireable that he should be on the ground fairly soon. I intended to have brought him home, but the circumstances which I have already mentioned will prevent me from so doing. I received James's letter on Saturday and was much obliged to him for it.

I am rejoiced to hear of your continued health. May the Lord sustain & comfort you under all your duties & trials. Elizabeth intends to write a few lines to Ma giving some account of the wedding. Must therefore bring my letter to a close.

Most affectionately yours

James

If you thought that you could make the ride next Saturday we should be most happy to have you make the attempt. My people love to have you with us on Communion Seasons, and it would be a great comfort and assistance to me. If you do not come out this week I trust nothing will prevent you from coming out at the meeting of Presbytery—

Elizabeth shared with her mother-in-law the details of the wedding to which James referred. Aurora was hosting a meeting of the presbytery and she too leaned on the senior Richardses' experience.

My dear Mother,

My Husband has left a little room on his sheet for me that I may give you some account of Miss Arms' wedding. She was married on New Years Evening to Mr. Van Vranken of Geneva. They were married very privately, no one being present except Capt Avery's family. I think I never attended such a pleasant wedding—all ceremony & parade were dispensed with as far as possible. Miss Arms has worn mourning a long time, & did not think best to lay it aside. She therefore appeared as usual in a black dress. We found her seated in the parlour with the [?] family when we went there, & she remained in the room both before and after the ceremony was performed & from her perfect ease and composure, no one would have imagined that we had assembled to witness her marriage. Mr. Richards spent the first part of the evening in the dining room with Mr. Arms & other gentlemen. At about 8 o'clock they went into the parlor & Mr. R was then introduced to Mr. Van Vranken & Mr. Arms then presented his Sister, & they were married. The exercises were very interesting & appropriate. (the fee was ten dollars) . . .

We hope it will be convenient for Father & yourself to be here at the meeting of the Presbytery. You have had so much experience in entertaining ministers & deacons, that I should be greatly benefitted by your advice & assistance at that time. . . .

Yours affectionately

E B R[36]

By now a year had passed since Elizabeth had given birth to little James. Dr. Richards noticed in the course of their visits that Elizabeth was suffering from a lung condition. He was sufficiently alarmed that he wrote to his son Henry who had struggled with tuberculosis for many years and had found Poughkeepsie a healthy place to live.

> I think he [James] ought not long to remain where he is on account of his wife's health. The lake air seems to be unfriendly to her constitution. She has had a hoarseness for a month or six weeks which indicates great delicacy & weakness of lungs. Indeed she has raised blood twice in small quantities which has [raised] our apprehensions. Should a door open for their removal to a more healthy location I should think they ought to improve it.

Dr. Richards noted a vacancy in the Presbyterian Church in Poughkeepsie. James's old friend Frame had been asked to fill it but had declined. Ever nervous about his ability in the pulpit, he had moved on to the editorship of the *New York Observer*. Dr. Richards sought Henry's opinion about Poughkeepsie as an opportunity for James.

> If I do not misjudge as to your brother's gifts and attainments, he would fill this vacancy at Poughkepsie acceptably. He has improved considerably since he first entered the ministry, and his improvement has been in the line of usefulness. I think he is every day becoming more spiritual and more devoted. From all that I can learn he is acquiring more and more influence among his people, and were it not for the apparent unhealthiness of the place I should not listen a moment to the proposition of a removal.

As it is I hardly know what to advise, so comfortably is he situated in many respects. In the first place he is solus; there is none to compete with, no jealousies, no rivalry. In the second place, he is universally and highly acceptable to the people. Again, they are not a large congregation and do not require such a multiplicity of parochial duties as to interfere with the labour of the study. He is near me and other judicious friends to whom he can easily repair for counsel in any special emergency. The salary is indeed small, but with the foreign aid[37] he receives he can live without getting into debt.

I have proposed this subject for your consideration, but I am not certain that it is best to seek any immediate action upon it. By the first of May, if the Lord pleases, your mother and myself will be on our Spring visit to our friends at the East & James and Elizabeth will accompany us. There will then be an opportunity for your congregation to hear him, & to take deliberate steps. But if they should be disposed to urge a hearing earlier, possibly he might leave home before the time I have specified and spend a Sabbath or two with them.

The leadings of Providence however must be respected in this thing. There must be no favoring of matters. If the door does not open naturally, it is not best to use violence to open it. I shall expect James here on Monday or Tuesday of next week. He will come for his wife who has been passing a few days with us, and weaning her little boy. . . .[38]

Whatever the merits of the proposal, nothing came of it, and they continued at Aurora for another year. Elizabeth may have resisted the thought of moving so far from her family. A brief respite was in store for her; Henry's son James would return to his parents for the summer at the end of the academy term.

In the meantime, Henry's wife wrote from Poughkeepsie to her stepson.

Pokeepsie Feby 29th 1840

My Dear Jas.

Your brother[39] has written you on the accompanying sheet a letter which I enclose without correction. It is all his own & written without any assistance & altho' somewhat stale as to its items of intelligence I think you will prize it more the less on that account. We recd. your letter on our return from N[ew] York & were much gratified to hear that you were well & happy. I hope you do every thing to please your Uncle & Aunt that your own good senses will suggest, that you are good tempered & obliging, doing every thing willingly that may be asked of you, & not be afraid to bring in the wood, go on errands, or take care of the house or any other little chore that your Uncle or Aunt would be pleased with. By so doing you will be acting the part of a clever & generous boy which character I am sure you would [not] forfeit for any selfish gratification.

      We are all doing about as usual. Bobby [his baby stepbrother] grows finely & says almost any thing. He says he loves "Father & Mother & Henry & Jimmy too" so that you perceive, that altho' absent from our circle, you are by no means forgotten. No my dear boy, you are constantly, most tenderly & affectionately remembered & we are beginning to count the weeks when we can once more welcome you to your father's roof & number you among our members. I enclose thirty dollars for your Uncle & will send him more. . . . [40]

In the fall of 1840 James moved on to a boarding school in Lee, Massachusetts,[41] and his place was taken in his Uncle James and Aunt Elizabeth's household by his brother Henry. Elizabeth was pregnant again and all talk of ill health disappeared from the correspondence. From his new school James wrote back to his younger brother and to young Anthony Dey. He had just turned thirteen, and although he wrote enthusiastically, his letters only become intelligible with some editing and added punctuation.

                                        Lee Mass Decem 23 1840
My Dear Youry [nickname for Anthony Dey]
      As you wrote a letter to me and as I expect that you think that I should answer it, I therefore take my pen in hand to comply with your wishes. In the first place, I feel an uncommon solicitude about

my hen and chickens which I left in their tender young age. I expect they, if they lived, are eaten but if they are not killed I expect that they are fine large chickens. How does your sled run this winter. I have got my cast iron sled up here and it runs very fast though I do not think that it runs as fast as the one I had last winter and it is a great deal heavier. . . . Who has got the fastest sled on the hill this winter. I guess that yours is the fastest because Henry cant steer as well as I can. I wish I had my old sled it runs so good. How does John Dogherty's sled run this winter. It did not beat mine last winter though he said it did have steel runners. Tell John Dogherty and Bill Morgan that if they will write a letter to me I will surely answer it. Give my respects to all those in the ladies department whom I have the honor to know. Tell Henry that I wish, that when he comes down in the spring, to fetch his sled along, for father thinks that he will keep him up there only this winter. My vacation is in April and we have only one month and I wish you and Henry would come down at that time so that I may see you both.

> your aff friend
> J. N. Richards

P.S. You must be sure to tell the boys what I told you. There is one thing which I have left out. This term we have been engaged in setting traps for squirrels and rabbits. We have caught about a dozen squirrels but no rabbits. We set our traps about a mile from home and go to them every morning early. I have got a new pair of skates this winter but they are a little too small for me but they would just fit you. They are like Jim Avery's only they have not got brass heels on them.

Give my love to Grandpa and Grandma the next time you see them and tell them that I am well and hope that they are too. Has Uncle got the same horse that he had before the old bay horse, and who takes care of him? Does Joshua?

As I have written such a long letter to you I expect to have a long one in return. I should like a longer one than you wrote before.

Give my respects to Miss Amanda Morgan.[42]

His accompanying letter to his brother included an engaging vignette of life with their father over the Thanksgiving vacation.

Lee Massachusetts December 23, 1840

My Dear Brother

I recieved [*sic*] your kind letter to gether with one from Aunt Elisabeth and Anthony while I was at home in the vacation and I now
take my pen in hand to inform you that I am well and also that I hope
you are enjoying the same blessings of life. When I was at home this
vacation I thought how happy I should be if you were there to play
with me. I had very fine times this vacation and in the latter end of it
I learned to shoot with a gun and I will tell you how I learned one
day when father had come up from New York [City]. He brought up
with him a large game cock and as he did not want any fighting to
be done he said that he wanted to have my old rooster killed and so
I asked father if I could not try my luck at shooting, taking him for a
mark. Father said I might, so I went and got the gun, and the old
rooster sat upon the rail fence near the big cherry tree, and I rested
the gun on the stone wall by the carriage house and took aim, and
good aim too if the good aim was showed by the shot striking the
mark as shure enough they did, and the old rooster fell off of the rail,
gave two or three kicks and died. After my first exploit in shooting
ended so well I felt very proud of it and as mother said that she would
like to have some birds to eat for dinner and after breakfast, I took the
gun and went out a shooting and shot some robins and a red squirrel.
But there is one thing that I have left out in my story which is that
we had the rooster for dinner, but he was so tough that we could
hardly eat a bit of it.

There are rather more scholars here this term than there were last.
The number last term was seven but this term it has increased to the
number of ten. . . . They are all clever boys here this term except one
whose name is Nicholas Phillips of Phillipsburg Orange County and he
is a very mean boy indeed. He tries to bully over the other boys but he
cant bully over me though he tries to. He has got a brother here who is
a very clever fellow and not at all like him.

Have you had any sleighing at Aurora yet or skating either? We have
had both here this winter. How do you like my sled? Is it a good one?
It used to be the fastest one there and I will leave it to Anthony if it
was not.

Give my love to Aunt Elisabeth and Uncle James and Believe me to be

> Your affectionate Brother
> James N. Richards

Master H. E. Richards
Aurora, Cayuga County, N.Y.   Merry Christmas[43]

Elizabeth did not share young James's enthusiasm for Anthony Dey, as she made clear in a letter to her sister Magdalena. She was concerned for her husband's sake about the impression the boys were making in the village and on her own account she found Anthony a particularly difficult child. Her pregnancy may have added to her touchiness and sense of being burdened.

> Since Papa was here Mr. Richards has had more trouble about Anthony than he anticipated. No event has occurred since we have lived in Aurora that has been such a severe trial to us as this. Mr. R. intends to write to Mr. Dey soon & he hopes some way will be provided for his removal. Please not to mention this to Brother Henry. Mr. R. had rather be the first to relate these circumstances to Mr. Dey. . . .

Elizabeth was always anxious for their reputation and it was not only the boys who threatened it.

> I do not expect to keep my woman but about one week longer. Some of my best friends in the village have thought that all the difficulties we have had in the government of our family have originated with her. Be this as it may it is certainly true that no one who ever lived with us before has brought such frequent complaints against the boys. I think it would be better for me not to have any domestic help, if by [having] it we must sacrifice our peace and quiet. A minister's "good name" is very necessary to his success & usefulness. His right to rule over his own house ought not to be questioned. . . .

All this took place against a background of solid happiness and the Richardses' good name never seemed to be in serious question.

> I can hardly realize that it is four months since you went from here. The summer has passed swiftly away from us and indeed the whole of my married life seems brief as a dream. I presumed I should have to remind you all that it will be four years tomorrow since we were married. "Goodness and mercy have followed us all our days."
>
> Tomorrow we expect Mr. Christopher Morgan (Congressman) to dine with us. He is only spending a few days in town; his wife & children are still at Auburn—[44]

Several months later Elizabeth was still dissatisfied with Anthony and the Deys, but this time her feelings about Anthony were mixed with some hope for his future. Her twelve-year-old brother Thomas was proving equally troublesome to her parents, but he seemed to be experiencing a change of heart. Why could this not happen to Anthony, too, however unlikely that appeared at present?

> Sabbath evening Nov. 15, 1840
>
> My dear Parents
>
> I have read and reread with the deepest interest the communication which I received from home last Saturday. No event could have occurred in our family, (save the hopeful conversion of someone yet living in impenitence) which would give me such cause for gratitude and rejoicing, as that therein narrated. I have been satisfied for a long time that Thomas was laying up anguish for the future. He seems now to feel like the Prodigal, who distant from a Father's house is made sensible of his wanderings and is brought back with due humiliation to acknowledge his departures from duty & to seek forgiveness. He has certainly exhibited the characteristics of true repentence & I trust his future course will test its genuineness.
>
> I should judge from all that I can learn that he is very well situated in every respect. I hope he will be under a decidedly religious influence. If so, by the blessing of God his submission to parental authority may be the first step towards his submission to his Father in Heaven. I never felt

before such a deep concern for his future welfare, as it respects this world and the next. His heart seems now to be softened, and his conscience tender, and if God in mercy interpose with a "new Character," I hope he may come with a renewed heart and be not only a dutiful son but an obedient kind humble child of God.

Altho I am quite young, (comparing my years with yours) yet I think I know, what that sorrow of heart is, which is occasioned by the ingratitude, & disobedience of one from whom we might have expected gratitude & love. The great change which has taken place in Thomas' feelings, has inspired me with the firm hope that I may live to see Anthony sensible of his departures from duty, and anxious by future obedience to make amends for past misconduct.

Her hope for Anthony was less than wholehearted. He finally left them with no regret on Elizabeth's part to go to a home in which she had little confidence.

Last week on Friday, we had a very unexpected visit from Richard Dey of Fayette, an uncle of Anthony, a man about 50 years of age, who has always lived single. He came to see us and to take Anthony home with him to spend a few weeks. We were very glad to have him go and we hope it will do him a great deal of good. He, however, did not care about going at all. When we were making preparations for his leaving, he asked how long he was to stay? I told him perhaps all winter, if his Uncle Richard was willing. He said he did not want to stay so long. He wept very much upon parting with us & seemed to feel very bad, but his tears have never affected me much for I have never before met with a child who was capable of practising so much deception. Altho I was anxious to have A[nthony] go away for a time, I regret that his associations at Fayette are very unfavourable. His relatives do not attend any church on the Sabbath & I do not know that there is one of his male friends who professes to have any respect for religion, or regard for the honour of God. I believe Papa knows that there is a Township of Land owned & inhabited by the different members of the Dey family. Anthony will probably visit among them all, and if it is as true now, as when Paul lived, that "evil communications corrupt good manners," I must expect that

AURORA

Anthony will be more or less influenced by them. Mr. Richard Dey is to be at Canandaigua next week to attend Court as a witness. I did not say anything about his going to your house, altho I did say that very likely he might meet with my Father as he was often in the Court Room.[45]

The accuracy of Elizabeth's assessment of Anthony's character and the effect of the move to western New York on Anthony's development are hard to gauge. Only one other letter about Anthony is preserved, a belated letter of thanks to James written by Anthony's mother, Lavinia Dey, a year after he left them. Her maternal impressions must be filtered through the possible distortions of time, distance, gratitude, and guilt, and Anthony may have contrasted his present circumstances with a romanticized memory of life in Aurora. Claiming that she had been ill and busy and therefore unable to write sooner, she then reported,

I have heard several times from my little boy since [he left your house]. He speaks with much gratitude and affection of Mrs. R. and yourself, and enumerates many, very many, kindnesses, which he has received from both—to Mrs. R. he says he owes every thing, as she has been his guide and instructress during the whole period of his residence with you; and that she has taught him nearly every thing he knows, he mentions her assistance while learning his lessons and says how much he feels the want of her instruction now as he has no one to ask when he wants information. From the general tenor of his letters, I feel that he is discontented . . . although he has not said so . . . but on the contrary says that his relations treat him very kindly. . . . I feel extremely anxious to see him, and at times scarcely know how to submit to the separation; had I known when we parted that three long years would have passed before we met again, I do not think my resolution would have sustained me, although I know it was for the benefit of my child. . . .

Please present my grateful acknowledgements that words cannot express the obligations I feel towards her for kindness to my darling boy, tell her she has made the Widow [full] with gratitude to that kind providence who raised up friends in time of trouble—pardon me but my feelings are too full and I must conclude. . . .[46]

With Anthony gone, Elizabeth could write about more comfortable and seemly news.

> Monday a.m. Mr. Richards went to Ith[a]ca on Saturday (and took his little nephew Henry Richards with him). I expect he will return this evening. Reverend Mr. Wisner is very unwell. In consequence of this the Elders of the Church at I[thaca] wrote to Mr. R. requesting him to come & preach for them. As all things were favourable he concluded to go. One of the Auburn students came & supplied our pulpit. He is quite a promising man by the name of Carr. He staid [sic] here, made quite a pleasant visit & left early this morning. As he was a very fine singer I thought he might possibly be a relative of Dr. Carr's. I therefore asked him where his Father lived. I found that he was born at Romulus, the village opposite us, so I conclude he is not connected with the Doctor's friends.
>
> Last week a family removed to our village. The gentleman's name is the Revd. Mr. Walker. He has been the settled minister in Pembroke a few miles west of Batavia. He is now employed by the State as an agent for the Improvement of Common Schools. I hardly know why, but he has concluded to make this village his headquarters. I am very much pleased with the appearance of himself & family. He has 5 children. One of the Boys staid [sic] here a day or two while they were regulating their affairs. They occupy the widow Wood's house which we once thought of renting.
>
> You inquire about my little James. He is learning to talk very fast indeed. He is very well & happy most of the time. The Boys have learned him to sing "Tippecanoe & Tyler too" and he has amused us very much indeed. I am very glad to learn that Mary's little boy has improved so much, & is able to walk. Remember us kindly to Dr. Carr & herself. . . .
>
> Did you hear of the return of the ship *President* that Mr. E[dward] C. Richards sailed in? He resailed on the 10th.
>
> Remember me with much affection to my Mother & Sister & regard me ever as your very affectionate & much obliged daughter.
>
> > Elizabeth
>
> I hope I may hear from home soon, the more letters I have the more I want. I will promise to answer all I receive.[47]

The everyday proximity of special friends like the Morgans gave a luster to life in Aurora. How distressing then when John Morgan died unexpectedly that winter. He had been a major reason for James's coming to Aurora three years before. The friendship was strong enough for James and Elizabeth to name their second child John Morgan Richards when he was born in February, a month after John Morgan's death. Although John Morgan left the church in Aurora $2,000 for the purchase of a parsonage and an additional $5,000, the interest of which was to be applied to the support of the pastor,[48] it was not enough to hold James in Aurora. This time it was not just that the farther fields looked greener but that Aurora had lost its former charms. Another parish in western New York, Penn Yan, needed a pastor and he was ready to act.

His father's unequivocal advice was to reject the offer.

> Since you were here I have learnt that Mr. Minor has concluded not to leave Penn Yan though dismissed from his former charge. His particular friends have rallied around him and promised to give him a support, and either have organized themselves or expect to be organized, as a congregational church. His old congregation are now looking out for a successor and from what I have heard it is possible they may make application to you. Should this be the case, my advice is to give them no encouragement, but kindly & respectfully to decline. This place cannot be a desireable one for the present, and those who are comfortably settled should leave it for others.

He was still concerned about Elizabeth's health. His advice to her in the same letter could only be given by a man little involved with the actual running of a household with small children.

> Tell Elizabeth that your mother and myself enjoin it upon her to take the best possible care of herself. This must be her first business, the great object to which every thing else must bend. Let things about the house put themselves to rights, if they get deranged, and let it be her care not to expose or fatigue herself till her usual strength is perfectly restored. . . .[49]

In the past his concern had suggested that they should move to the more congenial climate of Poughkeepsie. Knowing in addition that John Morgan's death had transformed the situation in Aurora and that James was ready for a greater challenge, he might have been expected to endorse the proposal. In order to understand why Dr. Richards was so adamant about rejecting the Penn Yan offer, it is necessary to go back to Auburn to see what had happened to the Presbyterian Church.

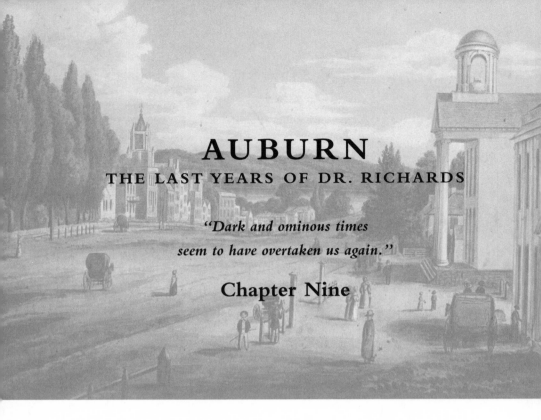

AUBURN
THE LAST YEARS OF DR. RICHARDS

"Dark and ominous times
seem to have overtaken us again."

Chapter Nine

W hat was it that made Dr. Richards so cautious about James's accepting the Penn Yan pastorate? The explanation undoubtedly lies in the tumultuous history of the Presbyterian Church in upstate New York over the previous decade.

In 1831, nine years before the crossroads in James's career, Dr. Richards could have looked back with some satisfaction at his life's work. His difficulties with Finney had not yet been fully resolved but the cause of religion had surely prospered in visible ways. The landscape was dotted with Presbyterian schools and seminaries, the number of professed Presbyterians had multiplied, voluntary societies were at work in every corner of the land, and closer to home, Auburn was turning out well-trained ministers in growing numbers.

His positive assessment of the value of the seminary's contribution to the cause is caught in a fund-raising letter he wrote in August 1831.

> What good has the seminary done or is likely to do? Allow me to say, it
> has sent forth more than one hundred and fifty preachers of the gospel,
> who are now lifting up their voices in Christ's name. Not a few of them
> have gone to the wide spread desolations of the West. More than thirty

are already in the great valley of the Mississippi; three have gone to the Sandwich Islands;[1] and two more expect to sail for the same destitute region sometime this autumn. Others have their hearts fixed upon a foreign mission and others still, though they wish to labour in our own country are ready to go to its utmost boundaries if they may serve the cause of their heavenly master. I could name more than thirty who have been blessed with extensive revivals under their ministrations and I speak soberly when I say that there are hundreds, nay thousands, and thousands of precious souls who we have reason to believe have been snatched from the burning lake through their instrumentality. May we not hope that the lovers of Christ and of his dear kingdom will look fairly at the call which the seminary now makes for assistance.[2]

In July 1832, he had reason to make a more disinterested assessment. He was visited by Alexis de Tocqueville and his friend Gustave de Beaumont. They were in America to investigate the American penal system, and Auburn's new model prison was naturally on their itinerary. The two young Frenchmen never lost an opportunity to talk with persons who could help them understand the country. Tocqueville noted, "Mr. Richards is an old man whose piety seemed to us sincere and even ardent (a rare thing in America). We asked him if in his opinion the religious principle was not losing its force. He replied, 'Perhaps in the large cities, not in the small ones and in the country. I believe that in the last thirty years, on the contrary, we have made some progress.'" Although Tocqueville added, "I am much afraid that he is mistaken," Richards could speak with authority about the small cities and the country; it was the area where he labored.[3]

Their conversation continued on the subject of the role of religion in society. Here Tocqueville found himself in total agreement with Richards when he said,

Alexis de Tocqueville. (Portrait by Theodore Chasseriau, Le Musee de Versailles, copyright 1988 Musees National)

> I don't believe that a republic can exist without morals and I do not
> believe that a people can have morals when it isn't religious. I therefore
> judge the maintenance of the religious spirit one of our greatest political
> interests.[4]

It was a commonplace of the age that a successful republic required citizens committed to the public good and that morality had its surest foundation in religion. Richards took additional satisfaction from his church activities when he saw himself in a civic light. This was part of his meaning when he wrote home to Caroline in August 1831. "How gladly would I employ my time at home if it were practicable, but being a public man, I am obliged to live for the public."[5]

Despite his firmly stated opinions about the strength and importance of religion in America, Richards knew that he only saw part of the picture. Even if he enjoyed a far flung correspondence and had friends and relatives who made their way in the commercial world, it was always a Presbyterian world that he saw. He knew that for many of his countrymen religion was becoming a private affair. He commented uncomfortably on a trip to New York in 1831:

> I have been continually among strangers since I left home; I have hardly
> met with a person whom I have known before. How many are good and
> how many bad, I know not. Whether they are Jews, Christians, or
> Mohamadans [sic], I cannot tell. A general civility has been manifest by
> those that I have met—but I may say nothing of religion. It is painful to
> intermingle with those who whatever they may be, discover no signs of
> their heavenly birth. A public vehicle however is not the place to learn
> the religious dispositions of men.[6]

The satisfaction he took in the progress of religion never led to complacency; life continued to throw up new problems. Slavery, for example, was increasingly coming to public consciousness. He had once been involved in Sunday School classes for "colored people" in Newark. Now there were "colored brethren" who were establishing churches for themselves, and at least one of these congregations applied to him for help. He wrote to Henry Dwight in January 1831:

The bearer of this is Israel Lewis the agent for the coloured colony now settling in Canada. He has a project for obtaining six or seven thousand acres of land, for his coloured brethren amounting to about 70 families and wishes the privilege of drawing your attention to it . . . I do not see why he should not be encouraged in this enterprise.[7]

While race prejudice was so common in the North that he made no comment about a congregation escaping the United States to settle in Canada, he must have been shaken by a letter he received in September 1831, from a fellow pastor in Alexandria, Virginia. The pastor had just survived the greatest slave revolt of the antebellum period, the one led by Nat Turner. The issue of slavery was becoming very real.

I presume you have seen accounts of the insurrections at the South. Since last Saturday our town has been in considerable alarm & every night we have a military patrol. The citizens also are furnished with arms which they keep in their houses in case of an attack. Some few think we are in no danger, being so far from the scene of civil war—but the great majority of our citizens are sufficiently alarmed to take every necessary precaution. Some families do not take off their clothes at night, & scarcely sleep at all. In Norfolk I am informed the people are afraid to go to church night or day & the churches are closed. Yesterday (Sabbath) we were not without apprehension of danger & thought it expedient to have our second service in the afternoon instead of the evening, as is our custom. We have understood that Wilmington N.C. is in ashes and that five counties in other parts of this state are in a state of insurrection; that many families have been butchered, etc. This is a state of things too bad to be borne, & I trust that God will overrule it so as to lead to our deliverance from the great national evil under which we have been long groaning.[8]

A darker, more contentious mood gradually took hold of the church as well. Richards was slow to adopt it, but was finally drawn in. When Finney removed himself from western New York following his defeats in Auburn and Oneida, he left behind numerous partisans. In Albany, Richards's friend Sprague was prepared to continue the battle with the Finneyites, and tried to enlist Richards's help. Richards replied in February 1832:

I rejoice that you have taken up your pen, as I doubt not in the defence of the truth. Let your argument be luminous and your points strong. Public discussion if sober and temperate will be beneficial. But nothing will be gained with those whom you would wish to correct by an appeal to authority. We live in new times, just upon the margin of the Millenium and it would be strange if we should not have new views and far outstrip any of our predecessors. What care we for what men thought fifty or an hundred years ago? Our appeal is to the Bible and to facts.[9]

Sprague had asked him to recount his earlier successes in New Jersey as an example of proper revivals, and Richards's response was decidedly lukewarm. He was sure that Sprague's strategy would not work. Even though he preached deference to his sons, his shrewd Yankee instincts told him that the new generation no longer listened to the voice of authority.

Despite his apparent equanimity, he sent and received a series of letters in 1832 that were ominous. The seminary was having real difficulty in replacing Dirck Lansing, and the difficulty increasingly centered on the orthodoxy of the candidates. After Dr. Gardiner Spring had rejected the seminary's offer three times, Dr. Skinner of Philadelphia was elected, but he also declined. Next the Reverend Edwards A. Park considered their offer but felt his education and convictions were too strongly Congregationalist to allow him to accept.[10] In a letter to his friend Henry Dwight on July 5, 1832, Richards described his difficulties in safely sorting out the new ideas afloat, including "Taylorism" which we have already seen was so disturbing to young Frame (see chapter 7).

Mr. Hopkins is much in favour of appointing Mr. Lindsley. . . . I feel somewhat embarrassed for though I would proscribe no man except a downright heretic, because he differs in theological opinions from me, yet I cannot but feel a delicacy in placing a man of questionable opinions in a situation where it would be easy for him in various ways to foster erroneous views. . . . I know we ought not to be overscrupulous in minor matters and that some latitude of opinion must in this important state of things be indulged, but where men are verging to a system which

our whole church as a body pronounces to be erroneous and of
dangerous tendency, it strikes me we should act with some degree of
caution. . . . I am you know a pretty divided Calvinist and I think I
can tolerate without much difficulty the many shades of difference
existing in this school. But when you go beyond this and touch upon the
precincts of Arminianism I stop with fear. . . . I do not say, nor do I
believe that Dr. Taylor is an Arminian, but he is cruising along the borders
of this deceitful sea. . . .[11]

In October 1833, he was still looking for a professor of Sacred
Rhetoric and Pastoral Theology and sharing his troubles with the
Reverend Leonard Woods of Andover, who was also trying to fill vacancies. Woods was as much at sea as Richards about the candidates outside his
own area and was seeking information. Woods's analysis of the available
candidates included a description of the increasingly polarized church in
Connecticut.

As to Mr. Park . . . I think you will do well to get him if you can. . . .
Dr. Porter [and I] both think him "pious and safe." . . . The next man to
him in my view is Nehem[iah] Adams of Cambridge. . . . I am not quite
certain that he has been rid of all his tendencies toward New Divinity tho'
I suppose he has. I should want to make a little more inquiry, for as you say,
it is difficult to know what men are.
    I suppose you found that the old school men in Conn[ecticut] are full
of zeal for a new Sem[inar]y [at East Windsor] They have already obtained
more than ten thousand doll[ars] towards a professorship. . . . But there
is danger of a most deplorable schism in Conn[ecticut]. . . . I observe
that some men, who have treated the proposal for a Sem[inar]y at Troy
with great candor & kindness, are very severe upon the plan at Windsor.
So it is. We are cast upon new times; times when boasting & ignorance &
impudence pass wonderfully well with multitudes.—I hope a new &
better order of things will arise out of all this disorder & confusion.
    I have thought it of immense consequence that the right man
should be elected for your new professor, because the time may come,—
yea, will come, when Auburn Sem[inar]y must be guided by a new set
of men. Your labors & your influence then will by & by be ended; & the

man who is now introduced may be the man to have a preponderating
influence on the right side, or on the wrong, after you are gone. . . .
The Lord raise up more men & better men for our colleges & seminaries;—men of strong minds & steady faith & warm & active &
consistent piety, & well balanced judgements,—men who may be
depended on in foul weather as well as fair,—in war, as well as peace.
Such men will be raised up just so fast & in just such number as God
sees best on the whole. It is all in his hand. . . .[12]

This letter witnesses vividly to the growing division within the Presbyterian Church. The situation was so fluid and confusing that Richards
himself did not know the orientation of the new seminary being founded
in Troy and had to write to his friend Sprague the next month to ask
about its "numbers, its prospects and its general estimation."[13] In a few
months, Lyman Beecher would be unsuccessfully tried as a heretic when
he took Taylor's ideas to Lane Seminary in Ohio. The Reverend Albert
Barnes, who had become an immensely successful revivalist and temperance man in Richards's old parish in Morristown, had already moved to
Philadelphia and been unsuccessfully tried as a heretic by the General
Assembly. He was to be tried again the following year. Lines were being
drawn and people like Richards and Woods were finding life increasingly
uncomfortable. They both taught in seminaries that tolerated a considerable diversity of opinion. Andover had been founded by a coalition of
Hopkinsians and "old Calvinists" to combat Unitarianism. Auburn was
founded under the Presbyterian-Congregationalist Plan of Union.
Although Richards leaned towards the more conservative thinking of his
current faculty, he had managed to work for a time with Lansing and had
worked over a long period with Perrine, who was clearly sympathetic
with the New Measures men.

   In the next phase of the search for a professor at Auburn, Richards and
Perrine mounted a campaign to woo Dr. Samuel Cox of the Laight Street
Church in New York. He was well-known to Richards, having been his
student back in Newark. Cox replied with many doubts about his duty,
the salary, the pressure to conform, and what kind of security Auburn
could offer. In the end he declined.

   The atmosphere of growing tension and division is evidenced by
another letter from Leonard Woods written on December 2, 1834. He was

interested in knowing about Albert Barnes for one of his vacancies at
Andover. Woods judged the opinion of "Dr. [Ashbel] Green's party and the
great body of the Presbyterian Church" that had just tried Barnes for
heresy to be so partisan that he wanted Richards's independent judgement.

> What degree of knowledge has he in Oriental literature? What are his
> habits of thinking, & the peculiarities of his preaching? How far has he
> adopted the new speculations of the Divinity School at New Haven?
> What is his influence & what is it likely to be in regard to the present
> controversy . . . between the peculiarities held by Dr. Taylor and Mr.
> Finney & their associates, & the settled theology of New England as held
> by Edwards, Bellamy, Smally and Dwight, etc. What would be the prob-
> able effect of his coming here on the character of this Sem[inar]y & upon
> its future prospects? In a word, what would you think of his being chosen
> a Professor here, & how w[oul]d it strike the great body of intelligent
> ministers who agree in sentiments with you? . . . I hear a new effort is
> making to get Dr. Cox. Is it so? I presume you will have him if you
> appoint him again.[14]

Auburn had resumed its courtship of the skittish Cox and put Perrine
in charge of the correspondence. His letters struck an entirely different
note from Richards's, at once whimsical and reassuring. Perrine, who was
at work on an *Abstract of Biblical Geography*, added charming little maps to
his letters.

Auburn Fe. 25th 1835

Dr. Brother Cox

    I have just recd. your esteemed favour of the 13th—It is written
pretty well, but I have some difficulty in reading it. Yes, I make it out
now. It is the genuine writing of brother C. I thought he was the same
good old friend & so he is—Well I will write another letter *simply* for
his eye. . . .

    1. I will send you a map of our village and it will afford all the infor-
mation you need.

    2. "What" you say "do you mean by my address at appearing on this
new stage" & I am rather ashamed of my blundering & fear I shall go on
blundering through life. I now see I awakened feelings in your mind

which I did not intend. In my folly I designed simply to remind you of an inaugural address which would be expected from you, & to express my desire that you should turn your thoughts towards it in due time. I truly meant nothing more nor less. As to your performances in the chair, or pulpit or your appearance or deportment among us *westerns*, I had them not in my mind. . . .[15]

There followed detailed information about every conceivable aspect of the operation of the seminary and its organization, and the house that Cox might buy or rent. This last was accompanied by the advice of Richards that "it will not be good policy to talk of purchasing at this moment as an effort is about to be made to obtain money for building two professors' houses on our own land." As a matter of fact the seminary was doing sufficiently well financially that year that full faculty salaries were restored in August after a lapse of five years.[16] To further reassure Cox, Perrine wrote three more detailed letters regarding transportation to Auburn, the seeds he would plant so that a garden would be in place upon his arrival, and the location and design of the garden fence.

The ground south & southeast of the house is such that in the arrangement of your garden you can display a *great deal* of taste—I wish your eye was upon it—& indeed upon the whole premises, & I could talk with you a few minutes—I know what I would do if I owned the lot & had the money in pocket—but your taste & judgement may be very different from mine. . . .

I have been out today to look for a cow, but have not met with such an one as I like—but shall endeavour to have one to introduce to you on your arrival. . . . I fear I shall not be able to obtain a cow of the first quality under $25 or $30. . . .

As to the inside of the house our women think that the present color of some of the rooms will not please Mrs. Cox & that she may wish to have them changed. . . . Tell Mrs. Cox I should have had the house painted throughout but our ladies advise to the contrary. They think Mrs. Cox had better direct in this matter. Now you know that women are the best judges in some things. . . .

As to help, if you can get a good colored man, not boy, it will be such help as you need. He can make your garden etc. but be sure to get such a one as possesses a good moral character & whose habits are fixed. The colored people here are vicious & will corrupt any one who is not protected by established principles of morality & religion. A good gardener would have work here in abundance & would get good wages. Such a one might do all your work, & be able to earn during the summer, a considerable amount by helping others etc. If you can procure good help, male or female, you better bring it with you.

I am surprised to learn from your letter that brother Lansing & family expect to accompany you.[17] Bravo. Come on dear brethren— we have room in our hearts & town for both of your families. . . .

Now be assured dear brother there are many here who are waiting your arrival with much impatience. We all want to see you & your family settled happily among us. . . .

Whatever enters your mind that you wish me to do, send it on with all possible promptitude. Speak—your brother hears.

You speak of being overwhelmed with business & with *feelings* at this crisis etc. & my Dr. Brother, I know something about your feelings & I feel for you. The hour of separating from your dear people & friends has not yet arrived—& of the feelings of that moment you are still ignorant. But you have done what you thought to be duty, & what I hope is peculiarly pleasing to your blessed Lord—Keep your eye fixed on him at the right hand of the Father & in the glories of his kingdom & not on the objects with which you are surrounded here.[18]

Cox finally arrived and was inaugurated June 16, 1835; a long-standing problem had been solved. And then within the year, Perrine died quite unexpectedly at the age of fifty-nine and the seminary had to face the same problem all over again. Perrine had been a professor from the beginning and the death of this much loved man left a serious gap in the ranks.

However, from the point of view of James Richards the division within the church was coming to a head and this took precedence over finding a replacement for Perrine. On the one side were the Finneyites and Taylorites, increasingly known as the New School, and on the other the doctrinal conservatives, known as the Old School. He wrote to his old friend Dr. Miller, who was still on the faculty of Princeton Seminary, presciently laying out the tragedy that was developing.

Auburn, March 5, 1835
I am distressed at the present state of things and at the prospect before us. I fully sympathise with you in the evils which threaten our beloved Ch[urc]h, and am equally at a loss for any speedy or specific remedy. I have thought of many things, but none of them seem to me exactly feasible or if feasible wise. I cannot go with our act and testimony brethren [a sobriquet for the Old School] though I sincerely support them and feel an inward and general leaning to their cause. . . . Produce the separation which our brethren seem to wish, and the individuals composing the new organization will be deprived of one half of their power—while hundreds in every direction who in all leading points are with them, but from a variety of causes cannot join them, will be thrown into the back ground, and their influence in a great measure nullified by the heterodoxy which surrounds them.

Did I think however that the corruption was as deep or as general as our act and testimony brethren suppose, I might possibly come to a different conclusion. But I can by no means persuade myself of this. I am certain indeed that in the immediate sphere of my observation it is not so. Western N[ew] York probably contains as much of the corrupt leaven as can be found in any equal portion of our Church. But the Church in this region is by no means as far gone in new measures and new opinions as has been supposed. As to the new measures they are evidently waxing old and ready to change; while new opinions are becoming the subject of more alarm, and many are calling out for the standards.

The P[res]b[ytery] of Geneva have lately lifted up their voice upon this subject and recommended to the Churches under their care a new and increased attention to the confession of faith and the catichisms [sic] of our Church. Several of the Pbys. to the West, Genessee, Niagara, and Buffalo are tending the same way and some of them with regard to Doctrine are fully prepared to take a stand. How near they approximate to the oldest of the old school I cannot say but

I understand that they mean to abide by *Calvinism* in all its essential features, a system which places God on the throne and the creature in the dust at his feet. The Pby. of Rochester I am told are improving in their doctrinal views; and that a certain brother hitherto not very stable, but possessed of speechifying power, is gradually losing his influence, both in the Pby. and in the synod. All this looks like a return to better days.

Another important fact is strikingly visible; protracted meetings and Evangelists and the whole system of machinery connected with them are fast losing their hold upon the public mind. People begin to inquire what *authority* is there for those things, and are their results on the whole *salutory*? I have rather been surprised to find some of our new measures men of late so much concerned for the honour of pastors and so desirous, if possible, to redeem their influence. Most of the revivals too in this part of the country for the last six months have assumed a more mild and orderly character and, what is no less gratifying, even new measure men speak of it with apparent satisfaction. Among several protracted meetings held in this vicinity this winter, two of which I myself attended, I saw and heard of nothing which any sober minded person would be likely to condemn. I speak of measures principally. There were no anxious seats, no calling out for prayers before or after the service, no numbering and displaying of converts, but rather a guarded silence on this subject. And this state of things occurred in places where formerly the greatest irregularities prevailed.

Surely our brethren are coming to their senses in these matters. And if I could say as much concerning doctrine my apprehensions for the future would in great measure subside. But this is a vastly more subtle and sturdy thing. The sorriest Pelagian & Arminian notions which are abroad in the land will not so suddenly disappear. While they enlist the pride and self sufficiency of men who wish to seem wiser than others, they draw to their aid all the hearts of the unsanctified. I loathe the system in all its forms, and none the less for the artful and crooked measures it adopts for its support and extension. But I do not see what hope we have of immediately escaping from its poisonous influence.

According to all human appearance there is and must be a conflict. The pulpit and the press will be compelled to engage in it. They must assume a bold and decided front, not pugnacious exactly, not vindictive, but tender, solemn, earnest and unflinching, looking to God for his blessing. He who has maintained his truth in past ages, can do it still. I do not dispond [sic]—though I fear and tremble. I know we deserve chastisement for our worldliness, and our criminal indifference to the cause of truth. Still I hope God will yet work for his great name.

But you will ask is there nothing to be done on our part; and what shall it be? I can only say *everything*, which promises success; be it argument, be it discipline or what it may. But I confess my chief hope, so far as means are concerned rests upon an honest and fearless exhibition of the truth. Let the true doctrines be set forth in their strongest & best lights—and sound and able answers returned to the false and dangerous opinions broached by our erring brethren. It strikes me that our reliance ought rather to be on argument than on authority. This is not an age to *awe* men by the influence of great names or by the decisions of Ecclesiastical counsels.

Not that I am opposed to discipline for heresy—I contend for it as truly in this case, as for immorality. But such is the temper of the times, that less is to be hoped from it than in some other periods of the Church. And for this reason too, great care must be taken in the *mode* of administering it. The manner must be clearly legitimate, fair and impartial. When this be done, let it be done, I will hold up both hands.

My hope however mainly fixes on an open and manly defense of the truth. Much has been done in this way already, by yourself and Coadjutors at Princeton—and a great deal more may yet be done. I wish to see pamphlets and small volumes of essays adapted to the times and coming forth in thick array. If judicious and of a popular cast they will have an influence which is wide and effective. I derive this opinion from what I have actually observed.

Whether anything can be done to satisfy our Old School brethren that we are friendly to truth & to Presbyterial order I am not certain. If they possess the spirit of Dr. Wilson of Cincinnati,[19] I should think it not very probable. I have no doubt however that there is a large majority in our Ch[urc]h who have more sympathy even with him than with *New Havenism*, where the system has been fairly unveiled. For myself at least I can say I consider him as standing much nearer the Ark than such men as I could name in Connecticut.

If by any act of the Gen[era]l Ass[embl]y an end could be put to the present "painful and agitating conflicts" I should rejoice. But I acknowledge I can see little hope of this. The evils are of such a nature that they seem to admit of no speedy cure. Well it would be if the sound and sober parts of the Ch[urc]h could be united in some general principles, though ultras on both sides should dissent. But I can think of no plan by which this union could safely and easily be affected; perhaps I should say formally. In my opinion it really exists now and will every day henceforth become stronger and more apparent. I calculate much upon this circumstance. It might work out good for us in the end. . . .

I do not expect to attend the next Gen[era]l Ass[embl]y, but I hope to be at N[ew] Y[ork] in the early part of May when I may have the pleasure of seeing you. What I have written has been in confidence and designed for your eye only.

With the sincerest affection I subscribe myself your brother in the Gospel.

Jas Richards[20]

This was the cry of a man deeply distressed, but not hopeless. The situation was reminiscent of his younger days when he had seen Timothy Dwight turn the unbelieving world at Yale to his way of thinking. Richards himself, by standing firm, had had a hand in moving western New York to the more reasonable views he saw developing. While he placed his confidence in an educated elite, one that he was committed to training, he was sensitive to the egalitarian currents of the age. He spoke not only as a keen observer, but as a man who found comfort in the long view. He was no fanatic; he could live with a variety of opinions even if he did not agree with them all. It must be acknowledged that deviations in doctrine bothered him more than deviations in evangelizing practice.

In April 1836, a year later, he was again writing to Miller, this time deploring just what he had warned against the previous year, an illegitimate show of power, unfairly applied by the very men with whom he agreed.

> I really tremble at the prospect before us. The Synod of Phil[adelphia] appear to me to have acted very unwisely, if not unconstitutionally in the case of brother Barnes. I am astonished that they did not clearly foresee they were putting their own cause to a fearful hazard by the course which they took. But the thing is done and must be met. . . .

He noted among the people of his region:

> a prodigious sympathy for Brother Barnes. . . . The delegates for our Presbytery are warm advocates of the new school. . . . My prayer and hope is that the great head of the ch[urc]h will vouchsafe his presence to the next Assby [Assembly] and give wisdom and grace needful for the great occasion. From movements in the city of N[ew] Y[ork] and in Illinois and in other places, it is easy to see I think that congregationalism is about to raise its multiplied and irresponsible head among us. If they would collect together the Finneyism and the New Havenism and relieve our church of the burden I for one would not complain.[21]

This is an obvious reference to the Plan of Union which he seemed ready to see disbanded.

Richards did not attend the General Assembly in the summer of 1836 despite the deteriorating situation. His health was poor. He went to Avon that summer where he noted:

> My appetite is good and the waters I think are beneficial but I am too far advanced in years to regain my strength as heretofore.[22]

By fall he was deeply immersed again in the precarious state of the seminary's finances. The trustees had decided to add a new building, Douglas Hall, and to call Luther Halsey to fill the chair that had been held by Professor Perrine. It was only a few months before the financial strain was felt and Cox announced that the seminary finances were too uncertain for him to be able to continue. He planned to resign in June 1837 to return to New York City at double his seminary salary. Richards wrote his friend Dwight in Geneva on January 26, 1837.

> Doctor Cox concluded to leave us. . . . Thus are we thrown upon the wide sea again—and shall have a new election on our hands, if another professor shall be deemed necessary. I hope however we shall have the wisdom to wait until the requisite funds are provided and that we shall not rely on any annual subscription. . . . His loss, however, I fear will unfavourably affect us; not altogether so deeply as if Doctor Halsey had declined our invitation. But we must submit to the Providence of God.[23]

His faith was firm; it always worked to persuade him that what might appear to be a personal or institutional failure was in fact a call to submission and a reason to rethink his approach.

By April, Halsey had arrived but had not been paid. Despite the fact that Richards had $12,000 subscribed, none of it was yet in hand. He chose to look at the brighter side when he reported to Dwight at the end of April.

> A very good junior class has already entered and more are expected. 16 have joined the seminary since the term began and it is gratifying to observe that they appear to be young men of more than ordinary promise.[24]

In May 1837 he left for a fateful meeting of the General Assembly. He travelled south with his wife, visited with his children, and then proceeded to Philadelphia apparently unaware of the Old School's plan to take control of the Presbyterian Church. Once in Philadelphia he wrote home:

> I reached Philadelphia about 5 o'clock, the afternoon I left you, safe and sound. Had a delightful passage and plenty of good company. I stepped into Mr. Brown's carriage as soon as I reached the wharf and they drove me immediately to Mr. T. Elmes . . . where I found my old friends glad to see me and ready to give me the best of quarters. My Rheumatism has almost entirely left me and my gen[era]l health I trust is improving.

I heard the opening sermon from Dr. Witherspoon, the last year's moderator; a production far below what might have been expected from his grandfather in similar circumstances. . . . The Old School carried their moderator by a majority of 31. . . . A good many of our old students are in attendance. It is pleasant to see them and take them by the hand once more.

This will be a highly important meeting of the Ass[embl]y. What precisely will be done is more than any of us can yet predict. Some talk loudly of division, others of cutting off some of the suspected members or branches of the Ch[urc]h. But no body knows what the issue will be. One thing is certain, the Gen[era]l Ass[embl]y will organize a Board of Foreign Mission to which I have no manner of objection. They will attempt too I think to cripple the Home Missionary Society and the N[ew] Y[ork] P[res]by[teria]n Education Society neither of which will they be able to do effectually. I hope it may please the Lord to pour upon them the spirit of wisdom and of a sound mind, the spirit of peace and of good will. . . .[25]

Richards was witnessing the opening guns of the Old School campaign, the election of a sympathetic moderator, and the striking down of the nonsectarian benevolent societies so dear to the heart of the New School. This was done on the grounds that they involved cooperation with other denominations and were therefore insufficiently Presbyterian in their inspiration. The next step towards purity was to purge themselves of their Congregationalist allies. By a vote of 143 to 110 they declared "that the Plan of Union adopted for the new settlements in 1801 was originally an unconstitutional act on the part of that Assembly and therefore . . . is hereby abrogated." They then resolved that "the Synod of the Western Reserve is . . . no longer a part of the Presbyterian Church in the United States of America." Finally the frenzy for doctrinal purity led the majority to declare that the Synods of Utica, Geneva, and Genessee were out of ecclesiastical connection with the Presbyterian Church. That same day they also dissolved the Third Presbytery of Philadelphia.[26] The four exscinded synods of western New York and the Presbytery of Philadelphia were stunned to find themselves outside the Presbyterian Church without formal charges having been preferred and without a trial.

Over the next few days the General Assembly published a list of sixteen alleged doctrinal errors that the exscinded group was supposed to hold. The banished group met each evening for consultation. Baxter Dickinson, previously the pastor of the Third Presbyterian Church in Newark and now a professor at Lane Seminary, drew up a rebuttal of the charges which in due course was presented to the Assembly. It was filed, but left unanswered. There was nothing further the group could do but go home, humiliated, angry, and cut off from their normal access to property, endowments, and the machinery of the church.[27]

The situation needed to be quickly regularized. The seminary rose to the occasion under Richards's leadership. It sent a circular to all the exscinded synods inviting them to send representatives to a convention in Auburn on August 17.[28] Richards's letter to his friend Dwight suggests the tone and attitude he wished the convention to adopt.

> It is desireable that there should be judicious and united action; and none can more properly move in it in the first place than those who have felt the severity of the blow. Auburn is central to the three synods in Western N.Y. who will naturally be represented in the Board of Commissioners assembling at our anniversary. Can there be a better time or place for such a convention if one is to be held. Please to give us your opinion and that of Mr. Hay and Mr. Hopkins on the subject. And if you are favourable to such a measure, be kind enough to say whether we may make use of your name in issuing a circular. We propose to say but little, and that of a dignified and general character.[29]

The synods hoped that the meeting would only need to provide a means for carrying on their work temporarily, and that if they publicized their treatment at the hands of the General Assembly, the great body of the church would rise up and reinstate their representatives at the next year's assembly. Richards was unanimously chosen president of the convention in view of his unquestioned orthodoxy, not to mention his reputation for prudence and patience. At the end of four days the convention, voting unanimously, issued a statement that the actions of the General Assembly had been unconstitutional and were therefore null and void. It called on the exscinded presbyteries to "retain their present organization and connexion without seeking any other and to send their commissioners to the next General Assembly as usual." Richards was appointed chairman of a committee to "take measures to secure the ends proposed by this convention"; Beecher headed another that was to contact the ministers and members of the Presbyterian Church; Cox's committee was to see to their legal rights; Halsey headed a committee on doctrine. This last committee prepared a statement known as the Auburn Declaration. Substantially the same as the one Dickinson had submitted in Philadelphia, this document in years to come became the statement of orthodoxy of the New School body.[30]

Richards described what he thought had been accomplished and where he thought things stood in a letter to Anna a few weeks after the convention.

> Much do I regret that there was any occasion for such a measure—but I hope the Lord will overrule it for good. Great harmony of sentiment and feeling prevailed among the members of the convention and a good spirit & trust towards our brethren of the Old School. They have acted we think under great misapprehension of the facts in the case. How strange does it seem that Dr. Miller and myself should be in opposite battallions in this spiritual conflict when our opinions probably are as much alike as any other two ministers in the Pby. church.[31]

Richards spent the year corresponding with colleagues in the East and South who wanted to know whether the accusations had any basis in fact. Many of these letters to him expressed the hope that he would be in Philadelphia the next year to give the gathering the benefit of his counsel and reassuring presence. He answered in much the same vein as he had written to Miller earlier. The more he examined the beliefs and practices of the churches in his area, the more he was persuaded of their orthodoxy. He even came to believe that "the Congregational Churches, as a general fact, are the most stable and thorough orthodox churches we have."[32] He assiduously avoided anything that looked like impatience in word and deed, or gave the appearance of pride in being considered a leader of the New School. On one occasion when asked by an old parishioner whether he was at heart an Old School man or a New School man, he replied, "My dear, I hope that I belong to the School of Christ."[33]

In the end though, his hope that the Old School would change its mind was sadly misplaced. If anything, the Old School men returned to Philadelphia even more intolerant of their New School colleagues than the year before. When a motion was made to enroll the commissioners from the exscinded synods, it was ruled out of order and they had no choice but to withdraw and hold their own assembly, "the only true General Assembly of the Presbyterian Church."[34]

On his return from Philadelphia he wrote to Dr. Sprague in June.

> Our old side brethren seem inclined to make thorough work in the business of reform. I do not see but they will drive the ploughshare of division—(I hope not of desolation) through every part of the Presbyterian Church. My consolation is the Lord even [?] Jesus reigns. Perhaps when old side and new get well apart, a better state of feeling will succeed. But it seems odd enough to observe what grouping there will be in the two parties, after the line of separation shall be well defined. The Princeton Professors on one side and the Auburn Professors on the other differing about as much in reality as each faculty differ among themselves. But so it is and so I suppose it must be. Possibly investigation may be promoted and truth become the gainer.[35]

There was nothing more to be done at the moment, but he held out for regenerative possibilities in the future, believing that the cause of religion could not be permanently hurt by denominational disputes.[36] The seminary returned to functioning as it always had. Once more Richards settled into preparing his lectures, attending to his students, advising his children, and taking pleasure in the arrival of more grandchildren.

The finances of the seminary never gave him rest. In January 1838 he heard bad news from the secretary of the American Education Society.

> We are deeply disturbed that we cannot pay our beneficiaries as usual. But our resources are dried up. We had placed much dependance upon the churches in this city but their contributions fall much below our expectations. In one Church that gave us last year nearly $3000 we shall

not this year receive $800—others will give about half the usual amount. . . . We have done what we could to provide funds but the churches cannot or will not respond to our calls. . . . Our hope is now in the country churches. If they do not come to our relief we cannot sustain our young men. . . . Our prospects are very dark, but I believe the Lord will sustain us. At Boston they are in similar difficulties.[37]

The problem did not stem from the divisions in the church; Richards was seeing the effects of the Panic of 1837. While the American economy had suffered from recurrent booms and slumps since its inception, this panic or depression was the most severe anyone had yet seen. By the fall of 1837 one third of America's workers were unemployed; wages fell 30 to 50 percent while the prices of necessities nearly doubled; New York banks lost an estimated $6 billion on defaulted loans; and it went on for seven years.[38]

Despite hard times, Richards welcomed a new member to the faculty, New School ally Baxter Dickinson, describing him to his friend Dwight in November 1839 as an excellent professor and a good businessman. Soberly he added:

Dark and ominous times seem to have overtaken us again. What will become of our country and our benevolent enterprises seems hard to tell. My greatest comfort is that God reigns, and that his revealed purpose is to bring good out of evil and light out of darkness.[39]

A few months later the general economic distress was striking much closer to home. Anthony Dey's financial affairs were in dire straits. The most enterprising member of the family had been the hardest hit. Anna wrote from Newark:

The girls passed several days in the city week before last. . . . They called to see their aunt—she was very much depressed. Henry Beals says Mr. & Mrs. Dey appear so generally—He saw them the night before Thanksgiving—Mr. Dey dined with us since I last wrote to you—he tried to be cheerful—but evidently made a great exertion—I told H. Beals I wished he would bring Caroline up to see us—he invited her—but she replied she did not expect to come this winter. I feel very sorry for them & do make every allowance. I shall not encourage the least alienation of feeling I assure you—I think Caroline's situation most trying—Mr. Dey an old man—so many young children—I hope sincerely he will get his charter[40] & think his soundest concern will succeed—& feel most anxious of all, that the dealing of providence may be sanctified—the Lord is able to make it a means of the richest blessing.[41]

However acceptable such sentiments may have been to her father, it is not surprising that Caroline wished to avoid her sister's pious comfort for the moment. Richards kept as close track of Dey's affairs as he could through the newspaper. In March of the next year he asked his son Henry, who was involved in helping Dey, to interpret what he was reading in the papers. It was frustrating to be so far away; there seemed so little he could do to help. In writing Caroline, he offered a perspective and much the same advice that Anna had proffered.

Great as your calamities are, they might be still greater. You might see yourself and your dear family devoted to immediate destruction in a burning ship, or buried in the ruins of a falling house, smitten by a tornado. . . . Be assured God's hand is in these events which are apparently so disastrous to you. They make a part of that wise and holy plan according to which from eternity he determined to govern the world; and besides you have the promise that they shall issue in your good, if you do but patiently submit to them.[42]

By June the disaster was in full flood; they lost the beautiful house in Colonnade Row and saw their possessions put up for auction at a sheriff's sale. At last able to offer concrete help, Richards arranged for Henry to buy his daughter's furniture for $600 so that it might not be lost for good[43] and then invited her to move to Auburn and live with him. She was hesitant, which provoked a sensitive and understanding response from him.

You speak of your distress at the prospect of being in a state of dependence. I fear you do not feel quite right upon this subject. We ought not

without great necessity to throw ourselves upon the kindness and sympathies of others; but when we can no longer help ourselves, it is a favor
that others will help us, and we should thank the Lord that he provides
such assistance, though it may not always be in a way the most congenial
to our feelings. Elijah was fed by ravens for a time but how clean their
talons or delicate their bills I know not; and when he was sent to the
house of a widow who was in possession of a barrel of meal and a cruse
of oil, we are not informed as to the style of cookery or the manner in
which his daily meals were served up. It was enough that in God's way
his wants were supplied.[44]

Caroline accepted his invitation and moved into her parents' house with
her three youngest children, aged six to ten, and one servant, Betsy; here
she lived for the next four years until Anthony Dey could see his way
clear to pay his debts and to reunite his family in a modest home in
Jersey City.[45]

The complicated situation in which Anthony Dey found himself
stemmed only in part from the Panic of 1837. It also reflected his enthusiasm for highly speculative ventures. He had invested in much more than
the land in Jersey City that had turned out so well. He had also bought
50,000 acres in St. John's County, East Florida; invested in land in Galveston, Texas, when the area was still owned by Mexico; and speculated in
gold mines on Cherokee land in Georgia.[46] Closer to home, he had
bought some 400 acres in the Hackensack Meadowland where he was
experimenting with blooded cattle and horses. He also had large holdings in Poughkeepsie, New York, that were less speculative.[47]

His daughter later claimed that he was worth over $800,000 before the
debacle,[48] but it seems probable that this figure was arrived at by opti-
mistically calculating the value of all these properties at their highest
potential sale price. In fact at his bankruptcy hearing, the court accepted
the fact that the Florida land was without value. It had been bought from
a Richard Hackley in 1822. He had received the title from the Duke of
Allegon, but the King of Spain had revoked the title and the United States
had refused to recognize it.

Dey's speculation in Galveston, Texas, was equally disastrous. He had
joined Samuel Swartout, a friend from the same old Dutch background,

To the Owners of Meadow Land, lying in the Township of Lodi, and County of Bergen, on the south side of the Post Road leading from New York to Newark, and within the Dyke commonly called "Swartwout's Bank."

TAKE NOTICE, That an application will be made to the Legislature of N. Jersey, on the second Tuesday of the next session, for a LAW to incorporate the owners of the said Meadow lying within the above mentioned boundaries, by the name and style of "*The Hackensack and Passaic Bank Meadow Company,*" with such provisions as are useful and necessary for such a Company to have and enjoy—and especially to raise a fund from the owners of the meadow for the preservation of the Bank or Dyke drains, dams, sluices and other waterworks, already made as contemplated by an act of the Legislature of the State of New Jersey, passed 5th February, 1816, entitled "an act concerning tide swamps and marshes between the Hackensack and Passaick Rivers.

ANTHONY DEY.

Dated Newark, 10th June, 1826 — 4w

Advertisement in the New Jersey Eagle, *July 7, 1826. (Courtesy—Collections of the New Jersey Historical Society)* in forming the Galveston Bay and Texas Land Company. Swartout was well-connected; he was a friend of Andrew Jackson and the Collector of the Port of New York. The company bought land for as little as ten cents an acre from *empresarios* or persons to whom the government of Mexico had ceded huge tracts of land on the condition that they attract settlers and establish colonies. The sale of these lands to specu-lators in New York was illegal unless the Mexican government approved of them. But Dey, along with Swartout and the others, had caught the Texas land fever and enthusiastically promoted the sale of the land to which they had such shaky title. The chance to make a killing was reduced when the Mexican government voided a number of the uncolonized empresario grants in an attempt to stop the influx of American settlers. Despite being refused official permission to send settlers to Texas, the investors continued to do so at the urging of the Americans who were already there. Swartout actively worked to raise money for the revolt of the Americans in Texas in the expectation that a government run by Americans would recognize his titles and repay him with still more land. As it turned out, by 1836 the new Texans had won their revolution, but they wrote into their constitution that "No alien shall hold land in Texas except by titles directly from this republic." Dey, Swartout, and the other speculators lost their entire investment.[49]

Dey's investment in blooded cattle never realized any money either. His interest in agricultural pursuits extended to manufacturing fertil-izer out of manure and night soil in a factory along the Hackensack River. His factory was called the Urate and Poudrette Company and later the Lodi Manufacturing Company. This too was a highly specu-lative venture as he found out "because of the want of knowledge among the Farmers and Gardeners of the value of the manures."[50] His timing could hardly have been worse; he was starting his company just before the Panic of 1837. He had procured the capital for his scheme by bonds and mortgages on his real estate and by selling stock in the company once it was incorporated. This was the charter to which Anna referred in her letter to her father. By November 1840, Dey was in deep trouble. He asked his creditors to postpone the payment of what he owed them and to invest in more stock so that he could have the working capital he needed to make a success of the company and have some hope of repaying them. As evidence that they would not be throwing good money after bad, he drew up a list of all his assets, and had Edward Richards, Henry Beals, and his cousin, Jacob Dey, hold them in trust. He then drew up a schedule of all his debts, assigning his assets to his creditors. At that time he could still show that his assets exceeded his debts.

The money did not come in. Perhaps he knew that it wouldn't. When he later filed for bankruptcy, a number of his creditors claimed that he had only created the trust to benefit a preferred list of his creditors, a list that included most of his friends and relatives. The precariousness of his situation can be seen in a letter he wrote to his daughter Carrie and her husband Howland Bill, who were then living in England.

New York 25 July 1840

My dear Children

At the close of the week and about the last act I expect to do before I go home this afternoon I sit down to answer Howland's letter by the *Leveen* of the 30 June and Carry's letter of the 2nd July by the *Brittannia*. I thank you my dear children for such kind and affectionate letters. They cheer me in the gloom and difficulty that surrounds me and now and then brings to my mind what I might and ought to have been if my advice could have been pursued some years ago. It is however in vain to look back upon past mistakes or to repine at what now cannot be helped. Four years ago I wished to retire upon what would have been an ample provision for myself in my old age to my large and helpless family. Now I cannot say what will be the result under the entire desolation that seems to surround me. I never saw anything like it.

I was compelled to make an assignment to save my property from sacrifice and destruction and have now nominally more than $200,000 worth of property over and above what will pay my debts. Yet I cannot sell anything or do anything at present to bring my business to a point. Business in New York in July to August even in the best of times is very dull, but at present I perceive the grass is growing in some of our streets. I hope in a few days to go west as far as Seneca and you must not be surprised if you should hear I had determined to locate my wife and 4 little girls and Rachel with Henry and Klause [upstate Dey relations] there.

Tuesday 28 July 1840

I had written this far when I was prevented from doing more. Your mother has been quite sick for a week past, hope she is better to day—has had an attack of Cholera moribus. Our children, that is to say, the three little girls, have remained all summer in the city. I think they are wilted down somewhat under this warm summer weather. The boys and Anna, because they could take care of themselves, have had a run at Pough-keepsie.

I am more and more at a loss what to do. Having assigned my property until it is sold and my debts paid, I have nothing to live on. Yet I think the best course will be for wife the 4 girls and Rachel to go to Geneva this winter where the children can be well educated and cheap and I can get them all boarded there for $10 a week, we finding our furniture and wood. It is certainly very cheap and it seems to me that if wife should like it there I may on winding up my affairs save enough to live comfortably there. In the meantime I must take rooms with my boys where we can sleep, eat Breakfast and drink Tea and get dinner down town at the ordinary.

You see what sacrifices we are driven to—especially in my old days when my comfort and happiness lies in my family around me.

XXXXXXXXXXXXXXXXXXXXXXXXXXXXXXXXXXXXXXXX[sic]

A. Dey[51]

Things did not improve, so in September 1842 Dey filed for bankruptcy under the new law that was passed in August 1841 to establish a uniform system of bankruptcy throughout the United States. A lawsuit followed that extended over the course of a year. After taking testimony from the creditors who were not assigned property from the trust he had established, the courts decided that he had indeed established the trust in anticipation of declaring bankruptcy in order to benefit a preferred group. He finally made arrangements that satisfied these creditors also and received his certificate of bankruptcy in the fall of 1843. His older children, his brothers-in-law Henry and Edward Richards and Henry Beals, as well as his business associates, had all testified for him, but it had been a difficult and humiliating experience. He had kept up his spirits remarkably well under the strain. At one point his wife had complained after a sleepless night, "Do you realize that you slept as quietly as a little child all night long and we are on the verge of ruin?" "Well," he replied, "would I be any better able to meet today if I had lain awake all night?"[52] Perhaps such resiliency explains his initial tendency to speculate so rashly as well as his capacity to survive and start over.

As part of the settlement, the Lodi Manufacturing Company remained in the family. It was not perceived to be a distributable asset. Not until thirty years later did it turn a profit for his son James.

During this time of deep concern for the Deys, James Richards felt the sting of an unexpected public attack. The New School, so identified with benevolent societies, took up the Abolitionist cause. Unbeknownst to his friends in western New York, James Richards still owned a slave back in Newark (see chapter 3). Abolitionist sentiment had reached new heights in the wake of the murder of the Presbyterian antislavery editor, Elijah Lovejoy, in Alton, Illinois, on November 7, 1837. When this became known, Richards was in danger of causing a public scandal and was called upon to give an explanation. Typically he fell short of the extreme abolitionist position.

Feby 6 1841

I can only say that there is a coloured woman in Newark N.J. who according to the laws of that state stands in the relation of a slave to me, but who in fact has been as free for nearly twenty years as she desired to be or as I could make her. When I moved into this state I gave her her choice to accompany me to Auburn or to stay among her friends without a master or supervisor, to work when she pleased and to play when she pleased without any will but her own to control her. She preferred the latter, though she has since expressed her regret that she did not remain in my family. She was too old to be manumitted according to law without bonds being given that she should not become a town charge and when the subject of manumission was proposed to her, she utterly declined it, saying that she knew her interest too well to be made legally free at her time of life.

Doubtless she judged wisely: for while she was able to work &
support herself, she was perfectly at her own disposal, had the benefit of
her labour; and when she became too infirm to do this she had a resort
to her master's [i.e. Richards's] funds which she has found adequate to all
her necessities. She lives among her relatives who provide every comfort
for her at my order and at my expense. As a friend of the coloured race
what could I do more: If I had manumitted her with or against her will,
she might have gone to the poor house in her old days, instead of living
among her friends in the most absolute ease & independence, with every
want cheerfully met and supplied.

But how came this woman into my possession & to stand in relation of a servant to me? It took place in consequence of her earnest
request & to promote what I then believed was her interest and my
own. She was then too old to be manumitted, a thing she did not desire,
but instead [she wished] to change masters for many reasons and among
others to be nearer to her husband and children. Such a change would
not increase the number of slaves while it would obviously ameliorate
their condition. Nor could it, as I supposed have any influence in
perpetuating a state of bondage. A gradual emancipation had already
been determined on & provision made by the laws of the State [of New
Jersey] for the freedom of every person to whom freedom would be a
privilege. The object then sought, has since been very nearly consu-
mated. The coloured people of that state, with the exception of a few
aged persons are now all free—and their freedom has been accomplished with less suffering to themselves and with more positive benefit
than if it had been effected in a single day. So I firmly believe: but
whether right or wrong in this opinion it has for its advocates the most
distinguished patriots. . . .

As to slavery in general I consider it a moral and political evil which
ought to be done away as soon as the interests of the slaves will permit,
and in that way in which the least injury to all parties concerned will be
sustained. I am inclined to the scheme of gradualism, rather than to that
of immediate emancipation yet I do not object to the latter when it can
be accomplished without violence. But great and sudden changes in
society are apt to be attended with evils and sometimes with evils which
overbalance the good.

I am not greatly concerned about the influence which abolition-
ists may exert against me or against the seminary. After a while I trust
they will become more calm, and be willing that other people should
think a little for themselves. In that state of mind I shall expect more
candour, and of course, a greater readiness to hear & receive explanations.[53]

There is no record of how this letter was received but perhaps silence
means that his characteristic calm and moderation carried the day. The
whole incident must have been distasteful in the extreme to a man who
was so mindful of his public appearance.

By now it was 1841. Richards was seventy-three years old and lived
in the knowledge that his life was running out. He seemed to be suffering
from some form of heart disease, although an autopsy performed after his
death suggested that his stomach was at the root of his medical problems.[54] He had certainly complained of bilious attacks and dyspepsia all
his life and his wife took the greatest care of his diet. He continued to
teach, but more and more he met his students at home in his study instead
of in the classroom. Here he wore his "double gown," a garment made of
calico in a large flowered design with a lining of a plain color, all fash-
ioned with carefully finished seams so that it could be worn inside out.
His granddaughter Julia thought he looked like an escaped sofa in it, but
one assumes that he wore the plain side out when he saw his students.
Every night a seminarian came to conduct prayers, and on Sunday
Richards catechized the Dey children.

These children were a source of great delight to their grandmother. Far
from resenting the extra work of an enlarged family, she taught the girls to
knit and sew, occasionally undermined Caroline's discipline by slipping
them forbidden cheese under the table, and enjoyed the stimulation and
companionship that her daughter's presence provided. As Richards became
increasingly unable to walk any distance, the children were set to work
rocking his chair half an hour at a time, an activity known euphemistically
as "grandpa's exercise."

One of the most pressing concerns towards the end of his life was the
state of the souls of his two unconverted sons. He had talked to James
about them four years earlier and his concern had not diminished.

I cannot tell you how anxious I feel for those two sons, advanced almost to the meridian of life without being secured in the fold of God's covenant. I earnestly and affectionately remember them at the throne of divine mercy. Nothing short of divine power can save them from the dominion of sin and from death eternal.[55]

His concern extended to other members of his family as well. Elizabeth was again in poor health. This was the year he had written her urging her to ignore her housework and "not to expose or fatigue herself till her usual strength is perfectly restored"[56] (see chapter 8).

Elizabeth recovered for the moment; it was the Beaches of Newark who now gave him reason for alarm. In October 1841 he wrote James:

A letter from Anna gives us the unpleasant intelligence of Mr. Beach's ill health. He still attends to his business, but is quite feeble and emaciated. They think of making us a visit at Auburn. His complaints are in my judgement of a very serious & threatening character such as might be expected from his severe sedentary habits.—of appetite, want of spirits— an incapacity to retain his urine, loss of voice, and an occasional diarrhea; all indicating that the system is running down, and this from over-working. I hope he may be persuaded to break away from his confinement, and take a month or six weeks relaxation. This is absolutely necessary—and I fear that even this will come too late.[57]

This letter was followed shortly by another.

I can scarcely realize the melancholy tidings which reached us this morning, and yet while I am writing our dear Mr. Beach lies a pallid corpse in the midst of his family, or perhaps his numerous friends and acquaintance are assembling to perform the last sad office in the power of earthly friendship to render. Seldom does death fall with so heavy a stroke or sunder ties at once so numerous or so tender. How much will our dear Anna feel it & how long will comforts & joys that are fled be remembered only to deepen the impression of her loss, and to add fresh poignancy to her grief. & our Caroline Amelia, attached as she was to her dear father, how will she endure this sudden and overwhelming bereave-ment. Now she will find the special need of support from on high. May we not hope that by the power of divine grace she will be led to seek a refuge in god. I feel for them all more than I can possibly express; but what can I do for them better or other than to commend them to him who has all power in heaven and earth and to beseech his eternal mercy in their behalf. He is the judge of the widow and the father of the fatherless in his holy habitation. I shall endeavour to write to them to morrow. In the mean time let our constant prayers ascend for grace to sanctify the event to us all & to afford all needed consolation and support.[58]

Richards continued at his post until the fall of 1842 when, while walking in the village after a long recitation, he was suddenly seized by what must have been a heart attack. The illness was diagnosed as a "determination of blood to the head and a subsequent suspension of arterial action." He never recovered entirely from the shock, feeling this was "a new sentence of death passed upon him by the voice of Providence." In the language of his faith it was the "occasion of manifest sanctification" and a warning to set his house in order and become "meet for the inheritance of the saints in light."[59]

Anna was visiting in Auburn at the time of his fall and she stayed on to help nurse him and comfort him. She wrote in detail to James to keep him abreast of the situation.

Our dear father seems quite comfortable today. He continued to improve rapidly until Saturday evening when about 11 oclock was seized with violent pain in his head. His feet were bathed immediately & he had a hot cup of tea which seemed to give relief—the last paroxym [sic] being so severe I feared it would throw him in spasms. We bathed his feet & applied drafts to his head also with camphor etc.

Dr. Pitney was called in & said from the strength of his pulse, concluded the pain originated from fullness of blood in consequence of taking too much animal food. Gave a large dose of medicine on Sabbath, next day he ordered a blister which dear father declined having used & then recommended 20 drops of morphine to be given as soon as the pain commenced & bathing his head with ether [?]. Both of which had the desired effect.

He was very calm all day yesterday—but exhilerated [sic] talked much—& very sensibly—full of reminiscences of former days—the children remained with him while we were at tea & Julia said she did not know but grandpa was going through the geography. He rested better last night. His appetite is better than before he was sick. He took 10 drops of morphine last night & 12 this morning. He appears stronger than he did—but has much to attribute to this opiate. I do not know—if its effects were entirely off could tell better. He has walked out into the back parlor this afternoon & went through the front room back to his study.

The young gentlemen are unremitting in their attentions. I think as far as I can judge there is a prospect of dear father's recovery from this fall—but that he will ever have [good] health is more doubtful. All depends on God's sovereign pleasure. The class in the seminary needs much his instructions—they often speak of it. Dr. Halsey does not return & the duties are rather arduous devolving on Drs. Mills & Dickinson—the latter not so popular as dear father, tho he does as well as he can under existing circumstances.

It was my intention to have returned this week. On suggesting it to dear father on Monday, he said he wished I would stay as long as I could—it was probably the last opportunity I would ever have of being near & about my father—that it was very pleasant to him to have his children near him particularly one so dear to him as I was. That he had been looking forward to this for some time. Perhaps the Lord was about to wind up the scene—perhaps he might be restored—He wished to leave his dependents in favourable circumstances as possible. Oh how calm he seems & submissive to the divine will. It will be a heavy blow to those who survive when it falls. My dear mother I feel much for. She has been very anxious. Dr. Pitney thought if these headaches cannot be subdued it would end in apoplexy. But the morphine has the desired effect. . . .[60]

James hurried to Auburn on receipt of this letter and wrote immediately to reassure his wife.

I arrived here a few moments since and have had a brief interview with my Father who, I am rejoiced to say, is better than [we] could have expected from the representations in Anna's letter which were far from being overdrawn. He is now bolstered up in the study and receives there all the attentions that his afflictive condition requires. . . . He is now comparatively free from pain and his medical attendants speak encouragingly of his symptoms. He knew at once when I entered the room and extended his hand, asked after you & the children, etc. Were it not for his advanced age & numerous infirmities there would be but little doubt of his speedy restoration. . . . Caroline has just come in and says that his pain is coming on now again much as it did last night . . . If there should be any unfavourable change I will let you know it immediately. I shall come home as soon as circumstances will admit of it.[61]

Richards regained some of his strength. Anna returned home, and life at the seminary resumed. On the 13th of December, without warning, Anna died in Newark. When the news reached Richards "he rose instantly from his seat and with a burdened heart and moistened eye, and hand raised toward heaven, exclaimed, 'My daughter! my first-born, and the beginning of my strength, the excellency of dignity and the excellency of power! Thou art gone to heaven and I shall meet thee there.'"[62] Whether or not this scene took place exactly as described, there is no doubt about how keenly he felt the loss.

For once the formulas of bereavement failed him. He asked his family to forbear all expressions of grief in his presence, so as to avoid the distress that their sympathy occasioned. After the lapse of a few days, he was able to write to Henry.

I need not say, that in the death of your sister we feel ourselves sorely bereaved. It is an exceedingly dark and trying dispensation of divine Providence, and is well calculated to teach us what an empty and uncertain portion the world is . . . Our dear Anna has been torn from us and her beloved family, suddenly and unexpectedly but not, I trust, without being essentially prepared. She has for thirty years given the most abundant proof that her piety was sincere. Very few were so conscientious, so consistent and uniform as she. Her meekness and gentleness, her humility and self denial told us whose spirit she had drunk, and in whose steps she was treading. I have not a particle of doubt that she has gone to be with Christ, which is far better. This greatly consoles us; but the event has fallen out under God's government, which is still a higher and stronger reason for our submission. May it please the Lord to sanctify this visitation to us all.[63]

He continued to prepare himself for what he felt would soon be the end, writing his will, and on several occasions giving parting words of advice to his son, James. And then another blow fell. At the end of April he received word that Henry's second son, young Henry, aged thirteen, had died by drowning in the Hudson River at Poughkeepsie. The circumstances of the accident were agonizing. The child was sailing with his older brother within sight of his father. The boat capsized, leaving the two boys struggling in the water, holding to the boat as best they could. Their father could not swim so ran for help. When he returned, little Henry was gone.[64] In the face of the gloom that spread through all the family, Richards tendered the following hard comfort to his son. He too was fresh in his grief for a child, albeit an adult one, but he knew that this was probably his last chance to move Henry into the ark.

A letter from your brother Edward informs us that the body of dear little Henry had not then been found—a circumstance which naturally augments your trial, and prolongs its anguish. But this too, is a part of

Poughkeepsie, home of Henry Richards and summer home of the Deys. (Courtesy— Dutchess County Historical Society)

God's wise design—a thing determined from eternity, and without which his scheme of government would be less perfect. How gladly would I be with you, in this hour of darkness and sorrow, but the state of my health forbids. . . . My prayer to God is, that he will be with and sustain you. It is infinitely easy for him to pour such a flood of light and peace into your mind, as not only to soften the anguish of your spirit, and enable you to bear without a murmur what he is pleased to lay upon you, but even to rejoice that he reigns and does all his pleasure, through all places of his dominion, leaving no one circumstance uncontrolled and undirected by him. Try my dear son, to come near to him and pour your sorrows into his bosom. He has a father's heart infinitely more tender than that of any earthly parent. He never mistakes either the means of our correction, the time, or the measure. You may, with great confidence, cast all your care upon him, and roll your burdens on his arm. . . . O that these repeated strokes of affliction might have their proper effect, by working in us the peaceable fruits of righteousness, and working out for us a far more exceeding and eternal weight of glory![65]

Henry was too far lost in his distress to make of this anything but confirmation of his own guilt as a worthless parent who had not adequately protected his child.

I have deferred writing from day to day in hopes of being able to communicate to you the intelligence of the recovery of the body of our dear Henry—But such is not the fact—Diligent search has been and is still pursued if possible to find it, but the water continues so cold and turbid that it may be, as I am informed by those experienced in matters of this kind, as late as the 1st of June before it will come to the surface. Yesterday I went to N. York . . . [by] boat & returned this morning. James [his first son] went down with me to return to school. In going down about ten miles below this place we discovered something that appeared like a floating body. Instantly my heart was in my mouth and it was not until we had passed it that I recovered sufficient composure to examine it more particularly & sufficiently so to make up my mind whether it could be it or not. If no tidings are brought me tomorrow, I think on Monday I will take a boat and go in search of it myself. I have issued handbills offering a reward to any person who will find it.

Oh it is indeed a heart rending struggle to yield my hold on that much
loved boy. I sometimes feel as if the infliction is too severe to be endured.
I know that Infinite wisdom has done it, that in mercy he has done it, for
he does not willingly afflict nor try the children of men. I regard it as a signal
rebuke for my own sins and my parental unfaithfulness. And my prayer is
that it may now be sanctified to me, to the children, to us all. . . .

I am dear Father with much love to all
your affectionate and afflicted son
Henry S.R.[66]

That same month Richards received word that his brother Abraham's
wife had died in New York. Here the traditional words of comfort rang
more naturally, reflecting his long preparation and anticipation of his own
death.

It is past all doubt, that she has gone to be with her Saviour—and them
that sleep in Jesus will God bring with him. You will naturally feel that
you needed her to accompany you in the few remaining steps of life's
journey; but God knows what is best for us and those we love. Submission to his will is equally our interest and our duty. You and I must
both feel that the morning cloud has veered far to the west, and will soon
disappear. It is high time for us to think much and well upon the hour
which will separate us from this world and fix our destiny for an
unceasing hereafter.[67]

Richards decided to tender his resignation at the next anniversary and
to retire to a new house he had built in Auburn. Before he could do so, he
died on August 2, as he had wished, "with his armor on, and at the head
of his troops." Professor Mills preached at the funeral on the text, "After
he had served his own generation by the will of God, he fell on sleep."
Resolutions of affection, respect, and admiration were passed by the seminarians, the alumni, and numerous Presbyterian bodies and a handsome
monument was erected in Auburn within the space of a few months.[68]

He left an estate of $15,503.14, a sum that included a detailed inven-
tory enumerating every object in the house down to items worth as little
as $1.00. He held bonds that were worth over $11,000. The bulk of his
estate and his household goods he left to his wife during her lifetime, and

James Richards's funeral monument on the far right, surrounded by those of his wife, his daughter Caroline, his son Henry, his son James, and his daughter-in-law Margaret, with the memorial inscription: "His Record in on High." (Courtesy—Elaine D. Baxter)

he gave each of his children a few of his valuable books. Although he wished to treat them equally, their circumstances were all different. Three of the children were to inherit an equal share on their mother's death. They were first to deduct the cost of their education or loans made to them, $500 in the case of Anna, $900 for Henry, and $800 for Edward's "mercantile education" and start in business. He considered Caroline's circumstances quite desperate so she was to receive the furniture that he had bought at auction for her when her husband had been declared bankrupt and a trust fund of $2,500 that her brothers were to invest for her benefit. James's situation was also special as his father had not only paid more for his education than for the others but had continued to support him in part. To make things even, James was to receive $1,500 and the bulk of his father's library. Richards's final concern was for Anna's wishes. She had died intestate, but on her death bed she had expressed a wish to do something for her sister and to leave $1,000 to charities of her father's choosing. Therefore her children's share of the estate was to be reduced by $1,300 so as to carry out her wishes. Three hundred dollars was to go to Caroline and then $200 each to the American Bible Society, the American Tract Society, the American Board of Commissioners for Foreign Missions, the American Home Missionary Society, and Auburn Seminary. It was a will that perfectly reflected his sense of justice vis-a-vis his family. However, it is curious that he left nothing himself to the church or to the benevolent institutions to which he had devoted his entire life. He did not find it necessary to explain. It is difficult to believe that he found his family more needy. Perhaps a lifetime of devotion was enough.

Some of his life purposes were not accomplished—three of his children were not within the ark, and the church was divided. But he had not despaired.

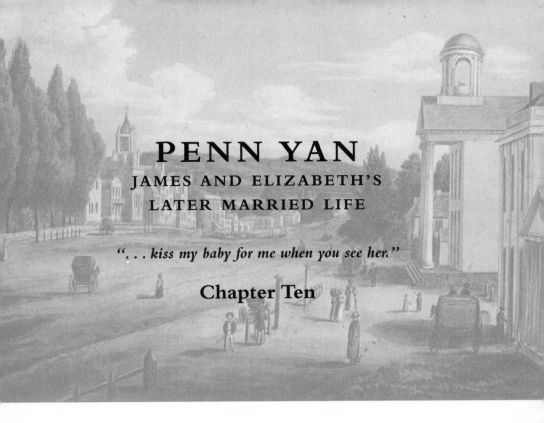

PENN YAN

JAMES AND ELIZABETH'S
LATER MARRIED LIFE

". . . kiss my baby for me when you see her."

Chapter Ten

espite his advice to the contrary, Dr. James Richards lived long enough to see his son James established as pastor of the Presbyterian church in Penn Yan. This was in 1841, two years before his death. Caroline Dey and her children were still living in Auburn, and Anna and Aaron Beach were both still alive.

Penn Yan had been settled three decades earlier by roughly equal numbers of Pennsylvanians and Yankees. The Presbyterian congregation had been formed in 1823. Now, after months of dissension along the familiar religious fault lines of the region and period, the congregation had voted to dismiss its pastor, the Reverend Ovid Miner. Miner, in response, had resolved to stay on in Penn Yan and shepherd his loyal minority of supporters in a new independent Congregational Church. It was this latter element of the situation that James's father, wary veteran of the burned-over days, Synod excision, and clerical rivalries going as far back as Newark and Griffin, had found so deplorable.

The son obviously saw the situation differently. His self-confidence buoyed by the regard of his friends, he seemed inclined to minimize the local controversy in favor of other considerations.

James and Elizabeth's first home at Aurora had been near Auburn. The move to Penn Yan was a move west that would put the young couple nearer Canandaigua, halving the distance between the fragile Elizabeth and her affectionate family, while moving them farther from Auburn with the effect of making James more independent. Unlike Aurora, Penn Yan had always supported its pastors without what the senior Richards called "foreign aid." This meant a more independent financial footing for a young minister with a growing family. Moreover, the larger size of the Penn Yan congregation, which at 230 was triple the size of his flock at Aurora, would give James's developing abilities a wider scope.[1] For Elizabeth, the call to Penn Yan was particularly timely. She was still recovering from the birth of their second son, and she could now rest at the Beals home in Canandaigua while James made arrangements for the move and his installation.

On June 9, 1841, just a few days shy of his twenty-eighth birthday, James Richards junior, was formally installed in his new pulpit. Neither his parents nor the ailing Elizabeth attended. Elizabeth wrote to James's mother that day, describing her own situation and taking pains to note James's great regret over his father's absence.

June 9, 1841

My dear Mother,

This is the day that my husband is to be installed at Penn Yan. I know he will feel even more regret than we do that we cannot be present on this interesting occasion. . . . My mother very strongly objected to my going until he could come for me . . . I was very ill . . . [but] for the last two days I have felt perfectly well, and I now consider it my duty as well as my privilege to go with my children to Penn Yan, and I have engaged an excellent girl to go with me. My husband is so anxious to go to Auburn to see father and yourself, that he hardly knows how to wait another week. . . . It was a great trial to him not to have his father present to take part in the services of his installation. The elders expressed a great desire to have father with them. . . .

I hope it will be consistent for father and yourself to come and see us very soon at our own home. We feel as if we should have one, even if we are for the present to be boarders, and [we] have made arrangements to have our friends well accommodated when they visit us. . . . After we get settled at Penn Yan, and I get accustomed to my new girl, I mean to leave her with the baby, and go to Auburn to spend a day . . . such fond anticipations I dare not indulge with any degree of confidence. You know how often I have been disappointed. . . .

My children are very well indeed. Whenever they see a grey-headed old gentleman they run up and say, "How do you do, grandpapa Richards?" . . . It is one month to-day since I came to Canandaigua. I have enjoyed the visit very much indeed. My health has been such that I have not made one call or one ceremonious visit. I have passed days with my sisters most pleasantly. Hoping to hear from you soon.[2]

July brought the usual visits of Beaches and Deys to western New York. Earlier, Dr. and Mrs. Richards had traveled east twice a year to visit their children and grandchildren, but these days the process was reversed. On July 6, Caroline Amelia Beach wrote to Elizabeth from Auburn.

July 6, 1841

Dearest aunt E.,

As Carry [nee Dey] and Mr. Bill [Carry's husband] leave this morning for Geneva & possibly for Pen Yan [sic], I cannot let them go without scribbling off a few lines . . . I presume your brother Thomas [age fifteen] has informed you of our arrival at Auburn. We came on under his protection & were well taken care of I can assure you . . .

I am rejoiced to hear that you are regaining your health. . . . I am very anxious to see you dearest aunt. . . . Your good husband too, I trust will not be backward to honor us with his presence. Grandma says you both must visit Auburn as soon as you can . . . also that you must make very small sleeves to your dress, as she is afraid you will not have enough for trimmings (rather a digression—but no matter). Carry has a very sweet babe—how are your dear little ones? My good parents send . . . love . . . Sarah [her sister] is just crazy to see you. . . .[3]

Caroline Amelia wrote again a few weeks later, observing in passing how much her grandfather missed James:

August 14, 1841

Dear aunt Elizabeth,

At Grandma's behest I have seated myself to write a few lines by your father (who has breakfasted with us). . . . We had a pleasant ride to Geneva . . . Yesterday morning Mr. and Mrs. Dwight and Mary came to see us immediately after breakfast and went with us through one of their hanging gardens. . . . When we arrived at Geneva our carpet bag was nowhere to be found and we were in a state of suspense as to its fate for several hours—but the returning train of cars brought it back from Seneca Falls, where it was found . . . I can assure you it was like meeting an old friend as we had not an article to change without it. . . .

Grandfather has been very unwell for the last few days & does not know how to get along without Uncle J. He says there are a great many strangers in town whom he is anxious for him to see & he must not fail to come. . . .

I am so glad that I have been to Canandaigua too. What a perfect paradise it is. . . . Your father is waiting, dear aunt & as I cannot write and talk too, I must close. . . . [4]

It took several months before James and Elizabeth were fully settled into their new place. Some of their goods were still arriving in the early fall. In his October 1 letter, Dr. Richards worried that "the effort was too much for Elizabeth's strength." Hearing that James contemplated missing the synod in order to attend to domestic matters, the older man felt compelled to disapprove, then softened to allow vaguely that the "circumstances may be such as to excuse a conscientious man. . . ."

In the same letter, Dr. Richards summarized the family news: He could report nothing new about Anthony Dey's complicated affairs in New York, but word had come from Newark that Aaron Beach was suddenly ill. Dey's son-in-law, Howland Bill, had sailed for England; however, Edward's trip to England now looked doubtful. He even had some Beals news: Elizabeth's brother Henry was engaged to marry Louisa Christie later that month.[5]

Despite the earlier report, notice of Mr. Beach's death a few weeks later came as a grim surprise. Anna Beach, forty-five years old, was the second

Richards of her generation to lose a spouse. Elizabeth felt the pressure of the sorrow in the Richards family, as she wrote to her father:

December, 1841

My dear Father,

Although I have but a few moments at my command, I feel anxious to acknowledge your very kind letter which I received by my brothers. It has afforded me very great pleasure to have a visit from Gorham and Thomas. . . . My husband's parents seem greatly to regret the distance between us; in every letter they allude to it, and urge us to improve the first favourable travelling to come and see them. The death of Mr. Beach has affected them much. When one is taken from a family, those who remain cling to each other with more affection. I feel deepest sympathy for Mr. Beach's family. I am very sorry they were obliged to move at such a bad season of the year. Mrs. Beach has always exhibited a wonderful degree of fortitude, and I hope it may not forsake her in this day of trial. . . .[6]

Winter saw James engrossed in care for his new congregation. The revival impulse, both orthodox and less so, was still alive in western New York in this postexcision period, as Elizabeth remarked in this letter to Auburn.

February 26, 1842

My dear Mother,

My husband is very anxious to have a letter sent to you by the mail to-day, and he finds that he has not one moment to spend in letter-writing, so he requested me to write for him. For the last week his engagements have been unusually pressing; meetings both for preaching and prayer have been multiplied. There is a very unusual interest felt on the subject of religion, and it seems to call for increased exertions. Besides the usual services on the Sabbath, Mr. R. preached three times this week, and attended two prayer-meetings. Since our last Communion season there has been an unusual seriousness exhibited by many. At that season one young lady was received into the Church and was baptized. The services were all very solemn. This seemed to arrest the attention of some of her young friends, and they have been led to inquire "what they must do to be saved. . . ." The elders have been visiting from house to house, and they find a readiness to receive instruction and to listen to warnings and entreaties. . . . The Congregationalists continue their meetings. They have public services twice every day, and occasionally three times. We hear that a number have been converted. . . .

I sometimes fear that Mr. R. will find his strength diminishing in consequence of his arduous duties. I hope he may be sustained, in answer to the prayers of his people. The Church is very much awakened; parents feel greatly anxious for the conversion of their children. We occasionally meet with an individual who seems bitterly opposed, and very much afraid that there will be an excitement, or that an attempt is made to work upon the sympathies or passions of men. These symptoms are, I believe, usually exhibited during a revival of religion. We do not, however, despair of the conversion of the boldest scoffer, for often cavillings plainly evince the strivings of the Spirit; those who now resist may be made humbly to submit. . . .[7]

By midwinter, James and Elizabeth and their two sons were at last well settled, and the Beals family kept in close touch via the Canandaigua stage line. Bundles were sent back and forth. Publications were exchanged with passages marked. Magdalena, Elizabeth's sister, sent articles of clothing for the little boys that she had made in her sewing society. Word came that their brother-in-law, Dr. Carr, was preparing a lecture for the literary society. News from their older brothers who were living in New York City was passed on regularly; Henry the merchant was getting used to married life, and Gorham was preparing to study medicine.

It turned out to be the news concerning the youngest Beals brother, sixteen-year-old Thomas, that soon riveted the entire Beals family. A troublesome boy for some time, Thomas was a great worry to his parents. For a few months now he had discussed his intention to go to sea, which was hardly the kind of maturing experience that the Beals family regarded as fitting for a Christian youth. All the same, the resolute boy in short order made his way to the New York docks, found a seaman's berth, and on a March morning sailed away. Henry Beals, embodying all the family's concern, came to the dock to see Thomas off, and afterwards reported at length on the scene in a letter to Canandaigua. With fascination, Henry

Elizabeth's sixteen-year-old brother, Thomas Beals, went to sea. (Illustration by E. Boyd Smith in Richard Henry Dana, Two Years Before the Mast, *Houghton Mifflin Company, The Riverside Press, Cambridge, 1911)*

described a daguerrotype of Thomas that he enclosed with his letter. Magdalena passed on the news to Elizabeth in Penn Yan.

March 14, 1842

My Dear Sister

You seem to feel bad concerning the plan Thomas pursued, but I can assure you, it was not entered upon without serious thoughts, nor without some knowledge of the trials & hardships a sailor is called to endure. Thomas was much interested in a book entitled "Two Years before the Mast" which with all its minute detail of a voyage at sea did not at all dissuade him from a desire to go to the "Mediterranean," as he expressed himself on Christmas day. . . . Thomas sent Mother his miniature, which is so perfect that it seems as though it was something more than a mere shadow. I will copy for you some parts of a letter which Henry wrote to sister Ann after Thomas had left for New York.[8]

Magdalena copied out the following:

Thomas has left with me a Daguerrotype likeness of *himself* which is a gift for *Mother*. It is taken with his sailor's rig and is *perfect*. To see it to good advantage you must sit with your back to the light and by close examination you will see the check stripe on his shirt, spots on his [handkerchief], the veins on his hands, & even the colour of his pantaloons is plainly discernible. It was taken in 45 seconds and just before he went to embark on ship board. His red flannel shirt is visible on his wrist but the colour is black on the picture. The man who took that got Tom to sit for another copy that he might keep it to exhibit in his shop.

Thomas wrote a letter in pencil which he put into my hand just as I was parting with him, express[ing] warmly his thanks for my attentions & he says "Words are too feeble to express my gratitude for all your kindness. Suffice it to say that I feel as though your attentions had been entirely unmerited & obligations are resting upon me etc. etc.—but the last and unlooked for kindness I consider greater than all as it affords not only gratification to me but will perhaps be more valued by *my dear Mother* for whom it is intended than you imagine." etc. etc. etc. And he concludes thus "And now my dear brother Adieu. I bid you farewell with no 'ordinary feelings.'"

I went with him to the ship. I heard the Captain took a great fancy to him & I was better pleased with [the Captain] than I was with the mate. The Capt. appears to be a man of good character, clever, gentlemanly etc. I should think he was a man of 45 years of age—a New Englander. I was quite amused with some of the purchases made for his comfort—a matress [*sic*] of straw, two blankets (no sheets), a tin cup (*quart measure* for his coffee), an iron spoon, etc. etc.

Henry reported that his brother-in-law, Mr. Christie, a minister, had visited the captain a few days earlier. They had bantered about Mr. Christie going to sea with them as chaplain, the minister adding more seriously, "I hope you will not forget to be your own chaplain." The captain's reply, "Very good advice, sir."

Henry, aware that their mother had given Thomas a Bible and some tracts before he left the house in Canandaigua, confirmed that Thomas had taken these with him to sea. Henry himself placed another large parcel of tracts in the bottom of Thomas's trunk, where he found

in a blank book a letter from Mother pasted on a leaf *directed* to "*my dear son*" containing extracts from Proverbs & signed from "your affectionate

Mother, Abigail Beals" It was written by Mother in her own hand. . . .
I know [Thomas] will value it coming as it does from one who I know
will not cease daily to remember her youngest son far away upon the
ocean but let us bear in mind that the same God rules the *seas* as the *land*
& therefore he is as safe there as here perhaps more so. . . .

Henry concluded by noting that among the ship's stores were ten hogs and
six sheep which meant fresh meat for the crew, "not a bad living."[9]

After Magdalena finished copying out Henry's account, their mother,
Abigail Beals, penned a postscript of her own. The rest of the family might
be making the best of Thomas's decision, but Mrs. Beals sensed that Elizabeth remained troubled about it.

You must not give yourself to much anxiety about Thomas. Remember
he is in the hands of God and not a sparrow fallen to the ground
without our heavenly father's notice. . . . I believe that if our Heavenly father has any thing for the child to do, he will preserve him,

Taking on livestock for the voyage. (Illustration by E. Boyd Smith in Richard Henry Dana, Two
Years Before the Mast, *Houghton Mifflin Company, The Riverside Press, Cambridge, 1911)*

through all the dangers and trials that he will be call[ed] to pass
through—if not it becometh me to be still and know that what the
Lord doeth is right. I have felt for the two years passed as if I had a
thorn in my flesh and it still remains I have no assurance that it ever
will be removed, but I am confident of one thing (that is) hitherto the
Grace of God has been sufficient for me . . . God sometimes brings
the blind by a way that they know not. From your affectionate Mother,
Abigail Beals[10]

Elizabeth must have cast back uneasily to conversations with Sam
Hopkins, who, during the time he worked for the Bethel Society, had
painted a distressing picture of the "moral wants of boatmen and sailors."

Thomas Beals had been prompted to try life at sea by reading *Two Years
Before The Mast*, Richard Henry Dana's account of his voyage to California
around Cape Horn. Dana was a young New Englander, not long out of
Harvard, whose background was not so different from that of young Beals.
The book won a wide audience, and Dana's compelling prose dramatized
for genteel readers the excitement as well as the grueling rigors of the
sailor's life.

Henry Beals watched Thomas go and perhaps imbibed the venturing
spirit; for eight years later, as a widower, he himself would take up a new
life in California in the aftermath of the Gold Rush.[11] For now, though,
he remained a merchant in the New York City flour trade, his Canandaigua
connections to Rochester, the "flour city," serving him well. Gorham, too,
had left the West for New York City and medical training at Columbia
College. None of the three Beals sons showed signs of succeeding to their
father's distinguished position in Canandaigua.

The Richards family was sorrowing over much sadder partings. From
the summer of 1842, family deaths exacted a toll on all. After the tragic
drowning of little Henry, James observed his father's declining strength and
tried to visit Auburn more often. The one source of family joy came in
November when Elizabeth gave birth to their first daughter, named Caroline Cowles Richards. Then, a month later, the sudden death of Anna, only
recently widowed, plunged the family once again into mourning. Anna
and James, the oldest and youngest children and the only converted ones,
had embodied the fondest of paternal hopes. James felt his father looking
to him for solace.

New family obligations weighed on a young man already fully stretched. In the early summer of 1843 he was completing his second year in Penn Yan. A heavy schedule often left him drained. Dr. Richards worried that James was pressing too hard.

Auburn July 26 1843

My dear Son

I rejoiced to hear that your health continued to improve. . . . You must avoid hard and protracted study. Keep much on horseback, your own or your neighbours, no matter which—but let this exercise be in the cool of the day. Attend to your diet, eating that wh[ic]h is nutritious and avoiding narcotics & stimulants. Above all, shorten your public exercises, your prayers and your sermons. I say this for the benefit of your people as well as for your own. Two public exercises on the Sabbath are as much as you can bear. If you attend a third service, let it be only to preside. . . .

Dr. Richards closed with an inquiry common between ministers, who were often called upon to supply character references.

I have been requested to inquire into the Character and circumstances of a Mr. Benham one of your neighbors as I suppose. His Christian name I do not remember, but he is a widower & report says is paying attention to Mrs. Munro of Elbridge. This request comes from a person who has a right to know what Mr. Benhams character & standing is, whether he is a correct and amiable man—what his reputation for piety, prudence & other good qualities. Let your statement be impartial & confidential & let it be by mail & as soon as your convenience will admit. . . .[12]

As it turned out, this was his father's last request of him. Dr. Richards had looked forward to seeing his minister son at the seminary anniversary in August; instead, a week later the old man died. The news came to James this way.

August 2d, 1843

Dear Brother in Christ

Through the request of your sister Mrs. Dye [sic] I address you with the afflicting intelligence that your dear father is no more on earth. He

passed peacefully away this morning about 6 oclock. For several days he
has been failing from the effects of diarrhea. A stupor had been upon him
for several hours the result of opium, in this state he died. Our loss is his
gain we can have but little doubt.

May the Lord abundantly sustain you and yours in this heavy
bereavement. Your friend and brother in Christ

I. Miles Gillett[13]

The letter contained a lock of his father's hair.

Again the Richards family put on the cloak of mourning, this time
for its patriarch. Relatives and a lifetime's friends gathered and paid
their tributes. The funeral coincided with the anniversary time of the
seminary, and Auburn bustled with visitors. It was only when James
returned home to Penn Yan that he began to absorb fully what had
happened. He wrote to his mother, feeling keenly the magnitude of
their shared loss.

August 21, 1843

My Dear Mother,

You have scarcely been out of my mind a waking moment since I left
you at Auburn. I have been fear-ful, lest, when the excitement of the
anniversaries should have subsided—and Henry, Sarah [Beach], & myself
gone and you were all quiet again, at home—that you would be so
oppressed with a sense of your loss as to be almost intolerable. I hope my
fears are groundless. That you will feel more & more the breach which
has been made by the decease of my dear Father I do not doubt. But if
with an increasing conviction of the loss you have sustained you are made
sensible of the Divine Presence proportionally, you will not sink under
your trials. . . . I hope you are able to carry all your sorrows to the
Lord—and that in doing so, you find the relief you seek. God is faithful
to his promises—and you may be sure that nothing will be withheld
which your real interest requires; and in no way can you better do
homage to his faithfulness and grace than to ask for a supply to your
wants as large and liberal as their multitude, their extent, and their variety
may demand. . . .

James did not dwell on the "duty of submission" that his father preached but instead spoke to his mother of the comfort her Lord could give her. As for himself:

> I feel as if I had begun the world anew. Every thing seems to wear a different aspect from what they have worn in times past. If the world shall continue to appear as empty—Eternity as near and as vast, important & solemn, I shall have reason to say "it is good for me that I have been afflicted."
>
> My family are all well—and every thing in the congregation is as favourable as I could expect considering my long absence from them & the variety of preaching they have had. Tell Caroline that Mrs Munro has been here to spy out the land—and the probability is that the marriage will not take place. Elizabeth and myself expect to go to Canandaigua to day. Mr. Christie is there with H. Beals & his wife. We shall return tomorrow—by leave of Providence. I want Caroline to inform me as soon as she hears of Edward's arrival. Mr. Dey, I suppose, will be at Auburn this week. Remember me to him affectionately and to all other inquiring friends.
>
> I shall let you hear from me very often and hope my dear sister C. will not be a tardy correspondent. I remain my dear mother most affectionately yours.[14]

In early October, his sister Caroline Dey was still with their mother. Fortitude was not Caroline's strong suit. She certainly had endured such real afflictions as typhoid, but her daughter Julia later described her as often "interestingly ill."[15] Her daughter Anna now wrote James their news:

> October 9, 1843
>
> My dear Uncle
> As mother does not feel able to write, she wished me to inform you that Uncle Henry arrived last Saturday night and as he hoped to get through with his business this week, wished you to come out immediately. Mother does not think she is any better—she does not

rest well and is very averse to taking morphine although prescribed by
the Doctor. Father did not come as we expected and I do not know
when he will come. . . .[16]

Dey was bringing his affairs at last into order, and his family in Auburn
anxiously awaited the resolution and their reunion after three years apart.

At this time James's mother arranged for some of the furnishings
from Dr. Richards's library to be passed to her minister son for use in
his new study, a detached structure built on the grounds of the
parsonage. Elizabeth referred to these items in a pre-Thanksgiving letter
to Auburn.

November 13, 1843

My dear Mother

Mr. Richards is very much engaged writing his sermon for
Thanksgiving, and he brought me this sheet to fill. . . . The new
study is finished . . . the library is arranged in much the same order
as when it was at Auburn. The old sofa and looking-glass came safely.
The former could not be carried through the door until it was taken
apart by a cabinet-maker. I think, if you could look into the room,
it would bring to your remembrance scenes and days which will
never return.

My baby sleeps now through the night without drinking at all, and
is growing finely. . . . I think she will run alone in a few days; she
walks about now by a chair. . . .

The return of Thanksgiving reminds us of the visits we used to
have from father and yourself when we lived at Auburn. It is very
pleasant to call to mind those days. . . . much love to sister C. and
all the family. James and John send their love to grandmother.[17]

A month later Elizabeth wrote a long letter to her sister Glorianna. Jane
Lightfoot, the young English servant woman who had lived in their
home and become exceptionally close to the family, had recently
married and returned to Canandaigua to establish a home of her own.
She was much missed.

November 6, 1843

My dear Sister,

I wish you would see Jane and send word to her, that in the basket under her fur cape is a small parcel, which I wish to have carried to Miss E. Wells at the [Canandaigua Female] Seminary. . . . I have been particular, because I thought it not unlikely that Jane might be very busy just now, getting her house settled, & would put her basket to one side, & not open it for some days or weeks. . . . I hope Jane has become quite reconciled to her new mode of living—if the sentence of death had been pronounced upon her she could not have looked more distressed than she did the morning she went away. I have thus far managed quite as well as I expected to, and even better. Jane Thatcher exerts herself to her utmost to please me, & altho she does not look as nice & tidy as I could wish & is not as particular in her way of doing work, yet I cannot complain.

The children all keep very close to me, even Jamie prefers being in the house since the weather has become cold. John has given up the idea of Jane's coming back & is perfectly satisfied to be Mother's Boy. He says his prayers two or three times a day—he stops very suddenly from his playthings, & comes & kneels down by my side & says, Jane told me I must not forget to say my prayers—I want to say "Our Father which art in Heaven etc." I hope he will always remember his early instructions. I intend to observe him carefully & see how long he will associate the performance of this duty with his recollections of Jane.

James [her son] has met with a great loss—his cat was found dead in the garden last Friday. When he looked at the cat & found it cold & stiff, he screamed & cried aloud for at least two hours. We could not quiet him with the promise of another, he said, it was his *dear* cat, that used to come to the table & get part of his dinner etc. I never saw such an exhibition of real grief from any child. He said, "he felt *awfully*" & his whole appearance certainly indicated it. He wanted to have the poor thing buried, where he could never see it again.

Last Saturday we had a very unexpected visitor, & not a very welcome one. I heard some one at the street door, & I opened it myself, Mr. Castleton stepped forward, & preached twice for Mr. Richards—his subject was the sanctification of the Lord's Day. I heard him in the evening, & did *not* get one new idea. I suppose I am too much prejudiced against the man to be much benefitting by his preaching. . . . I am very sorry he was ever received into the Presbyterian Church, I think he mistook his calling when he entered upon the work of the ministry.

Like the late Anna, Elizabeth did not shrink from making intellectual demands on her ministers or declaring her disappointment, within the family at least, when they fell short.

If either you or Magdalene have an opportunity to come & see me, I hope you will improve it. The weather just now seems very unfavourable for travelling and with us, it is so cold as if it was Christmas. I am afraid we are to have "nine months of hard winter," as the British soldier once said, when writing from New England to his friends at home.

I had quite a generous present from Mrs. Welles last Saturday. She sent a loaf of Refined White Sugar, about 10 lb. Brown Sugar, & 2 lb. Green Tea and 1 1/2 doz. Sperm Candles. She did the same last year. She is a most valuable friend & neighbor, & I feel much indebted to her for her kindness.

Mr. Richards had a letter from his Mother last week—they are enjoying tolerably good health. Mr. Dey has been up to see them. He has received his discharge under the "Bankrupt Law." He feels now as if there were a prospect of his doing something successfully.[18]

On February 14 of the new year, 1844, Glorianna wrote to Elizabeth after her return from a visit in Penn Yan. The family had recently welcomed Thomas home after his ten months at sea.

February 14th, 1843

My Dear Sister

I arrived home safely at ten minutes of six on Monday evening. The ride was very pleasant though the sleighing was all gone in several places; if we had waited until the next day we should have had to come home on bare ground. . . . when I think of my coming home it seemed as if I was *blown here*, we came so rapidly.

I want to hear from you very much, to know, if your *face has burnt* any more. It seems quite lonely not to have any children around. Mother says you can keep that *flannel nightgown* as long as you wish to. I suppose in your confusion when Thomas came you did not read the news in Mag's note which is "that Sophia Johns has a daughter about two weeks old"—I thought you would like to hear this important item of news.

Sister Ann sends her love to you and says it would give her a great deal of pleasure to spend a Sabbath with you, but it is such cold weather she does not feel as though she could leave the children over night, but if there should come a pleasant day she might come and make you a call.

It was apparently not uncommon for a mother to leave her young children in the care of family or trusted servants for a few days of unaccompanied visiting. Glorianna continued:

Dr. Hamilton of Rochester . . . has written Dr. Carr a letter saying that he is going to Europe in March and that he (Dr. Carr) must go with him. The invitation is very pressing and if he can raise the money he will go & he is very anxious to do so. Dr. Hamilton said in his letters that he might raise some objection to going on account of his family but he said, "I have a wife and child so have you but my wife is anxious I should go, so that I can tell her all about my travels when I come home. . . ."

Father received a letter from Gorham [in New York City]; he and his wife [Mary Mollar] are very well and happy. Mag received a short letter from her, she . . . wants to have Mag come and make her a visit.

Mrs. Christie [Henry Beals's mother-in-law] wrote Father a letter giving her views of Henry & Louisa going to keep house . . . in the Spring. She had a great deal to say about "the baby," and spoke as though there never was *such a child*.[19]

Sea voyages and European tours began to exercise a great hold on the imagination of the prosperous American middle class male in the 1840s.

James himself was considering a trip. Thomas Beals, whose generation had
not known such a fashion, was circumspect about expressing his view. In a
letter to his daughter Elizabeth a month later, he let a member of the
Richards family of his own generation speak for him:

> Mr. Richards says he has given up his foreign voyage—I thought he
> would, but did not like to say anything to influence him, but it being now
> settled, I will tell you what his Uncle Abraham Richards said to your
> brother Henry a week ago when he called to spend a sociable hour with
> him. He said "as for James, he had better not go abroad; that it was quite
> essential to the welfare of his flock that he should remain at home," and
> I have no doubt it is a sound opinion. . . .

Beals was much more sympathetic to James's and Elizabeth's plan to
go to New York that spring on a family visit, and he encouraged them to
go without their children:

> I think you had better shut up your house and bring the children
> here—with the help of Jane, I think we can manage them—I do not
> know what are your views on this head, but I would advise that you go
> from home without any incumbrance, & having no anxiety about the
> children.[20]

He suggested an early visit, before Edward Richards and Henry Beals
moved to new houses on the customary May 1 moving date. The young
couple much looked forward to the trip, as Elizabeth wrote to her father
on March 25:

> We expect to get all things ready to leave on Wednesday morning. Our
> friends are so anxious to show their kind feelings by coming to see us,
> that they hardly allow us the requisite time to prepare ourselves. I feel,
> my dear father, under much increased obligations to you for your kind-
> ness and liberality. . . .
>   I received a letter this morning from Mrs. Coan, a missionary at the
> Sandwich Islands. I will carry it to C[anandaigua] that you may read
> it. She is never allowed the pleasure which I am anticipating, of leaving

all her cares, and of spending a little season of recreation in visiting friends . . .

The Society are now collecting Mr. R.'s salary, and we have every reason to believe that they will furnish the means of defraying the expense of our journey.[21]

No sooner were James and Elizabeth returned from this excursion than Beals proposed that Elizabeth join him and Magdalena on a trip to his native Boston. Elizabeth replied:

I am very much obliged to you for your invitation. . . . It would give me very great pleasure to go with you, but I believe it is best for me to decline—I have recently allowed myself three weeks relaxation from all the cares & labours of a family that I feel now that it is my duty to remain at home—I feel however that while I decline going with you *this summer,* that I should like to have the privilege kept in reserve—and that if our lives are spared we may at some other convenient season take a journey together to Boston—I have a great veneration for the home of my Father—there is not a spot on earth that I should be more delighted to visit. . . . [Magdalena] is now about the same age that I was when I went to New York the first time under the care of my Father—the visit I shall never forget—it was one of the happy portions of my life. . . .[22]

In midsummer, James and Elizabeth once more looked forward to visits from some of the older Beach nieces and nephews. Caroline Dey and some of her children were still—or again—in Auburn. James wrote to his mother "in the constant expectation of welcoming some of you at our house."

I hope [the Beaches] do not intend to pass more than half of their time with you, and if this is the arrangement I shall be satisfied. Our claim on them is in my judgment equal to that of yours and I think they will so regard it. I have two spare bedrooms & if necessary a third which shall be most cheerfully devoted to them as long as they can make it agreeable to themselves to remain with us. I have a first rate horse & my waggon has recently been fitted with an extra seat so that we can give them all a fine ride as often each day as they may find it convenient to go out. Our garden was never in a better condition—and I may say that our "help" was never *stronger*—if not better. So that I hope you will come out with them. If Caroline will leave [her] children with Betsy [the longtime Dey servant]—I see not why you could not *all come*. I will gladly meet you at Geneva & bring you here any day that you may appoint. . . .

James cheerfully played the matchmaker for his nephew, Anna's oldest son, only a few years younger than himself.

Tell James [Beach] that mother Benham alias Monroe lives opposite my house and every facility will be afforded him for pressing his suit for the daughter through the Mother—the only way in which one can rationally hope to succeed in these days—

I do not think that I shall be able to visit Auburn before the anniversary—I am then to preach before the alumni—and have not written the first word as yet—though I intend to commence next week if I am spared and shall take it quite leisurely.

It was a pious convention to say "if I am spared," but life events tended to vivify such expressions:

I cannot tell you how often I am reminded of the sad changes which have occurred in our family within the last two years—I shall never be able to think of the anniversary season at Auburn without associating it with the *scenes* of the *last*—and when I think of that—other events of a *like character* are *at once* recalled & with a melancholy pleasure reviewed— What changes another year shall disclose is known only to him who seeth the end from the beginning & in whose nature & purposes there is not even the shadow of turning—Our safety & happiness lies in cultivating the feeling that we are in a dying world & nothing here is permanent & abiding. Let it be our chief concern to have our conversation in heaven and our *treasure & heart* there. . . .[23]

James preached this fervently but it did not keep him from taking immediate pleasure and comfort in the thought of having so much of his family about him again. With his father dead, the Beaches orphaned, and the Deys uprooted, James and Elizabeth now became the emotional center of gravity for the extended Richards clan. The summer reunion in Penn Yan was followed by their own visit that autumn to Auburn. Caroline Dey had left with her children for a visit in New York, and James's widowed mother was anxious to fill the house with his young family.

Oct. 1844 Friday morning

My dear James

I received your letter yesterday morning and was very much disappointed in not seeing you all in person. I had been looking for you every plesant [sic] day since Caroline left. . . . she went in company with Mrs. John Porter and Anna, her daughter. . . . They were expecting Mr. Stearing to have been their protector but he disappointed. After seating herself in the [railway] cars, [Caroline] looked around to see if there was any one she could recognize, [and] the first person she saw was Mr. Young, Mary Dwight's father in law; and his daughter a very beautiful girl of seventeen. . . . He recognized her immediately and asked her if she had any gentleman with her, she told him they had been disappointed in their escort, he then said he would be very happy to take charge of them, and was very attentive to them indeed—to cut the matter short, they were very much pleased with *him* and he appeared so with *them*. They parted with Mrs. Porter at Albany, Mr. Young took care of them and their luggage and put them on board the Knickerbocker. Caroline says she never received more attention and kindness from any one in her life.

And now my dear James there is nothing in the world would give me more pleasure than to visit you while Caroline is gone, but I do not *see* how it is *possible*. I have business which *must* be attended to before Henry leaves for the South. Mr. Wright wishes to take up his Mortgage among my papers. . . .

Tell dear Elizabeth I shall be greatly disappointed if you do *not all* come here next week. . . . kiss the dear chicks for me. . . . I should like you to bring Sarah with you if it is perfectly convenient, and you do not find it too expensive, however I would like you to act your own pleasure about it. . . . Remember me to Sarah and Patrick [servant and gardener].[24]

After this visit took place, James's mother wrote again. She had begun sorting through the sermons and papers of her late husband and wished to draw James's attention to those works she particularly loved. She also praised her son for a sermon she had recently heard him preach in Auburn.

October 28 1844

My dear James

By my not hearing from you since you left us, I conclude you got home safe, without any bones broken or little Jimmys neck which I considered in so much danger—I felt very gloomy the day you left us after having so plesant [*sic*] a visit from you and Elizabeth, and I hope it wont be long before you repeat it. . . .

My object in writing to you now is to propose to you to copy two or three of your dear fathers sermons, one of them is on the *worth* of the *soul*. The other is "When Christ who is our life should appear then we also shall appear with him in glory."—"My peace I leave with you" is a very good one, the first ones are most exelent [*sic*]. The one on the worth of the soul is one of your fathers most solemn sermons, there are so many good ideas in it. Your worthy sermon, as I call it, [that] you preached here last spring is one of your best, it was fine—very much liked here. I wish when you write again you would tell me where the text can be found. I wish also you would copy those verses your father used to repeat so beautiful[ly] in the first sermon mentioned above. I do not wish my dear son to interfere with any of your matters, but I must say that I feel a deep interest in every thing respecting yourself and family. Remember me very affectionately to Elizabeth and all the children and tell them their grandma loves them very much. . . .[25]

James and Elizabeth were preoccupied that fall by renovations to their Penn Yan church. The inside of the original structure was all torn away in order to put on an addition of twelve feet. During the construction, James held prayer meetings in his new study and in private houses. Elizabeth's sewing society transferred their meetings to the court house; there forty or so women met and sewed together to raise money to furnish the renovated

Elizabeth and her church circle sewed and exchanged notes on their reading. (Woodcut in Marshall B. Davidson, Three Centuries of American Antiques, *Bonanza Books, New York, 1979)*

church. Elizabeth related all this in a letter to one of her sisters. She also noted with interest, and without disapproval, the considerable number of wagers laid on the 1844 presidential election, in which they and many of their friends had supported the losing candidate, Henry Clay.

> Miss M. has been quite ill for some time past; I do not know, but she was so much elated with the result of the election, that her health was affected by it. I hope you have borne the defeat with your usual dignity. Some of our good people have been dreadfully disappointed. Mr. Tunnicliff has lost a large sum of money by bets; this, too, is the case with others. You will not have to inquire after this "Who is Jim Polk? . . ."
>
> My little Caroline does not forget you; it is a daily occurrence for her to sit by a table or chair and finger as if she was playing on a piano, and accompany her feigned music with her voice, and now and again she will turn to me and say, "Aunty does so." She is now two years old, and she makes herself well understood in her attempts at talking.[26]

Sometime during that fall, James's nineteen-year-old nephew, Henry Beach, made a visit to Penn Yan. While he was there, the recent graduate of Princeton "lectured" on the subject of temperance. His grandmother Richards and his aunt Caroline Dey looked forward to hearing Henry repeat the performance when he passed through Auburn. A letter from Caroline playfully cautioned Henry to "shield his *heart against the fascinations* of some of the Penn Yan ladies." They were aware that Henry Beach's older brother James had been smitten on recent visits there by a young woman discreetly referred to as "Cynthia." To her own brother James, Caroline shifted tone and scolded:

> You promised to write very often but you do not do it. As Mama is so very anxious to hear how Elizabeth continues to be—once a week at least if it is only ten lines.
>
> Mama wants to know how father's memoirs are coming on and when they will probably come out—you must be very careful what you put in of mine, as I am not willing some things should be put in—it requires great judgement I think . . .[27]

Shortly before his death, Dr. Richards had spoken to James about publishing his lecture, "On the Will," along with a few others. James, in consultation with his brothers, now pursued the project in earnest and added to his usual workload the task of supervising the transcription of his father's lecture notes. His literary nephew, Henry Beach, had come to help him.

The final volume was to include a biographical sketch of Dr. Richards by the Reverend Samuel Gridley, and for this purpose, James was supplying Gridley with family letters and other pertinent documents. His sister Caroline was wary of this part of the project. Perhaps in response to her concern, Gridley eventually restricted himself to quoted excerpts of the letters and used generic descriptions of their recipients, e.g. "to his daughter." Gridley later noted in his preface: "It may be thought strange that the writer has dealt so largely in extracts, and so sparingly in entire letters. . . ." He pleaded limitations of space and personal preference.[28]

In her letter expressing concern over the "memoirs," Caroline made the first surviving reference to their brother Edward's wife, Emily:

I have heard from both Henry and Edward since I last wrote. Henry writes that he is very comfortable for him, still feels that his life is very precarious—Edward is as usual—Anna [Dey, her daughter] is with him and she says her uncle is very kind and indulgent & sister Emily is very kind indeed to her. . . .[29]

Emily Matilda Ferris was the oldest of eight children of Benjamin Ferris, a lawyer in the city of New York. The Ferris family had strong ties to the city's political and commercial establishment.[30] Edward and Emily may have married relatively late. Years later when Edward and Emily were in their fifties, a niece from upstate who visited their home in the city wrote in her diary that they were "stylish and grand but I don't mind." Aunt Emily she found "reserved and dignified but very kind."

Now thirty-four, Edward was four years older than his wife. The couple remained childless and partly for this reason may have been absorbed into the large circle of Emily's relations in the city.[31] This might account for the relative lack of news about them in the surviving Richards correspondence, which in the 1830s and 1840s was centered on western New York, a place they seldom visited.

By contrast, the Deys actually lived in Auburn for three years and several of the Beaches came regularly for long and short visits. In December, a letter from Henry Beach, back in Newark, brought news of Aaron and Anna Beach's nine orphaned children, whose ages ranged from eight to twenty-six. In the two years since their mother had died, the older Beach offspring had managed so far to carry on the household and to keep the family together. It was not easy, and like his uncle, Henry felt deeply the changes in the Beach-Richards family circle, especially at Thanksgiving time. Since it would not do to dwell on sorrows without remembering mercies, he wrote hopefully of the "remnant" of the family, using a word with biblical overtones of solidarity and resolution.

December 17, 1844

Dear Uncle James

I make it a matter of duty & conscience to fulfill my engagements. When you were last visiting us just before you left I engaged to write you a letter, upon condition of receiving an answer—my part of the contract I hereby meet.

It is winter in right good earnest. We are persuaded so by the nipping, pinching cold, the occasional appearance of snow clouds & flake showers. . . . "Thanksgiving" too has come and gone—that good old-fashioned custom handed down to us from our Puritan ancestors. Yet it is not kept in our community, I regret to say, as it is reverently observed in Puritan New England. Still it is a festive occasion even we rejoice to have return, for it brings back to us the hallowed recollections of other days. Though changes have occurred to break in upon our family circle, which when formerly complete was one of the happiest it is still a pleasure for the remnant to gather together & renew the pledges of fidelity & love, ask after each others welfare & exchange those glances so full of meaning more easily understood than expressed & repeat to each other the heartfelt "Godspeed" for encouragement in the way. But the absence of "old-familiar faces" is mournfully felt.

The Newark relations always regretted that James had not taken the pulpit at neighboring Bloomfield, as David Frame once proposed. Henry Beach alluded to this as he broached the topic most urgently on his mind, his younger brother Newton.

I wish you could have spent the day with us, which you could have done if you were now the shepherd of a Bloomfield flock instead of tending the flock in Penn Yan's pastures. We have much to be thankful for—as well as our sore trials to profit by. One of our sorest trials is with Newton who has become so contaminated by his associates here that his morality has become decidedly vitiated and his conduct extremely reprehensible. We know not what to do with him, so reckless has he become. He feels that he is accountable to no one, since his parents are gone, & no restraint binds him—neither having the fear of God before his eyes, nor regard for us. Dr. Brinsmade [their minister] has expostulated [with] him in vain. Only fifteen years old! he has made up his mind not to study, altho it was his parents expressed wishes that he should receive a liberal education; he does not spend his evenings home as we wish, keeps company with such boys as are baneful to the virtuous & is contrary in almost all his ways—This is indeed a sad picture—would that it was too highly wrought! The truth is Newark is one of the worst places to bring up boys that can be found on this continent—It has always been so, especially so now. James [his older brother, twenty-five] has felt the vicious influence of its society of youth. . . .

One year ago Newton was not inclined to disobedience, or to go astray. He has some most valuable traits of character, which with proper training would make him an ornament to society and the pride of virtue—This he never will become here. The only hope of reformation is in his removal from these evil influences. I would not trouble you with this recital, but from the hope of your cheerful cooperation in the work of reform. Dr. Brinsmade . . . wishes to know if it be practicable . . . to place him upon a farm in western New York in your vicinity. Where you could exercise a supervision over him, where he would be under wholesome restraint, his time fully occupied with useful employment, away from the society of vicious boys & under good family influences, religious & social—Can such a place be found? I am aware that it would be difficult at this season of the year—but something always is to be done—He is capable of doing work & could work efficiently & well. Perhaps after a year's employment in this manner he might readily incline to study & sobriety—or it may be if this course is not adviseable, that it would be a judicious plan to send him to school in your village & receive him into your family if you could be prevailed upon to do this much for his own sake, for our sakes & for the sake of our deceased parents.

We feel that something must be done for him & done now . . . and if done he may live to bless us rather than be our disgrace. . . .

Thus were James and Elizabeth appealed to once again to look after one of the family's difficult-to-manage young. The tranquility of country life, the ruggedness of farm labor, the kindly attentions of a clergyman's loving young family—it was a popular formula applied to many a wayward youth of this period coming to manhood in a fluid society with few benchmarks.[32] Henry Beach showed no awareness that his admired Uncle James had provoked similar family consternation fourteen years earlier when he was about Newton's age. The letter continued:

James [his brother] now expects to come out West in January & if so it would present a favorable opportunity to make the proposed "transfer"—What say you? will it not be well? Do help us to some advice—I regret the necessity which makes it incumbent upon me to give such an account of Newton, when he might be such a comfort to us.

Sister Sarah [about twenty-three] has been unwell. . . . She has recovered now & again resumed her domestic duties & cares which in the interim devolved upon our friend, Martha Grant, who is spending the winter with us. . . . she is a lovely girl, very companionable & is an agreeable acquisition to our family circle. She desires her love to Aunt Elizabeth, whom she has met at Mr [Henry] Beals'.

Can you write anything encouraging to James in reference to the lunar goddess Cynthia, his satellite? Her brother we have heard has been recently married much against their wishes. Jas' chance is good yet, I suppose, good as ever! They are about to enlarge their business in N[ew] Y[ork] by taking in another partner & transacting the Grocery in conjunction with the Commission business. He can tell you his plans more fully when he visits you.

James Beach had already left Newark for the grocery business in New York, and a year and a half later Henry would join him there to study law. The two brothers would find lodgings together in the fast-growing city of Brooklyn and ride the ferry into Manhattan. Newark's old Puritan character was being overwhelmed by rapid industrialization and an influx of immigrants; and the brothers' family ties to Newark, so altered by the death of their parents, failed to hold them there.

For now, though, Henry Beach remained in Newark, soaking up the available cultural influences:

I am frequently inquired of touching the progress of Grandpa's memoirs—may I be permitted to report progress! It ought not to be lost sight of but something should be done towards rearing such a monument from his valuable writings as will endure when tradition shall cease to repeat his praise or mention his venerable name. "The great man never falls" as William Lord "the wild eagle poet" (of whom you shall hear in my next) has sung in this exquisite verse "on the defeat of Henry Clay"—he calls "the dear people" a blind giant—published in [the] Newark Daily.

1. "Fallen? How fallen? States & empires fall
Our towers and rock-built walls
And perished nations, floods to tempests call
With hollow sound along the sea of time
The great man never falls—
He lives, he towers aloft, he stands sublime—
They fall who give him not
The honor here that suits his future fame—
They die and are forgot

2. O giant! loud & blind! The great man's fame
Is his own shadow & not cast by thee
A shadow that shall grow
As down the heaven of time the sun descends,
And on the world shall throw
His god-like image, till it sinks where blends
Time's dim horizon with Eternity—"

I have copied these verses not as apropos of the fame of him of whom I had just been writing—for different far is his fame—greater perhaps in Heaven's eye, but aside from the obscurity of the first four lines of the first stanza, on account of the extreme beauty & vigor & uncommon merit of the poetry. I promise in my next letter to speak more at large of him whose poetic genius will astound the world ere long.

The Rev. Dr. Baird has been delivering one of the most entertaining & instructive courses of lectures in this city I ever attended. His subjects were the moral, social & political condition of the several states of Modern Europe. I wish you could have heard him. You would have a larger, more comprehensive view of things. He let us into the secrets of nations & we learned that which we could learn no where else, his personal recollections. His qualifications for such a course of lectures

surpass any one in this country or even in the world—for he has been
in the acquaintance and even confidence of the crowned heads of
Europe. But I must hasten to close with much love to Aunt Elizabeth,
the little ones & yourself from all your aff[ectionate] nephews &
nieces—

Yours truly, Henry Quill

This is the sobriquet Martha has given H.N.B.[33]

Henry Beach typified a rising generation who looked for the United
States to take its place among nations by erecting its own literary
monuments. He quoted the above poem by the twenty-five-year-old
New Yorker, William Lord, from the newspaper, though he apparently
knew that the poet's first book of poems was about to appear; and
indeed upon its publication Lord was briefly acclaimed by some as
"the American Milton." Poe, whose work Lord had parodied, dissented
in a scathing criticism.[34] Henry's other new hero, Dr. Robert Baird,
was a Presbyterian minister currently making appearances on the
lyceum circuit. For several years the Princeton-educated Baird had been
the principal American liaison to European Protestant brethren doing
missionary work in some of the Catholic countries of continental
Europe. In evangelical circles, he was for a time a prominent interpreter
of cultures on both sides of the Atlantic.[35]

Henry Beach would be freed to explore this and other enthusiasms
once a place could be found for young Newton; indeed, it would lift a
great responsibility from the young shoulders of all the Beach brothers
and sisters. James and Elizabeth probably felt obliged to consider taking
Newton in, but it was hardly a propitious time: James was busy with a
larger congregation, church renovations, local rivalries, and his father's
memoirs; and Elizabeth, unlike the early days of marriage, now cared for
three young children of her own and suffered from poor health. They
must have been much relieved, then, when a place was found for
Newton with an upstate farm family. Expressing satisfaction at this
arrangement, Elizabeth mentioned in a February 13, 1845, letter to
James's mother a recent visit from another nephew, Henry Richards's
oldest son, James Nicholas, their former charge in Aurora. He was now
the same age as Newton Beach and as unruly as ever. The visit had
confirmed them in their decision not to have Newton live with them.

"James' visit has satisfied me that Penn Yan is not a desireable residence for a young man whose habits are unsettled."

In the same letter, Elizabeth also recounted a recent visit with a dear old friend of both the Richards and the Beals families, Mrs. Henry Dwight of Geneva.

> I think Mrs. D. appears in her usual health. I could perceive that her whole frame was somewhat tremulous, and I thought her step was not as quick as formerly; but she is very cheerful, and talks as much as ever. . . . She gave me every particular of her late sickness—told me how she felt when she supposed that she was about to pass away into another world. I think she must have been wonderfully composed, from her own account of herself. She knew everything that was done or said, and was perfectly self-possessed all the time when she was unable to converse. When I see you I can tell you what I have not room or time to write now. . . .

Those near death could be subjects of special revelations, and their demeanor was watched for signs. Elizabeth had reason to be specially attentive beyond her fondness for Mrs. Dwight. Death, she knew, could brush quite close. For one thing, she was pregnant again in an age when childbirth could mean for any woman her own mortal end. For another, Elizabeth felt increasingly her own vulnerability in the grip of a chronic illness no one had yet identified. She admired Mrs. Dwight's composure under trial and meant to imitate it.

Continuing her letter, Elizabeth told how a terrible storm had extended their stay in Geneva and affected the return trip to Penn Yan. Despite the coming of the canal and the railroad, much rural travel was still by sleigh and stage and was sometimes frightening in bad weather.

> Our ride from Geneva was very tedious—we came through in about five hours. There were three sleighs following each other, our own the last, and we of course had the benefit of the track made before us; we were thrown out once into a deep snow-drift, but suffered no especial inconvenience from it. I suffered more in mind than in body, for I was fearing something dreadful would happen all the time. It was nearly eight o'clock

in the evening when we reached home, and the last six miles of our way was on the tow path of the canal, this being the only road that could be opened to travellers . . .

I had a letter this evening from my brother Henry [Beals]; he writes to inform me that he has another daughter. His wife went to church the day before! . . . Mr. R. would gladly have written to you this week, but he has been unusually occupied—a great deal of company, and preparation to make for the Sabbath. With much love from us both. . . . [36]

In March, Elizabeth's middle brother, Gorham, brought his bride Mary to the West on her first visit. A few days of pleasant weather helped to create the usual favorable impression on Mary that pleased the family so much.[37]

Meanwhile, Henry Richards, James's older brother in Poughkeepsie, who had contended with tuberculosis for over a decade and a half, seemed to be entering a new phase of the battle. Their literary nephew in Newark, Henry Beach, had observed in his December letter an uncharacteristic desperation in his Uncle Henry's need for hope and reassurance.

Uncle Henry & family sailed last week for Curacao in good spirits. Before he left he consulted Dr. Brewster, Sister Caroline's physician, who told him that he has not got the consumption, that the bronchial tubes may be inflamed, but it all originated from a diseased spine etc. & so convincing were his reasons for such an opinion that Uncle H. who is not easily duped, you know, firmly believes it & only regrets that he did not consult him sooner so as to save the necessity of going South this winter . . .[38]

Here is a rare family reference to the word consumption, a diagnosis that left the sufferer to alternate sometimes for years between periods of weakness and strength. Henry Richards was a prime example of the seesaw nature of the illness. During his years of affliction, he had managed to keep up his law practice, and, in his second marriage, had fathered four more children in six years.

But three months after Henry Richards's December sailing to Curacao, the raised hopes then reported by his nephew were being quietly dashed. A letter from Caroline Dey brought news that Henry was "gradually failing" and that his family in Poughkeepsie "expressed the strong desire" that his mother, sister, and brothers "should come to him as soon as they can." Elizabeth wrote to Magdalena, "They have concluded to go this week."[39]

James's journey to Poughkeepsie meant a postponement of the dedication of the new church. Of course, the congregation could use the basement of the church a while longer, but though she did not refer to it, Elizabeth was already six months pregnant and this pushed the occasion closer to the period of her confinement.

While James was gone, Elizabeth kept busy with spring house-cleaning and soap-making, while also seeing to the sewing of a wedding dress for a servant who was soon to marry and leave. Again the problem of help arose, and this time her husband's absence, her pregnancy, and the unreliability of her own strength made the prospective loss of a servant especially worrisome. Her father had hired an Irishman named Patrick as gardener and carriage driver, and she now cast her net wider in search of good servants. ". . . I have thought that I would like to try a *German* girl if you could find one qualified to do my work," she wrote home, "I have heard that they would work for less wages than American or English." She asked if her family at Canandaigua could send her someone by the first of May, and she looked to Magdalena for help in July when her baby was due.[40]

On the morning of James's return two weeks later, Elizabeth wrote appreciatively to Magdalena of his efforts to get home as soon as possible.

Friday Morning 19 April 1845

My dear Sister

I would have answered your letter yesterday but I was sick all day, and not able to do any thing. To-day I feel quite like myself again, and am very glad to inform you that Mr. Richards has returned—he came with three or 4 gentlemen who hired a private conveyance at Geneva, and came directly through. It was 3 o'clock this morning when he arrived—he left Poughkeepsie at 10 o'clock on Wednesday eve'g. He made no delay on the way—his Mother & Sister did not return with him. . . . Mr. R. left his Brother in a very feeble state, and feels as if he had taken a final leave of him. We are very thankful to be together again as a family—I believe I never passed such a long fortnight—I am glad it is over—

Judge Ellsworth called . . . and brought your most acceptable offering—I feel exceedingly obliged to you for the loaf of cake. I owe you a thousand thanks and more for [daughter] Caroline's little dress, and the collar for me. The satisfaction of knowing that I am remembered at home, and that I share in its blessings, adds greatly to the value of the presents. I call the cake Dedication Cake, and have laid it away for that great occasion. . . .[41]

On the last day of June, Elizabeth was delivered of another daughter, named Anna Beach for James's deceased older sister. The baby was healthy, but Elizabeth was so weak afterward that she could not care for her new child. So the newborn Anna was sent to Canandaigua and put in the charge of the much-loved Jane Lightfoot, who had recently had a child of her own. Jane was one "whom we all desire to honour as a nurse—who was all but mother to" Anna, a grateful family member later wrote.[42] Elizabeth now depended on her sisters in Canandaigua for every bit of news about her baby.

The seriousness of Elizabeth's condition seems not to have been appreciated right away. She was not really recovering from Anna's birth, and family members were slow to recognize the recurrence of symptoms that had laid her low on and off since the birth of her first baby. James's mother, for example, wrote to say how much she longed to see her and her "dear babe" and hoped they would come for a visit in Auburn.

Mrs. Richards was clearer about the condition of Henry in Poughkeepsie, who, she reported, was better, but not expected to make it through "another winter, dear child." She hoped he was "prepared for his great and last change. He said he was more comfortable in his mind than he has been." She added, "I pray God to prepare him and us for what ever he in his providence shall appoint. . . ."[43]

In this period of intensified concern for his wife and his brother, James received two letters bound to stimulate reflection and uneasiness about the circumstances of his ministry. The first of these letters illuminates the unpleasant factionalism to be endured in Penn Yan and its environs, while

the second points to the chilly relations that had developed between
Princeton and Auburn in the eight years since the excision crisis. James had
begun his ministry in 1837, the very year of the excision, and had elected
to stay near his father in western New York. Yet by theology, acquaintance,
and aspiration, he seemed increasingly to cherish his ties to the Old School
orthodoxy of Princeton and the eastern seaboard, now represented intellectually by Charles Hodge. Hodge was laying out the main critique of the
modified Calvinism that Nathaniel William Taylor had developed at Yale.

The first letter James received came from the Reverend Thomas
Lounsbury, a neighboring Presbyterian pastor and the favorite minister of
Caroline Dey. Religious division had persisted within the New School
after excision, and the village of Penn Yan illustrated that division: James,
his father's son, was in the conservative wing of the New School that felt
sure of its orthodoxy and to that extent felt closer to Princeton Presbyterianism than Princeton itself recognized. Ovid Miner, James's predecessor
and a dissatisfied radical, had done what Dr. Richards had wished others of
his ilk would do; he had gone over to Congregationalism, where
Finneyism and New Haven theology were willing bedfellows (see chapter
9). Writing to James against this background, an acerbic Lounsbury scorned
the presumption of the Reverend Miner to speak on behalf of New School
Presbyterianism.

Ovid May 1 1845

Dr Brother
    I received the other day a printed letter from the Rev. O. Miner on
the subject of perfection by which it would seem that he has taken the
ministers and churches of Yates County under his Episcopal supervision, whether of all denominations or of the Presbyterian only I am
unable to say. . . . In said letter however he affirms that a precious
revival of religion has commenced in Pen Yan [sic], which he trusts will
continue under the wing of perfectionism as . . . perpetuated by
Miner. You would confer a favour on me by stating if convenient, some
of the facts in the case. Is there really a revival of religion in Pen Yan, or
only an excitement under the influence of a New ism? If an excitement
even how great is it? The letter itself besides a series of misstatements, I
consider deeply tinctured with strong Pelagian tendencies. The radical
point upon which his whole argument turns, if argument it may be

called, is "that God requires no more of the creature than he be able to perform." If this be true what becomes of the surety ship of Christ? What becomes of the atonement? What becomes of the whole system of grace? If man is able to perform all that God requires of him then the atonement is surely a work of superarrogation. I think the dogma neither honorable to Christ, nor safe for man, and yet the said diocesan [Ovid Miner] would persuade . . . that such is the undoubted faith of New School Presbyterians.[44]

James's other letter came from George Schenk, a graduate of Princeton and Princeton Seminary who for a time taught school in western New York in Stockport, Aurora, and Penn Yan. Schenk and James, the same age and both married, had become close friends. When James and Elizabeth moved to Penn Yan in June 1841, George and Catherine Schenk moved there, too. Two years later the couple returned to Princeton so that Schenk could complete his theological training. Schenk opened his letter to James with expressions of sentiment and duty in the playfully orotund manner familiar from the letters of David Frame.

                                                    Princeton N.J. May 6 1845
My dear Friend,
      I still retain the old practice of commencing a letter with that expression of friendship contained in the words "my dear friend" notwithstanding "res cum tempore mutandur" [things change with time]. . . . how long it has been since I recd. your last . . . I did intend to sit down immediately & write to you saying "that I had such confidence in you as a friend that I could not be induced to believe that you would injure me in feeling by not writing to me unless you had reasons" for in fact during 3 or 4 months before I recd. yours I began to think that some malicious person had influenced you to give credence to one of those P[enn] Y[an] fabrications which ought not to be minded. But your letter dispelled all such surmise & as you *asked* my forgiveness you *have* it freely & fully upon this condition that you will forgive *me* for being dilatory in the same way.
      A little after I recd. yours my wife's sister was taken very ill with the heart complaint & died very suddenly the day before Christmas & buried the day after, sermon by the Rev. Dr. Alexander—text "be ye

also ready" etc. compared life to a journey & carried out the allegory in the minutiae—need of preparing—inquiring the nature of the country to be visited etc. This of course rendered me indisposed for a time to write letters & in addition the duties of my school & the studies of the Semy. a very thorough course of Theology with Dr. [Charles] H[odge] & other professors caused my time to pass away almost to the neglect of my correspondence & I have continued waiting for a *good* opportunity to sit down *leisurely* & write you a *long* letter & yet after having waited a long time I have at last concluded to write *in haste* rather than wait any longer although we are now on the point of examination in the Theo. Semy.

In regard to the publication of some of the writings of your venerable father, I may safely say that he is held in such high esteem by all classes & denominations who "hold the truth in the love of it" that such a book would be eagerly bought. I believe there is no doubt of his orthodoxy & it has been matter of wonder that he has managed so well in a section of the country so full of error. I think after talking to some of our professors that they do not know exactly what is now taught at Auburn. I think that many people in your section are entirely mistaken as to what our professors mean by the doctrine of limited atonement. . . .

Here Schenk reviewed the argument: Christ died for all, but in his omniscience knew who would be influenced by his grace to accept. James had obviously sounded out his friend about how his father's writings would be received there. Despite the present estrangement between the two seminaries, Schenk was reassuring.

Such are my reasons for thinking that there is a nearer coincidence than you may have supposed of the views of your father with those of Princeton. However I tell you what I do by way of inference as I did not like to ask the professors pointedly whether they agreed with Auburn. . . .

I really hope you will publish your father's works: *all* of them—if you come through Princeton be sure to come & see us. We live in a little yellow cottage surrounded by lattice work on the road leading to the railroad stopping place—you can walk up in a few minutes or ride in the hack & take the evening train & be in Phil[adelphia] almost as soon as if

you had kept on—i.e. if you happened to be in haste—but what we
should like would be to have you stay over Sabbath & preach. Dr. [John
Holt] Rice is very unwell & has been away some months & just returned
almost as sick as when he started: if he should give up I should like to
have you step into his place. I think you would suit us exactly. Dr. Rice
does not visit as much as is desireable; but the people here do not expect
half as much as the P[enn] Y[an] people. You would have to preach only
once a week as there are so many others to be invited & sometimes only
once a fortnight. My wife says you come next to Dr. Alexander as the
preacher of all the ministers she ever heard . . . no flattery—I think the
same. My wife sends a great deal of love to Mrs. R. & the children & all
inquiring friends. We shall never forget the kindness of yourself & family &
some other[s] in P.Y. when we were among strangers & far from home.[45]

As Frame had once pushed James for Bloomfield, now Schenk proposed
him in the most flattering terms as successor to the eminent Dr. Rice for
the Presbyterian pulpit of the town of Princeton. The ministry, as it had
professionalized since the beginning of the century, had lost some of the
sense of calling and developed more of the sense of career. In their *inter pares*
communication, ministers now readily described the sizing-up process
between congregations and prospective pastors—the Princeton flock would
be less demanding than the people of Penn Yan, said Schenk. The dignified,
even high-flown language about "the Lord's work" characteristic of Dr.
Richards's generation had receded; the younger ministers were less apt to
discuss the overall state of that work and the question of where each one
could be most "useful."

It was also true that many different spheres were open to James's generation of ministers. A few became foreign or home missionaries. Some went
into journalism. Many more taught in private academies. David Frame edited
the Presbyterian *New York Observer* for a while before becoming the principal
and proprietor of an "English and Classical Boarding School for Young
Gentlemen" at Bloomfield.[46] Some worked in the various nondenominational societies that formed a structure parallel to, but separate from, the
churches. Sam Hopkins did this for a while, before settling down to teach for
the rest of his life at Auburn Seminary.

Moreover, in a mobile and competitive society demographically dominated by its young adult population, a young minister was schooled in the

same personal ambition that was developing elsewhere. He, too, wanted to see his life as a progress to greater and greater responsibility and competence, not just a linear series of useful labors some of which the Lord would bless and others not. The pressure for individual recognition was even greater perhaps because the public influence of the profession as a whole was declining in relative terms.

In these new circumstances, however, James seemed positioned to do well. In an age of oratory, he had the gifts of eloquence and presence. He was attentive and energetic. He had an excellent helpmeet in Elizabeth, who was said, for example, to be "a kind and friendly critic of sermons [such] as a sensitive or despondent pastor needs."[47] Attractive and well-liked, he had numerous friends in different sections of the country. His father's reputation, as Schenk's letter shows, transcended the distaste some felt for the church of western New York. Indeed, his father's steadiness, judgment, and exceptional practical sense were well remembered and no doubt enriched observers' impressions of the younger James Richards.

Lounsbury had mirrored for him the frustrations of his Penn Yan ministry, and Schenk had opened a window on another possibility. Much as these letters might have impressed James, however, it was not the time to pursue a pulpit in Princeton. Elizabeth's condition and the need to stay near her helpful family and their new baby ruled it out.

His mother, too, needed him. In September, she wrote to him from Auburn, "My family is small now to what it has been." She wanted to visit them "while your peaches and plums are in such fine order," but she and Caroline Dey were without servants and she could not leave Caroline alone in the house. She was glad Elizabeth was "improving," though not yet "recovered." She still seemed unsure of Elizabeth's exact condition. Even as she knew that her daughter-in-law was too weak to care for her new baby, Mrs. Richards again wrote hopefully of having Elizabeth visit her in Auburn. In large part, she simply missed them all. "How is Jimmy and Johnny and dear little Cary? . . . I long to see . . . dear *little Anna*. I never wanted to see a child so much before."[48]

This letter from James's mother illustrates what a riddle consumption presented. Elizabeth's condition was hard to sort out from the weakness that followed childbirth, which in pre-antiseptic days still presented a serious peril of its own. Her brother-in-law and fellow sufferer, Henry Richards, who might have known better, did not seem to identify her symptoms with his own, but rather thought they resembled an ailment of his late wife, Margaret, from which she had eventually recovered. He said he believed Elizabeth would recover, too. Of his own health, Henry, no longer at death's door, gave a mixed report, "I am gaining a little strength, my appetite is excellent and digestion good, still my cough is just the same . . . and expiration quite as bad as it was months ago." He hoped the coming cold weather would brace him up, then said his doctor recommended spending another winter in the warm South. The two courses seem contradictory, but then consumption was a fickle disease. Strength came and went. New cures were constantly looked for. Henry was only recently virtually given up, yet now, feeling "a little strength," he announced he would go down to New York City for the sale of his late mother-in-law's estate and then go on to Princeton to see his son, James, who was a student there.[49]

James Nicholas Richards, the surviving son from Henry's first marriage, was now seventeen. As a younger boy, he had known foster care with his aunt and uncle and then life at a boarding school. He was fourteen when his younger brother drowned, and this loss may have left him further adrift in the busy household in Poughkeepsie centered on an ill father and a covey of small children. Elizabeth found him still a youth of "unsettled habits." It must have gratified his father when he entered Princeton, for Henry himself had done so well there. But James was more like the rogues of his father's day than like his father. He was soon cited for repeatedly breaking the rules. Three months later, the college requested his father "*not* to allow [the] son to return."[50]

Even before his son's virtual expulsion, Henry suffered a relapse and took again to bed, suffering great fatigue and recurrent hemorrhaging. James was asked to visit them again. "Your presence and conversation might be a great comfort." Elizabeth, meanwhile, had written Henry a letter that moved him to respond, though in a feeble, shaky hand so different from the vigor and grace of his usual handwriting. Poor punctuation and touches of incoherence suggest that the tuberculosis now affected his nervous system and made it difficult for him to think clearly.

> My dear Elizabeth
>   I have taken my pen in hand to thank you for your very acceptable letter you cannot conceive how delighted we were to receive a letter

from you in your own handwriting and as you said nothing about your health we are in great hopes that it is improving. a letter from you is a great treat to me as we see each other so seldom.

I am glad the children were pleased with the few things their father caried [*sic*] them, & I have a little present for Cary which I shall send her the first opportunity that presents I long to see you all very much I think it is most time for James to come and see us again I think little Cary has good health. . . . I long to see you all I wish you could send her to me I should like to look at her I think her good health must improve her very much. Your little Anna must have grown very much I would give most any thing to see her I am glad she is where you feel no anxiety about her I received a long letter from Edward last week he has given up visiting Auburn this winter provided I will make them a visit in the spring he is very anxious I should do so he wants me to come down to New York and have my likeness taken to put with your fathers. Caroline has written to him and told him that my mind was not made up on the subject that if I went at all I could not go till the weather became warm and settled in the spring or summer[51]

The family seemed to expect Henry to rally once again and be ready to travel. Edward's interest in having his likeness taken may reflect a hedge against these hopes.

In the meantime, Elizabeth, who could not care for her own baby, somehow expected to keep on hosting visiting family members. Perhaps their help and company offset any extra duty. She kept at the household chores.

Saturday afternoon, Nov. 2, 1845

My dear Mother

Mr. Richards just came from his study and requested me to answer your letter . . . It is so near the close of the week, that he must necessarily employ every moment in making preparations for the Sabbath. . . . I am very sorry that you did not come home with us. As Caroline has concluded to stay a little longer in New York, I think it would have been pleasant for you and for us if you could have been here for at least a week. . . .

. . . my little Caroline . . . has a very heavy cold. I have some reason to fear that she has the whooping cough. A good many children in the village have this complaint; and if she has it, of course the little boys will have it. I do not think they will go to school any more this winter. . . .

We have been making soup this week. Yesterday [servant Sarah] thought she would like to try her skill, and she made a kettle full that was quite creditable. I think it is well for her to learn how to do such things. I hope she may be very useful to you at some future time. You must excuse me for writing about such a trivial matter: such little affairs are of great consequence to housekeepers. . . .

Mr. R. says he will comply with your requests about his father's manuscripts; he has transcribed one of those to which you referred. You ask for the text to one of his sermons. You will find it in Hebrews vi. 12.

I hope you will not forget your promise to come and see us soon, and take us all by surprise. It would be a delightful surprise. You do not know how easy it would be for you to get here if you could only make up your mind to give up your cares at home for a little while . . . [52]

One visitor who did make it soon to Penn Yan was Henry Beach, "Henry Quill." From there, he went to Auburn where he spent Christmas Eve in a family party "with whom Cynthia united in adding to the 'good cheer' & holiday festivity." He added, "I was much disappointed in her & cannot say that I am sorry the future marks her as Mrs. Burnet—not Mrs. Beach." Boarding the train that night, he was pleased to meet Auburn's leading citizen, Governor William Seward. They rode the train together to Albany and New Haven and then took the same boat to New York. For the Albany-to-Hartford leg of this trip, young Beach rejoiced even more at having the company of the esteemed Robert Baird, "who filled up the time so cheerfully" with his "anecdotes, & views of men & places, in a word his graphic conversation. . . . Was it not a treat?" Henry was flattered by the atmosphere of "mutual confidence" and especially Baird's "kind & confiding familiarity—& the freedom with which many things were expressed 'inter nos'. . . ." Having lost his parents, Henry responded eagerly to the attentions of such elders.

Once back in Newark at the beginning of the new year of 1846, he wrote up these details in a lively letter to his Uncle James, indulging in all the flourishes of the literary man. Duties awaited him in the Beach household, now managed jointly by the older brothers and sisters in their twenties who wrestled at times with the issue of authority. The Newark scene contrasted sharply with Henry's fond images of his stay in Penn Yan where he could sit relaxed at the family table and be cared for by a solicitous aunt and uncle.

Newark Jany 2 1846

Very Dear Uncle,

I have been home five days & not unemployed a moment scarcely, since I crossed the threshhold of No. 4 Fulton St. Things were at loose ends and seemed in patient waiting for *me* to tie them up again. My return trip was no less delightful than . . . my visit. Take it all in all no one ever enjoyed anything more than I did my Western Excursion—full of incident, as it was, at once novel & various—and long long indeed shall I cherish a grateful recollection of your own & Aunt E's kindness & attention in anticipating my wants & comforts & in affording a ready supply—& be assured that I hold you all in constant remembrance—not forgetting "the little joys"—the ruddy & hale James Jr, the delicate & grave Johnny Morgan, & the wee sparkling "I did just as you did"—& last, tho' not least the tiny innocent of whom as yet we know nought but her name & the beamings of the Immortal in the intelligent expression of her sweetly pretty countenance. I prize highly the more intimate acquaintance which has by my sojourn in your cheerful abode been opened to my mind & heart, & count it "an additional cause for *thanksgiving*"—

Henry Beach had heard his uncle preach at Auburn and had sensed in him an uncertainty about its success. Perhaps James had found himself comparing the sermon with his father's efforts which he was currently editing. In broaching the topic, young Henry Beach affected a breezy tone of reassurance, seeming to downplay his usual earnestness. With his

Uncle James he enjoyed another confiding relationship of obvious importance to him.

> I had almost forgotten to tell you that after you left me at A[uburn] several times during the day I heard your sermon which you delivered on Tuesday Evening, very highly commended—So you perceive I was not mistaken in the estimate I put upon it. . . . Were it mine to deliver the mandate, I should say as was said to those having the ark in charge among Israel's hosts—"Go forward"—I understand that *your* Thanksgiving discourse has been republished in the Evangelist—tho' I have not seen it—if so it must have been approved. They were pleased with it at home. . . . Not a question was asked, no doubts raised—but it seemed perfectly intelligible—Originality, veracity, no less than beauty are ascribed to *your effort*—"Solon" is not always a failing prophet. . . .

Henry seemed to attract nicknames ("Solon," "Henry Quill"). He was proud of his uncle's growing reputation and of his role in the family's publication project, ". . . I shall proceed with my transcribing labors as speedily as possible & then seek an opportunity of sending you the Copies. . . ."

The new generation observed Christmas, once shunned for its "papist" associations, though Thanksgiving still held precedence as a family celebration. Henry had missed out while he was away on a much anticipated yuletide party hosted by his brothers and sisters. Certain aspects of the party took him by surprise when he learned about them, and he confided to his aunt and uncle his relief at not being present. The absence of the older generation was clearly felt.

> The party came off on the Evening after Christmas as I was apprised & it was one of the most successful & happy parties ever held in town—so our guests uniformly expressed themselves either earnestly or in the cant of "politeness"—But I am glad that I was not at home—James would have Champagne & Dancing—contrary to the girls' remonstrances—in opposition to the temperance sentiment for which our parents when living declared—& in violation of the church regulations. . . .

Henry had arrived in time for another large affair at Alex Pennington's and for making the customary "New Year's calls." He was looking forward to yet another party that very evening, this time at the home of Henry and Louisa Beals. Seventy invitations had been issued. "We are hoping for something of a frolic—particulars hereafter."

He knew his Aunt Elizabeth craved all the family news he could supply, and as he had sensed his uncle's need for reassuring praise, so he acknowledged in her a need for distraction or encouragement when her health or good cheer failed. "I shall occasionally send Aunt E. a newspaper to engage her attention when in one of those peculiar moods."[53]

A hint of such a mood can be found in Elizabeth's letter a few weeks later to Glorianna:

> Penn Yan, Jan. 27, 1846
>
> My dear Sister Glorianna,
>
> I presume you have read the widow's letter in the "New York Observer" of the 17th. She concluded by saying that "she had been fed upon Irenaeus' letters." If you have ever depended for aliment upon my letters, you must by this time be famishing. The great difficulty to find anything to write about that would interest you has hitherto prevented my answering two of your letters, which merited immediate notice. . . .

The familiar passing reference to Irenaeus, one of the early church fathers, suggests again the theological attainments of this female circle. Elizabeth had chanced to read in the newspaper about the death of Gorham's father-in-law, and asked Glorianna, "Was the event very unexpected? Mary Beals [Gorham's wife] was probably absent, as when you last wrote she was at Tarrytown. If she was absent, the event will on that account doubly afflict her." Of her own health, Elizabeth noted: "The doctor has consented to have me go out, and I have taken one short ride. It did not hurt me at all, and I had [a] better rest than in a long time before." Still she was not strong. She wrote that her friend Eliza

> . . . has been twice to see me since her return. On Saturday she brought me a cap as a present from herself; it is very pretty, and designed to be worn every day. She is very kind, and I feel almost oppressed with the

obligations she has laid upon me. I really needed it, for I have to keep myself looking "pretty smart," as the saying is. I have a great many calls, and if I am not positively sick I dare not refuse to see people. Sometimes I am very glad to see my friends, at other times I think it would be the greatest luxury imaginable to be quite alone, except to have one close by to whom I can whisper "solitude is sweet."

It is impressive that Elizabeth had to give up the care of baby Anna but could not escape the obligation to receive callers and even look "smart" doing so. Her sisters knew how much she missed Anna and regularly included reassuring news about the infant's progress. A knowing realism and a quiet pathos characterize Elizabeth's concluding remarks and imply a silent protest against the abnormal separation of mother and child.

> I believe we are apt to leave until the last that which we consider of the most consequence. I now refer to my dear little Anna. I am very thankful that you always happen to find her so happy. I presume she is not so unlike the rest of her race, but that she sometimes cries. I am glad she is so good. Ask Jane if the child has cut a tooth yet? I believe James had two when he was five months old.[54]

In a letter from Glorianna, Elizabeth was touched to learn something else about baby Anna. She wrote to her mother the following week.

> Monday evening, Feb. 2, 1846
>
> My dear Mother,
>   I have received a letter from brother Henry this afternoon, which he has requested me to enclose and send to you. I am glad to . . . acknowledge Glorianna's letter . . . I feel much indebted to her for writing. I think my baby is quite young to answer to her own name. I am glad she has been so early taught to know the name of "Anna." My other children have all been called "Baby" until they were one or two years.

To have to depend on others for such vital information must have grieved her sorely. She was pleased to hear from her brother Henry, but became understandably nettled by his lapses in naming and numbering her children, and told her mother so.

> I wish G. would be so kind as to tell brother Henry, in her next letter to him, how many children we have, and what their names are. I hope Uncle David will get out his genealogical table, for Henry's benefit. Our own family is increasing so rapidly, that one generation can scarcely remember the names of those who are to immediately succeed them. . . .

She was realizing herself here how numerous and scattered the family had become. "Uncle David" was her mother's nephew, David Field, who, in addition to being the family genealogist, was an eminent lawyer and codifier of New York State law.

As Elizabeth could not fend off callers, she was also at the mercy of everyday pressures like the outbreak of childhood illnesses.

> My little children are getting over the chicken-pox, except little Caroline: she looks "like a fright," the boys say, and surely she does. Her whole face is covered with sores, and she has not been able to find a place for her father to kiss for the last day or two. She has been fretful and complaining since Saturday. . . . Mr. R. expects to leave tomorrow for Waterloo, to attend Presbytery; he will be absent until Thursday. I have not felt as well as usual for a week past. I believe I saw too much company. I had a long visit from Mrs. Hudson, and she gave me a history of nine weeks in Philadelphia. . . . I am going to take rest all this week. . . .[55]

Elizabeth's symptoms were diffuse and varied, suggesting that the tuberculosis bacterium was not confined to her lungs. As was the case with her brother-in-law, her energy came and went. After her children's chickenpox and the out-of-town visitors, she had several days of letdown. During this period she received a letter from her sisters in which Magdalena described an illness of her own. Elizabeth was moved to compare their symptoms, and the effort evoked from her a more sustained reflection on the nature of her illness than she had ever put

Doctors paid a surprise house call on Elizabeth. (Courtesy— New York Academy of Medicine Library)

down in a family letter. Soon afterward two physicians made a surprise call in order to examine her. The occasion absorbed her and drew from her this extraordinarily detailed account.

Penn Yan, Feb. 13, 1846

My dear Mother,

I received a joint letter from M[agdalena] and G[lorianna] on Tuesday evening, and would gladly have answered it before this present, if I had had the full command of my time. Since I last wrote to you I have had several sick days, when I have not felt *bodily* able to write; as soon as I was better, my kind friends came in to express their sympathy:—thus I have been occupied. . . .

You will remember that when I last wrote I was promising myself a "week of rest"—I had it in part; The Doctor called the morning Mr. R. left home and found me not quite as well as usual, he thought my Liver was in fault; and he told me to raise a Blister on my right side, which I did, with good effect.

I suspect from Magdalena's account of herself, that she has the same disease from which I have been suffering a long time. I feel much sympathy for her, but I think that her age makes her case less serious than my own: in her case only one organ (the stomach) seems to be diseased, while I have a complication of diseases; and when I am relieved in one part, another suffers in consequence—this makes my situation ten fold worse than her own—I hope Magdalena will attend to the Doctor's directions. Here I am going to give her a little advice, as the result of my own experience—I would not allow myself to sit still too much nor would I use a needle and thread or a book all the time, give the mind and body rest, never allowing yourself to be in a hurry to complete a piece of work of any kind within a *given time*—I am confident I have injured myself in that way—so much to Magdalena, and now to appeal again to my Mother, I presume it is almost useless for me to inquire if you recollect the state of my health during the winter previous to my marriage? I was reminded of my feeling at that time when I was reading Magdalena's description of her own case—I date the commencement of my ill health as far back as the winter of 1836; in confirmation of the fact that some of my ails are the same now that they were then, I would add that the same remedies are proposed to me now, which were then.

Monday a.m.—Last week on Tuesday, Dr. Oliver came to see me, and brought with him the elder Doctor Spencer of Geneva—Dr. S. was sent for expressly to give Professional advice in the case of Mrs. Tunnicliff, a member of our church. . . . The Doctor's visit upon me was very unexpected, but not the less timely and acceptable. On Tuesday morning I saw a carriage stop before our house, a Lady & Gentleman came in whom I did not recognize. Sarah came in & told me that Dr. Spencer & Mrs. Van Vranken wished to see me. I received them very cordially, the Dr. said he would leave Mrs. V. with me, while he went to see some of Dr. Oliver's patients, & would call for her in a few hours. I invited the Doctor to return & dine with us a 1 o'clock—he half accepted my invitation & left. . . .

At one o'clock precisely, my dinner was announced—and at the same moment Dr. O. and Dr. S. presented themselves. Mr. Richards gave the gentlemen a very hearty welcome, and said we were much gratified to have them dine with us—Dr. Oliver said in his usual blunt way "we have had our dinner, we came to see *you*" pointing at me. Mr. Richards observed my agitation, and relieved me at once by inviting Mrs. Van Vranken to take my seat at the Dinner Table—While the family were dining in the back room, I was left alone with the Doctors in the Parlour.

Dr. Oliver's *first* remark was "we make minister's wives a gratuitous visit" (perhaps the Dr. had an idea, that I would not be benefitted by the advice if I expected to have to pay for it) I told the Dr. I was very grateful for the attention, and should be glad to have Dr. Spencer's opinion of my case. Dr. Oliver observed a little agitation (for my pulse was so much quickened by the excitement that they could not judge of me at all from that); said "we are grey-headed old men you must tell the whole story without any reserve." Dr. Spencer gave me a most thorough examination. I have not had as many questions asked me in one day since I was one of Miss Upham's pupils; in some instances I hardly knew how to answer him.

Dr. Spencer's first inquiries were relative to the disease of the Stomach and Bowels—he remarked that as it first presented itself, it was in many particulars like the disease which afflicted Edmond Dwight some years ago—he added that a sea voyage cured him and that it probably would me, if I was disposed to make a trial of it.

Upon a more careful examination the Dr. found a difficulty with my Lungs. He decided that it would not be safe to check the Diarrhea suddenly: the system has become accustomed to a drain and if it should cease, the Lungs being in a delicate and perhaps diseased state . . . increased action or inflammation of that organ would inevitably ensue. Dr. Spencer reccommended [sic] for the disease of the Bowels a "Nitre Muriatic Bath"—for the Lung complaint dry cupping, and the "Balsam of the Wild Cherry"—I am to omit the use of the Iron which has been my exclusive medicine since Nov. 1—and for a strengthening medicine take a table spoon full of Brandy, three times a day.

I believe that favourable results will follow Dr. Spencer's visit to me. I have much confidence in his judgment, Dr. Oliver agrees with him perfectly . . . They do not promise me entire restoration to health, but they are disposed to believe that when Spring returns, I may reasonably hope for a comfortable health. Dr. Spencer said he did not wish to have me confined to my room or my house but wished me to interest myself in what was passing around me, and to cultivate a cheerful spirit. He said my restoration to health depended very much upon my being cheerful & not allowing my mind to dwell upon any subject that would depress the spirits. He also desired me to take an occasional ride when all things were favorable.

You will be surprized [*sic*] to know that Dr. Oliver has consented to my going to C[anandaigua]. I am so very desirous to go & see my dear Baby, that I am strongly tempted to avail myself of the permission granted. . . .

By the way, our little Johnny is just five years old today—the return of his Birth Day has brought to my recollections all of the events connected with his Birth, and my protracted illness which followed. It has pleased God to raise me up, more than once when I had felt that my own case was hopeless. It may be that the Lord has more work for me to do. I desire to be passive in His Hands, and know no will but His.

I hope Jane is very well—and my little Anna I am delighted to know that she thrives so well with Jane's good nursing. When I have a very well day—I feel as if I wanted to have my Baby in my arms—duty and affection prompts such a wish. But I let my infirmities press upon me, and my first thoughts are "Oh how thankful I am that my Baby is so well provided for" —I am sure no child could be better situated if necessarily deprived of a Mother's care. . . .[56]

Toward the latter part of March, James received a letter from the irrepressible Henry Beach. The move to Brooklyn was imminent, ending the forty-year presence of the Richards family in Newark. There seemed to be no regrets about the move. Henry could think only of his upcoming trip to Europe in the company of Robert Baird, the American envoy to continental Protestants.

Saturday March 21 1846

Dear Uncle J.—

The passage marked in [Senator John C.] Calhoun's interesting speech will remind you of a certain thanksgiving sermon once preached in your church—a striking illustration of coincidence of thought in great minds.

We shall move to Brooklyn probably next week on Thursday, the 26th of March—On the 6th or 10th of April, Providence permitting, I shall sail for Europe in company with Dr. Brinsmade [his Newark pastor] & Rev. Ed. Rankin—with a view of travelling thro'out Great Britain & on the continent, North & South, for Seven months, designing to embark on return from Liverpool in Steam ship Oct. 31, 1846—Would you not like to go if it were practicable? *Dr. Baird will be our accomplished guide on the Continent.* We expect to be present at the "World's Convention" in Aug[ust]—to be introduced to some of the European Courts en route—& see all that is to be seen—learn all that is to be learned by observation, & mature, profitable conversation. Our plans will be unfolded more in detail by the girls when you visit them. I would love to have taken a farewell from Aunt E. & yourself, Grandma & Aunt C.—but fear I will not be privileged so to do.

You will perhaps be disappointed & surprised to hear that I have not completed the work I brought home to do—but shall I say—the Fates have been against me. If I am returned in safety & health—I shall consider myself bound to execute it then. I would like to have been in N.Y. to superintend in some measure the publication forthcoming. You may have calculated upon it—but the opportunity offered to make this tour is *rare* indeed, & may never be presented again—& I think could you have been here you would of [*sic*] advised me to go by all means.

I would give anything to see you—Remember us all in your prayers—With love to all of your dear family in wh[ich] the girls unite. I must bid you an affectionate adieu—as ever Yours[57]

So "Henry Quill" departed for European adventures and put aside efforts to help his Uncle James with transcriptions of his late grandfather's lectures. James seemed to anticipate something of the sort, for he had already hired a local young woman to assist him. "Miss Mary Ann Hall came here today," Elizabeth had written soon after their nephew's return to Newark, "She has taken up the work which Henry Beach left undone, and will probably complete it." Elizabeth found her "a quiet, amiable girl" and praised her handwriting, "handsome as copperplate."[58]

In May, Glorianna tried to cheer Elizabeth with a letter full of family news and scenes. Despite references from time to time to improvement in Elizabeth, her overall condition had continued to worsen.

>   Canandaigua May 4 1846
> My dear Sister,
>   We received Mr. Richards letter this noon and are very glad to know that you are much better. This weather is very favourable for invalids and I hope you will be invigorated by it. This morning Mother and Mag took a ride, the latter being *driver*—Ma has quite recovered from her cough. Mag's is almost gone. . . .
>   On Saturday afternoon I went to Jane's and found her and the children very well—Little Anna seemed to feel very happy and looked the picture of health. Jane had cleaned her front room during the past week; every thing was in the nicest order you can imagine, but I cannot describe the cleanest of every thing. . . .
>   Mr. Richards inquires what Dr. Carr thinks of "The Balsam of wild cherry"? he says this bark of the wild cherry is a very good tonic, but there is *no* such thing as the "Balsam of wild cherry."
>   I was very much pleased to see the letter written by Jimmy [seven years old] and could hardly believe that he could write so well—I think he deserves a great deal of credit—& I am afraid none of his cousins would prove very good correspondents. . . .
>   Mother has put some figs into the valise, and says you can eat them or give them to the children—Mag eats them quite freely and thinks they do her good. . . .[59]

Most of Elizabeth's surviving correspondence was with Magdalena and Glorianna, her unmarried sisters living at home. Her older married sisters were busy with their own families. As a sign that the family saw Elizabeth taking a turn for the worse, Ann Field and Mary Carr now made unusual exertions to be in touch with Elizabeth and to visit little Anna. In the middle of May, her eldest sister Ann, exhausted from nursing her children through the whooping cough, lovingly assured Elizabeth of her concern.

Canandaigua May 15th 1846

My dear Sister Elizabeth

I do not like to have the week close without giving you some *tangible* proof of my affectionate remembrance.—I cannot bring myself, to believe for a moment, that you can doubt the anxiety I have, *constantly* for you— or the regret I feel that my domestic cares are such that I cannot leave for *one* day, *unencumbered*, to see you—But it is so.—and for the last month I have been so much broken of my usual rest, and sleep, at night, with the children & coughing, that I have been almost unfitted for my daily duties, but I hope they will soon be better. On Wednesday Sister Mary called over here with your letter, and we walked together, down to Janes to see your little Anna,—We found her very well and looking so happy. She was not afraid to come to us. Jane's little girl seemed very fond of the baby. The little bonnet fitted nicely, and is very pretty—Jane was all smiles—I hear from the baby every morning, Henry [Field, her son] goes down there.

I know not when I have so much [been] astonished at any thing as the letter your James wrote to his Aunt Mary. He must be precocious. I am sure, for Henry cannot do much better now and he is over 12 years of age—It must be very gratifying to you—Tell Johnny, *he* must write his first letter to his Aunt Ann—

Do you hear often from New York? Henry & Gorham are not very good correspondents, but I suppose they are like the rest of us, taken up with the cares and business of life. . . .

Ann had news that she thought would interest James. Her husband had just returned from Philadelphia, where he had heard that a friend of James, the Reverend Thompson, was having such difficulty in his church that he told his people he would leave them in a fortnight if something wasn't done about it. On a different plane, Ann also reported that the Reverend and Mrs. Daggett in Canandaigua had recently built a verandah over the front door of the parsonage. It was painted green and very pretty and done "at their own expense, I *believe*."

I intend in the morning to put a few tulips and some apples for your children in a basket and send you with this letter.—I wish there was *something* I could do for you—Do you think of any thing I have, or can

*James and Elizabeth's sons, James and
John Morgan Richards. (Taken from
Caroline Cowles Richards, Diary
1852–1872, copyright 1908)*

procure that you could relish or would add to your comfort in any way?
If so will you oblige me by letting me know what it is that I may have
the pleasure of sending it to you—If you feel able to write a few lines,
I should be glad to receive it.

My love to Mr. Richards and the children. . . . Good night, my
dear Sister, I hope this letter will find you improving in strength,—and
may the Blessed comforter be near to strengthen and sustain at all times
is the prayer of your sister Ann.[60]

Two weeks passed before Elizabeth was able to reply. It would be her
last surviving letter. The pangs of separation from her baby Anna now
served to awaken her to the coming final separation from all of those
whom she loved.

My dear Sister

It is just a fortnight since I received your letter, with the flowers and the fruit and the cakes for the children. We were all very much pleased. I have been trying to think of something with which to fill the basket, that would afford you and yours equal pleasure. For the letter I feel especially grateful. I was very miserable and weak on the day of its reception. The sympathy and affection you expressed for me seemed to revive and animate me very much. . . .

I feel considerably better than when I last wrote to you. The means used to cure my mouth and throat have proved successful. I can now take a little comfort in eating, and I have a pretty good appetite. I began eating little birds, wild and tame pigeons. I think it will not be many days before I shall be able to eat ordinary food with the family. I have been out to ride every day this week. I rode five miles yesterday. My cough has not left me, but we think it gradually abates. I raise more or less every day, and not unfrequently a small quantity of blood.

Elizabeth's sister, Ann Fields. (Taken from Caroline Cowles Richards, Diary *1852–1872, copyright 1908)*

While this continues I must of necessity be very weak. I never expect to have perfect health. I think I may be comfortable while the mild weather continues.

I look upon my situation with calmness and submission; I feel as if God has laid his afflicting hand upon me, but yet I have not been left to *murmur*, but enabled to say, I love the Lord. . . .

If I should see you, I could not tell you how I have felt or do feel: my voice is so very feeble, that I cannot say to my husband one half that I should be glad to. When we are riding I cannot make myself heard at all unless the waggon is stopped.

How is my little Anna this morning? When her father prayed for her at our morning devotions, my heart was full. I hope she will live to comfort her father; but I feel she will never know that she had a mother, except as her friends shall tell her how early she was taken from the paternal roof.

Dr. Oliver has told Mr. Richards that he wished me to take a short journey, to try my strength a little. . . . some time next month. We hope Mrs. Dr. Richards will spend next week with us.

I feel under great obligations to you for what you have done in clothing my little Anna. It was entirely unexpected to me, but not the less acceptable, as I have not been able to provide for her wants. I was writing when sister Mary came in. What I have not strength to write, Mary will tell you. If I should not be able to come and see you, I hope you will come to me. My sisters are very dear to me. I wish I could enjoy more of their society. . . . Give my love to Jane, and kiss my baby for me when you see her.[61]

As her son James wrote many years later in a memoir, "Her disease assumed a very serious aspect from this time, and her decline was marked and rapid. She lived exactly a fortnight. . . ."[62] Elizabeth died on June 13, 1846; she was thirty-two years old. She had years before arranged and set aside "grave clothes."[63] She had designated certain "sisters of the church" to prepare her body for burial. James had once wanted to have her portrait painted, but she had refused. On the day of her death, he called in a man to take a plaster mold of her face from which a bust was made. She was buried in a place she had chosen, under a large walnut tree. In James's pocket Testament, she had placed a poem cut from *The Philadelphia Gazette*, "I See Thee Still."[64]

When her sister Lucilla had died some years before, Elizabeth had expressed confidence that the Lord would raise up people to care for Lucilla's children. This had been her experience with little Anna, the baby she hardly saw and never stopped asking about. There was no question but that family members would help now with the rest of her children, who were all under the age of seven.

But for Lucilla's husband, Elizabeth had worried: Would there be any consolation equal to his grief? Possibly she had imagined to herself how James would take such a loss. Her surviving kin likewise feared for James's state of mind. His losses had been so many. In five years the train of Richards family deaths included his brother-in-law, his sister, his twelve-year-old nephew, his father, his wife; and as he began his mourning for Elizabeth, his brother Henry lay dying in Poughkeepsie.

Marble bust of Elizabeth done at the time of her death. (Taken from John Morgan Richards, With John Bull and Jonathan, *D. Appleton, New York, 1906)*

Two days after Elizabeth's death, her sister Ann wrote to James:

                                        Canandaigua June 15 1846
My dear Brother
   I know not how to address you, but yet feel constrained to tell
you how much my feelings are in unison with yours in this time
of our deep bereavement and affliction.—The sad news yesterday
completely overwhelmed me. I found I was entirely unprepared for
it, perhaps more so, that if I had not so recently enjoyed such a
sweet interview with our dear Elizabeth—when I parted with you,
on Thursday evening I felt confident that this week the object we
had so long desired of seeing the dear *invalid* in our own homes
would be realized.
   I know not why I was so deceived in her appearance, but she
seemed so cheerful and calm—there was such a lovely look about your
yard and garden—the cottage so comfortable and so neat, the air
seemed so bland, and the children so interesting, that it seemed that it
could not *be* as we have feared.

   "When life with opening hopes is full.
   How *hard* it is to die"

   These thoughts were in my mind, the whole way home. I think I half
persuaded the friends here to think that Elizabeth would be herself
again.—but alas I sought to claim a June spirit just ready for Heaven to
this troubled sphere. I cannot tell you how impatient I am to see you—
I hope my visit did not excite her too much, that she was not grieved
that I left without a parting word Oh, how little I thought I had taken
my *last* look.—
   And now would that I could comfort you but you know where to
go.—and those dear children, truly bereaved.—Oh! that I could do
something for them, and for you—It is not thought best for me to go
now, as I cannot leave my babe, but at anytime, if it would meet your
wishes or be a comfort to you in any way, I would be glad to come and
stay a few days.

I am afraid that I do not feel submissive to this chastisement, nor sufficiently impressed with the eternal realities of which Elizabeth had entered repose. Oh! that I had more of her sweet resignation, as she expressed in a beautiful letter received from her a fortnight since. "I feel that God has laid his afflicting hand upon me, but yet I have not been left to *murmur*, but enabled to say, I love the Lord."

I can add no more but an assurance of tender sympathy and love from your Sister Ann B. Field[65]

Only one other message of condolence survives, a letter from one of James's colleagues, a minister in Trumansburg, New York:

Trumansburg June 23, 1846

Reverend and Dear Sir

When at Auburn a few days since I learned the melancholy intelligence of the death of your wife.

Dear Sir my regard for the person and memory of your venerated and deceased Father and for his family—and the frequent and pleasant occasions of friendly intercourse which by their kindness I have enjoyed with them—my slight but agreeable acquaintance with your deceased wife—and especially the very kind and generous and to me most grateful and welcome sympathy which you have *personally shown me* make me feel that I *have sympathy* to share with you and condolence to offer which I hardly know to conceal—

And Sir I am not *all unused* to sorrows like your own—True, God has not taken from me the wife of my Youth and left me desolate as You now are—but often—alas—how often have I been compelled to tear her from my heart and give her up to God—and even now I feel each day that she is only lent, a precious boon from heaven—a little season in answer to my prayers and tears—soon to be resumed by God.

Permit me then Dear Sir to offer You my sincerest sympathy & condolence. May the Lord sustain You in Your hour of trial—Oh this is a hard rugged life of ours—God grant Dear Brother that You may not sorrow as those who have no hope—but assuredly believing that they who sleep in Jesus will God bring with him, that You may have strong consolations—and lay hold on the hope that when He who is our life shall appear You and Your departed wife shall also appear with him in glory—

Affectionately Your Brother in the Lord

D. H. Hamilton[66]

With Elizabeth's death, the surviving Richards correspondence, with few exceptions, comes to an end. Henry died a month later.

WANDERINGS

JAMES'S LATER CAREER

"Your friend Richards is drunk."

Chapter Eleven

J ames Richards Jr. had experienced three turning points in his life thus far. The first was his youthful conversion. The second was meeting and marrying Elizabeth Beals, who had influenced him to enter the ministry. The third was her untimely death. With her solid support of his ministerial vocation, he had seemed to thrive. In their ten-year marriage (1836–1846), they had created a partnership that became the emotional focus of the extended Richards family, especially after Anna's death and the gradual dissolution of the Beach household in Newark. Now James had to face his loss and recast his life. Just as his case of smallpox had been followed by conversion, love, and profession, it was possible that this latest, most painful trial would in time give way to renewed happiness and success.

Instead, he found himself on a different road, facing a thirty-year battle against alcoholism and struggling for self-respect and survival in his profession. His father fought institutional battles; it became his lot to fight personal ones. Church and family continued to be the crucial contexts of his life.

The period of his mourning, from the little we know, he weathered well. Caring friends lent him encouragement and by the end of the summer of Elizabeth's death he was again traveling and exchanging pulpits. ". . . Now [won't] you come[?] . . . [we] will endeavor to make you comfortable. . . ." wrote the Reverend John Bradford, inviting him in September to preach in Geneva. "Come directly to my house, and I will see your horse is provided for."[1]

Keeping busy on many fronts, the Penn Yan pastor engaged a house-keeper and enrolled precocious James and little John Morgan at the local Dame's School while continuing to look after his elderly mother, who remained in Auburn.[2] His bereavement did not delay the appearance later that summer of his father's seminary lectures. Published by M.W. Dodd in New York, the final work included a ninety-page biographical sketch of Dr. Richards by the Reverend Gridley and twenty-two of Dr. Richards's lectures on such topics as the will, creation, the fall of man, native depravity, the extent of the atonement, election, justification, the prayer of faith, apostasy, and ability and inability.

With the death of their elder brother Henry, James and Edward drew closer. From his vantage point in the city, Edward watched over the prospects of their father's book, and in a September letter, expressed concern that Dodd was not doing enough to secure a review of it. He urged James to come visit him that fall, "It is some time since I have heard from you and I feel anxious to hear how & what you are doing. . . ." He inquired when James had last been to Auburn to see "our dear Mother."[3]

Caroline Richards died the next year, on October 8, 1847, having reached the age of her late husband, seventy-six. Her death removed James's last blood connection to western New York. The ranks of his kin by marriage were also thinning there. Though Thomas and Abigail Beals remained in Canandaigua, their sons Henry and Gorham were still living in New York City. Young Thomas would eventually go to Indiana. As for the younger sisters of Elizabeth whom James knew best, they, too, left the scene that year: Magdalena succumbed to tuberculosis, and Glorianna married a Mr. Rogers and departed with him for a new life in Wisconsin.

These developments favored James's long-contemplated return to the East. Interested friends moved on his behalf, and in late October came stirring news. James was called to the Presbyterian pulpit at Morristown, where his father had begun his ministry fifty years before and where the elder Richards had once said he expected to end his days. Only the pulpit at Newark could carry for James a similar emotional charge.

The solitary life of a widower did not suit James, and society encouraged prompt remarriage. A year and a half after Elizabeth's death and a month after accepting the call to Morristown, James was wed to a member of his congregation, the daughter of a Penn Yan lawyer and the niece of the Reverend William Wisner, one of Auburn's founding trustees.

It was said of widowers that they chose ever younger brides. James's new wife, Sarah Wisner, was eighteen years old. Anthony Dey and Henry Richards had likewise married much younger second wives. The general opinion was that a younger woman would prove more adaptable to the requirements of an established household headed by an older man more fixed in his ways. It was not easy: Caroline Dey had suffered the uncertainty of mixed loyalties, and Henry Richards had never quite made the families from his first and second marriages cohere. Some benefits may be noted, however. The younger second wife was getting a husband who was mature but not old—James was thirty-four—whose qualities were demonstrated and not merely "promising"; and the husband acquired a companion of youthful attractions and energy. Energy counted, for Sarah would find her hands full with James's four small children, the youngest aged two.

Earlier in life, Elizabeth Beals had brought a steadiness and purpose to an ambitious, high-spirited, less-focused young man of her own age. In a sense, the adult James had been formed by that marriage. This second union had to be different. Sarah Wisner, whatever her own capacity and maturity, would be called to a more adaptive role than to a mutually educative one. She was inexperienced and once in Morristown would be without the support of her own relatives. They were married in Penn Yan on November 16, 1847, and left the familiar small towns of western New York shortly thereafter for a place richly furnished in Richards family history.

Morristown was now a town of 2,500 inhabitants. James was formally installed at the end of December. The Reverend Dr. David Magie preached the charge, hailing at length the elder Richards, Edward Griffin, Asa Hillyer, et al. as "a bright constellation—you may look far and scarcely find their equals," but none so wise as James's father, and "may the son be like him."[4]

The new pastor needed no prompting to feel the full weight of these expectations. For the last four years the figure of his father had been much before him as he edited the Auburn lectures and reviewed his father's life in correspondence with Gridley. In addition, he had recently perused a new volume of his father's sermons brought out by his father's old colleague at Albany, William Sprague. The publication that year of these two books, one of lectures and one of sermons, had served to recall in the late Auburn professor's large circle a vivid sense of his worthiness.

James's new position yielded an annual salary of $900 paid quarterly and the use of the parsonage. Money was tight, and family expenses included the fees at the Morris Academy, where the boys, James and John Morgan, attended school. Ministers' incomes did not match those of other professionals and merchants with whom they shared leadership in the town. To supplement the pastor's salary, members of the congregation brought many practical gifts to an annual "Donation Party" held at the parsonage. James's son John later remembered the teasing and embarrassment connected with wearing second-hand clothing from which "my stepmother was not altogether exempted." On one occasion, the previous owner of a gown Sarah Richards was wearing stepped up to her and remarked that she had seen that dress before. "There was a titter among those present; but my [step]mother replied with great composure: 'You certainly showed good taste,' and passed to her seat in church." For all her youth, Sarah was not easily intimidated.[5]

Sarah gave birth to two daughters in quick succession, first Lizzie, perhaps named for James's first wife, followed by Julia. They had been in Morristown only a year and a half when Sarah realized she had more than a houseful of children, straitened finances, and the new public role of minister's wife to handle. She had a husband in trouble.

Something was going seriously wrong with James. The elders of his congregation began to note erratic behavior that suggested he was on occasion drinking spirits heavily. At those times he was simply not himself. When Sarah became pregnant the second time in the winter of 1849–50, the four older children from the first marriage were sent to live with their grandparents in Canandaigua. It was a familiar recourse, taken up in part to spare the children anxiety, but especially to relieve the pressure on James and Sarah. The consumptive Henry had done the same in the early years of his second marriage. A quieter house did not help James much. Soon afterward, in a drunken rage, he assaulted the pregnant Sarah in the presence of Ira Whitehead, the chief elder.

James and Elizabeth's daughters, Caroline and Anna, at the time they were sent to their Beals grandparents. (Taken from Caroline Cowles Richards, Diary 1852–1872, copyright 1908)

Oddly, in the midst of these wretched developments there occurred an event that should have buoyed James up: Lafayette College awarded him an honorary doctorate. What prompted the Lafayette decision is not at all clear. College records show only that when the trustees voted on the degree, discussion was waived, a procedure noted as "unusual."[6] In the light of James's recent behavior, it seems at least possible that the degree was arranged by friends anxious to arrest or buffer the fall he seemed headed for.

Disturbing incidents multiplied, and the concern felt in many hearts turned into full-scale alarm. For a clergyman in a temperance age, drunkenness was "criminal" enough. The profanity and domestic violence that often went with it created a serious public scandal. Making matters worse, whenever James was confronted about his behavior, he would vociferously deny the problem. Church leaders worried over what to do.

These events took place within a climate of changing public attitudes toward the consumption of alcohol. Earlier in the century, Western farmers began to take the surplus of grain they could not sell and distill it into whiskey. As a result, cheap spirits flooded the market, and whiskey replaced rum and hard cider as the national drink. The earlier American practice of imbibing small quantities of rum throughout the day in shop or workplace was succeeded by the practice of heavy after-hours drinking in the tavern, with pernicious effects on family life and public order. Young men detached from their families who went on drinking binges to show off their independence and relieve their loneliness were a special concern in scattered western settlements. Unsurprisingly, those who promoted the civilizing influence of churches soon embraced the temperance movement as well. The most ardent revivalists moved on to outright prohibition.[7]

James had come to young adulthood in the midst of the change. At the end of the 1820s, the decade in which per capita alcohol consumption peaked, he began frequenting taverns as a college youth. After his conversion, such behavior on his part seems to have ceased. Sentiment for temperance permeated the air in his Aurora and Penn Yan years. The Beaches embraced the cause of abstinence, and James's nephew Henry Beach became a public advocate. At the same time, it seems clear that spirits remained easily available and valued for their medicinal and relaxing properties. Elizabeth's doctors had prescribed a daily dose of brandy to alleviate her symptoms. Dr. Richards had warned James at one point to guard his health by avoiding "stimulants." It is hard to know if he saw in James a special susceptibility or if this was just of a piece with his advice to get enough rest. His counsel taken as a whole might also be seen as a caution to someone prone to nervous exhaustion.

In Morristown, all those most close to James could see that he was getting worse. He himself seemed to realize that he had to do something. On January 13, 1851, only four months after receiving the Lafayette honor, he wrote to the session, the elders who were the governing body of his congregation, declaring that "under present circumstances, I had better resign." He said that he intended to offer his resignation to the presbytery at its April meeting.[8]

With this cryptic notice, the formal undoing of James's once-promising career began. On February 4, the session met at the home of Ira Whitehead to acknowledge the pastor's stated intention. Whitehead had taken the unusual step of inviting the trustees, whose normal responsibilities were church buildings and finances rather than governance and discipline, to be present. James himself was absent; he was probably not invited. Upon hearing James's letter read, the session agreed to supply the pulpit in the interim "while [the pastor] seeks to regain his health."

James took immediate offense at both the eagerness to replace him and at the buzz of gossip precipitated by the presence of so many at the meeting. In a second letter to the session, he demanded an inquiry into the charges circulating against him and served notice that he wished to rebut them. Furthermore, he insisted that he could continue for the present to fill the pulpit himself. If his offer to resign had been a feint to evoke entreaties to stay, Ira Whitehead had maneuvered to keep the pressure on.[9] The chief elder had enough experience with James to realize that he might not hold to his decision. Alcohol induced shifting perceptions of reality; James seemed to glimpse the truth of his situation, then lose track of it.

On March 13, the session met again, this time at the parsonage. James was present and immediately sought to invalidate the session's last meeting with a volley of procedural objections that centered on the irregular presence of the trustees on that occasion. He was directed to put his protest into writing for the session meeting of April 2, and a three-man commission was appointed to reply. The commission rejected his protest.

Thus stymied, James went ahead with his resignation to the presbytery on April 15, which that body accepted, "on the ground that a release from all pastoral cares and responsibilities is indispensable to his complete restoration of health and to his permanent usefulness in the ministry." Apparently for now he had waived his demand for an inquiry.

His resignation accomplished, James retired with Sarah and their infant daughters to western New York to rest and reflect. Three months passed. Anxious and angry, he began to confuse effect with cause and to blame his troubles on shoddy treatment by others. He determined to renew his demand for an inquiry, this time appealing beyond the session to the presbytery. On August 6, baby Julia's first birthday as it happened, he wrote from Penn Yan to the Reverend Alfred Chester, moderator of the presbytery. He summoned forth his most reasonable manner for this task.

My Dear Brother
    I shall endeavor to be with you at your special meeting of Presbytery at Morristown on the 14th. Could you not make out a call for another

special meeting of Presbytery to attend to the rumours which are now being scattered far & wide with reference to my Christian & ministerial character, & which are most seriously affecting my usefulness & happiness as well as dishonoring to the cause of God. Please to make the request in your own way. Obtain the requisite signatures, & fix it at such time & place as in your best judgment & that of Dr. Magie or other brethren shall be most expedient. For me it is desireable to have matters investigated as speedily as is possible. Too many interests are involved to allow of any delay.

I am, dear Bro., yours in the best of bonds

J. Richards

James's need for vindication turned what had still been a relatively discreet parting from the Morristown church into a complicated public proceeding that commenced on August 19. James was present as the moderator called on the appointed committee of two ministers, Mr. Blauvelt and Mr. Bond, to report the charges. The general charge involved the nebulous but critical issue of reputation: "Common fame charges the Reverend James Richards D.D. with criminal conduct, & conduct unbecoming a Christian, & minister of the Gospel, especially." There then followed five specific charges, each with particulars of time and place: (1) drunkenness, (2) lewd and profane language, (3) abusing his wife by frequently defaming her character, assaulting her person, and striking her with violence, (4) prevarication and falsehood, and (5) attempting to have illicit intercourse with Nancy Willis in his own house.

The presbytery directed that a copy of the charges and the names of the "witnesses to sustain" be placed in the hands of Dr. Richards, and cited him to appear before the Presbytery at 11:00 A.M. on September 2 in the lecture room of his former church at Morristown. The moderator would issue summonses for the witnesses named in the specifications and such witnesses as Dr. Richards desired to call. "[T]he Reverend Dr. Brinsmade [the Beaches' pastor at Newark], & the Reverend R. S. Finley were, at the request of the Reverend Dr. Richards, appointed to assist him in his defence." Blauvelt, who had served on the charges committee, and another minister were appointed to conduct the prosecution.

The judicial proceeding in James's case was a considerable affair, lasting for two and a half months, from September 2 to November 15, and involving scores of witnesses. Convening usually at eight o'clock in the morning, the presbytery heard testimony in nineteen sessions, meeting on average twice a week. All ministers within the presbytery and one elder from each parish were expected to attend, and any visiting clergy from outside the presbytery were commonly invited to sit as corresponding members—two or three were present at most sessions.

Twenty-three ministers and fourteen elders assembled for the opening session on September 2. Before the proceeding began, the presbytery intended to control the notoriety of what would follow by resolving "that the investigation . . . be conducted with closed doors." Once assembled, the presbytery rescinded this resolution. What altered the presbytery's judgment on this matter is unknown, but it is easy to conjecture that many churchmen had hoped James would withdraw his request and spare the church this painful proceeding. When he did not, they gambled that making it public would pressure him to reconsider. Again he did not back down.

The best extant source on James's church trial at Morristown is the minutes of the presbytery, which only summarize actions taken and refer the reader to "files" for the verbatim testimony. These files do not survive. The eighty-odd witnesses included several ministers, elders, and other church members; James's friends and family, including Caroline and Anthony Dey, his brother Edward, and his nephew Henry Beach; his mother-in-law, Mrs. Wisner; and the Nancy Willis who figured in the adultery charge.[10]

James and his defense team advanced a quasi-medical explanation for his behavior. He pleaded mental derangement, which was evidently preferable to being considered a simple drunkard. The particulars of this defense are undetailed in the minutes, but we know that a Dr. Richard Stevenson submitted an affidavit, and that an E. A. Darcy, M.D., presented "a medical volume of Copland" to explain his opinion in the case. To depict James's state of mind, the defense introduced several of his letters into the record. Questions were raised as to whether James's aberrant behavior had grown increasingly flagrant. The defense also submitted letters from James's mother-in-law concerning James's recent months in

Penn Yan, which presumably buttressed defense assertions about his mental condition.

There was much defense testimony from older, pre-Morristown friends and family attesting to James's "general character and exemplary deportment." When Henry Beach expatiated in this vein, the prosecution cut him off, objecting that there was enough of this already in the record.

Summations began in the morning session of November 14. For reasons unspecified, the counsel for the defense declined to sum up the case. "Dr. Richards was then heard in review of the testimony. . . ." Perhaps there had been a falling-out with Brinsmade or Finley, but it is just as likely that James placed great confidence in his own ability to plead his case.[11]

The evening session began at six. The prosecution made closing remarks, "the parties then withdrew," and the roll was called for individual remarks. These remarks continued into the next morning's session. In the afternoon of November 15, votes were recorded on each charge. The minutes reported the findings thus:

> The Presbytery after a patient & prayerful investigation of the case of Dr. Richards have come to the conclusion that some of the facts tabled in the charges are sustained by the evidence. But we are persuaded that Dr. Richards has been the subject of such aberration of mind at the times of the commission of the acts charged that he ought not to be held responsible & cannot be considered guilty.

The vagueness of this finding aroused vehement objection. The protesters insisted that the presbytery make a more systematic consideration of the charges. The discussion that followed produced a sharper finding that did not muddle the issue of James's responsibility. Those more inclined to leniency prevailed in the matter of most importance to James and his supporters, the sentence.

> After its reconsideration, it was on motion Resolved 1st. That the 1st. & 2nd. charges [drunkenness and profanity] are proved: that the 3rd & 4th charges [abuse of his wife and prevarication] are proved in part: and that the 5th charge [attempted adultery] is not proved at all. But that the criminality of Dr. Richards is in the view of Presbytery greatly

modified on the ground of insanity. [Resolved] 21y. That the judgment of this Presbytery in view of the whole case is this: that Dr. Richards be requested & he is hereby enjoined to demit the functions of the ministry until the meeting of this Presbytery in October 1852. And he is hereby affectionately advised to spend the intervening time in efforts to regain his health by travel, exercise, abstinence from close study, & from those causes of nervous excitement to which he is predisposed; and if in the meantime nothing occurs in the conduct of Dr. Richards to render necessary in our judgment the continuance of the demission of the duties of his office, Presbytery will cheerfully permit him to resume them.

The "reconsideration" did not conciliate everyone. Four ministers and one elder dissented even from this judgment, and these five were joined by five more in protesting the proceedings as irregular "on the ground that no formal vote was taken & recorded as to the guilt or innocence of the accused as to the charges on which he has been tried."

James was called in and the judgment duly announced to him. He replied that he submitted to their decision and "would endeavor to conform himself to their advice according to his ordination vows." He then asked "for himself their sympathies & prayers in the difficult & trying circumstances in which he was placed." The presbytery adjourned.

Despite the cavillings of the hard-nosed minority, it is hard to escape the conclusion that many in the presbytery were loath to examine the issues in much depth. In some sense the church old-boy network enfolded one of its errant own in the interest of mutual protection. Christian forgiveness was a factor as well, and James's contrite demeanor undoubtedly helped his cause.

He passed his twelve-month probationary period in Princeton, in a different presbytery, out of the immediate Morristown circle and away from all family.[12] Sarah remained for the present with their two daughters in Penn Yan. This makes it seem that their marriage had by now completely broken down.

James's four children by Elizabeth continued in the care of their grandparents at Canandaigua. Their grandfather, Thomas Beals, believing in the value of out-of-door labor as part of a sound rearing, sent the boys to separate farms in a neighboring village to live with farm families and work at chores for their room and board.[13] It is worth noting that Henry, Edward, and James Richards seem to have escaped any acquaintance with farm labor. Perhaps a minister like their father, conducting his business within the parsonage, could more easily keep an eye on his sons. A merchant and banker like Thomas Beals, busy in the town, could not so conveniently do so and may have instituted this kind of regimen for his own sons Henry, Gorham, and Thomas as a substitute for the supervision he had known in his father's tailoring shop in Boston. His youngest son still managed to have a rough passage to manhood; yet if the hard life of a sailor had helped young Thomas through, this could only reinforce for Beals the value of hard manual work. Moreover, through James and Elizabeth, he had noted how young Anthony Dey, James Nicholas Richards, and Newton Beach had seemed to flounder when fatherly supervision departed from their lives. Such examples would have confirmed his decision to send James and Elizabeth's boys off to farms for a year.

At the end of his year of probation, James was restored to his normal ministerial functions by the Elizabeth presbytery.[14] Princeton was a nerve center of the Presbyterian Church, and during his year there he would have learned about opportunities for redemptive service in frontier areas and in newly settled districts such as the lower Mississippi Valley. Looking for a fresh start, he informed family members in New York and Canandaigua of his plan to go to New Orleans, taking thirteen-year-old James and eleven-year-old John Morgan with him. Caroline and Anna stayed in Canandaigua and continued to be raised by their Beals grandparents. Lizzie and Julia remained with their mother, Sarah, in Penn Yan.

The 1,600-mile river journey to New Orleans along the Ohio and Mississippi Rivers took eight days. James stopped short of New Orleans and accepted a teaching position at Planter's College, in Port Gibson, Mississippi, a cotton town on the Mississippi River, between Vicksburg and Natchez. Here, for the next few months, he taught a course called Moral Philosophy and Belles Lettres.[15]

College life was disrupted in July 1853, when yellow fever came to Port Gibson after first appearing in May at New Orleans.[16] For refuge, James took his boys inland, away from the Gulf, to a place called Woodbine

This sketch depicts two children returning home with coffins for other members of their family. New Orleans newspapers carried appeals on behalf of the many children orphaned by the epidemic. The yellow fever came to Port Gibson from New Orleans. (Taken from John Duffy, Sword of Pestilence: The New Orleans Yellow Fever Epidemic of 1853, *Louisiana State University Press, Baton Rouge, 1966)*

Plantation. When John Morgan had been on the upstate New York farm, he had listened to the farmer's wife read aloud by the evening fire from *Uncle Tom's Cabin.* "I remember that we never heard, at any one time, quite enough of that remarkable story. Our sympathies were strongly aroused in favour of the slaves. . . ." Woodbine had "about 300 negroes on the estate" but he saw "neither cruelty nor torture practised" there. "We greatly enjoyed our visits to the negro quarters, and their songs, music, and dancing."[17]

After the episode of yellow fever, the minister-turned-professor perhaps concluded that the climate was too unhealthy to keep his sons in Mississippi, for by the end of August, James and John were back in New York, living with their Uncle Edward. From Edward's house on Courtlandt

Street, John wrote to his little sister Caroline. He delighted in telling her about his new slippers, an understandable enthusiasm after years of wearing hand-me-downs.

> Dear Caroline—
>
> My slippers were finished having been at the Shoemakers being footed, they are very nice indeed & the most comfortable things I ever had on. I have had various pairs of slippers in my life, some too big, some too little & most every kind but a pair made on purpose for me. . . .
>
> How very kind Grandpa is to make you girls so many nice presents—you in return ought to make as little trouble as possible, to part pay back. . . .
>
> There is nothing of particular interest going on in the city at present—Everything goes on about the same every day—I will enclose a note for Anna—Much love to Grandpa & Grandma . . . and all the Aunts etc.
>
> Your aff[ectionate] brother   J.M. Richards
>
> P.S. [Don't] show my letters as they are written bad and no one cares to see them any way J.M.R.[18]

In the seven years since his mother's death, John Morgan had been shuttled from Penn Yan to Morristown to Canandaigua to farm room-and-board to Port Gibson to Woodbine Plantation to New York City. How easily he might feel that "no one cares." Yet, he and his brother James had already seen enough of life's uncertainty to appreciate their relative good fortune in having kindly family members like Uncle Edward and Grandpa and Grandma Beals. He encouraged in his sisters a similar sense of gratitude ("to part pay back") for the stable and comfortable life that their grandparents were able to give them.

In early 1854, James, probably through the offices of the Reverend Dr. William Anderson Scott, received a call to become pastor of the Third Presbyterian Church at New Orleans. New Orleans was still part of the Mississippi presbytery; Third Church was a new congregation and James would be its first settled pastor. Scott, the same age as James, had studied at Princeton Seminary a few years earlier when George Schenk was also there.[19] He would certainly have known James's father, and he would have heard the younger Richards's preaching praised by Schenk and others. The boys now rejoined their father and were present at his installation on April 16, 1854.

That Scott and his colleague, the Reverend Woodbridge, were also conversant with James's recent history might be inferred from the contents of the sermon and the charges they gave at James's installation. Woodbridge's first charge to James was: "Take heed unto thyself." He cautioned against pride and the spirit of self-justification, using as metaphor, "Intoxication is the result, and the inebriate fancies he is every inch a king." In his charge to the congregation, Woodbridge emphasized the importance of not overburdening the pastor: "Be not exorbitant in your demand for visits, relieve him from pecuniary care, relieve him from all services which are not essential to his office, etc." As his final charge, Woodbridge reminded the people of the "duty of encouraging your spiritual guide."[20]

From the start, the congregation, numbering forty or fifty, was set to wondering about James. Only a week before his installation, the ruling elder, a Mr. Stringer, had watched his new pastor at a Wednesday evening lecture and realized that he was intoxicated. James, complaining of sickness, had then dismissed the congregation. Afterward, a concerned Stringer approached another minister, Mr. Hart:

> [I] thought the installation of Dr. Richards should not be proceeded with. Mr. Hart thought otherwise, and spoke to Dr. R. who positively asserted that he had not been drinking. On assurance given, I passed it over, and the Installation was proceeded with. . . .[21]

Stringer saw Richards again afterward and told Hart that Richards's sickness "was from drunkenness & drunkenness only." But the two men chose to overlook the situation.

Their concern was well-founded, for James lasted just short of a year. His pastoral relation to Third Church was officially dissolved in March 1855. It was hardly a clean break, and James did not wait around. Claiming ill health, he borrowed enough money to sail to England. His son James had already returned north to study at Princeton, but he left John Morgan, aged fourteen, behind with friends. Meanwhile, the New Orleans presbytery

laboriously proceeded to investigation and trial.

Once in London, James
decided to return to New York
rather than New Orleans. He sent
John Morgan instructions to pack
up their library of three thousand
books, along with other personal
effects, and arrange freight terms
and passage north. On the Fourth
of July, the boy arrived by steamer
in New York to be reunited with
his father at the home of Uncle
Edward. Though this is in some
ways a story of flight and abandon-
ment on his father's part, in telling

Edward Richards in middle age. (Taken from
Caroline Cowles Richards, Diary 1852–1872,
copyright 1908)

these events years later, John Morgan recalled instead the pride he felt in
executing this commission. The episode echoes his grandfather's early
experience of teaching school at the same age during the Revolutionary
War. Edward now stepped into the situation, and from this time forward
assumed financial responsibility for both of James's sons. He gave John
Morgan the choice of entering college like his brother or training for the
commercial life. The boy chose the latter. For the next few years, John
worked as office boy and clerk for an agricultural supplies warehouse. In
the evening hours, he collected rents from his Uncle Edward's tenants,
several of whom were performers in stage and minstrel shows. John
Morgan acquired a lifelong love of the theater, an interest previously
discouraged in families like his.[22]

James, meanwhile, had found a temporary teaching position and awaited
news from New Orleans about his church trial. Within a few days of his son's
return, an elder of the New Orleans church delivered in person a citation to
appear at trial in November. James set the citation aside, unanswered, for
several months. The New Orleans situation was difficult to face; in Morristown, at least, he had had many supporters. At the eleventh hour he put
together a reply, giving his return address as the Humboldt Institute on
Fourth Avenue in New York City:

November 20, 1855

Dear Brother:

A communication dated the 7th of May 1855 . . . presenting a
serious charge & specification against me & citing me to appear at
N[ew] O[rleans] and answer the same . . . was placed in my hands
some time in the early part of July by Mr. Henry Thomas, an Elder.
. . . I have several times determined in the absence of all light, as to the
view which was taken of my case, to visit New Orleans in person &
await the issue of the investigation. But the distance from this city, where
I am now located, is so great, and I am so constantly occupied in
teaching (having virtually two Seminaries in my hands) this being the
only business that I can now attend to profitably & usefully, that it is
manifestly impossible for me to obey the Citation in person without an
immense sacrifice. . . .

James suggested that a written statement from him might do instead.

Permit me then, my dear Brother, to assure you that I am greatly
surprised and deeply grieved at the charge & specifications which are set
forth. It seems to me that in several instances refered [sic] to by the
witnesses named, they do attribute that which was caused by physical &
mental derangement to a very different cause, so that I cannot admit the
correctness of all things which are set forth. . . . Such however has
been my physical & mental condition for some time past, at home &
abroad, that I know not what to admit & what to deny. I am certain,
however, of this fact that the painful situation in which I have been
placed has frequently produced a state of mental alienation, and in this
state I have resorted to stimulants, & in some instances to intoxicating
drinks by means of which I have been thrown into a state of insensi-
bility. I have felt & do still feel the incompatibility of such liabilities with
the faithful discharge of the duties of the Gospel ministry. All this is as
evident to my own mind as it is to the minds of the members of the
Presbytery.

Things are so changed now that I hope for better days. I am now
among friends & relations. I have a pleasant home in a private family. My
mind is constantly occupied in teaching. My domestic unhappiness is in
some measure relieved by a Divorce. My pecuniary liabilities are in a fair

way to be cancelled so that I hope to be subject to these distressing &
horrible states of mind & body no longer. But at the same time I freely
& fully admit it to be reasonable and just & right that the Presbytery
should have evidence of this fact, before they restore me to the . . .
duties of a Christian Pastor. This evidence can only be furnished by time
& the kind Providence of a merciful God.

And now, dear Brethren, if these admissions . . . should be
deemed . . . a sufficient basis to justify [Presbytery] in the consideration of my suspension, until evidence is furnished that I am in a
suitable condition to resume . . . ministerial duty, I shall make no
opposition to such a course, but will cheerfully submit to their action;
for although it may be painful to my feelings, distressing to my friends,
& mortifying to my young & interesting family, I shall consider it
necessary and right. May the Great Head of the Ch[urch] guide us all
in the right path. For my own part, I deeply feel my need of your
prayers. I remain as ever your friend & afflicted Brother. . . .[23]

James hoped that by admitting frankly to the worst, he might make
his judges grateful for sparing them opposition. As at Morristown, he
pleaded mental derangement, making plain, as the Morristown documents do not, what he considered the causes of his mental state—his
failed second marriage and his accumulated debts. He took the view
that the two difficulties affected his mind and that in turn led to his
drinking. Divorce and cancellation of the debts were now alleviating
both of these and considerably brightening his outlook. In his new
mood, he persuaded himself that the authorities in New Orleans would
deal kindly with him in the light of his genuine contrition and these
concrete corrective steps.

Although no record of a divorce has been found, a mutual agreement
to that effect seems likely. Calvinist tradition treated marriage as a contract
of reciprocal obligations rather than a sacrament. Although adultery was
the sole grounds for divorce in New York State, Connecticut had a liberal
divorce law as did many of the western states.[24]

Sarah remarried three years later when she was twenty-nine. She may
have met her new husband, Michael Shoemaker, in Michigan, perhaps on
a visit there as early as 1854. Little Julia died that year while James was in
New Orleans. Sarah and Shoemaker were married in Penn Yan in 1857

and left to live out their days in Michigan, where Shoemaker was a mill owner and a merchant who later became a state senator. They had nine children together, of whom three survived to adulthood. Sarah's other daughter by James, Lizzie, ten years old when her mother remarried, stayed on with her Wisner grandparents in Penn Yan and kept up her connection to her half-brothers and especially to her half-sisters in Canandaigua, who also lived with their grandparents. The willingness of the Wisner and Beals grandparents to take over child rearing in both instances made it possible for their adult children to try for new lives.[25]

The divorce was a personal relief to James, but he had little idea how irrelevant a development it was in the face of all that had occurred in New Orleans. Distance clouded his perceptions, if they had ever been sharp, of how thoroughly he had exhausted everyone's understanding there. He apparently looked for a resolution similar to that in Morristown, suspension and eventual restoration.

The New Orleans presbytery held trial at last in January 1856, and in James's absence heard the testimony of ten witnesses. The verbatim transcript of this proceeding survives, and it dramatizes the issues confronting the parishioners. Stringer's statement that Richards's sickness "was from drunkenness and drunkenness only" addressed the central issue at the trial: Was Richards's problem drunkenness or insanity? Implied in the question was the view that drunkenness was a moral weakness subject to the will, while insanity was an organic condition that was not subject to the will. At Morristown, the presbytery had declared James "predisposed" to nervous excitement. At least five of those who had sat in judgment had found this explanation overly permissive.

The trial record in New Orleans leaves the impression that the members of Third Church had been at pains from the start to act with considerable patience, tact, and charity toward their minister during the year he served them. The very compassion they for so long extended to their troubled pastor may have worked against him when the time of judgment came.

Mr. Toy, the church organist, told of Richards visiting him at his office, his breath smelling of rum, his manner and language violent. They had "a considerable altercation." James left, and the concerned Toy had an office boy follow him. Richards returned later, much changed, and cordially invited Toy to take tea with him.

Mr. Lugenbuhl testified to finding Richards in the Exchange Alley leaning against a wall, intoxicated. Lugenbuhl "was shocked and thought what I could do to prevent his being disgraced." He watched Richards stagger into the Continental Coffee House, where the keeper "refused to give him any more to drink and assisted him to a chair." When Lugenbuhl went over to his pastor, he found him "stupid and asleep." It was three o'clock in the afternoon. Richards's son was with him, and he sent the boy for a cab. Together they brought the pastor to his house on Greatman Street. Lugenbuhl stayed at the house till late at night.

Mr. Stickney reported trying to avoid Richards outside the post office when he saw the pastor was not quite right. Stickney's companion, however, went up and spoke to the minister, then came back to Stickney and said, "Your friend Richards is drunk." Stickney "asked him to say nothing about it."

Another parishioner, Mr. Raymond, told of calling on his minister at Greatman Street and finding him in bed. "[He] looked very badly—eyes bloodshot." His breath smelled of drink. Raymond "covered him as he was naked."

Several witnesses testified to Richards's intoxication while in the pulpit. On those occasions he might announce one set of Psalms and read from another, or lose his place in the reading, or lecture in a disconnected way. A disheveled appearance—heavy eyes and thick voice—often gave him away.

The testimony noted that in the autumn James accompanied his older son on a journey north where the younger James entered the freshman class at Princeton. Upon his return to New Orleans, James changed his lodgings and roomed thereafter with his younger son in the house of Captain and Mrs. James M. Whann. This couple was mindful of the pastor's tendencies, and protective. On one evening, Captain Whann testified,

> . . . my wife after dinner said [the pastor] had been drinking and requested me to ask him to take no more, as he had to preach that night. I told him—he was angry. . . . Think he ordered me out of his room— then followed me, altered his tone, & was very friendly—got him to walk out. He preached well that night.

On another evening James performed less well. The Reverend Hart, who was present, went home with him. "He lay down. He asked 'what did

The levee at New Orleans. (Taken from Illustrated London News *XXXII, June 5, 1858)*

I say? How did I appear?' and declared he had not been drinking, without being questioned on the subject . . ." Mr. Raymond added, "Upon several occasions when charging Dr. Richards with intoxication, he always denied it, even though I specified the times."

Whatever his other troubles in New Orleans, there were no accusations of violence or attempted seductions. James may have been lonely, but when intoxicated he did no more than embarrass himself on the subject of the opposite sex. Toy told how Richards once requested him to see two females "and find out about them." Then Richards mused on about another "Young Lady of good character" and stammeringly asked, "Toy, how do you think she would do for a pastor's wife?" He would also at times hold forth too frankly on his marital troubles. Another parishioner, Mrs. Colson, who once went into Richards's yard on Greatman Street and found a tub full of empty bottles, reported that, on a visit to her house, Richards "was very flighty, used improper language concerning his wife, said things very improper. . . ."

After his trip north, James's weaknesses became more public and scandalous, despite the precautions and interventions of lay supporters. One night he was arrested and confined to the Watch House. Stringer informed him that the story was in the papers. James seemed unaware of what had happened, exclaiming, "Good God, is it so, [and] had I any friends to defend me?"

Worse was in store. Hart substituted for him on a lecture evening when he "was not in a state to do it." Hart told him to drink no more, and James consented to give Mrs. Whann his keys to search his room. She found no liquor. The next day, Richards went off earlier than usual to visit, he said, many families in his congregation. For the first time, he stayed out all night. Whann went looking for him the following day. At the telegraph office, Whann met Stickney and asked if he had seen anything of Richards, observing, "The doctor is let down again." The two soon spotted their pastor staggering out of the post office. Richards's face was bloody and dirty. "[He] told me," Whann testified, "he had been in the Calaboose. Said they did not know him at the Calaboose—said he gave his name Richardson, not wanting to be known." Whann took him home in a cab. ". . . [he] went into bed with his boots on. He looked like a man who had been on a spree."

Among the most affecting testimonies is one that records the tension and anguish of John Morgan Richards, at fourteen struggling on his own to cope with his father's troubles. One evening both Lugenbuhl and Stringer called on the pastor and found him showing every sign of a man "after a debauch." Richards stated he was unconscious of having drunk liquor. He "appealed to his son," and "requested him to speak the truth. [John Morgan] burst into tears, and said he had gone to the Coffee Houses with his father, and that when[ever] his father had gone alone, he had returned with a bottle of brandy."

John Morgan Richards as a boy. (Taken from John Morgan Richards, *With John Bull and Jonathan, D. Appleton, New York, 1906)*

James experienced again one of those shocks of illumination when he seemed to realize the effects of his drinking episodes on those around him. Going some way toward acknowledging the seriousness of his condition, he agreed in December to sign a written, witnessed agreement with another gentleman not to use intoxicating drinks. It seems not to have helped.

Since James always insisted that his main problem was mental derangement, Dr. Woodbridge in his examination of witnesses at the church trial sought opinion on the issue. The ruling elder, Stringer, of course emphatically declared the problem was drunkenness, not insanity. Lugenbuhl equivocated, "I cannot say that he was partially insane, but I say that at certain periods his mind was not properly balanced. . . ." The organist, Toy, considered Richards "flighty even in his sober moments."

For four months James lived with the Whann family. Dr. Woodbridge inquired of Whann, "Was Dr. Richards' deportment, while in your family, such as you would expect from a Christian Gentleman?" Whann replied that the doctor was always gentlemanly and behaved himself well. The captain found it of interest to note that his lodger "seldom talked on religious subjects" and "spent little time in his study."

The most thoughtful observations belonged to an Episcopalian clergy-man, Dr. J. H. Lewis, who had befriended James. Lewis specifically attributed some of his behavior to an excitable temperament. Perhaps under pressure the high spirits noted in his youth had taken on a more manic aspect. Lewis's extended remarks conclude the recorded testimony:

[Testimony by Dr. J.H. Lewis, Episcopalian, graduated at Paris—studied here, & at the North]: . . . The first time I saw Dr. Richards he appeared in a state of mental excitement, which I attributed partly to temperament, & partly to family troubles. I am not suspicious. Dr. Richards' loquacity, imaginativeness (& being badly marked with small Pox, which disease often affects the disposition) I attributed to nervous excitable temperament. One day I called to see him—he was speaking at random—spittle thick & frothy—spoke of things disagreeable to me, and which I did not wish to know. As I was leaving, he called to his son, and said, give the Dr. 100, 200 dollars, which startled me. I then thought he was under the influence of drink. Spoke to him—he burst into tears & acknowledged he had been drinking. I then reminded him of his position & prospects, & the example he was setting. He wept, & frankly confessed. I saw him frequently after that, laboring under excitement— never saw him intoxicated, but stimulated so as to be indiscreet. Did not approach him near enough [to] smell his breath. Dr. Richards said he drank to drown troubles. . . .

[Question by Dr. Woodbridge]: Do you think Dr. Richards' constitution so broken as, aside from his drinking, not to be a reliable man?

[Answer]: From my intercourse with Dr. Richards I have remarked powers & cultivation of mind of no ordinary kind. He has, in every instance, shown great excitability of mind—but never a loss of logical reasoning, except in the instances mentioned. The peculiar wildness of his eye—his expression, and the fact of his having had the small Pox in a severe degree led me to suppose that there might be some organic or constitutional disorder of his mental faculties, but to be positive would have required opportunities for studying him which I never had.[26]

During James's brief ministry at Third Church, New Orleans had become an independent presbytery, albeit a small one compared with Elizabeth, New Jersey, where he had been tried before. On January 17, 1856, seven ministers and four elders voted unanimously to sustain the general charge of drunkenness and to impose a severe sentence: deposition from the gospel ministry. In essence, James was defrocked. None of the pressures for mitigation present at Morristown operated on his behalf at New Orleans.[27] The sentiments of the presbyters in the case of Common Fame vs. James Richards D.D. were so aroused over the "aggravations of the offense, as proven" that the sentence was amended five days later as follows: "Resolved, that the sentence be interpreted to include excommunication." This, too, won unanimous approval. James was expelled from the Presbyterian Church!

The news must have arrived in New York as a thunderbolt. The church had been his home, and the ministry had been the organizing principle of his life. Simply to support himself, he would have to find another line of work. The most obvious choice was schoolmastering, this time in earnest and not just as a temporary expedient. It was not an attractive prospect. In the middle of the nineteenth century, much schoolteaching still tended to be seasonal, poorly paid, and lonely work. It was known for attracting misfits, and heavy drinking was all too common. To slip into this category meant a sure drop in status.[28]

The best way to make schoolkeeping respectable was to preside over a private academy. His friend David Frame, who shrank from the public exposure of the pulpit, had found this to be a worthy alternative career. To start up a private school, however, required capital and connections. James, just relieved of his burden of debt, could have done nothing on his own. His most likely backer was his brother Edward, who had recently retired from the woolens business to devote himself to his considerable real estate interests.

By the following year, 1857, James seemed to have landed on his feet. He had returned to Connecticut, his parents' native state, to establish himself as the superintendent of a boarding school in Litchfield. The Litchfield Female Academy, which had flourished under the Misses Pierce thirty years earlier when Henry Richards briefly attended Litchfield Law School, had recently closed. The timing was good for James, who took over the abandoned facility and started a new boys school called Elm Park Commercial, Agricultural, and Collegiate Institute. The

Elm Park Collegiate Institute. (Courtesy—Litchfield Historical Society)

school catalogue of 1857 lists a faculty of six. James's oldest son, the Princeton student now nineteen, served as an assistant teacher of mathematics. There was a chaplain named Hempstead who also taught Greek and Latin. James concentrated on administration and taught English, philosophy, history, and geography. The school accommodated both day students and boarders.

The superintendent, the catalogue noted, desired to instruct "not merely from books, but from nature." The instructors would live with the students as their "guardians, companions and friends and . . . exert over them a discipline, directed mainly to the conscience and affections." The school would be Christian in its character, "the Bible being a daily textbook—but is under the control of no sect or party, either religious or political." The nondenominational character of the school was consistent with the contemporary emphasis on moral training rather than religious doctrine, and it certainly suited James by removing him from the direct scrutiny of church judicatory bodies. For references and testimonials, the catalogue listed, among others, James's nephews, Henry N. Beach and James R. Dey, now both lawyers in New York City; two Cowles cousins; and the Reverend Dr. Sprague, still at Albany. James was relying on his oldest circle: only one person from New Jersey and none from New Orleans were among the twenty-five or so names.[29]

Heading the school's Examining Committee, and perhaps an influential mover in promoting James's enterprise, was the Reverend Leonard Bacon. Bacon, born the son of a missionary in the Old Northwest Territory, had been for over thirty years the pastor of the First Congregational Church in New Haven, known for its historic connection to Yale College. He was admired as a diplomat among churchmen, yet he was on record as one who had judged the Plan of Union experience of cooperation with the Presbyterians, 1802–1837, a wrong turn for his fellow Congregationalists. In 1848 he became editor of *The Independent*, a newspaper that championed Congregational independence, a cause that James Richards was now prepared to embrace.[30] Such a consideration had no doubt played a role in his decision to return to the New England of his forebears where the heavy hand of meddlesome presbyteries had little writ. Or so he may have supposed.

Bacon may have been a special ally for another reason, less well known. He had a brother, David Bacon, the same age as James and also the youngest child of his family, who at the age of twelve was drinking and running with the village rowdies. David was sent to live with his older brother, Leonard, then just beginning his distinguished ministry in New Haven. Bacon was severe with his clever younger brother, but failed to rescue him from lifelong alcoholism. In time, David became one of those hard-drinking schoolmasters, and the parents of his pupils eventually dismissed him for it. He later studied medicine and traveled on a messianic mission to Liberia. There he drank and quarreled with everyone, and the work came to nothing.[31]

David Bacon exemplified a trend toward solitary drinking, distinct from workshop or saloon conviviality. In the go-ahead antebellum period, there were many like him who struggled with the gap between inflated expectations and disillusionment. Drinking offered such men temporary relief from internal pressures and responsibility. Though David Bacon never enjoyed the success that James had known after his conversion and his first marriage, Leonard Bacon may have sensed similarities between the two men. There is no way of knowing if James took the New Haven pastor into his confidence, as he had the Episcopalian clergyman in New Orleans. Bacon may simply have been predisposed to assist a talented man who reminded him of the lost David.

Now that he was free to do so, James wasted no time in marrying again. He had met Helen Lawrence Franklin in New York. She was thirty-eight years old; he was forty-four. On July 20, 1857, they were wed in Litchfield by Bacon.[32] The marriage certificate specified Helen's marital status as widow; James's marital status was left blank.

Not since Penn Yan had James taken on so many new things at once. Though he was unable to care for his own children, he adopted Helen's twelve-year-old son from her first marriage. For years he had kept up with his daughters in Canandaigua chiefly by post. His sons were often with him, but they were supported by Edward. Whatever these anomalies, this was a time of promise, and September brought a rare family reunion when James's daughters, Caroline and Anna, came to Litchfield for a visit.[33] Anna and her new stepbrother, George Franklin, were the same age.

For two years James ran his school more or less successfully. His discontent in the role was poorly disguised, however. Feeling trapped in work he felt unsuited for, he would explode at his hapless charges, sometimes throwing inkstands at them.[34] This was not the kind of educator he set out to be when he wrote in the school brochure of discipline directed mainly to the conscience and the affections.

People in Litchfield remained unaware of the actions taken against him by the New Orleans presbytery. Although he honored the sentence handed down there to the extent of not seeking a specifically Presbyterian pulpit, he did not disturb the local assumption that he was a minister in good standing. He joined the Litchfield South Association made up of the local Congregationalist clergy and began to preach occasionally in local pulpits. He was not satisfied to forego the full-time ministry and continued to search for ways to serve in that capacity. He even explored his acceptability to Connecticut Lutherans, drafting a letter to a Lutheran clergyman named Pohlman:

December 15, 1857

Rev. and Dear Sir

Will you be so good as to accept a Catalogue of our Institute which I send you by the mail of today. If you have the minutes of your last Synodical meeting, I should be most happy to receive a copy—if it can be shared. I am seriously contemplating a union with your Evan[gelical] Luth[eran] ch[urc]h *provided a door of entrance & of utterance could be spared to me.*

Three years ago, under *very trying circumstances* at the South—and just before my *departure for Europe*, I declared myself an *Independent*, and since *that time* I have ministered almost every Sabbath in some *Congregational Church*—and am now *preaching* as a stated supply to the 1st chh. of Wolcottville—five miles distant.

My *health* is *entirely* restored & my *domestic* peace & comforts are once more established—and *now* it seems to me that if my *ecclesiastical relations* were *agreeable*, I could labour with unfainting assiduity—with success & with delight, in the *work of the ministry exclusively.*

My prospects here as a *mere Educator* are of the *most flattering* character—but my *heart* is not so much in this work, as in that of the *ministry.* To herald that Saviour whom I hope one day to meet in the clouds of heaven, has been the *chosen* and *loved occupation* of *fourteen years of my life,* without the *interruption* of a Sabbath—and to spend the remainder of it in the *same holy calling*—tho' in circumstances the *least attractive* to the *eye & observation* of man, would be all that my *ambition* would crave.

The feature which most pleases me in the Lutheran Chh. is its *liberality*, kindly extending the hand of kindred & of fellowship to all who hold the great and fundamental doctrine of the gospel—justification by faith alone. This feature I *love* as exhibiting *preeminently* the Sp[iri]t of our L[ord] J[esus] [Chris]t. I have been delivering two or three Lectures on the prominent events in the life of the great Reformer and shall probably deliver one or two more. The people are much interested in them—as much as they could be in this decidedly New School & Congregational region.

I should be gladly received into fellowship with any of the Congregational associations here, if I should apply—but I think I could not be so happy among them or labour with as much efficiency and success as among the Evangelical Lutherans. My trials since 1850 have been very great—and at times I have been led to exclaim "verily thou art a God that *hides* thyself—O God of Israel [?] Saviour"—But the clouds are being dispersed and I now feel that the day is not far distant when my "righteousness shall be brought forth as the light & my judgment as the noon day."

I should be very glad to hear from you—if you can share a few moments from your very pressing duties to attend my inquiry. I am dear Sir with real respect & affection—yours in the best of all bonds, James Richards[35]

James had hit upon the strategy in Connecticut of asserting that it was personal dissatisfaction with the Presbyterians in New Orleans that had led him to declare himself an independent. Fighting to regain a footing in his chosen profession and to preserve his dignity and self-regard, he was sometimes given to boasting and flattery. The note of modesty, when sounded, rang false, for he was clearly not content to preach at tiny Wolcottville. James was agile, though, and probably believed in his own seriousness, when, in approaching the Lutherans, he tried to demonstrate an intellectual grounding in that branch of the Reformed tradition. In any case, it is unclear whether he actually followed through on this inquiry, and it certainly bore no fruit.

James's misrepresentations finally caught up with him in the late fall of 1859. Someone who knew the facts about New Orleans found out about his pulpit activities in Connecticut and began to talk.

Getting wind of the crisis, James pursued two tacks. He applied at once to the Congregationalists as a candidate for their ministerial license, hoping to regularize his standing with them. At the same time, he petitioned the presbytery at New Orleans for restoration, which, in the absence of evidence of his repentance, it swiftly and unanimously denied. New Orleans must have apprised the Litchfield Congregationalists of this action, for the latter, referring to James's "moral unfitness," now refused him standing in their church. Interestingly, they focused, not on his "crimes" at New Orleans, but on his failure to honor his covenant with the Presbyterian Church: "Richards refuses to respect the discipline of that body whose discipline he had solemnly covenanted and promised to obey, and continues to exercise the public functions of the ministry as he finds opportunity."[36] The omission of any reference to James's alcoholism suggests it may not have been an issue at Litchfield as it was in Morristown and New Orleans.

Despite their unwillingness to have him as a formally recognized colleague, the Congregationalists showed extraordinary forbearance. If he would henceforward "desist from his scandalous course," they would not act against him for past misrepresentations. They balanced this with a harsh warning. Any further act of public ministry on his part would prompt the Association to notify the public in specific terms of his past: the charge and sentence at New Orleans, his defiance of the sentence, his falsehoods, and his contemptuous disregard of covenanted authority. A letter would be sent to eight different newspapers, including the *New York Observer* and *The Evangelist*, publicizing his misdeeds.

James, however, did not desist. And so, in January 1860, a lengthy denunciation of him in smiting language worthy of seventeenth-century divines was published in the several papers. It read in part:

> From the first planting of these churches, the trust has been reposed in the hands of the Associated Pastors, of examining and recommending suitable candidates for the ministry, and of ascertaining the character and standing of ministers coming among us from abroad. . . .

And inasmuch as the said Richards has endeavored to break the force of the censure which rests upon him by calumnious aspersions against the body which deposed him, and by other false assertions, and lest any church should still be beguiled by such means into receiving him into their confidence, we add that we have conclusive evidence that he has been guilty of deliberate and aggravated falsehood in our presence; and without exception, so far as our careful and impartial inquiries have extended, those who have known him best from the outset of his ministry—men of the highest standing in the church of Christ, and of the weightiest character for integrity and wisdom, and, withal, men who have no personal feeling but a friendly one toward Dr. Richards—solemnly declare that his character for truth and veracity is bad.

We have long forborne this public action, hoping to escape the painful necessity of it. But the contumacy of Dr. Richards in disobeying that discipline to which he had solemnly vowed and covenanted to submit, his evasion of trial by withdrawing successively from the jurisdiction of one body after another, before which the charges against him were about to be investigated, and his pertinacious attempts to impose on the confidence of the churches, notwithstanding our repeated remonstrances, leave no other course open. . . .

In conclusion, brethren, we pray you to be vigilant against *any person* who, by seeking to evade the safeguards of the ministry, gives presumptive evidence of his unfitness for it; and always to remember the words of the Lord Jesus, how he said, "Beware of false prophets who come to you in sheep's clothing, but inwardly they are ravening wolves. Ye shall know them by their fruits."

The grace of our Lord Jesus Christ be with you all. . . .[37]

James, Helen, and fifteen-year-old George hung on in Litchfield for at least another half-year following this latest crisis. James's sons by Elizabeth were also with them. The census lists James, twenty-two, as a lawyer, and John Morgan, twenty-one, as a merchant. In addition, there were two young teachers and five Irish-born servants also living on the grounds of Elm Park Institute. The 1857 catalogue had listed thirty enrolled students and their hometowns; only seven came from outside Connecticut. By the time the enumerator for the national census called at the school, on June 16, 1860, the out-of-state student body had risen to twenty-three. There is no way to know if local day-student enrollment suffered in the face of the headmaster's recent notoriety.

The record on James Richards after 1860 is elliptical. A memoir written many years later by his merchant son, John Morgan, helps to pick up his trail. In 1863, midway through the Civil War, John Morgan and his fiancée, a young woman from East Boston, visited his family "in Connecticut and New York." So perhaps James Richards maintained his school in Litchfield a few years more. In 1867, a prominent New York druggist needed a sales and advertising manager for his London branch, and John Morgan took the job. He recalled saying goodbye at that time to his father, who was now, he noted, a pastor in East Boston. He made no mention of Helen Richards, for at some point during these years she had a stroke and resided thereafter in a New Hampshire hospital. As had been the case with several other family members, Edward Richards supported James's widow to the end of her days.[38]

The records of the Congregational Church of East Boston do not mention the service of James Richards before January 19, 1870. It is possible that he acted as "temporary supply" there prior to a formal call in 1870.

The exact whereabouts of James Richards between 1860 and 1870 thus remain a mystery. There is one tantalizing piece of gossip that bears a few marks of plausibility. In the alumni files of Auburn Seminary is a letter dated October 9, 1886, eleven years after James's death and some twenty years after the period in question. The writer, the Reverend S.W. Boardman, was a former pastor of Second Church at Auburn, and the recipient was a professor on the Auburn faculty, Willis Beecher, who was at the time the biographer of the seminary alumni.

Boardman told of meeting the wife of a village school teacher who had known James Richards "2d" in Morristown. "It has occurred to me that it might be worth while to send to you in permanent record, what might otherwise fade . . . from my memory, the affectionate testimony of this parishioner to the excellencies of that strange man whose career was so deeply clouded." The first of her recollections that he recorded does not square with established facts: She seemed to confuse James's smallpox with typhus fever, which "left him insane," and she placed him in New Jersey when he was still in western New York. Her next recollection was also faulty—she had his second marriage failing *prior* to his call to Morristown. She believed that his second wife's consorting with another man drove him "again insane." Whatever his troubles, in Morristown she had found him a good pastor. "James Richards didn't do anything which he didn't do well." She knew about his drinking and "vertigo" in New Orleans. "Later still he came through N[ew] J[ersey] lecturing as a Reformed Drunkard. His friends considered it one of his crazy turns."

At this point in the letter, Boardman interjected, "I told her how I met him, while [he was] an inmate of the Inebriate Asylum at Binghamton." Out of a composite of facts, half-truths, and misstatements leaps this intriguing first-person testimony. But that is the end of it. The pastor concluded his account:

> She seemed to consider his strange aberrations through life to be connected with fits of insanity. And looking up very earnestly after all, she said, "I never had a pastor that I looked up to with so much *reverence* as to James Richards." It was a pleasant testimony from one who knew so fully his checkered career, and let me hang it as a wreath upon his monument.[39]

The letter illustrates the affection, sympathy, and respect that this bedeviled man consistently managed to evoke. It seems quite possible that after a quiet and discreet stay at the asylum in Binghamton, he may well have made a lecture tour of the type described. A private dedication to dealing with his alcoholism may explain the barren public record between Litchfield and East Boston. His wife was hospitalized in New Hampshire, his sons were grown up, and he had no work; it was a good time to try to do something.

Helping to bring the matter to a head may have been the fact that the Richards family had two other alcoholics on its hands. Henry's two youngest sons, Henry and Pierre, were both arraigned in court actions for public drunkenness and disorderly conduct around this time. One incident involved gunshots. Edward was attending to their cases.[40] In 1865, the court remanded Henry to the Inebriate Asylum in Bing-hamton. This may have brought the institution to the family's attention. The

late John Morgan's older brother
Edwin of Aurora was also one of
its founding trustees. James was
now past fifty. Edward and other
anxious friends might well have
prevailed on James to enter the
Binghamton facility, where his
dignity and privacy would be
respected.

The New York State Inebriate
Asylum was the brainchild of Dr.
Edward Turner, a New York City
physician who came to look upon
alcoholism as a remediable sickness. Energetic and persuasive, he
garnered philanthropic support for
an institution that would provide a

*Edward Richards as an older man. (Courtesy—
Laura S. Seitz)*

regimen of treatment intended to restore its inmates to productive lives in
society. Begun in the early 1850s, the hospital catered to the higher classes
of businessmen, doctors, and ministers who would commit to a minimum
of a year of care and who could afford to pay six months' fees in advance.
The hospital occupied 250 acres of high ground two miles east of Binghamton. Illustrations in an 1869 issue of *Harper's Bazaar* showed a reading
room, a dining room with chandeliers and tablecloths and waiters, a chapel
with vaulted ceiling, a billiard room, a bowling alley, a gymnasium, a reception room, and a patient's single room with wardrobe, desk, and daybed as
well as regular bed. The patient could not leave the grounds, however, and
was not allowed money or postage stamps. Only close relatives could visit.
Boardman might have seen him with a visitor in the public reception
room.[41]

Perhaps it was after James passed a year or more at Binghamton that his
son John found a new opportunity for his father in his wife's home church
at East Boston. It must have been exhilarating for James to be again in
charge of a parish. "Under the powerful preaching of the new minister, the
congregation revived," reported the church historian.[42] Not many months
after James took the pulpit, however, a great fire swept through the streets
and destroyed the "White Church," as it was known. James rallied his flock.

NEW YORK STATE
INEBRIATE ASYLUM!
Binghamton, Broome County, N. Y.

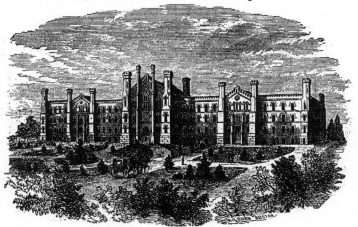

This Asylum is admirably situated, overlooking a fine section of country, and is complete in all the appointments of a first-class home, with ample means to meet the wants of every case. It is located three miles from the city, and removed from all temptation. Its management is the same as all other State charities, under the control of a Board of Managers appointed by the Governor. The law provides for the maintenance of indigent inebriates, similar to that of the insane, and whenever a vacancy occurs, patients from other States may be admitted.

The experience of this Asylum, for the past nine years, indicates an increasing usefulness and necessity for such institutions, and the original intention of making this an Asylum Hospital, where this disorder may be thoroughly understood and treated on broad scientific principles is nearer realized than ever before. All rules are strictly enforced, and no patient permitted to go beyond the Asylum grounds without permission from the Superintendent, or in the care of an attendant.

THE CHARGES FOR BOARD

Will be less to residents of the State, and will include medical care, washing, lights, fuel, etc., with ordinary attention. The exigencies of each particular case will be acted upon, as it may present itself, to those of moderate and limited means as well as the rich.

Special Terms will be made to Non-residents of the State.

All inquiries and applications for admission should be addressed to the Superintendent.

DANIEL H. KITCHEN, M. D., Supt.,   WILLARD PARKER, M. D.,
    Binghamton, Broome Co., N. Y.   New York, N. Y.
                               President Board of Managers.

New York State Inebriate Asylum. (Advertisement, 1877 New York City Directory, as printed in Harper's Bazaar, 1879)

Funds were raised and a building committee oversaw the restoration of the edifice, which was dedicated in November 1871. But the strain had been too great. James's drinking again became an issue, and he resigned. The official history of the church recalls him this way:

> The people, to whom he had endeared himself by many noble qualities, parted from him with much sorrow. He was in many respects a remarkable man, and left a deep impression on this community. He was tall, of commanding figure, and by gift and training, a pulpit orator of high order. He was the son of one of the grandest men the Presbyterian church this country has produced, and gave early promise, by the splendor of his powers, of eclipsing even his illustrious father. There was a time when he stood at the head of the pulpit in New Orleans, and held in his choice high positions in the church throughout the land. His impulses were quick and generous, his sympathies broad and tender, his mind clear and logical, his culture high and his information extensive and varied. He possessed that rare combination of powers which fitted him to be a ruler among men. Many of you remember the power of his eloquence on those days during which the church lay in ashes, when, roused by the emergency, he delivered those powerful sermons which so thrilled the people and awoke their enthusiasm in building again the sanctuary of the Lord. One weakness, however, marred his life, blighted his early promise, and led to his resignation of this congregation. . . .[43]

The weakness was, of course, unspecified. This thoroughly appreciative account of his tenure suggests that his East Boston congregation did not have their sympathies for him blunted by feelings of having been deceived and manipulated. Perhaps the stay at Binghamton had humbled him and allowed the church to restore him formally to the ministry. There is no record, though, of restoration, and it remains possible that he again bluffed his way into the pulpit and departed before his problem took on the dimensions of scandal. The observation that he "held in his choice high positions in the church throughout the land" sounds like one of his exaggerations, a bit of wishful thinking. Still, the Boardman letter and the East Boston parish history affirm the genuine high regard that others regularly reflected back to him.

In the summer of 1872, James traveled to Auburn where his four children by Elizabeth had gathered for a family reunion.[44] Seminary connections seemed to have opened the door for him one last time. He was called to be pastor of the Kanawha Presbyterian Church in Charleston, West Virginia, the new capital of the state created by the divisions of the Civil War.

The Scotch-Irish Presbyterians of West Virginia had settled in the poorest backcountry of the Old Dominion of Virginia. Charleston could not have been an especially refined place. James's new congregation of twenty-five consisted of the remnant who had declined to affiliate with the Southern Presbyterians, preferring to retain instead an association with the General Assembly in Philadelphia. They had no church, and James conducted his first service in the Senate Chamber of the State Capitol. A new building was begun after his arrival, but with the panic of 1873 "all enterprise and growth in the community were checked for a while."[45]

James still cut an impressive figure. He had taken to wearing his beard full and tapering in the postbellum style. When it was learned that he had relatives in London, he was offered a commission from the state government to go to Great Britain for the purpose of recruiting immigrants to the state.

He arrived in London in the spring of 1875. Encouraged by his family, he used some of the time there to put together a collection of his sermons, which was published in London in July under the title, *The Safe Side*. He dedicated the volume to his son, John Morgan, and to his brother, Edward. In the author's note dated July 21, he noted his ministry of forty years and hoped that "these familiar discourses may be loved, maintained, and vindicated by those loved ones, and by their children, and children's children, when the hand that penned them shall be motionless, and the tongue that uttered them is stilled in death."[46]

A few days later, having turned over his collected sermons to the publisher, James traveled alone by train to Edinburgh in execution of his commission. On July 30, he fell in the railway station and hit his head against a concrete abutment. He was taken to the Royal Infirmary, where he died. The surgeon certified the cause of death as "Concussion of the Brain and Shock, superinduced by Deceased falling on his head apparently accidentally while under the influence of drink."[47] He was sixty-four years old.

We have often seen the human face of this man's excuses and evasions. Despite everything, his family never deserted him, and he managed to hold on to the cherished title of minister. As a Christian and a clergyman, he felt the need to look at what had happened to him in religious terms. How did he understand his own life? In what ways did religious faith sustain him or rebuke him? A few clues lie in the final product of his life, the sermons published in London.

In the title sermon, "The Safe Side," James addressed the religious doubts sewn in the post-Darwinian intellectual climate of the 1870s. Fully acknowledging

James Richards Jr. in later life. (Taken from James Richards Jr., The Safe Side, *London, 1875)*

the contemporary confusion, he pressed upon his hearers to choose the life of Christian faith for safety's sake. It was a strategy akin to Pascal's wager without Pascal's metaphysical imagination, and it was a far cry from his father's conviction. By necessity James spent his life as a wanderer among the clergy, and safety eluded him after the death of Elizabeth. The instability of his own life surely gave to assurances of safety a heightened personal value.

In another sermon, "The Great Battle of Life," James represented the Christian life in a radically different way. Faith was not a refuge, but a summons to battle. He called attention to St. Paul's habit of picturing life as a contest. Everyone has to "contend eventually with his own self-esteem, conscience, and the higher energies of his nature . . ." James dwelled on the Christian as agonist. But the arena was not the world so much as one's own nature. Arrestingly for those who know his story, he evoked the figure of the prodigal son. After sinful self-indulgence, the prodigal is brought to

> a sense of wasted talents, of self-degradation, by the reproaches of conscience, by the remembrance of home, by the well-known hopes of a fond father, by the memory of a sainted mother . . . still there is resistance. . . . No one becomes a drunkard or a debauchee in a day . . . some time must elapse before we can see the fully developed fruit. . . .

In James's sermon, the "daily fight" of the wandering sinner is with the "sense of shame, the sense of sin, and the remonstrances of love."[48]

Intellectually restless to some degree, James seemed to find comfort in Christianity as the basis of a literary culture. His father had been at home in a theological world that valued the systematic exposition of the major truths of the gospel. James belonged to a generation that often plucked fragments from the sacred texts and adorned them with eloquence and sentiment. In another treatment of the text on the prodigal son, James focussed not on the central figure of the wayward son forgiven by his father, but on the peripheral figure of the elder brother who envies the attentions to the prodigal: "And he was angry, and would not go in" (Luke 15:28). James's sermon was a plea for a forgiving heart that forsakes envy.

In Edward, he himself had found such an elder brother, who, with no children of his own, cared for all the rest of the family. As guardian, bene-factor, or business partner, Edward over the years assisted, in addition to James, his bankrupt brother-in-law Dey, his ambitious nephews starting out in business, his alcoholic nephews in trouble with the law, and his brothers' widows. In later life, when his sister Caroline had a falling-out with her son, she found a home with Edward in her old age. A vivacious niece, who remembered how he arranged for her to meet her soldier-fiancé on leave during the Civil War, treasured her uncle's attentions while she was still a girl and wrote in her childhood diary. "I wish all the little girls in the world had an Uncle Edward."[49] With the sermon above and the dedication of the entire volume, James acknowledged all that Edward had done.

In the last sermon of the collection, James returned again to the theme of moral struggle and to the religion of the heart that had come to char-acterize so much of American Protestantism in the late nineteenth century. He concluded:

> A Christian is a sinful man who goes to Christ for the honest purpose of becoming better. The prodigal son could not go back to his father at one step, but he could determine to perform the whole journey, and take the first step, and the next, and the next, perseveringly, and in good earnest; and though a good way off, his Father will have compassion on him, and fall on his neck and forgive him.[50]

To the end of his life James was still hoping—and still drinking. The religion that sustained him was different from his father's religion. Both father and son worshipped at "the Throne of Grace," but for the senior Richards, grace came in God's good time, not when the sinner called upon it. Although the younger Richards had been theologically somewhat conservative in his early ministry, in practice he had moved closer to Finneyism and so had America. Indeed, this religion of compassion in many ways made it possible for him to go on functioning as a minister.

The senior James Richards favored intellectual preparation and distrusted the excitations of the individual heart as self-serving and self-deceiving. He accepted the discipline of covenant and community. The younger James Richards found that a more individualistic, imaginative, emotional approach met the conditions of his life. This approach set aside theological formulations and community sanctions that seemed to encumber the free personality and block the open exercise of his obvious ministerial gifts.

For James Richards, the son, it was also a religion of solace for his many losses, not least among them a vision that he once held of himself as minister, husband, father, and scholar. Perhaps the last sermon in his collection on the prodigal son became for him an eloquent, impersonal, and literary means by which he might "testify" with seemly dignity to the possibilities of grace. He could preach such a sermon with the conviction that his father brought to the animating doctrines of the will and the atonement and the absolute sovereignty of God.

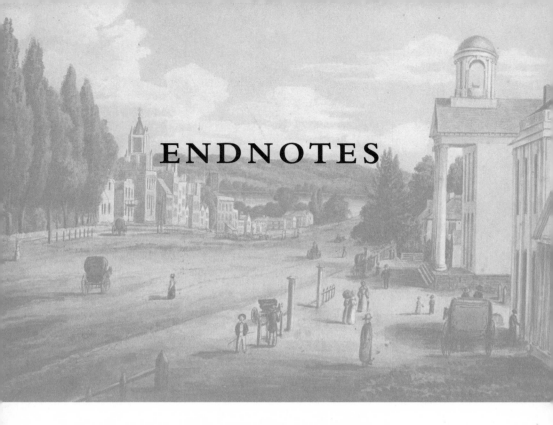

ENDNOTES

Chapter 1. Connecticut: Beginnings and Conversion

1. Harriet M. Stryker-Rodda, *Ancestors and Descendants of Frank Lusk Babbott Jr., M.D. And His Wife Elizabeth Bassett French* (Princeton: Polyanthos, 1974), pp. 298–300.

2. Mary Louise King, *Portrait of New Canaan, The History of a Connecticut Town* (Chester, Pa.: New Canaan Historical Society, John Spencer, Inc., 1981), p. 81.

3. Stryker-Rodda, *Ancestors and Descendants,* p. 298.

4. Samuel Gridley, *Mental Philosophy and Theology: James Richards, D.D. Sketch of his Life* (New York: M.W. Dodd, 1846), p. 10.

5. Stryker-Rodda, *Ancestors and Descendants,* p. 300.

6. King, *Portrait of New Canaan,* p. 12.

7. Gridley, *Mental Philosophy,* p. 10. Except where otherwise noted, the material on James Richards's early life can be found in this source.

8. Ibid., p. 12.

9. Ibid., pp. 12–13.

10. King, *Portrait of New Canaan,* p. 36.

11. Gridley, *Mental Philosophy,* pp. 13–15.

12. Ibid., p. 16.

13. Abner Morse, *Genealogical Register of Descendants of Several Ancient Puritans* (Boston: 1861), p. 218.

14. Stryker-Rodda, *Ancestors and Descendants,* pp. 206–207.

15. Gridley, *Mental Philosophy,* p. 18.

Chapter 2. Morristown: Early Ministry

1. *History of Morris County, New Jersey, With Illustrations and Biographical Sketches of Prominent Citizens and Pioneers* (New York: W. W. Munsell & Co., 1882), pp. 133–134.

2. *Minutes of the First Presbyterian Church of Morristown,* archives of the Presbyterian Historical Society, Philadelphia. Minutes of the Session and of the Trustees for the pastorate of James Richards are found pp. 21–32. *History of Morris County, New Jersey*, pp. 133–135.

3. Gridley, *Mental Philosophy,* p. 19.

4. Jedidiah Morse, *The American Universal Geography* (Boston, 1805).

5. *History of Morris County*, p. 134.

6. Gridley, *Mental Philosophy,* p. 134.

7. Stryker-Rodda, *Ancestors and Descendants,* p. 207.

8. Gridley, *Mental Philosophy,* p. 20.

9. Ibid., p. 20.

10. Ibid., p. 22.

11. Ibid., pp. 21–22.

12. Ibid., p. 22. A full account of these revivals occurs pp. 22–23.

13. Malachi 3:2–3, "But who can endure the day of his coming, and who can stand when he appears? For he is like a refiner's fire and the fullers' soap; he will sit as a refiner and purifier of silver, and he will purify the descendants of Levi and refine them like gold and silver, until they present offerings to the Lord in righteousness."

14. Richards to Griffin, February 23, 1803, Gratz Collection, Historical Society of Pennsylvania, Philadelphia.

15. *History of Morris County*, p. 35.

16. Gridley, *Mental Philosophy,* p. 23.

17. *Minutes of the General Assembly*, 1803.

18. Richards to Miller, April 26, 1803, Gratz Collection.

19. *Minutes of the General Assembly*, 1804.

20. Seven letters between Woodward and Richards written 1805–1810 may be found in the Gratz Collection.

21. Bellamy was an eighteenth-century New England theologian whose works were popular into the nineteenth century.

22. Griffin to Richards, March 21, 1807, Newark. Griffin to Richards, April 17, 1807, Newark. Both letters are in the Gratz Collection.

23. Richards to Green, May 12, 1806, Morristown, Gratz Collection.

24. Thomas Jefferson Wertenbaker, *Princeton 1746–1896*. (Princeton: Princeton University Press, 1946), pp. 138–142.

25. *Trenton True American,* May 11, 1807, quoted in Wertenbaker, p. 142.

26. Miller to Griffin, quoted in Wertenbaker, p. 145.

27. Gridley, *Mental Philosophy,* p. 24.

28. Ibid., p. 27.

Chapter 3. Newark: Church Leadership

1. John T. Cunningham, *Newark* (Newark, 1966), pp. 1-19; Susan E. Hirsch, *Roots of the American Working Class: The Industrialization of Newark, 1800–1860* (Philadelphia, 1978), p. 3.

2. Morse, *American Universal Geography*, p. 529.

3. Burr had come under the influence at Yale of a young contemporary, David Brainerd. The author of *Divine Grace Displayed* and a missionary to the Indians of Connecticut, Brainerd died at the age of twenty-nine. Jonathan Edwards later wrote an account of Brainerd's brief but impressive life that was published along with Brainerd's journal. This work was received among many as the life of a Puritan saint. Brainerd had been engaged to another of Edwards's daughters at the time of his death.

4. The junior Aaron Burr, Richards's contemporary, had narrowly lost the presidency to Jefferson in 1800, and in 1804 had ruined his political career by killing Hamilton in a famous duel. He was now wandering the West in search of profit and power.

5. That is, Princeton became the chief institutional training ground. It provided a liberal arts education, specifically a foundation in rhetoric and languages, that suited the Presbyterian ministry. Princeton graduates headed for the ministry then went on to train professionally in this period under the close personal supervision of a pastor on the apprenticeship model.

6. Around the time Richards and his bride settled in Morristown, Griffin was ordained and soon married to a minister's daughter who was the niece and adopted daughter of Samuel Huntington, governor of Connecticut and a signer of the Declaration of Independence. Although James Richards and

Caroline Cowles came from solid farmer and merchant families, theirs were not families that boasted ministers and governors. William B. Sprague, *Annals of the American Presbyterian Pulpit, or Commemorative Notices of Distinguished Clergymen of the Presbyterian Church in the United States from the Early Settlement of the Country to the Close of the Year 1855 with an Historical Introduction* (New York: Carter and Brothers, 1866) (hereafter cited as *Annals*).

7. Lefferts A. Loetscher, *Facing the Enlightenment and Pietism: Archibald Alexander and the Founding of Princeton Theological Seminary* (Westport, Connecticut, 1983), p. 141.

8. In 1800 Griffin published what an admirer called a "somewhat minute account" of the New Hartford revival in two issues of the *Connecticut Evangelist Magazine*. The same admirer noted its value "as a record of Divine grace and as exhibiting the human instrumentality then employed." Quoted in Sprague, *Annals,* p. 28.

9. Rev. Z. M. Humphrey, D.D., *Biographical Sketches, New School Branch, Presbyterian Reunion Memorial Volume, 1837–1871,* (New York).

10. William B. Sprague, *The Life of Jedidiah Morse* (New York, 1874), pp. 65–66.

11. Quoted in Sprague, *Jedidiah Morse,* p. 109.

12. Griffin to Richards, letter, April 8, 1809, Seitz Collection, Luce Library, Princeton Theological Seminary, Princeton, N.J.

13. Contract signed by Edward Dorr Griffin and James Richards, May 26, 1809, Gratz Collection. The terms of this transaction anticipated a statute passed by the New Jersey legislature in 1820 that made free every child born of slave parents subsequent to July 4, 1804, males upon the age of twenty-five and females upon the age of twenty-one. The Quaker influence in New Jersey had been discouraging slavery for over a century; and in the period 1790 to 1820, the number of slaves enumerated in the census declined by almost a third.

14. Gridley, *Mental Philosophy*, p. 28.

15. Hirsch, *American Working Class*, p. 11.

16. Cunningham, *Newark*, pp. 82-83.

17. The new congregation was formally organized in 1811 on completion of the new church building in south Newark. First Church set aside one-third of its income to provide for the infant congregation of ninety members. See "The Old First Presbyterian Church, The Founding Church of Newark, 1666–1966," in *Newark*.

18. Seven letters from Hannah Kinney to James Richards written between 1810 and 1822 may be found in the Seitz Collection, Luce Library, Princeton Theological Seminary, Princeton, N.J.

19. Letter signed with the names of seventeen deacons, elders, and trustees, Newark, August 22, 1809, Gratz Collection.

20. James Richards, "The Duty of Submission," in *Sermons by the late Rev. James Richards, D. D., with an Essay on His Character,* William B. Sprague (Albany, 1849).

21. Richards to Caroline Cowles Richards, September 7, 1810, Seitz Collection, Luce Library, Princeton Theological Seminary, Princeton, N.J.

22. Mark A. Noll, *Princeton and the Republic, 1768–1822* (Princeton, 1989), p. 261.

23. Loetscher, *Facing the Enlightenment,* p. 126.

24. Griffin to Richards, November 24, 1810, Gratz Collection.

25. Humphrey, *Biographical Sketches,* p. 212.

26. Griffin to Richards, March 13, 1811, Gratz Collection.

27. Griffin to Richards, n.d., probably 1810, Gratz Collection.

28. Wertenbaker, *Princeton,* p. 153.

29. Richards to Green, March 24, 1812, Gratz Collection.

30. Griffin to Richards, April 22, 1812, Gratz Collection.

31. Griffin to Richards, May 2, 1812, Gratz Collection.

32. Richards's involvement in this controversy was due in part to the fact that New York and New Jersey were still joined together in one synod. The Synod of New Jersey did not become separate until 1823.

33. Loetscher, *Facing the Enlightenment,* p. 133.

34. James Richards to Caroline Cowles Richards, May 29, 1812, Seitz Collection, Luce Library, Princeton Theological Seminary, Princeton, N.J.

35. Ibid.

36. James Richards to Caroline Cowles Richards, September 18, 1810, Seitz Collection, Luce Library, Princeton Theological Seminary, Princeton, N.J.

37. James Richards to Caroline Cowles Richards, September 7, 1810, Seitz Collection, Luce Library, Princeton Theological Seminary, Princeton, N.J.

38. On the centennial of the Old First Sunday School, the congregation erected a tablet to honor "Anna Richards" who "began Sunday School work" at the Newark church in 1814, "gathering fourteen children for religious instruction." The inscription praised her "faith, fidelity, and enthusiasm."

39. Richards, "Address on the Death of Mrs. Cumming," in *Sermons.*

40. Richards to McDowell, March 27, 1813, Collections of the Office of History, Presbyterian Church U.S.A., Philadelphia, Pennsylvania.

41. Griffin to Richards, April 12, 1814, Gratz Collection.

42. Richards to Green, March 13, 1810, Gratz Collection. Blackburn was serving simultaneously as pastor of a congregation, missionary to the Cherokee, and general fund-raising agent for the missions. When he complained in a letter to the New Jersey Mission Society of failing health and resources, the local people responded by raising over two hundred dollars for the cause. The situation prompted Richards to plead the case to Green for giving Blackburn a "salary sufficient to induce him to give himself wholly to the work—to leave the congregation where he now labours, and move into some part of the Cherokee nation, and devote himself entirely to their instruction." He felt that if Blackburn resigned as he now talked of doing, it might "have an unhappy effect on the cause of missions in our part of the country." He also reported that some in the New Jersey Mission Society found fault with the present plan of the mission: "They wish to see more pains taken with adults."

43. This stood in contrast to the Calvinist leaders of the previous generation like John Witherspoon and Timothy Dwight. See Noll, *Princeton and the Republic, 1768–1822*.

44. Richards, "The Spirit of Paul and the Spirit of Missions," in *Sermons*.

45. Richards to [probably Richard Salter] Storrs, December 19, 1814, Gratz Collection. Storrs was at this time a pastor in Longmeadow, Massachusetts.

46. Richards to Morse, March 10, 1815, Gratz Collection.

47. Morse to Richards, March 17, 1815, Morse Family Papers, Yale University.

48. Only three of Morse's eleven children survived to adulthood, including the inventor and painter Samuel F. B. Morse. The Reverend Morse was six years older than Richards and his sons were already young men.

49. By then, the 1820s, however, the Reverend Lyman Beecher, eight years younger than Richards, had moved to Boston to marshall the forces of orthodoxy in a way that coalesced many elements in the strategy that regional leaders like Richards had nurtured in the decade preceding.

50. William Rankin and David R. Frazier, "The Presbyterian Church in Newark, New Jersey, During the Nineteenth Century," *Annals of the Theological Seminary*, July 11, 1901, Princeton, New Jersey.

51. For those master shoemakers and bootmakers who got overextended and then fell into debt, Newark still maintained a debtor's prison into the 1820s. See Hirsch, *Roots of the American Working Class: The Industrialization of Newark, 1800–1860.*

52. Diana Richards to James Richards, March 7, 1816, Seitz Collection, Luce Library, Princeton Theological Seminary, Princeton, N.J.

53. Kinney to Richards, April 18, 1816, Seitz Collection, Luce Library, Princeton Theological Seminary, Princeton, N.J.

54. Cunningham, *Newark,* p. 88.

55. This story is told by Julia Dey, one of the daughters of Caroline and Anthony Dey, in a privately printed memoir entitled *The Childhood of Julia Norton Dey 1829–1919* that is included as an appendix in Stryker-Rodda, *Ancestors and Descendants*, pp. 473ff.

56. Richards to Green, November 4, 1817, Dreer Collection, Historical Society of Pennsylvania.

57. Green to Richards, June 14, 1817, The Ashbel Green Collection, Princeton University Library.

58. As quoted in a circular on the subject of the Education Society signed by Asa Hillyer, James Richards, Matthew LaRue Perrine, and Gardner Spring to answer Samuel Miller and Archibald Alexander of Princeton, April 13, 1819, Library of Princeton Theological Seminary.

59. Perrine to Richards, March 14, 1821, Seitz Collection, Luce Library, Princeton Theological Seminary, Princeton, N.J.

60. Moreover, the practice of regular pulpit exchanges, while addressing the issue of a "hireling clergy," obviated any resort to itinerant preachers, whose excesses in the 1740s and 1750s many still recalled with acute distaste. In the case of a prolonged absence of a pastor, the church now made temporary appointments, known in church parlance as "stated supply," to avoid such potentially dangerous freelancers.

61. Griffin to Richards, March 30, 1821, Gratz Collection.

62. Sprague, *Annals,* p. 32. Williams and Amherst were both established in the Massachusetts Connecticut Valley by orthodox Calvinists who no longer wished to entrust their sons to Harvard. See Christopher Jencks and David Riesman, *The Academic Revolution*, Garden City, New York, 1968, pp. 156–160.

63. Green to Richards, November 23, 1819, Ashbel Green Collection, Princeton University Library.

64. Green to Richards, October 24, 1821, Ashbel Green Collection, Princeton University Library.

65. John Demos, *Past, Present, and Personal: The Family and the Life Course in American History*, New York, 1986, p. 46.

66. Henry Richards to James Richards, November 26, 1821, Seitz Collection, Luce Library, Princeton Theological Seminary, Princeton, N.J.

67. Sprague, *Annals*, pp. 465–468.

68. However, the proportion of graduates entering the ministry had risen from a tenth to a quarter during Green's tenure. See Noll, *Princeton and the Republic*, p. 282.

69. Henry Richards to James Richards, January 8, 1823, Seitz Collection, Luce Library, Princeton Theological Seminary, Princeton, N.J.

70. Henry Richards to James Richards, March 22, 1823, Seitz Collection, Luce Library, Princeton Theological Seminary, Princeton, N.J.

71. James Richards to Caroline Cowles Richards, May 9, 1823, Seitz Collection, Luce Library, Princeton Theological Seminary, Princeton, N.J.

72. Lindsley to Richards, June 11, 1823, General Manuscripts Collection, Princeton University Library.

73. Richards to McDowell, July 8, 1823, Collections of the Office of History, Presbyterian Church (U.S.A.). Elsewhere, Richards commented, "The Church has had an awful sifting. . . . It is dark as night to look without, and notice the state of the congregation and the town." Quoted in "The Old First Presbyterian Church."

74. James Richards, "Statistical Account of the 1st Presbyterian Church, Newark, N.J. from October 1801 to August 1823," in *Church Manual for the Members of the First Presbyterian Church, Newark, N.J.* (Newark, 1827).

Chapter 4. Auburn: Settling In

1. Gary B. Nash, et al., *The American People: Creating a Nation and a Society* (New York, 1986), pp. 275-276.

2. John Quincy Adams, *A History of Auburn Theological Seminary, 1818–1918* (Auburn, N.Y.), p. 19.

3. Ibid., p. 21.

4. Ibid., p. 37. The material on the founding of the seminary can be found on pp. 32–48.

5. Ibid., p. 50.

6. Jonathan Edwards was the leading theologian of the first Great Awakening and Joseph Bellamy wrote a popular commentary on the Bible.

7. Perrine to Richards, Auburn, July 15, 1820, Gratz Collection.

8. Adams, *History of Auburn,* pp. 55–58.

9. Perrine later taught Biblical Geography, publishing *Abstract of Biblical Geography in 1835 to which is added a Comprehensive View of the Modern Geography of Europe, Asia, and Africa.* Adams, *History of Auburn,* p. 79.

10. Perrine to Richards, Otisco, March 14, 1821, Archives and Manuscripts, The Auburn Theoogical Seminary Collection, Archives of the Burke Library, Union Theological Seminary in the City of New York.

11. Employees were required to pledge not to drink alcohol, to go to two services on Sunday, and then to give a summary of the sermons they had heard on Monday morning.

12. Adams, *History of Auburn,* p. 58.

13. The Auburn system became one of the two great ways of controlling and rehabilitating criminals in America. In contrast to the Philadelphia system where prisoners lived cooperatively, Auburn practiced total isolation and silence.

14. Caroline Richards to Anna Beach, Auburn, November 23,1823, Seitz Collection, Luce Library, Princeton Theological Seminary, Princeton, N.J.

15. Julia Norton Dey, *The Childhood of . . .* , in Stryker-Rodda, *Ancestors and Descendants.*

16. Records of The Auburn Historic Preservation Society suggest that Richards's interest in planting elms was due to a boost to civic pride that resulted from John Quincy Adams's visit to the village and an increase in economic prosperity that took the form of repairing and widening the streets. John R. Stilgoe, *Borderland: Origins of the American Suburb, 1820–1939* (New Haven), p. 988, finds that in the first quarter of the nineteenth century horticultural pursuits were considered good for the political safety of the Republic. They were associated with the permanence of the Constitution and patriotism. A conscious effort was made to beautify villages and towns with American trees: birches, elms, cherries, poplars, maples, etc.

17. James Richards to Anna Beach, Auburn, November 23, 1823, as postscript to letter of Caroline Richards to Anna Beach on the same date, Seitz Collection, Luce Library, Princeton Theological Seminary, Princeton, N.J.

18. Diana Richards to James Richards, New Canaan, December 20, 1823, Seitz Collection, Luce Library, Princeton Theological Seminary, Princeton, N.J.

19. Mr. Seymour was the treasurer of the seminary.

20. James Richards to Caroline Richards, Utica, February 5, 1824, Seitz Collection, Luce Library, Princeton Theological Seminary, Princeton, N.J.

21. The Greek war of independence was taking place and had been greeted with considerable sympathy in western New York.

22. James Richards to Caroline Richards, Troy, February 14, 1824, Seitz Collection, Luce Library, Princeton Theological Seminary, Princeton, N.J.

23. James Richards to Caroline Richards, Albany, February 18, 1824, Seitz Collection, Luce Library, Princeton Theological Seminary, Princeton, N.J.

24. Gridley, *Mental Philosophy,* p. 37.

25. Hillyer to Richards, Orange, February 16, 1826, Gratz Collection.

26. Hillyer to Richards, March 11, 1824, The General Manuscripts Collection, Princeton University Library.

27. Henry Richards to James Richards, Newark, August 18, 1824, Seitz Collection, Luce Library, Princeton Theological Seminary, Princeton, N.J.

28. The letter begins with Richards telling Sprague that he is sending him three discourses that he has asked for. ". . . I am not very anxious to defend to posterity in this way; but I think your design laudable, and have no doubt your collection will be found not only the means of gratifying curiosity but of benefiting the Institution which shall be fortunate enough to receive your deposit." Sprague's unrivaled collection of sermons, tracts, and memorabilia eventually found a home in the library of Princeton Theological Seminary.

29. Richards to Sprague, Auburn, March 1, 1824, Yale University Library.

30. James Richards to Caroline Richards, Newark, June 2, 1824, Seitz Collection, Luce Library, Princeton Theological Seminary, Princeton, N.J.

31. James Richards to Caroline Richards, West Springfield, June 1824, Seitz Collection, Luce Library, Princeton Theological Seminary, Princeton, N.J.

32. James Richards to Caroline Richards, Boston, July 3, 1824, Seitz Collection, Luce Library, Princeton Theological Seminary, Princeton, N.J.

33. It was Dr. Codman who so promptly contributed $1,000 to Princeton Seminary in answer to Lindsley's plea of the previous year. See chapter 3, p. 43.

34. James Richards to Caroline Richards, Boston, July 9, 1824, Seitz Collection, Luce Library, Princeton Theological Seminary, Princeton, N.J.

Chapter 5. New York City: The Richards Children, 1823–1833

1. Quoted in Gridley, *Mental Philosophy,* p. 74.

2. Joseph A. Scoville, *The Old Merchants of New York City,* 2nd ser., (New York, 1863), p. 240.

3. Robert Greenhalgh Albion, *The Rise of New York Port, 1815–1860* (New York, 1939), p. 241.

4. The two brothers were living in Savannah, with its population of about five thousand, as early as 1804. *The Columbian Museum and Savannah Advertiser* of October 8, 1806, reported on their new store at Telfair's Wharf "opposite their old stand" with a stock of goods such as brown sugar, loaf sugar, Jamaican rum, brandy, wines of different kinds, Negro cloth and blankets, teas in cotton bagging, hoes, cotton cords, and lead. Both Richardses became active in Savannah civic life. The two served together on the board of the New England Society of Georgia and helped to incorporate the Savannah Poor House and Hospital Society. Silas also served on the chamber of commerce. Appearing on the list of tax defaulters one year did not prevent him from being elected alderman the following year. A few years later, Abraham was one of sixty "citizens and merchants" to incorporate the Insurance Company of the City of Savannah. When he moved back to New York, he became involved in other insurance ventures that were covered by the Savannah press. See newspapers of the Wayne-Stites-Anderson Collection, the Georgia Historical Society.

5. Launched in 1822, the *Silas Richards* was a 454-ton vessel built by the master shipwright Webb. For ten years the ship was part of the Fourth or Blue Swallowtail Line of the packet service, sailing from New York on the 8th of the month and from Liverpool on the 24th of the month. She averaged thirty-nine days on her westward passages and was deemed a "slow sailer." Her best crossing was twenty-five days, her worst was sixty-seven. Though slow by transatlantic standards, she set the record in 1837 of ninety-one days for the run from Canton to New York, a record not broken until 1845. After service in the China trade, she ended her days as a whaler. An 1825 Liverpool newspaper noted that a bust or a kind of bas-relief of the merchant Silas Richards adorned the ship's wide stern. See Carl C. Cutler, *Queens of the Western Ocean: The Story of America's Mail and Passenger Sailing Lanes* (Annapolis, 1961), pp. 377–378, and William Armstrong Fairburn, *Merchant Sail,* vol. 4, p. 1102.

6. *The Georgian,* August 26, 1823.

7. He married in that year and afterwards maintained his family on an eight-acre farm outside the city walls that he purchased from Simon Congo, "a free negro." Information on the early history of the Dey family in America comes from Stryker-Rodda, *Ancestors and Descendants,* pp. 210–33, unless noted otherwise.

8. However, the last of the Indian wars in that vicinity prohibited for a few years any Dutch settlement there. Meanwhile, Dirck purchased a house and lot on Heere Street (present-day Broadway). When the English took over New Amsterdam in 1674, Dirck's name appeared on the list of "best and most affluent inhabitants of the colony."

9. Laidlie had served in Holland before his call to America around 1764. Manuscript Collection, Dey Family Box 3, New York Historical Society.

10. As Varick was a former mayor of New York, so Radcliff would become a future mayor of New York, serving from 1810 to 1817. Alexander Hamilton, who would have known Varick since their common service on General Washington's staff and who had his own Jersey connection through his wife, examined the title. Dey conducted the actual negotiations for the purchase. See Daniel Van Winkle, *History of the Municipalities of Hudson County* (Jersey City, 1924), and William H. Shaw, *History of Essex and Hudson Counties* (Jersey City, 1884).

11. "Mrs. Anna Beach" is recorded as the treasurer of both the Female Association of Newark and the Newark Ladies Clothing Society. Records of the Presbyterian Education Society, Library of Princeton Theological Seminary.

12. Joseph Bellamy was the author of *True Religion Delineated,* first published in 1750 and for several generations thereafter perhaps the most enduringly popular of serious American theological works. In her 1869 novel about the Calvinist world of her grandparents entitled *Oldtown Folks,* Harriet Beecher Stowe named an entire chapter after an edition of Bellamy known to the narrator as "My Grandmother's Blue Book." The grandmother, this narrator recalls, set aside time every afternoon for reading; she "delighted in history and biography and followed with keen relish the mazes of theology." To Calvinists of that day, Bellamy stood for a hard-edged theology that was in sharp contrast to the softer theologies soon to be on the rise in the Second Awakening with their emphasis on the individual will or to sensual, superstitious Catholicism. "They never expected to find truth agreeable. . . . They wanted no smoke of incense

to blind them," wrote Stowe. Though the novelist, writing after the Civil War, had put considerable distance between herself and the rigorous Calvinism of her youth, her so-called "local color" novel is mostly sympathetic in its treatment. Anna Richards Beach, thirteen years older than Stowe, came out of the same background but seems to have experienced fewer internal conflicts. See Harriet Beecher Stowe, *Oldtown Folks* (Cambridge, 1966).

13. Anna Beach to Caroline Cowles Richards, letter, October 1, 1824, Seitz Collection, Luce Library, Princeton Theological Seminary, Princeton, N.J.

14. *New York City Directory*, New York, 1821, New York Public Library.

15. Stryker-Rodda, *Ancestors and Descendants,* p. 232. This appointment provides another example of the easy congress between Calvinist congregations.

16. The naming of this second child was probably meant as a tribute to Dey's dowager mother-in-law and an attempted solace for her losses. She had survived all of her children, and her other losses included the stillborn older twin of Richard Varick Dey who had been intended to bear the Laidlie name. To Americans of a later day, this deference to old connections may seem a striking approach to the blending of families. In accounting for this deference, it is well, perhaps, to remember that Caroline was twenty years younger than her husband and that old Mrs. Laidlie was twenty-five years older than Caroline's own mother. Also, this was consistent with conventions of naming that connected a child above all to family and community.

17. Anna Beach to Caroline Cowles Richards, October 1, 1824, Seitz Collection, Luce Library, Princeton Theological Seminary, Princeton, N.J.

18. James Richards to Caroline Cowles Richards, April 28, 1825, Seitz Collection, Luce Library, Princeton Theological Seminary, Princeton, N.J.

19. Henry Richards to James Richards, August 18, 1824, Seitz Collection, Luce Library, Princeton Theological Seminary, Princeton, N.J.

20. Henry observed that ten pages of an oration by Hooper Cumming, the former pastor at Second Church, had been "stolen" from an unpublished address delivered in 1818 by Theodore Frelinghuysen, a Newark lawyer and Presbyterian lay leader who later became governor of New Jersey and United States Senator.

21. Anna Beach to Caroline Cowles Richards, letter, October 1, 1824, Seitz Collection, Luce Library, Princeton Theological Seminary, Princeton, N.J.

22. James Richards to Henry Richards, n.d., but dated by a later hand, probably Henry's, as November 1824, Seitz Collection, Luce Library, Princeton Theological Seminary, Princeton, N.J.

23. Henry Richards to James Richards, December 7, 1824, Seitz Collection, Luce Library, Princeton Theological Seminary, Princeton, N.J.

24. Henry Richards to James Richards, December 23, 1824, Seitz Collection, Luce Library, Princeton Theological Seminary, Princeton, N.J.

25. James Richards to Henry Richards, January 29, 1825, Seitz Collection, Luce Library, Princeton Theological Seminary, Princeton, N.J.

26. Henry Richards to James Richards, March 18, 1825, Seitz Collection, Luce Library, Princeton Theological Seminary, Princeton, N.J. Henry wrote in a beautiful, well-spaced, and regular hand that shows the marks of careful labor over a final copy.

27. James Richards to Henry Richards, January 29, 1825, Seitz Collection, Luce Library, Princeton Theological Seminary, Princeton, N.J.

28. Henry Richards to James Richards, March 18, 1825, Seitz Collection, Luce Library, Princeton Theological Seminary, Princeton, N.J.

29. Henry Richards to Caroline Cowles Richards, September 19, 1825, Seitz Collection, Luce Library, Princeton Theological Seminary, Princeton, N.J.

30. Records of the Chancery Court of New York, BM-961-S, 1825, and BM-562-R, 1826, detail the facts and quoted testimonies.

31. James Richards Jr. and James Richards to Henry Richards, April 17, 1826, Seitz Collection, Luce Library, Princeton Theological Seminary, Princeton, N.J.

32. Samuel H. Fisher, "The Litchfield Law School, 1775–1833," Tercentenary Commission of the State of Connecticut (Yale University Press, 1933).

33. The Richards family here reflected the "kinship mentality" of eighteenth-century Yankees, which was not "diffuse and general" but "intense and focused nearly exclusively on children." The struggle of some of the Richards children to emerge from the well-knit nuclear family reflects the transition to nineteenth-century individualism that the near exclusive orientation of parents to their own children may have fostered. See Daniel Scott Smith, "All in Some Degree Related to Each Other," *American Historical Review* 94, no. 1 (February 1989): p. 73.

34. Anna Beach to Henry Richards, July 25, 1826, Seitz Collection, Luce Library, Princeton Theological Seminary, Princeton, N.J.

35. Henry Richards to James Richards, July 26, 1826, Seitz Collection, Luce Library, Princeton Theological Seminary, Princeton, N.J.

36. James Richards to Caroline Cowles Richards, letter, August 25, 1826, Seitz Collection, Luce Library, Princeton Theological Seminary, Princeton, N.J.

37. Of the Demings's eight children, only one survived infancy. Four of Caroline Richards's five older sisters were at least ten years older than she and thus into their seventies.

38. James Richards to Caroline Cowles Richards, September 16, 1826, Seitz Collection, Luce Library, Princeton Theological Seminary, Princeton, N.J.

39. *New York City Directory*, New York, 1827, New York Public Library.

40. Henry Richards to James and Caroline Cowles Richards, February 19, 1827, Seitz Collection, Luce Library, Princeton Theological Seminary, Princeton, N.J.

41. *History of Dutchess County, 1683–1882* (Poughkeepsie, 1882).

42. *Newark Intelligencer*, March 15, 1827.

43. Henry Richards to James Richards, July 26, 1826, Seitz Collection, Luce Library, Princeton Theological Seminary, Princeton, N.J.

44. James Richards to Edward Richards, March 4, 1828, Seitz Collection, Luce Library, Princeton Theological Seminary, Princeton, N.J.

45. James Richards to Edward Richards, November 2, 1829, Seitz Collection, Luce Library, Princeton Theological Seminary, Princeton, N.J.

46. Anna Beach to Henry Richards, July 25, 1826, Seitz Collection, Luce Library, Princeton Theological Seminary, Princeton, N.J.

47. Anna Beach to James and Caroline Cowles Richards, March 22, 1830, Seitz Collection, Luce Library, Princeton Theological Seminary, Princeton, N.J.

48. Henry Richards to James Richards Jr., July 23, 1830, Seitz Collection, Luce Library, Princeton Theological Seminary, Princeton, N.J.

49. Henry Richards to James Richards, December 25, 1830, Seitz Collection, Luce Library, Princeton Theological Seminary, Princeton, N.J.

50. Henry Richards to James Richards, February 10, 1831, Seitz Collection, Luce Library, Princeton Theological Seminary, Princeton, N.J.

51. James Richards to Edward Richards, April 6, 1831, Seitz Collection, Luce Library, Princeton Theological Seminary, Princeton, N.J.

52. Sprague, *Annals*, p. 111.

53. Richards to Davis, January 31, 1831, Henry Davis Papers, Hamilton College.

54. These two sums taken together amounted to a tenth of Dr. Richards's annual salary.

55. Richards to Davis, March 11, 1831, Henry Davis Papers, Hamilton College.

56. Richards to Davis, April 22, 1831, Henry Davis Papers, Hamilton College.

57. James Richards to Caroline Cowles Richards, n.d., Seitz Collection, Luce Library, Princeton Theological Seminary, Princeton, N.J. Though the letter is undated, internal evidence indicates that the letter falls into this period.

58. Richards to Davis, June 12, 1831, Henry Davis Papers, Hamilton College.

59. Richards to Davis, August 1, 1831, Henry Davis Papers, Hamilton College.

60. George Henry Woodruff, "Some Recollections of Hamilton College, Sixty Years Ago," March 13, 1890, publication of Hamilton College.

61. Quoted in Gridley, *Mental Philosophy,* pp. 75–76.

62. Ibid., p. 74.

63. Ibid., pp. 73–74.

64. James Richards to Caroline Cowles Richards, August 23, 1831, Seitz Collection, Luce Library, Princeton Theological Seminary, Princeton, N.J.

65. Geoffrey C. Ward, *Before the Trumpet* (New York, 1985), pp. 26–28.

66. Henry Richards to James Richards, December 20, 1831, Seitz Collection, Luce Library, Princeton Theological Seminary, Princeton, N.J.

67. Richards to Sprague, February 8, 1832, Yale University.

68. Henry Richards to James Richards, December 20, 1831, Seitz Collection, Luce Library, Princeton Theological Seminary, Princeton, N.J.

69. Richards to Henry Dwight, July 1833, Gratz Collection.

70. Henry Richards to James and Caroline Cowles Richards, July 22, 1833, Seitz Collection, Luce Library, Princeton Theological Seminary, Princeton, N.J.

71. James Richards to Edward Richards, n.d., Seitz Collection, Luce Library, Princeton Theological Seminary, Princeton, N.J. Internal evidence indicates that the letter was written in August 1833.

72. Morse, *Genealogical Register*, vol. 3.

73. *New York City Directory*, 1834.

74. Their house on Nassau Street may have suffered damage from the great fire of that year that swept through lower Manhattan. When the area was rebuilt, it became almost exclusively commercial as it remains to this day.

Chapter 6. Auburn: The Finney Controversy

1. Sprague, *Annals* pp. 224–227.

2. Charles Hawley, *The History of the First Presytery Church, Auburn, The Daily Advertizer* (Auburn, 1875), p. 45.

3. Richards to Davis, Auburn, January 10, 1826, Davis Papers Notebook Manuscript Collection, Hamilton College.

4. Eight students from the class of 1827 and two from the class of 1828 signed a statement on March 7 stating that, although they respected Mr. Lansing as a gentleman and a Christian, on the basis of his public performances and published sermons they were unable to give him their approbation as a professor of Sacred Rhetoric. Gratz Collection.

5. Richards to Davis, Auburn, March 9, 1826, Henry Davis Papers, Hamilton College.

6. Richards to Caroline Richards, Geneva, March 18, 1826, Seitz Collection, Luce Library, Princeton Theological Seminary, Princeton, N.J.

7. Richards to Caroline Richards, Geneseo, March 25, 1826, Auburn Theological Seminary.

8. Richards to Caroline Richards, Canandaigua, March 26, 1826, Seitz Collection, Luce Library, Princeton Theological Seminary, Princeton, N.J.

9. R. K. Richards to James Richards, New Canaan, March 11, 1826, Seitz Collection, Luce Library, Princeton Theological Seminary, Princeton, N.J.

10. Richards to Davis, Auburn, April 3, 1826, Henry Davis Papers, Hamilton College.

11. Whitney R. Cross, *The Burned-over District: The Social and Intellectual History of Enthusiastic Religion in Western New York, 1800–1850* (Ithaca, N.Y., 1950), p. 153.

12. David MacMillan, unpublished essay on the confrontation between Charles Grandison Finney and James Richards between spring 1826 and summer 1841. Written in 1983, this manuscript can be found in the library of the Auburn Seminary. The description of Finney's failure at Hamilton is

based on letters from H. H. Kellogg to Finney between May and late August 1826, Charles G. and Lydia Finney Manuscript Collection, Oberlin College.

13. Gridley, *Mental Philosophy,* p. 43.

14. MacMillan, essay, p. 67. He quotes from an unsigned manuscript diary from the "Autographs" Collection of Oberlin College Library. He identifies the author of the diary as Silas Clark Brown, a recent graduate of Union College who entered Auburn in the fall of 1826. In the First Great Awakening of the seventeenth century, the average age of converts was the late twenties, while in the Second Awakening, the average age was more typically under twenty.

15. Hawley, *History,* pp. 46–47.

16. Morse, *Genealogical Register,* p. 217.

17. *Letters of the Reverend Dr. Beecher and Rev. Mr. Nettleton on the "New Measures" in conducting Revivals of Religion.* (New York: 1828), G. and C. Carvill.

18. Richards to Dwight, Auburn, July 5, 1832, Gratz Collection.

19. Charles E. Furman to Asahel Nettleton, Auburn, October 11 and November 6, 1826, Asahel Nettleton Papers, Hartford Seminary Foundation Library. Furman was graduated from Auburn in the class of 1828.

20. Richards to Griffin, Auburn, July 27, 1826, Gratz Collection.

21. *Auburn Alumni Catalog,* pp. 22–35.

22. Blackburn to Richards, Louisville, May 17, 1826, Dreer Collection, Historical Society of Pennsylvania.

23. Cross, *Burned-over District,* p. 234.

24. Charles Finney to Theodore Dwight Weld, Auburn, March 30 1831. See Dwight L. Dumond and Gilbert H. Barnes, eds., *Letters of Theodore Dwight Weld, Angelina Grimke Weld, and Sarah Grimke, 1822–1844.* (Gloucester, Mass.: Peter Smith, 1965), p. 45.

25. Robert H. Abzug, *Passionate Liberator Theodore Dwight Weld and the Dilemma of Reform.* (New York: Oxford University Press, 1980), p. 87.

26. MacMillan, essay, p. 135. This conclusion is based on a number of letters exchanged between Gale and Finney.

27. Richards to Nettleton, Auburn, February 22, 1827, March 1, 1827, June 23, 1827, Asahel Nettleton Papers, Hartford Seminary Foundation Library.

28. Cross, *Burned-over District,* pp. 163–164.

29. Gridley, *Mental Philosophy,* p. 43.

30. *American Education Society Quarterly* (October 1828): p. 141.

31. Ibid., (January 1829): pp. 144–150. Article by E. Porter, Andover Seminary, December 1828.

32. Gridley, *Mental Philosophy,* p. 42.

33. Walter Pilkington, *Hamilton College 1812–1962.* (Clinton: Hamilton College, 1962), p. 101.

34. Sprague, *Annals,* pp. 106–112.

35. Ibid., p. 108.

36. Gridley, *Mental Philosophy,* p. 94.

37. Sprague, *Annals,* Vol. 4, p. 112.

38. Sprague, *Sermons by the Late Rev. James Richards., D.D.,* p. 26-27.

39. Sprague, *Annals,* p. 110.

40. Sprague, *Annals,* p. 111.

41. Richards to Davis, Auburn, July 6, 1827, Henry Davis Papers, Hamilton College.

42. Julia Norton Dey, *The Childhood of . . .*, in Stryker-Rodda, *Ancestors and Descendants.*

43. Adams, *History of Auburn,* pp. 93, 96; *American Education Society Quarterly,* no. 11 (October 1827): p. 1; Ibid., no. 1, "Health of Literary Men," (August, 1830).

44. This was the moment when Rev. Axtell, Dey's future son-in-law, was called to Auburn to lead the newly formed Second Presbyterian Church.

45. MacMillan, essay, pp. 128, 129. Based on minutes of the Session of First Presbyterian Church, Auburn, from April 1828 to April 1829.

46. Gridley, *Mental Philosophy,* p. 45–48.

47. Adams, *History of Auburn,* p. 92.

48. MacMillan, essay, pp. 136–140.

49. First Presbyterian Church Records, Auburn, New York.

50. Perrine was so fearful that he would not get a New Measures man for First Presbyterian that he wrote Finney on July 14, 1830, asking him to to persuade Hopkins to come. Charles G. Finney Papers, Oberlin College Archives.

51. Hopkins to Finney, Auburn, November 19, 1830, and December 13, 1830, Charles G. Finney Papers, Oberlin College Archives.

52. Richards to Davis, Auburn, January 31, 1831, Henry Davis Papers, Hamilton College.

53. Richards to Davis, Auburn, March 11, 1831, Henry Davis Papers, Hamilton College.

54. Hopkins to Finney, Auburn, October 1, 1830, and February 3, 15, 19, 1831. The letter of February 19 has a postscript from Perrine, Charles G. Finney Papers, Oberlin College Archives.

55. MacMillan, essay, p. 148.

56. Weld to Finney, Apulia, N.Y., March 29, 1831, Dumond and Barnes, *Letters,* pp. 44–45.

57. Finney to Weld, Auburn, March 30, 1931, Charles G. Finney Papers, Oberlin College Archives.

58. Adams, *History of Auburn,* p. 83.

59. Richards to Davis, Auburn, December 21, 1831, Henry Davis Papers, Hamilton College.

60. Richards to Davis, Auburn, October 27, 1832, Henry Davis Papers, Hamilton College.

61. Richards to Davis, Auburn, November 30, 1832, Henry Davis Papers, Hamilton College.

Chapter 7. Canandaigua: Elizabeth Beals and Her Family

1. *A Memorial of Mrs. Elizabeth Beals Richards, Wife of the Reverend James Richards, D.D.,* privately published (London, 1872), p. 2 of the introduction written by her son, James Richards (hereafter cited as *Memorial*).

2. James Richards to Caroline Richards, Canandaigua, March 26, 1826, Seitz Collection, Luce Library, Princeton Theological Seminary, Princeton, N.J.

3. Samuel Beals named his youngest son Isaac Nuvis Cardoza after a Jewish cloth merchant in Charleston with whom he had dealings.

4. Caroline Cowles Richards, *Village Life in America* (New York, 1913), p. 167.

5. Information on the founding and early history of Canandaigua as well as the role played by Thomas Beals is drawn from George S. Conover, ed., *The History of Ontario County, New York* (Syracuse, N.Y., 1893), Prof. W. H. MacIntosh, *The History of Ontario County, NY, 1788–1876* (Philadelphia, 1876). See also the obituary of Thomas Beals found in Caroline Cowles Richards, *Village Life,* pp. 167–169.

6. Caroline Cowles Richards, *Village Life,* p. 169.

7. Ibid., pp. 38, 222.

8. Henry M. Field, *The Family of the Reverend David D. Field, D.D. of Stockbridge, Massachusetts,* printed privately, 1860.

9. Beals genealogy comes from family papers.

10. *Memorial,* p. 9.

11. George McG. Hayes, *History of Banking in Canandaigua from 1813–1951,* n.p., n.d.

12. This refers to leas of beer.

13. Elizabeth Beals to Ann Field, Canandaigua, April 18, 1833, Seitz Collection, Luce Library, Princeton Theological Seminary, Princeton, N.J.

14. Since the person referrred to was still alive in Canandaigua, the editor did not mention her name so as not to offend her should she happen to see the memorial book. This occurs in several other letters.

15. Elizabeth Beals to Ann Field, Canandaigua, October 27, 1833, in *Memorial*, p. 28.

16. Elizabeth Beals to Ann Field, November 16, 1833, in *Memorial*, p. 24.

17. Elizabeth Beals to Ann Field, December 5, 1833, in *Memorial*, pp. 27-28.

18. Elizabeth Beals to Ann Field, December 24, 1833, in *Memorial*, p. 34.

19. Elizabeth Beals to Ann Field, December 24, 1833, in *Memorial*, pp. 32–35.

20. Elizabeth Beals to Ann Field, May 28, 1834, in *Memorial*, pp. 32–35.

21. James Richards to Caroline Richards, Geneva, January 10, 1835, Seitz Collection, Luce Library, Princeton Theological Seminary, Princeton, N.J.

22. *Memorial,* p. 11.

23. Caroline Amelia Beach to James Richards Jr., n.d., Newark, Seitz Collection, Luce Library, Princeton Theological Seminary, Princeton, N.J.

24. Caroline Dey to James Richards Jr., n.d., Seitz Collection, Luce Library, Princeton Theological Seminary, Princeton, N.J.

25. This refers to the rage for phrenology.

26. Caroline Richards Dey to James Richards Jr., August 10, 1835, Seitz Collection, Luce Library, Princeton Theological Seminary, Princeton, N.J.

27. Thomas Beals to James Richards Jr., Canandaigua, April 23, 1836, Seitz Collection, Luce Library, Princeton Theological Seminary, Princeton, N.J.

28. A description of the wedding can be found in *Memorial*, pp. 11-12, and Caroline Cowles Richards, *Village Life,* p. 84.

Chapter 8. Aurora: James and Elizabeth's Early Married Life

1. Richards, *Village Life,* p. 56.

2. Thomas Beals to James Richards Jr., Canandaigua, September 14, 1836, Seitz Collection, Luce Library, Princeton Theological Seminary, Princeton, N.J.

3. Thomas Beals to Elizabeth Beals Richards, Canandaigua, September 20, 1836, Seitz Collection, Luce Library, Princeton Theological Seminary, Princeton, N.J.

4. Thomas Beals to James Richards Jr., Canandaigua, August 26, 1836, Seitz Collection, Luce Library, Princeton Theological Seminary, Princeton, N.J.

5. Lyman Beecher, for example, was an enthusiastic supporter of Taylor before he was ready to accept Finney, as seen in chapter 5.

6. David Frame to James Richards Jr., East Windsor, January 4, 1837, Seitz Collection, Luce Library, Princeton Theological Seminary, Princeton, N.J.

7. New Testament reference to "No man is a prophet in his own country."

8. Frame to James Richards Jr., Meriden, April 20, 1837, Seitz Collection, Luce Library,.Princeton Theological Seminary, Princeton, N.J.

9. Frame to James Richards Jr., East Windsor, June 1, 1837, Seitz Collection, Luce Library, Princeton Theological Seminary, Princeton, N.J.

10. *Memorial,* p. 13.

11. Also known as the hypo or hypomania, a nineteenth-century word for depression.

12. This refers to staying up with the sick.

13. Stryker-Rodda, *Ancestors and Descendants,* p. 232.

14. Elizabeth Beals Richards to Thomas Beals, Aurora, September 28, 1837, Seitz Collection, Luce Library, Princeton Theological Seminary, Princeton, N.J.

15. James Beach to James Richards Jr., Newark, October 26, 1837, Seitz Collection, Luce Library, Princeton Theological Seminary, Princeton, N.J.

16. Richards to James Richards Jr., Auburn, November 24, 1837, Seitz Collection, Luce Library, Princeton Theological Seminary, Princeton, N.J.

17. He was the professor of Church History and Church Polity at the seminary since 1836.

18. Elizabeth Beals Richards to Thomas and Abigail Beals, Aurora, December 26 1837, from *Memorial,* p. 37.

19. Elizabeth Beals Richards to Caroline Cowles Richards, Aurora, January 22, 1838, from *Memorial,* p. 41.

20. Sam Hopkins to James Richards Jr., Steamboat Commerce on the Chatahoucher River, April 15, 1838, Seitz Collection, Luce Library, Princeton Theological Seminary, Princeton, N.J.

21. Henry Channing Beals to James Richards Jr., New York, May 25, 1838, Seitz Collection, Luce Library, Princeton Theological Seminary, Princeton, N.J.

22. Stryker-Rodda, *Ancestors and Descendants,* p. 232.

23. Edmund Platt, *Eagle's History of Poughkeepsie from Earliest Settlement 1683–1905,* (Poughkeepsie, 1906), p. 282.

24. Elizabeth Richards to Caroline Cowles Richards, Aurora, August 7, 1838, from *Memorial,* p. 40.

25. Frame to James Richards Jr., New Jersey, October 1, 1838, Seitz Collection, Luce Library, Princeton Theological Seminary, Princeton, N.J.

26. A letter normally consisted of a folded sheet of paper sealed with wax and addressed on the exposed surface. Since there was no envelope, other letters could not be enclosed. Letters were not forwarded unless they were included in a package.

27. Elizabeth Beals Richards to James and Caroline Cowles Richards, Aurora, January 25, 1839, Seitz Collection, Luce Library, Princeton Theological Seminary, Princeton, N.J.

28. Frame to James Richards Jr., Succusunna, Morris County, N.J., January 28, 1839, Seitz Collection, Luce Library, Princeton Theological Seminary, Princeton, N.J.

29. Elizabeth Beals Richards to Abigail Beals, Aurora, March 3, 1839, Seitz Collection, Luce Library, Princeton Theological Seminary, Princeton, N.J.

30. James Richards Jr. to Caroline and James Richards, Aurora, March 8, 1839, Seitz Collection, Luce Library, Princeton Theological Seminary, Princeton, N.J.

31. James Richards Jr. to Thomas and Abigail Beals, Aurora, March 8, 1839, Seitz Collection, Luce Library, Princeton Theological Seminary, Princeton, N.J.

32. Edson Carr to James Richards Jr., Canandaigua, March 10, 1839, Seitz Collection, Luce Library, Princeton Theological Seminary, Princeton, N.J.

33. Hopkins to James Richards Jr., Geneva, March 12, 1839, Seitz Collection, Luce Library, Princeton Theological Seminary, Princeton, N.J.

34. Thomas Beals to Elizabeth Beals Richards, Canandaigua, October 17, 1839, Seitz Collection, Luce Library, Princeton Theological Seminary, Princeton, N.J.

35. Presbyterians took Communion twice a year after rigorous preparation.

36. James Richards Jr. to James Richards, Aurora, January 6, 1840, Seitz Collection, Luce Library, Princeton Theological Seminary, Princeton, N.J.

37. The church in Aurora may have received outside missionary funds or he may be referring to his and the Beals's supplement.

38. James Richards to Henry Richards, Auburn, March 7, 1840, Seitz Collection, Luce Library, Princeton Theological Seminary, Princeton, N.J.

39. This refers to little Henry Richards.

40. Mary Richards to James Nicholas Richards, Poughkeepsie, February 29, 1840, Seitz Collection, Luce Library, Princeton Theological Seminary, Princeton, N.J.

41. James could have been sent as a day student to the Poughkeepsie Collegiate School, a school founded by Charles Bartlett in 1836 to educate the sons of Hudson River gentlemen in a less punitive style than was usual. In contrast, Mr. Alexander Hyde's school at Lee, Massachusetts, was known for its firm control of troublesome boys and its strong emphasis on religion. James Roosevelt, another youngster from Poughkeepsie, was also sent there in 1841. Geoffrey C. Ward, *Before the Trumpet* (New York: Harper and Row, 1985), pp. 22–25.

42. James N. Richards to Anthony Dey, Lee, Massachusetts, December 23, 1840, Seitz Collection, Luce Library, Princeton Theological Seminary, Princeton, N.J.

43. James N. Richards to Master H. E. Richards, Lee, Massachusetts, December 23, 1840, Seitz Collection, Luce Library, Princeton Theological Seminary, Princeton, N.J.

44. Elizabeth Beals Richards to Magdalena Beals, Aurora, August 26, 1840, Seitz Collection, Luce Library, Princeton Theological Seminary, Princeton, N.J.

45. Elizabeth Beals Richards to Thomas and Abigail Beals, Aurora, November 15, 1840, Seitz Collection, Luce Library, Princeton Theological Seminary, Princeton, N.J.

46. Lavinia Dey to James Richards Jr., New Brunswick, July 17, 1841, Seitz Collection, Luce Library, Princeton Theological Seminary, Princeton, N.J.

47. Elizabeth Beals Richards to Thomas and Abigail Beals, Aurora, November 15, 1840, Seitz Collection, Luce Library, Princeton Theological Seminary, Princeton, N.J.

48. *Memorial,* pp. 13, 14.

49. James Richards to James Richards Jr., Auburn, March 12, 1841, Seitz Collection, Luce Library, Princeton Theological Seminary, Princeton, N.J.

Chapter 9. Auburn: The Last Years of Dr. Richards

1. This is an early name for Hawaii.

2. Richards to the Reverend John W. Adams, Auburn, August 31, 1831, Gratz Collection.

3. George Wilson Pierson, *Tocqueville and Beaumont in America* (N.Y., 1938), pp. 214–215.

4. Ibid., p. 214.

5. James Richards to Caroline Cowles Richards, Oswego, August 23, 1831, Seitz Collection, Luce Library, Princeton Theological Seminary, Princeton, N.J.

6. James Richards to Caroline Cowles Richards, Albany, n.d., probably 1831, Seitz Collection, Luce Library, Princeton Theological Seminary, Princeton, N.J.

7. Richards to Dwight, Auburn, January 24, 1831, Collection of the Office of History, Presbyterian Church, Philadelphia.

8. Wiliam C. Walton to Richards, Alexandria, September 19, 1831, Gratz Collection.

9. Richards to Sprague, Auburn, February 8, 1832, Beinecke Rare Book and Manuscript Library, Yale University Library.

10. Adams, *History of Auburn,* pp. 82-83.

11. Richards to Dwight, Auburn, July 5, 1832, Gratz Collection.

12. Woods to Richards, Andover, October 28, 1833, Gratz Collection.

13. Richards to Sprague, Auburn, November 5, 1833, Yale University Library.

14. Woods to Richards, Andover, December 2, 1834, Gratz Collection.

15. Perrine to Cox, Auburn, February 25, 1835, Auburn Theological Seminary Library.

16. Adams, *History of Auburn,* pp. 92-93.

17. After leaving Auburn in 1829, Lansing served as a pastor in Utica and Brooklyn. He was now retiring to Auburn.

18. Perrine to Cox, Auburn, March 24, 1835, Auburn Theological Seminary Library.

19. He was the dogged prosecutor of Lyman Beecher at Lane.

20. Richards to Miller, Auburn, March 5, 1835, Samuel Miller Papers, Princeton University Library.

21. Richards to Miller, Auburn, April 22, 1836, Samuel Miller Papers, Princeton University Library.

22. James Richards to Caroline Cowles Richards, Avon, July 4, 1836, Seitz Collection, Luce Library, Princeton Theological Seminary, Princeton, N.J.

23. Richards to Dwight, Auburn, January 26, 1837, Gratz Collection.

24. Richards to Dwight, Auburn, April 30, 1837, Gratz Collection.

25. James Richards to Caroline Cowles Richards, Philadelphia, May 19, 1837, Princeton University Library.

26. Minutes of the General Assembly, 1837.

27. Adams, *History of Auburn,* p. 106.

28. Ibid., pp. 108, 109.

29. Richards to Dwight, Auburn, June 26, 1837, Gratz Collection.

30. Adams, *History of Auburn,* pp. 109–111.

31. James Richards to Anna Beach, Auburn, September 1, 1837, Park Family Papers, Yale University Library.

32. Gridley, *Mental Philosophy,* p. 56.

33. Ibid., p. 57.

34. Adams, *History of Auburn,* p. 111.

35. Richards to Sprague, Auburn, June 15, 1838, Yale University Library.

36. The church was reunited in 1868, twenty-five years after his death.

37. B. Labaree to Richards, New York, January 15, 1838, Gratz Collection.

38. Nash, *The American People,* pp. 412, 413.

39. Richards to Dwight, Auburn, November 1, 1839, Gratz Collection.

40. Anthony Dey was trying to incorporate or charter a manufacturing company.

41. Anna Beach to James Richards, Newark, December 3, 1839, Seitz Collection, Luce Library, Princeton Theological Seminary, Princeton, N.J.

42. Gridley, *Mental Philosophy,* p. 81.

43. This is referred to in the will of James Richards.

44. Gridley, *Mental Philosophy,* p. 81.

45. Julia Norton Dey, *The Childhood of . . . ,* p. 24.

46. Records of his participation in the Georgia Elrod Gold Mining Co. are in the Manuscript Collection of the Dey Family at the New York Historical Society.

47. A description of Anthony Dey's assets and their value forms part of the court record in his application for bankruptcy.

48. Julia Norton Dey, *The Childhood of . . . ,* p. 23.

49. Leo Hershkowitz, "The Land of Promise: Samuel Swartout and Land Speculation in Texas, 1830–1838," *New York Historical Society Quarterly,* 48, no. 4 (October 1964): pp. 307–327.

50. Circular, November 4, 1840.

51. Copy of a letter from Anthony Dey to Howland Bill and his wife in the court record of Anthony Dey's bankruptcy proceedings.

52. Julia Norton Dey, *The Childhood of . . . ,* p. 24.

53. Richards to Charles Merwin, Auburn, February 6, 1841, Seitz Collection, Luce Library, Princeton Theological Seminary, Princeton, N.J.

54. Gridley, *Mental Philosophy,* p. 59.

55. James Richards to James Richards Jr., Auburn, November 24, 1837, Seitz Collection, Luce Library, Princeton Theological Seminary, Princeton, N.J.

56. James Richards to James Richards Jr., Auburn, March 12, 1841, Seitz Collection, Luce Library, Princeton Theological Seminary, Princeton, N.J.

57. James Richards to James Richards Jr., Auburn, October 1, 1841, Seitz Collection, Luce Library, Princeton Theological Seminary, Princeton, N.J.

58. James Richards to James Richards Jr., Auburn, n.d., Seitz Collection, Luce Library, Princeton Theological Seminary, Princeton, N.J.

59. Gridley, *Mental Philosophy,* p. 59.

60. Anna Beach to James Richards Jr., Auburn, November 16, 1842, Seitz Collection, Luce Library, Princeton Theological Seminary, Princeton, N.J.

61. James Richards to Elizabeth Beals Richards, Auburn, Wednesday evening, Seitz Collection, Luce Library, Princeton Theological Seminary, Princeton, N.J.

62. Gridley, *Mental Philosophy,* p. 60.

63. Ibid., pp 60-61.

64. Ibid., p. 62.

65. Ibid., p. 62.

66. Henry Richards to James Richards, Poughkeepsie, May 13, 1843, Seitz Collection, Luce Library, Princeton Theological Seminary, Princeton, N.J.

67. Gridley, *Mental Philosophy*, p. 63.

68. Ibid., pp. 66–69 describe the last moments of Dr. Richards and the funeral arrangements.

Chapter 10. Penn Yan: James and Elizabeth's Later Married Life

1. James H. Hotchkin, *A History of the Purchase and Settlement of Western New York and the Presbyterian Church in that Section* (New York, 1848), p. 397.

2. Elizabeth Beals Richards to Caroline Cowles Richards, June 9, 1841, Seitz Collection, Luce Library, Princeton Theological Seminary, Princeton, N.J.

3. Caroline Amelia Beach to Elizabeth Beals Richards, July 6, 1841, Seitz Collection, Luce Library, Princeton Theological Seminary, Princeton, N.J.

4. Caroline Amelia Beach to Elizabeth Beals Richards, August 14, 1841, Seitz Collection, Luce Library, Princeton Theological Seminary, Princeton, N.J.

5. James Richards to James Richards Jr., October 1, 1841, Seitz Collection, Luce Library, Princeton Theological Seminary, Princeton, N.J.

6. Elizabeth Beals Richards to Thomas Beals, December, 1841, from *Memorial,* pp. 42–44.

7. Elizabeth Beals Richards to Caroline Cowles Richards, February 26, 1842, Seitz Collection, Luce Library, Princeton Theological Seminary, Princeton, N.J.

8. Magdalena Beals to Elizabeth Beals Richards, March 14, 1842, Seitz Collection, Luce Library, Princeton Theological Seminary, Princeton, N.J.

9. Henry Beals to Beals family, as quoted by Magdalena Beals to Elizabeth Beals Richards, March 14, 1842, Seitz Collection, Luce Library, Princeton Theological Seminary, Princeton, N.J.

10. Abigail Field Beals to Elizabeth Beals Richards, March 14, 1842, Seitz Collection, Luce Library, Princeton Theological Seminary, Princeton, N.J.

11. Obituary of Henry Beals, *Ontario County Times*, New York, February 12, 1896. The obituary tells of Beals's early years in the New York City flour trade and his migration in 1851 to California, where he became editor of the *Commercial Herald*, a leading business newspaper. He was "a great church worker" with the Flower Mission and was connected with St. John's Presbyterian Church "since its beginning."

12. James Richards to James Richards Jr., July 26, 1843, Seitz Collection, Luce Library, Princeton Theological Seminary, Princeton, N.J.

13. I. Miles Gillett to James Richards Jr., August 2, 1843, Seitz Collection, Luce Library, Princeton Theological Seminary, Princeton, N.J.

14. James Richards Jr., to Caroline Cowles Richards, August 21, 1843, Seitz Collection, Luce Library, Princeton Theological Seminary, Princeton, N.J.

15. Julia Norton Dey, *The Childhood of . . .* , in Stryker-Rodda, *Ancestors and Descendants.*

16. Anna Dey to James Richards Jr., October 9, 1843, Seitz Collection, Luce Library, Princeton Theological Seminary, Princeton, N.J.

17. Elizabeth Beals Richards to Caroline Cowles Richards, November 13, 1843, Seitz Collection, Luce Library, Princeton Theological Seminary, Princeton, N.J.

18. Elizabeth Beals Richards to Glorianna Beals, November 6, 1843, Seitz Collection, Luce Library, Princeton Theological Seminary, Princeton, N.J.

19. Glorianna Beals to Elizabeth Beals Richards, February 14, 1844, Seitz Collection, Luce Library, Princeton Theological Seminary, Princeton, N.J.

20. Thomas Beals to Elizabeth Beals Richards, March 13, 1844, Seitz Collection, Luce Library, Princeton Theological Seminary, Princeton, N.J.

21. Elizabeth Beals Richards to Thomas Beals, March 25, 1844, Seitz Collection, Luce Library, Princeton Theological Seminary, Princeton, N.J.

22. Elizabeth Beals Richards to Thomas Beals, May 30, 1844, Seitz Collection, Luce Library, Princeton Theological Seminary, Princeton, N.J.

23. James Richards Jr., to Caroline Cowles Richards, July 19, 1844, Seitz Collection, Luce Library, Princeton Theological Seminary, Princeton, N.J.

24. Caroline Cowles Richards to James Richards Jr., October, 1844, Seitz Collection, Luce Library, Princeton Theological Seminary, Princeton, N.J.

25. Caroline Cowles Richards to James Richards Jr., October 28, 1844, Seitz Collection, Luce Library, Princeton Theological Seminary, Princeton, N.J.

26. Elizabeth Beals Richards to Magdalena or Glorianna Beals, November 19, 1844, in *Memorial*, pp. 55–57.

27. Caroline Richards Dey to James Richards Jr., n.d., Seitz Collection, Luce Library, Princeton Theological Seminary, Princeton, N.J.

28. Gridley, *Mental Philosophy.*

29. Caroline Dey Richards to James Richards Jr., n.d., Seitz Collection, Luce Library, Princeton Theological Seminary, Princeton, N.J.

30. Emily's father, Benjamin Ferris, served several terms as sheriff and member of the state assembly. The Ferris family seat was in the town of Cortlandt in northern Westchester County, which probably influenced Edward's decision later in life to buy land and settle there. Emily's mother, Anna Maria Schieffelin, was the daughter of Jacob Schieffelin, who in 1794 founded what became one of the leading mercantile houses of the city of New York. See Floyd I. Ferris, *Jeffrey Ferris Family Genealogy* (Ithaca, 1963); Isaac J. Greenwood, *Jacob and Hannah (Lawrence) Schieffelin of New York* (Boston, 1897).

31. A notice of the death of Emily's widowed mother, Anna Maria Schieffelin Ferris of 770 Broadway, appeared in the *New York Evening Post,* October 23, 1843.

32. See Joseph F. Kett, *Rites of Passage: Adolescence in America 1790 to the Present* (New York, 1977).

33. Henry Nathaniel Beach to James Richards Jr., December 17, 1844, Seitz Collection, Luce Library, Princeton Theological Seminary, Princeton, N.J.

34. James D. Hart, *Oxford Companion to American Literature*, 5th ed. (New York, 1983).

35. Baird had just published a detailed description of the American religious scene for the benefit of his continental audience, emphasizing the positive significance of the "voluntary principle" in contrast to the workings

of an established church on the European model. It became quite influential. His lecture tour no doubt contributed to the impact of the work. See Robert Baird, *Religion in United States of America* (New York, 1844).

36. Elizabeth Beals Richards to Caroline Cowles Richards, February 13, 1845, in *Memorial*, pp. 57–60.

37. Elizabeth Beals Richards to Magdalena Beals, April 1, 1845, Seitz Collection, Luce Library, Princeton Theological Seminary, Princeton, N.J.

38. Henry Nathaniel Beach to James Richards Jr., December 17, 1844, Seitz Collection, Luce Library, Princeton Theological Seminary, Princeton, N.J.

39. Elizabeth Beals Richards to Magdalena Beals, April 1, 1845. The information in Caroline Dey's letter regarding Henry Richards is reported in this letter.

40. Ibid.

41. Elizabeth Beals Richards to Magdalena Beals, April 19, 1845, Seitz Collection, Luce Library, Princeton Theological Seminary, Princeton, N.J.

42. Introduction, *Memorial*, p. 14. The introduction was written by her eldest son, James, who at the time of writing was a lawyer in the New York City firm of Coudert Brothers.

43. Caroline Cowles Richards to James Richards Jr., July 11, 1845, Seitz Collection, Luce Library, Princeton Theological Seminary, Princeton, N.J.

44. Thomas Lounsbury to James Richards Jr., May 1, 1845, Seitz Collection, Luce Library, Princeton Theological Seminary, Princeton, N.J.

45. George Schenk to James Richards Jr. May 6, 1845, Seitz Collection, Luce Library, Princeton Theological Seminary, Princeton, N.J.

46. The same November 20, 1841, issue of the Newark newspaper, *The Sentinel of Freedom*, that carried the death notice of Aaron Beach also carried an advertisement for this school. "D. A. Frame" is noted as the "principal and proprietor."

47. Introduction, *Memorial*, pp. 7–8.

48. Caroline Cowles Richards to James Richards Jr., September 8, 1845, Seitz Collection, Luce Library, Princeton Theological Seminary, Princeton, N.J.

49. Ibid.

50. Student record of James Nicholas Richards, citing faculty minutes of December 19, 1845, Princeton University.

51. Henry Richards to Elizabeth Beals Richards, October 6, 1845, Seitz Collection, Luce Library, Princeton Theological Seminary, Princeton, N.J.

52. Elizabeth Beals Richards to Caroline Cowles Richards, November 2, 1845, in *Memorial*, 61–63.

53. Henry Nathaniel Beach to James Richards Jr., January 2, 1846, Seitz Collection, Luce Library, Princeton Theological Seminary, Princeton, N.J.

54. Elizabeth Beals Richards to Glorianna Beals, January 27, 1846, in *Memorial*, pp. 66–67.

55. Elizabeth Beals Richards to Abigail Field Beals, February 2, 1846, in *Memorial*, pp. 66–67.

56. Elizabeth Richards to Abigail Beals, February 14, 1846, Seitz Collection, Luce Library, Princeton Theological Seminary, Princeton, N.J. An edited version also appears in *Memorial*.

57. Henry Nathaniel Beach to James Richards Jr., March 21, 1846, Seitz Collection, Luce Library, Princeton Theological Seminary, Princeton, N.J.

58. Elizabeth Beals Richards to Glorianna Beals, January 27, 1846, Seitz Collection, Luce Library, Princeton Theological Seminary, Princeton, N.J.

59. Glorianna Beals to Elizabeth Beals Richards, May 15, 1846, Seitz Collection, Luce Library, Princeton Theological Seminary, Princeton, N.J.

60. Ann Beals Field to Elizabeth Beals Richards, May 15, 1846, Seitz Collection, Luce Library, Princeton Theological Seminary, Princeton, N.J.

61. Elizabeth Beals Richards to Ann Beals Field, May 30, 1846, in *Memorial*, pp. 71–73.

62. Ibid.

63. Ibid.

64. Ibid.

65. Ann Beals Field to James Richards Jr., June 15, 1846, Seitz Collection, Luce Library, Princeton Theological Seminary, Princeton, N.J.

66. D. H. Hamilton to James Richards Jr., June 23, 1846, Seitz Collection, Luce Library, Princeton Theological Seminary, Princeton, N.J.

Chapter 11. Wanderings: James's Later Career

1. John M. Bradford to James Richards Jr., September 2, 1846, Seitz Collection, Luce Library, Princeton Theological Seminary, Princeton, N.J.

2. John Morgan Richards, *With John Bull and Jonathan: Reminiscences of Sixty Years of an American's Life in England and in the United States* (New York, 1906), p. 7.

3. Edward Richards to James Richards Jr., September 7, 1846, Seitz Collection, Luce Library, Princeton Theological Seminary, Princeton, N.J.

4. Rev. Dr. David Magie, "Sermon at Installation of the Reverend James Richards Jr.," Records of First Presbyterian Church of Morristown, New Jersey, December 28, 1847.

5. John Morgan Richards, *With John Bull*, pp. 9–11.

6. Archives of Lafayette College, Easton, Pennsylvania. Recommendations for an honorary degree were usually submitted three months in advance. There is no record in the college minutes of such a prior recommendation.

7. W. J. Rorabaugh, *The Alcoholic Republic: An American Tradition* (New York, 1979).

8. The information on James's ordeal and trial in Morristown, except where otherwise noted, comes from the minutes of the Elizabeth Presbytery.

9. Ira Condict Whitehead was a lawyer who, according to First Church records, served as ruling elder from 1846 until his death in 1867. He was fifteen years older than James Richards Jr. These records describe him as ". . . abrupt and positive in declaring his opinions (perhaps his one fault). . . ."

10. A separate but related piece of business occupied the presbytery in its afternoon session: An elder of the Morristown church presented that congregation's formal call to James's successor, the Reverend John H. Townley, and arrangements were made for his installation. It is unclear if James was present to witness this or whether the timing was anything but coincidental.

11. Although motions were often entered into the record without affixing names to them, the names of the dissenters and protestors were entered into the minutes.

12. The General Assembly minutes of 1852 confirm his residence in Princeton that year. His friend George Schenk had died there two years before.

13. John Morgan Richards, *With John Bull,* p. 12.

14. Extract from Elizabeth Presbytery Minutes, signed by stated clerk, Joseph T. English, October 5, 1852.

15. The school was actually still known at this time as the Southern Scientific Institute. The State of Mississippi granted change of name in 1854.

16. H. S. Fulkerson, *Random Recollection of Early Days in Mississippi*, (Vicksburg, 1885).

17. John Morgan Richards, *With John Bull,* pp. 14–15.

18. John Morgan Richards to Caroline Cowles Richards, August 27, 1853, Seitz Collection, Luce Library, Princeton Theological Seminary, Princeton, N.J.

19. Clifford M. Drury, *William Anderson Scott* (Glendale, Calif.: H. Clark Co., 1967).

20. "Dr. Scott's Sermon, with the Installation Charges in the Third Presbyterian Church, Rev. Dr. Richards's," New Orleans, printed at the office of "The Creole," 1854.

21. Records of the New Orleans Presbytery, Montreat Study Center, Montreat, N.C., p. 44. All quotations that deal with the relations of James Richards Jr., to the New Orleans Presbytery are drawn from this source.

22. John Morgan Richards, *With John Bull,* p. 16, pp. 124–137.

23. Records of the New Orleans Presbytery, pp. 35–36.

24. All of the northeastern states except New York allowed divorce on a wide variety of grounds, and Indiana was a virtual divorce mill. In 1849 Connecticut had added an omnibus provision that included "any such misconduct as permanently destroys the happiness of the petitioner and defeats the purpose of the marriage relation." For the next three decades the topic received much attention. Between November 1852 and February 1853, Horace Greeley debated against easy divorce with the elder Henry James on the pages of his *New York Tribune.* See Glenda Riley, *Divorce: An American Tradition* (New York: Oxford University Press, 1991).

25. *American Biographical History of Eminent and Self-Made Men of the State of Michigan* (Cincinnati, Western Biographical Publishing Company, 1878). *History of Jackson County, Michigan, vol. 1* (Chicago, 1881). The latter lists Sarah Wisner as a pioneer who arrived there in 1854, though a New York State census had her still in Penn Yan in 1855. Shoemaker was active in Democratic politics in Michigan and distinguished himself as a Union colonel with the Thirteenth Michigan Volunteer Infantry in the Civil War.

26. Records of the New Orleans Presbytery, pp. 47–48.

27. James's patron, Dr. Scott, had been called to a church in San Francisco and was no longer on the scene. Scott became pastor of St. John's Presbyterian Church, where Henry Beals coincidentally was a founding member and elder.

28. Rorabaugh, *Alcoholic Republic,* p. 145.

29. *Catalogue of the Elm Park Commercial, Agricultural, and Collegiate Institute,* Litchfield, 1857.

30. Henry Warner Bowden, *Dictionary of American Religious Biography,* Westport, Conn., Greenwood Press, 1977, p. 23.

31. Rorabaugh, *Alcoholic Republic,* pp. 164–167.

32. One month later, on August 25, his former wife Sarah married Michael Shoemaker in Penn Yan. The close timing of the two marriages suggests that a legal divorce was indeed granted.

33. Caroline Cowles Richards, *Village Life,* p. 89.

34. Alain C. White, *The History of Litchfield, Connecticut, 1720–1920* (Litchfield, Enquirer Printing, 1920), p. 236.

35. Richards Jr., to Rev. Pohlman, Litchfield, Conn., December 15, 1857, Historical Society of Pennsylvania, Philadelphia, Pa.

36. "The Documents in the Case of James Richards," The Litchfield South Association, New Haven, 1860. The document quoted here is dated December 6, 1859.

37. Ibid.

38. Will of Edward Cowles Richards.

39. S. W. Boardman to Willis Beecher, Stanhope, N.Y., October 9, 1886, Alumni Files, Auburn Theological Seminary, Union Theological Seminary in the City of New York.

40. See case of Pierre T. C. Richards, Court of Common Pleas, New York City, October 8, 1865; order of Justice Didge in the case of Henry S. Richards, Second District Police Court, New York City, May 20, 1867; and "In the Matter of Henry S. Richards, a Supposed Habitual Drunkard," heard before three commissioners of the Court of Common Pleas, New York City, December 10, 1867.

41. See "Regulations and Rules of the New York State Inebriate Asylum," adopted September 29, 1864; *Binghamton Daily Republican*, November 25, 1858; *Harper's Bazaar*, 1869.

42. "History of East Church," Boston.

43. Ibid.

44. It was on this occasion that the children, now in their thirties and late twenties, decided to publish privately a number of their mother's letters as a memorial.

45. Jean M. Brown, *A Brief History of Kanawha Presbyterian Church*, (Charleston, 1930).

46. James Richards Jr., *The Safe Side* (London, 1875), author's n.

47. Register of Deaths, No. 005515, District of Canongate, Burgh of Edinburgh. There were in fact two death certificates, one dated August 2 and another dated August 18. The second was written as a "result of a precognition" and added the information about the "influence of drink."

48. James Richards Jr., *The Safe Side*, p. 26.

49. Caroline Cowles Richards, *Village Life*, p. 19.

50. James Richards Jr., *The Safe Side,* pp. 243–244.

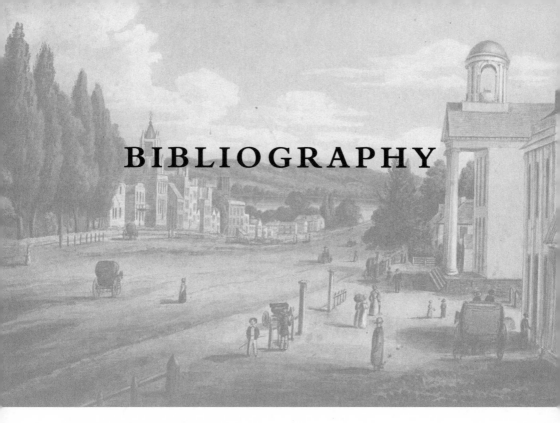

BIBLIOGRAPHY

Letters and Family Papers

Correspondence (150 letters) of James Richards, D. D., and his family in the possession of his descendants.

Correspondence of James Richards at Yale University, Auburn Library of Union Theological Seminary, Princeton University, Princeton Theological Seminary, Presbyterian Historical Society, Historical Society of Pennsylvania, and Hamilton College.

French, Eleanor G. *The Childhood of Julia Norton Dey 1832–1919*. Montclair, New Jersey, 1934. A memoir by James Richards's granddaughter.

A Memorial of Mrs. Elizabeth Beals Richards. London, 1872. A privately printed collection of the early letters of James Richards's daughter-in-law, Elizabeth Richards.

Richards, Caroline Cowles. *Village Life in America*. New York, 1913. This memoir by James Richards's granddaughter of her childhood in Canandaigua, New York, has been continuously in print since its publication.

Richards, James, D. D. *Lectures on Mental Philosophy and Theology, with a Sketch of His Life*. By Samuel H. Gridley. New York, 1846.

———. *Sermons by the Late Rev. James Richards, D. D., with an Essay on His Character*. By William B. Sprague. Albany, 1849.

457

Richards, James, D. D. Additional sermons in the Princeton Theological Seminary Library.

Richards, James, Jr. *The Safe Side*. London, 1875. A collection of sermons by James Richards's son.

Richards, John Morgan. *With John Bull and Jonathan: Reminiscences of Sixty Years of an American's Life in England and in the United States*. New York, 1906. A memoir by one of James Richards's grandsons.

Sources of Archival Materials

Auburn Theological Seminary alumnae records, early pamphlets, letters, etc.

Court records of New York City.

Federal court records of bankruptcy proceedings in Bayonne, New Jersey.

Libraries: New York Public Library; New York Genealogical Society Library; Wood Library of Canandaigua, New York; Jersey City Public Library; South Street Seaport Museum Library; Hartford Seminary Foundation Library; Oberlin College Archives; Lafayette College Archives.

Local church records in Morristown, Newark, Canandaigua, Aurora, Penn Yan, East Boston, Kanawha.

Local Historical Societies of New Canaan, Connecticut; Litchfield, Connecticut; Canandaigua, New York; Auburn, New York; and Broome County, New York.

National Archives of the United States for maritime information.

Presbyterian Church records in Lexington, Kentucky.

Presbyterian Historical Society records at Montreat, North Carolina, and Philadelphia of clergy, seminaries, church governing bodies, and other organizations.

Princeton Theological Seminary records.

Probate Court records in the following New York localities: White Plains, Poughkeepsie, Canandaigua, Auburn, and New York City.

State Historical Societies of New Jersey, New York, Michigan, Mississippi, Pennsylvania, Georgia, and California.

Union College.

Unpublished Manuscripts

Blauvelt, Martha Tomhare. *Society, Religion, and Revivalism: The Second Great Awakening in New Jersey, 1780–1830*. Princeton University dissertation 1974.

McMillan, David. Essay on James Richards and Charles Finney.

General

A Brief History of Kanawha Presbyterian Church, 1930.

Adams, John Quincy. *A History of the Auburn Theological Seminary 1818–1918.* Auburn, 1918.

Albion, Richard G. *The Rise of New York Port, 1815–1860.* New York, 1939.

Baird, Robert. *Religion in the United States of America.* New York, 1844.

Baird, Samuel J. *A History of the New School and of the Questions Involved in the Disruption of the Presbyterian Church in 1838.* Philadelphia, 1868.

Beecher, Lyman. *Autobiography and Correspondence,* ed. Barbara Cross. Cambridge, 1961.

Betts, John Rickards. "American Medical Thought on Exercise as the Road to Health, 1820–1860," *Bulletin of the History of Medicine* (Mar.–Apr. 1971).

Bledsoe, Burton J. *The Culture of Professionalism: The Middle Class and the Development of Higher Education in America.* New York, 1976.

Bonomi, Patricia U. *Under the Cope of Heaven: Religion, Society, and Politics in Colonial America.* New York, Oxford, 1986.

Bowden, Henry Warner. *Dictionary of American Religious Biography.* 1976.

Bushman, Richard. *From Puritan to Yankee: Character and the Social Order in Connecticut, 1690–1765.* Cambridge, 1967.

Calhoun, Daniel. *Professional Lives in America: Structure and Aspiration, 1750–1850.* Cambridge, 1965.

Cole, Charles C. *The Social Ideas of the Northern Evangelists.* New York, 1954.

Cott, Nanay F. *The Bonds of Womanhood: Woman's Sphere in New England 1780–1835.* New Haven, 1977.

Cross, Whitney R. *The Burned-Over District.* Ithaca, 1951.

Cunningham, John T. *Newark.* New Jersey Historical Society, Newark, 1966.

Demos, John. *Past, Present, and Personal: The Family and the Life Course in American History.* New York, 1986.

Doherty, Robert W. "Social Bases for the Presbyterian Schism of 1837–1838: The Philadelphia Case," *Journal of Social History* (fall 1968).

Douglas, Ann. *The Feminization of American Culture.* New York, 1977.

Dwight, Timothy. *Travels in New England and New York,* ed. B. M. Solomon and P. M. King. Cambridge, 1969.

Ferris, Floyd I. *Jeffrey Ferris Family Geneology.* Ithaca, 1963.

Finney, Charles G. *Lectures on Revivals of Religion*. Ed. and intro. William G. McLoughlin Jr. Cambridge, 1966.

———. *Memoirs*. New York, 1876.

Fisher, Samuel H. *The Litchfield Law School 1775–1833*. New Haven, 1933.

Fliegelman, Jay. *Prodigals and Pilgrims: The American Revolution Against Patriarchal Authority, 1750–1800*. Cambridge, 1982.

Foster, Charles I. *An Errand of Mercy: The Evangelical United Front, 1790–1837*. Chapel Hill, 1960.

Gridley, Samuel H. *Lectures on Mental Philosophy and Theology, with a Sketch of His Life*. New York, 1846.

Hareven, Tamara K., ed. *Anonymous Americans: Explorations in Nineteen Century Social History*. Englewood Cliffs, 1971.

Hershlowitz, Leo. "The Land of Promise: Samuel Swartwout and the Land Speculation in Texas, 1830–1838," *New York Historical Society Quarterly*, 47, no. 4 (October 1964).

Hirsch, Susan E. *Roots of the American Working Class: The Industrialization of Newark, 1800–1860*. Philadelphia, 1978.

History of Morris County, New Jersey, 1882.

Hotchkin, James H. *A History of the Purchase and Settlement of Western New York and the Presbyterian Church in that Section*. New York, 1848.

Johnson, Paul E. *A Shopkeeper's Millennium*. New York, 1978.

Keller, Charles H. *The Second Great Awakening in Connecticut*. New Haven, 1942.

Kett, Joseph F. *Rites of Passage: Adolescence in America 1790 to Present*. New York, 1977.

King, Mary Louise. *Portrait of New Canaan: The History of a Connecticut Town*. Chester, Pennsylvania, 1981.

Larkin, Jack. *The Reshaping of Everyday Life, 1790–1840*. New York, 1988.

Loetscher, Lefferts A. *A Brief History of the Presbyterians*, fourth ed. Philadelphia, 1978.

———. *Facing the Enlightenment and Pietism: Archibald Alexander and the Founding of Princeton Theological Seminary*. Westport, Conn., 1983.

Marsden, George. *The Evangelical Mind and the New School Presbyterian Experience*. New Haven, 1970.

May, Henry F. *The Enlightenment in America*. New York, 1973.

———. *Ideas, Faiths, and Feelings: Essays in American Intellectual and Religious History, 1952–1982*. New York, 1983.

McLoughlin, W. G., Jr., and Lipsitt, L. P. "Evangelical Child-rearing in the Age of Jackson," *Journal of Social History* 9 (1975).

McLoughlin, William G. Jr. *Revivals, Awakenings, and Reform.* Chicago, 1978.

Mead, Sidney E. *The Lively Experiment.* New York, 1963.

————. *Nathaniel William Taylor 1786–1858: A Connecticut Liberal.* Chicago, 1942.

————. "The Rise of the Evangelical Conception of the Ministry in America (1607–1850)," in Niebuhr, H. R., and Williams, D. D., *The Ministry in Social Perspective.* New York, 1956.

Miller, Douglas T. *Jacksonian Aristocracy: Class and Democracy in New York, 1830–1860.* New York, 1967.

Miller, Perry. *The Life of the Mind in America from the Revolution to the Civil War.* New York, 1965.

Minton, Steven, and Kellogg, Susan. *Domestic Revolutions: A Social History of American Family Life.* New York, London, 1988.

Morse, Jedidiah. *The American Universal Geography.* Boston, 1805.

Noll, Mark A. *Princeton and the Republic, 1768–1822.* Princeton, 1989.

Pessen, Edward. *Riches, Classes, and Power Before the Civil War.* Lexington, Mass., 1973.

————. "The Wealthiest New Yorkers of the Jacksonian Era: A New List," in *New York Historical Society Quarterly,* 54, no. 2 (April 1970).

Pierson, George Wilson. *Tocqueville and Beaumont in America.* New York, 1938.

Pilkington, Walter. *Hamilton College, 1812–1962.* Clinton, 1962.

Princeton Theological Seminary Biographical Catalogue, compiled by Joseph H. Dulles. Trenton, 1909.

Richards, Caroline Cowles. *Village Life in America: 1852–1872.* New York, 1913.

Richards, James. *Lectures on Mental Philosophy and Theology, with a Sketch of His Life by Samuel H. Gridley.* New York, 1846.

Richards, John Morgan. *With John Bull and Jonathan: Reminiscences of Sixty Years of an American's Life in England and in the United States.* New York, 1906.

Riley, Glenda. *Divorce: An American Tradition.* New York, 1991.

Rorabaugh, W. J. *The Alcoholic Republic: An American Tradition.* New York, Oxford, 1979.

Rothman, David J. *The Discovery of the Asylum: Social Order and Disorder in the New Republic.* Boston, 1971.

Ryan, Mary P. *Cradle of the Middle Class: Family in New York 1790–1865.* New York, 1981.

Scoville, Joseph. *The Old Merchants of New York.* New York, 1866.

Silverman, Kenneth. *Timothy Dwight.* New York, 1969.

Sklar, Katherine Kish. *Catherine Beecher.* New Haven, 1973.

Smith, Daniel Scott. "All in Some Degree Related to Each Other," in *American Historical Review*, 94, no. 1 (February 1989).]

Sprague, William B. *Annals of the American Presbyterian Pulpit.* New York, 1866.

————. *The Life of Jedidiah Morse.* New York, 1874.

————. *Sermons by the Late Rev. James Richards, D. D., with an Essay on His Character.* Albany, 1849.

Stowe, Harriet Beecher. *Oldtown Folks.* Ed. and intro. Henry F. May. Cambridge, 1966.

Stryker-Rodda, Harriet M. *Ancestors and Descendants of Frank Lusk Babbott Jr., M.D., and His Wife, Eliza-Bassett French.* Polyanthus Princeton, 1974.

Taylor, George R. *The Transportation Revolution, 1815–1860.* New York, 1951.

Trollope, Frances. *Domestic Manners of the Americans.* New York, 1984.

Ward, Geoffrey C. *Before the Trumpet: Young Franklin Roosevelt.* New York, 1986.

Wertenbaker, Thomas J. *Princeton: 1746–1896.* Princeton, 1946.

White, Alain. *The History of the Town of Litchfield, Connecticut, 1720–1920.* Litchfield, 1920.

Wilentz, Sean. *Chants Democratic: New York City and the Rise of the American Working Class, 1788–1850.* New York, Oxford, 1984.

Wilentz, Sean, and Johnson, Paul E. *The Kingdom of Matthias.* New York, Oxford, 1994.

Woody, Thomas. *A History of Women's Education in the United States,* 2 vols. New York, 1966.

INDEX

BEALS

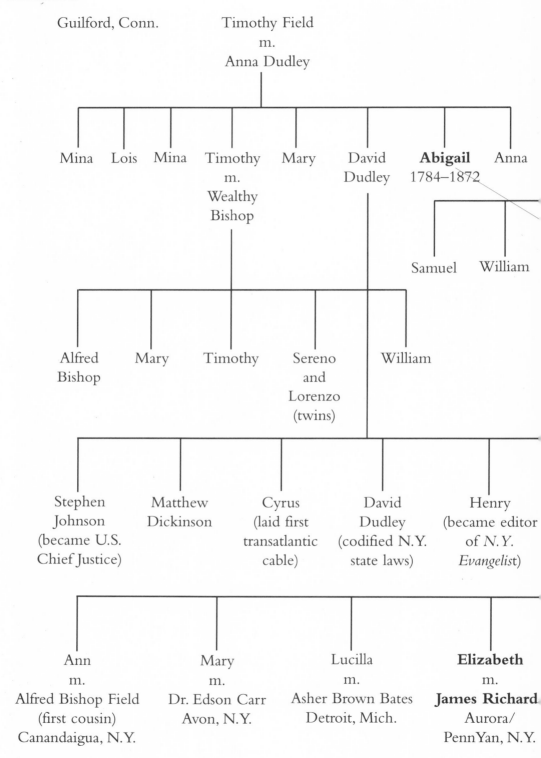

Guilford, Conn. Timothy Field
m.
Anna Dudley

Mina Lois Mina Timothy Mary David **Abigail** Anna
m. Dudley 1784–1872
Wealthy
Bishop

Samuel William

Alfred Mary Timothy Sereno William
Bishop and
Lorenzo
(twins)

Stephen Matthew Cyrus David Henry
Johnson Dickinson (laid first Dudley (became editor
(became U.S. transatlantic (codified N.Y. of *N.Y.*
Chief Justice) cable) state laws) *Evangelis*t)

Ann Mary Lucilla **Elizabeth**
m. m. m. m.
Alfred Bishop Field Dr. Edson Carr Asher Brown Bates **James Richard**
(first cousin) Avon, N.Y. Detroit, Mich. Aurora/
Canandaigua, N.Y. PennYan, N.Y.